WONDER WOMAN
AGENT OF PEACE
VOL. 2

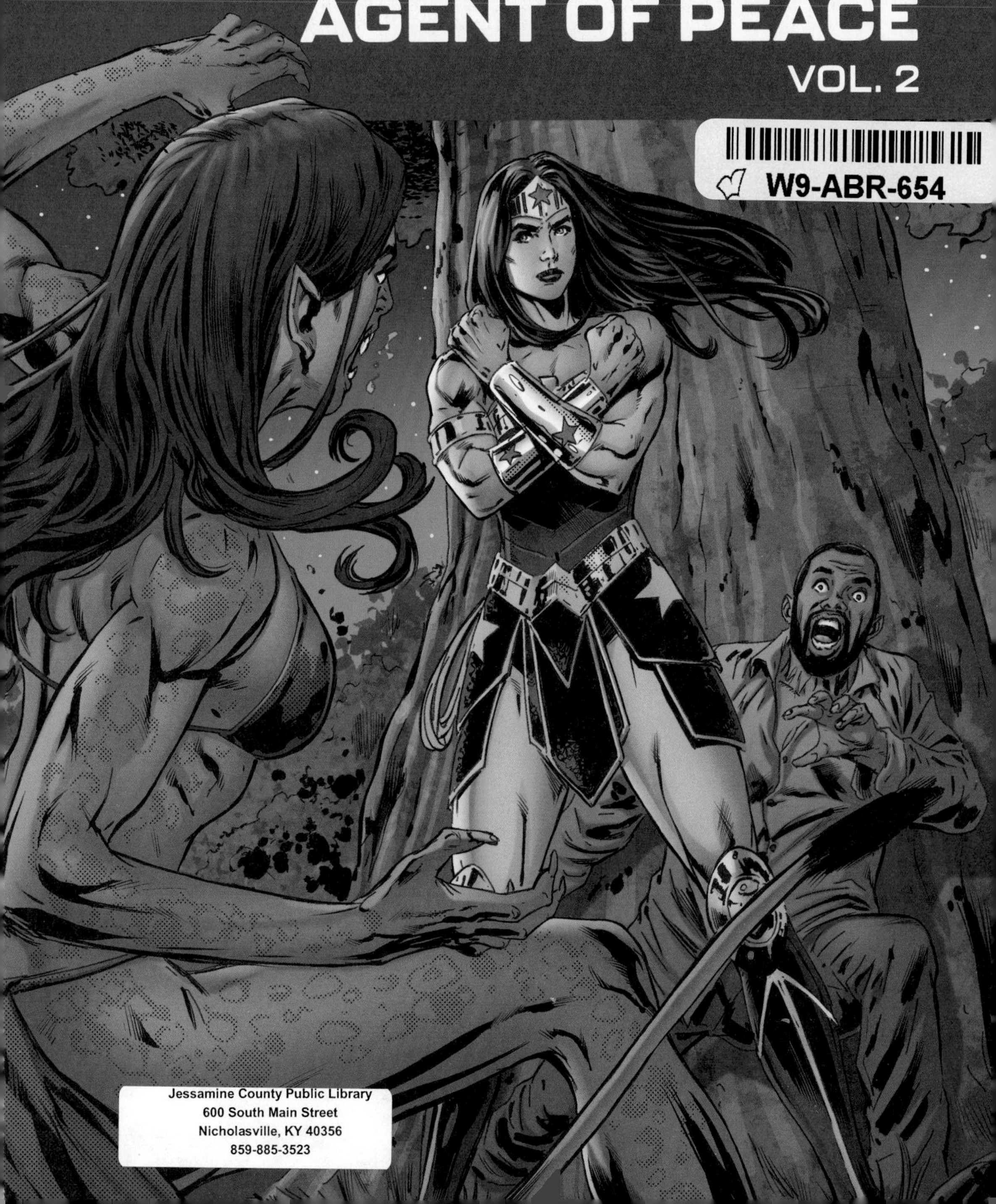

WONDER WOMAN

AGENT OF PEACE

VOL. 2

Liz Erickson, Ivan Cohen, Amanda Diebert,
Danny Lore, Andrew Wheeler, Andrea Shea,
Cavan Scott, Bryan Hill, Tim Seeley,
Dan Abnett, Josh Trujillo, Christos N. Gage
writers

Jose Luis, Pop Mhan, Aaron Lopresti,
Maria Laura Sanapo, Paul Pelletier, Isaac Goodhart,
Andrea Broccardo, V. Kenneth Marion, Tom Derenick,
Hendry Prasetya, Neil Edwards
pencillers

Jonas Trindade, Pop Mhan, Matt Ryan,
Maria Laura Sanapo, Norm Rapmund, Isaac Goodhart,
Andrea Broccardo, V. Kenneth Marion, Tom Derenick,
Hendry Prasetya, Neil Edwards
inkers

Hi-Fi, Rex Lokus, Wendy Broome, Adriano Lucas,
Cris Peter, Sian Mandrake, Emilio Lopez,
Ulises Arreola, Jeromy Cox
colorists

Janice Chiang, Travis Lanham, Becca Carey,
Carlos M. Mangual, Andworld Design
letterers

Simone Di Meo
collection cover artist

Wonder Woman created by William Moulton Marston.

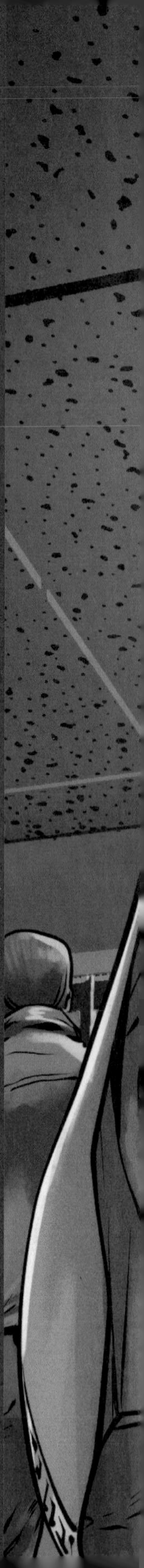

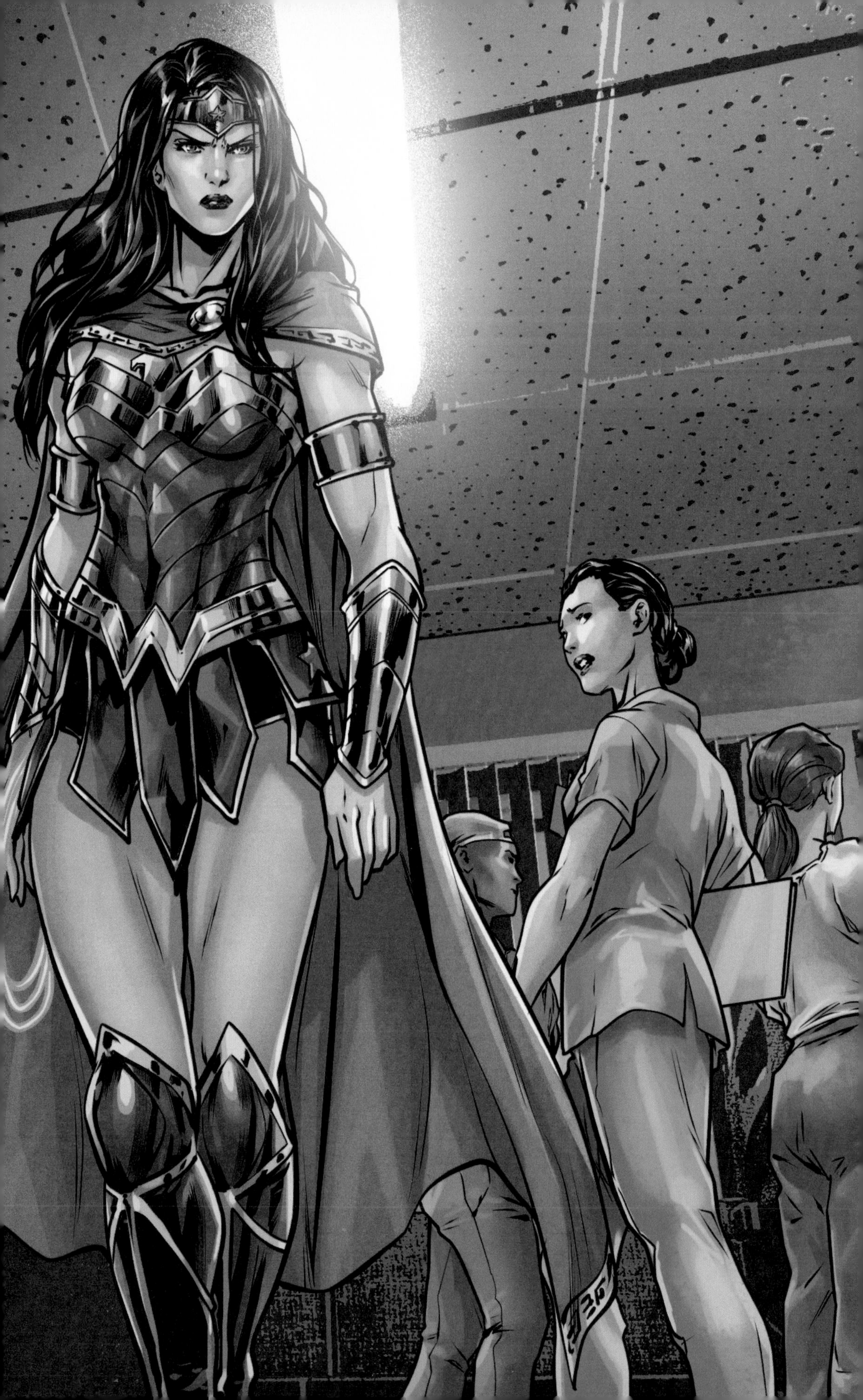

Michael McCalister
Editor – Original Series & Collected Edition

Steve Cook
Design Director – Books

Megen Bellersen
Publication Design

Erin Vanover
Publication Production

Marie Javins
Editor-in-Chief, DC Comics

Daniel Cherry III
Senior VP – General Manager

Jim Lee
Publisher & Chief Creative Officer

Don Falletti
VP – Manufacturing Operations &
Workflow Management

Lawrence Ganem
VP – Talent Services

Alison Gill
Senior VP – Manufacturing & Operations

Jeffrey Kaufman
VP – Editorial Strategy & Programming

Nick J. Napolitano
VP – Manufacturing Administration & Design

Nancy Spears
VP – Revenue

WONDER WOMAN: AGENT OF PEACE VOL. 2

Published by DC Comics. Compilation and all new material Copyright © 2022
DC Comics. All Rights Reserved. Originally published online as *Wonder Woman:
Agent of Peace* Digital Chapters 12-23. Copyright © 2020 DC Comics. All Rights
Reserved. All characters, their distinctive likenesses, and related elements
featured in this publication are trademarks of DC Comics. The stories, characters,
and incidents featured in this publication are entirely fictional. DC Comics does
not read or accept unsolicited submissions of ideas, stories, or artwork.
DC – a WarnerMedia Company.

DC Comics, 2900 West Alameda Ave., Burbank, CA 91505
Printed by Solisco Printers, Scott, QC, Canada.
2/11/22. First Printing.
ISBN: 978-1-77951-509-4

Library of Congress Cataloging-in-Publication Data is available.

PEFC Certified

This product is from
sustainably managed
forests and controlled
sources

PEFC/26-31-02   www.pefc.org

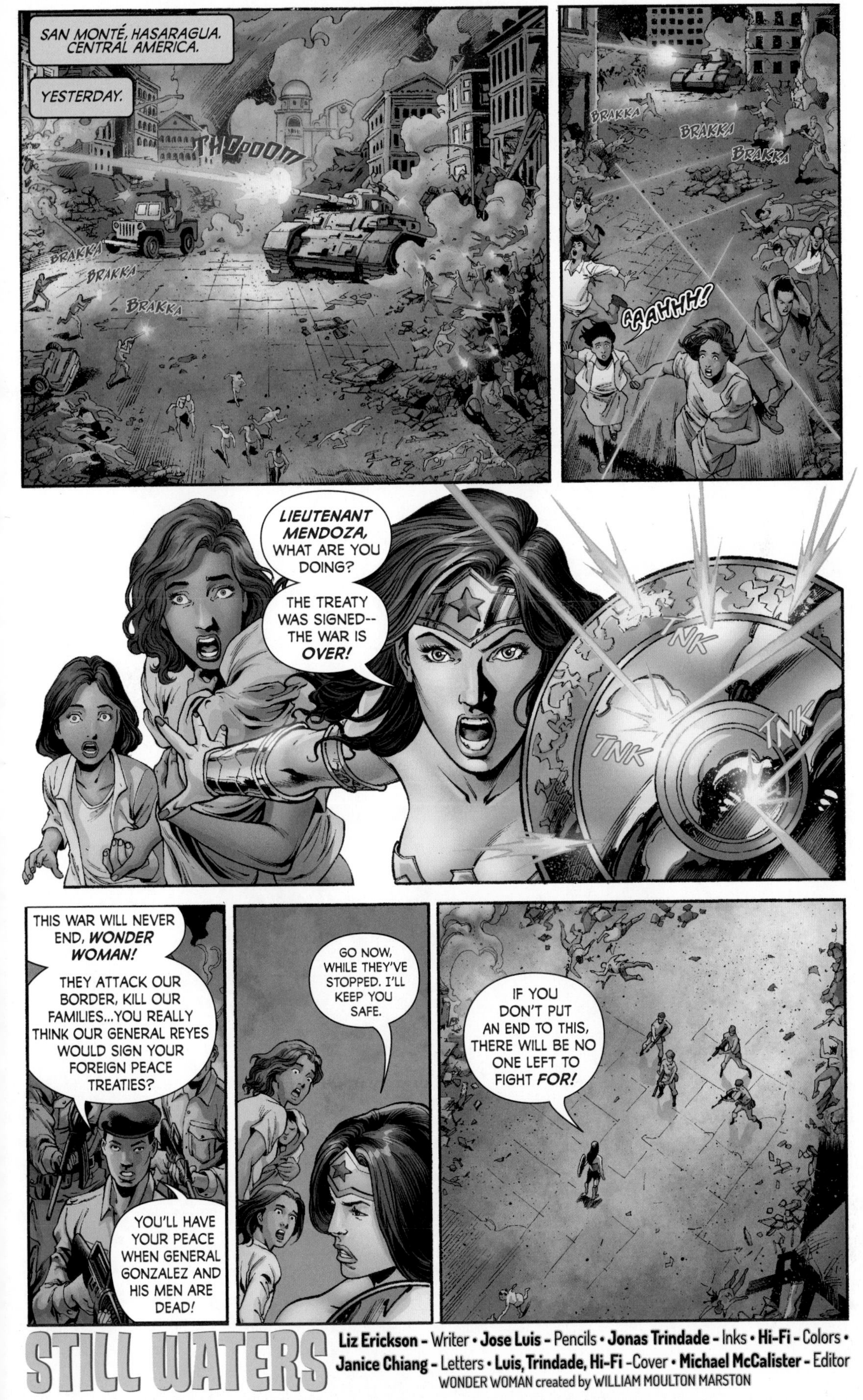
SAN MONTÉ, HASARAGUA. CENTRAL AMERICA.
YESTERDAY.
THOOOOM
BRAKKA
BRAKKA
BRAKKA
BRAKKA
BRAKKA
BRAKKA
AAAHHH!
LIEUTENANT MENDOZA, WHAT ARE YOU DOING?
THE TREATY WAS SIGNED-- THE WAR IS OVER!
TNK
TNK
TNK
THIS WAR WILL NEVER END, WONDER WOMAN!
THEY ATTACK OUR BORDER, KILL OUR FAMILIES...YOU REALLY THINK OUR GENERAL REYES WOULD SIGN YOUR FOREIGN PEACE TREATIES?
YOU'LL HAVE YOUR PEACE WHEN GENERAL GONZALEZ AND HIS MEN ARE DEAD!
GO NOW, WHILE THEY'VE STOPPED. I'LL KEEP YOU SAFE.
IF YOU DON'T PUT AN END TO THIS, THERE WILL BE NO ONE LEFT TO FIGHT FOR!

STILL WATERS

Liz Erickson - Writer • **Jose Luis** - Pencils • **Jonas Trindade** - Inks • **Hi-Fi** - Colors • **Janice Chiang** - Letters • **Luis, Trindade, Hi-Fi** -Cover • **Michael McCalister** - Editor

WONDER WOMAN created by WILLIAM MOULTON MARSTON

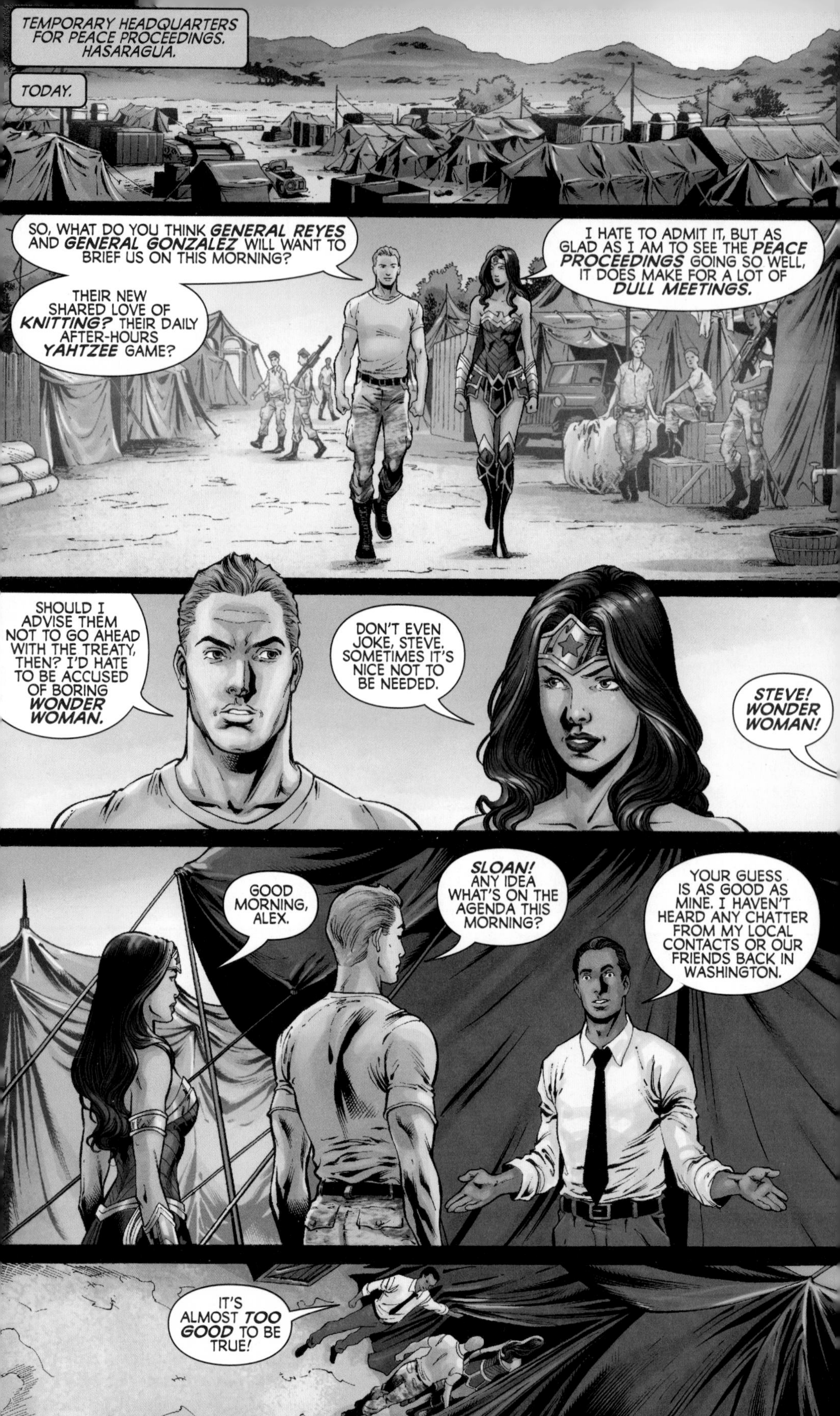
TEMPORARY HEADQUARTERS FOR PEACE PROCEEDINGS. HASARAGUA.
TODAY.
SO, WHAT DO YOU THINK GENERAL REYES AND GENERAL GONZALEZ WILL WANT TO BRIEF US ON THIS MORNING?
THEIR NEW SHARED LOVE OF KNITTING? THEIR DAILY AFTER-HOURS YAHTZEE GAME?
I HATE TO ADMIT IT, BUT AS GLAD AS I AM TO SEE THE PEACE PROCEEDINGS GOING SO WELL, IT DOES MAKE FOR A LOT OF DULL MEETINGS.
SHOULD I ADVISE THEM NOT TO GO AHEAD WITH THE TREATY, THEN? I'D HATE TO BE ACCUSED OF BORING WONDER WOMAN.
DON'T EVEN JOKE, STEVE. SOMETIMES IT'S NICE NOT TO BE NEEDED.
STEVE! WONDER WOMAN!
GOOD MORNING, ALEX.
SLOAN! ANY IDEA WHAT'S ON THE AGENDA THIS MORNING?
YOUR GUESS IS AS GOOD AS MINE. I HAVEN'T HEARD ANY CHATTER FROM MY LOCAL CONTACTS OR OUR FRIENDS BACK IN WASHINGTON.
IT'S ALMOST TOO GOOD TO BE TRUE!

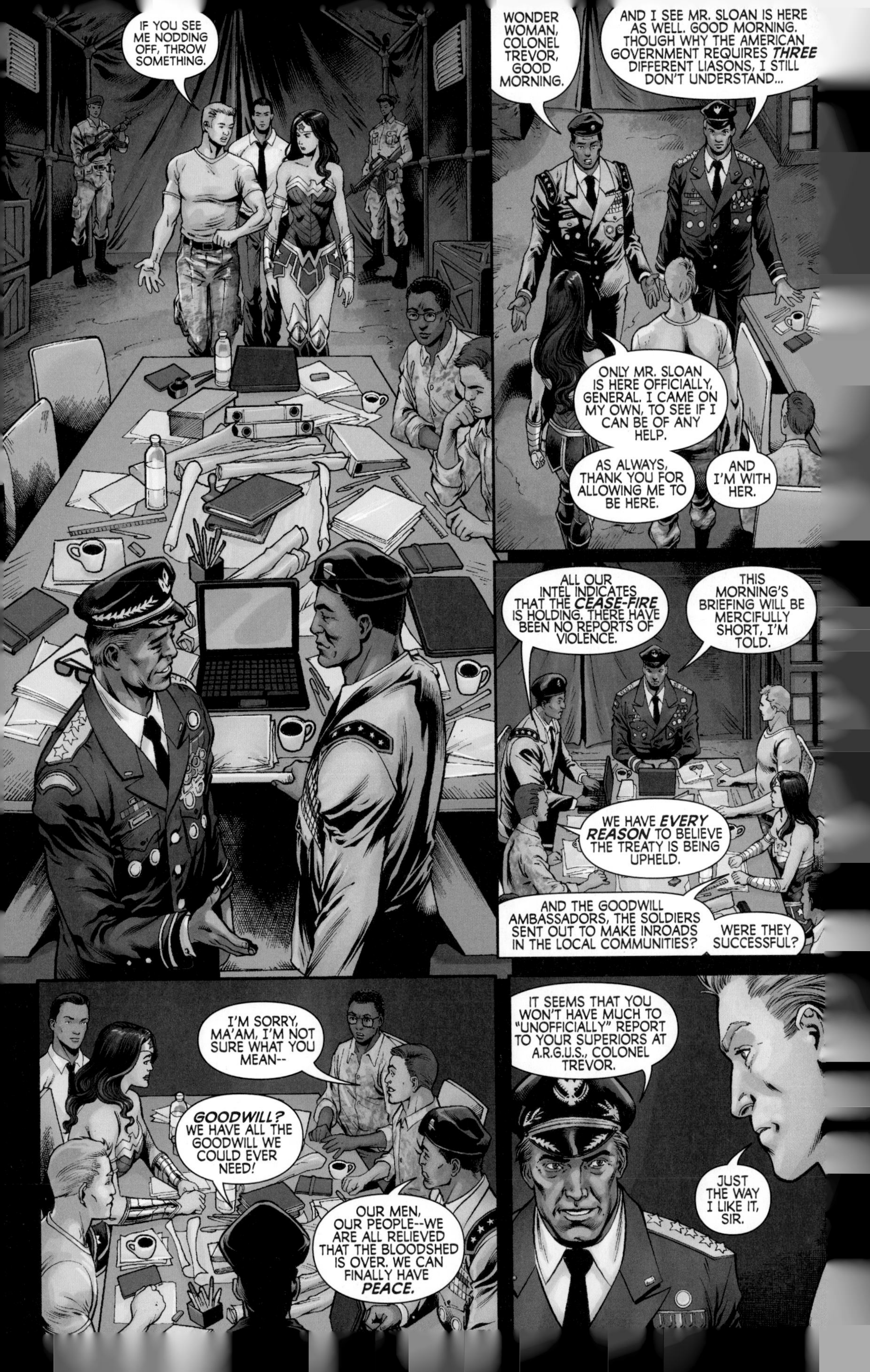

IF YOU SEE ME NODDING OFF, THROW SOMETHING.
WONDER WOMAN, COLONEL TREVOR, GOOD MORNING.
AND I SEE MR. SLOAN IS HERE AS WELL. GOOD MORNING. THOUGH WHY THE AMERICAN GOVERNMENT REQUIRES THREE DIFFERENT LIASONS, I STILL DON'T UNDERSTAND...
ONLY MR. SLOAN IS HERE OFFICIALLY, GENERAL. I CAME ON MY OWN, TO SEE IF I CAN BE OF ANY HELP.
AS ALWAYS, THANK YOU FOR ALLOWING ME TO BE HERE.
AND I'M WITH HER.
ALL OUR INTEL INDICATES THAT THE CEASE-FIRE IS HOLDING. THERE HAVE BEEN NO REPORTS OF VIOLENCE.
THIS MORNING'S BRIEFING WILL BE MERCIFULLY SHORT, I'M TOLD.
WE HAVE EVERY REASON TO BELIEVE THE TREATY IS BEING UPHELD.
AND THE GOODWILL AMBASSADORS, THE SOLDIERS SENT OUT TO MAKE INROADS IN THE LOCAL COMMUNITIES?
WERE THEY SUCCESSFUL?
I'M SORRY, MA'AM, I'M NOT SURE WHAT YOU MEAN--
GOODWILL? WE HAVE ALL THE GOODWILL WE COULD EVER NEED!
OUR MEN, OUR PEOPLE--WE ARE ALL RELIEVED THAT THE BLOODSHED IS OVER. WE CAN FINALLY HAVE PEACE.
IT SEEMS THAT YOU WON'T HAVE MUCH TO "UNOFFICIALLY" REPORT TO YOUR SUPERIORS AT A.R.G.U.S., COLONEL TREVOR.
JUST THE WAY I LIKE IT, SIR.

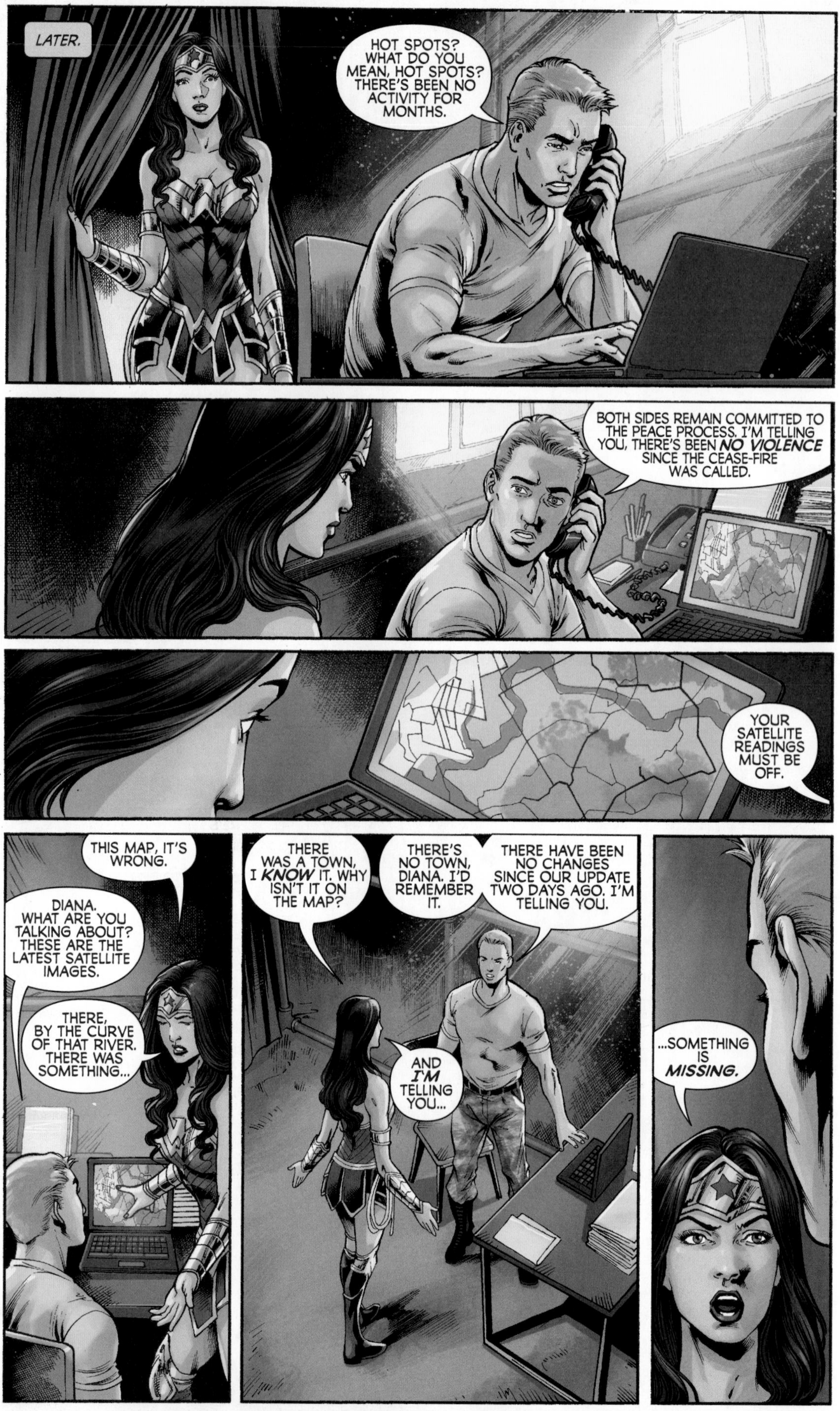
LATER.
HOT SPOTS? WHAT DO YOU MEAN, HOT SPOTS? THERE'S BEEN NO ACTIVITY FOR MONTHS.
BOTH SIDES REMAIN COMMITTED TO THE PEACE PROCESS. I'M TELLING YOU, THERE'S BEEN NO VIOLENCE SINCE THE CEASE-FIRE WAS CALLED.
YOUR SATELLITE READINGS MUST BE OFF.
THIS MAP, IT'S WRONG.
DIANA. WHAT ARE YOU TALKING ABOUT? THESE ARE THE LATEST SATELLITE IMAGES.
THERE, BY THE CURVE OF THAT RIVER. THERE WAS SOMETHING...
THERE WAS A TOWN, I KNOW IT. WHY ISN'T IT ON THE MAP?
THERE'S NO TOWN, DIANA. I'D REMEMBER IT.
THERE HAVE BEEN NO CHANGES SINCE OUR UPDATE TWO DAYS AGO. I'M TELLING YOU.
AND I'M TELLING YOU...
...SOMETHING IS MISSING.

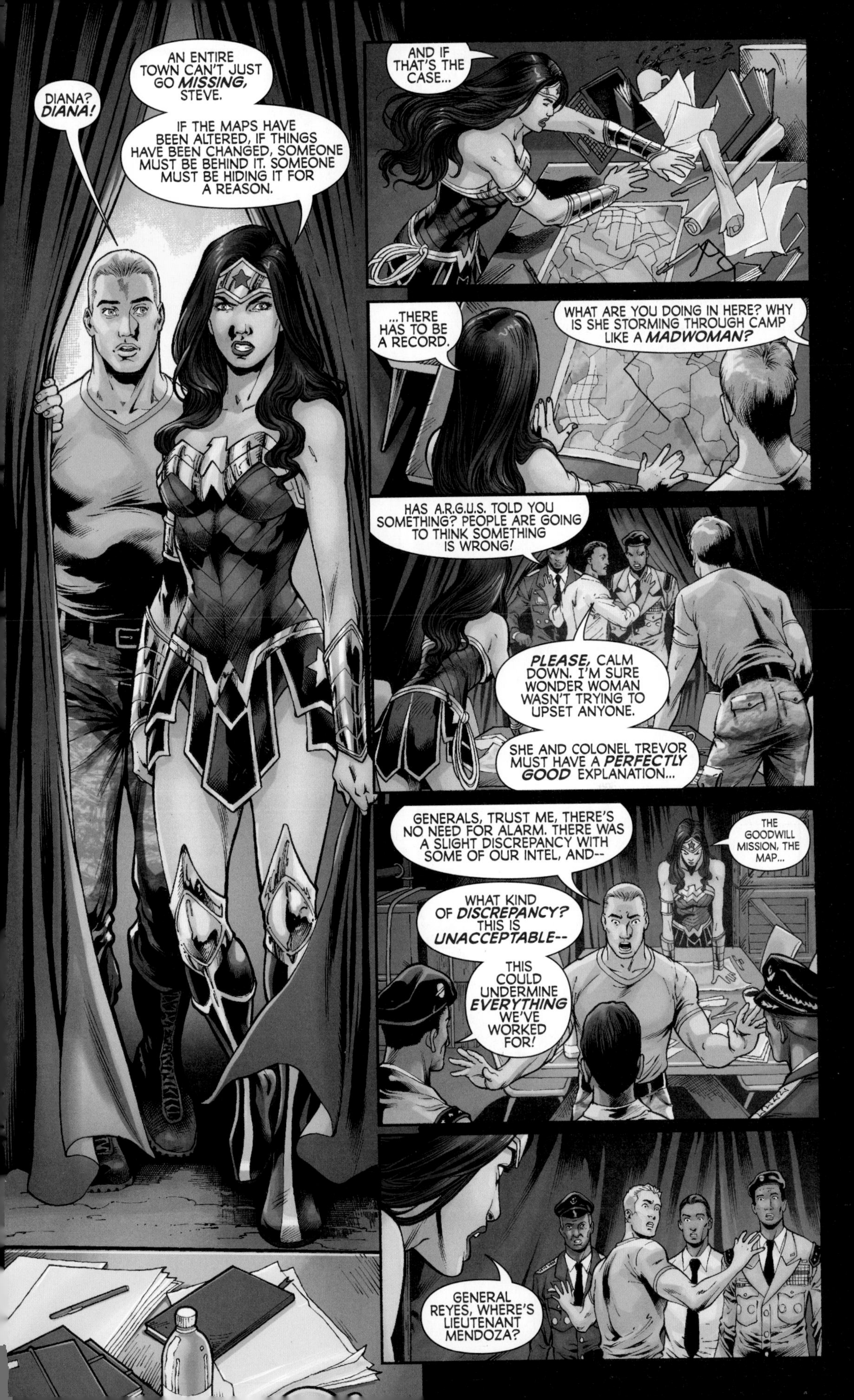
DIANA? DIANA!
AN ENTIRE TOWN CAN'T JUST GO MISSING, STEVE.
IF THE MAPS HAVE BEEN ALTERED, IF THINGS HAVE BEEN CHANGED, SOMEONE MUST BE BEHIND IT. SOMEONE MUST BE HIDING IT FOR A REASON.
AND IF THAT'S THE CASE...
...THERE HAS TO BE A RECORD.
WHAT ARE YOU DOING IN HERE? WHY IS SHE STORMING THROUGH CAMP LIKE A MADWOMAN?
HAS A.R.G.U.S. TOLD YOU SOMETHING? PEOPLE ARE GOING TO THINK SOMETHING IS WRONG!
PLEASE, CALM DOWN. I'M SURE WONDER WOMAN WASN'T TRYING TO UPSET ANYONE.
SHE AND COLONEL TREVOR MUST HAVE A PERFECTLY GOOD EXPLANATION...
GENERALS, TRUST ME, THERE'S NO NEED FOR ALARM. THERE WAS A SLIGHT DISCREPANCY WITH SOME OF OUR INTEL, AND--
THE GOODWILL MISSION, THE MAP...
WHAT KIND OF DISCREPANCY? THIS IS UNACCEPTABLE--
THIS COULD UNDERMINE EVERYTHING WE'VE WORKED FOR!
GENERAL REYES, WHERE'S LIEUTENANT MENDOZA?

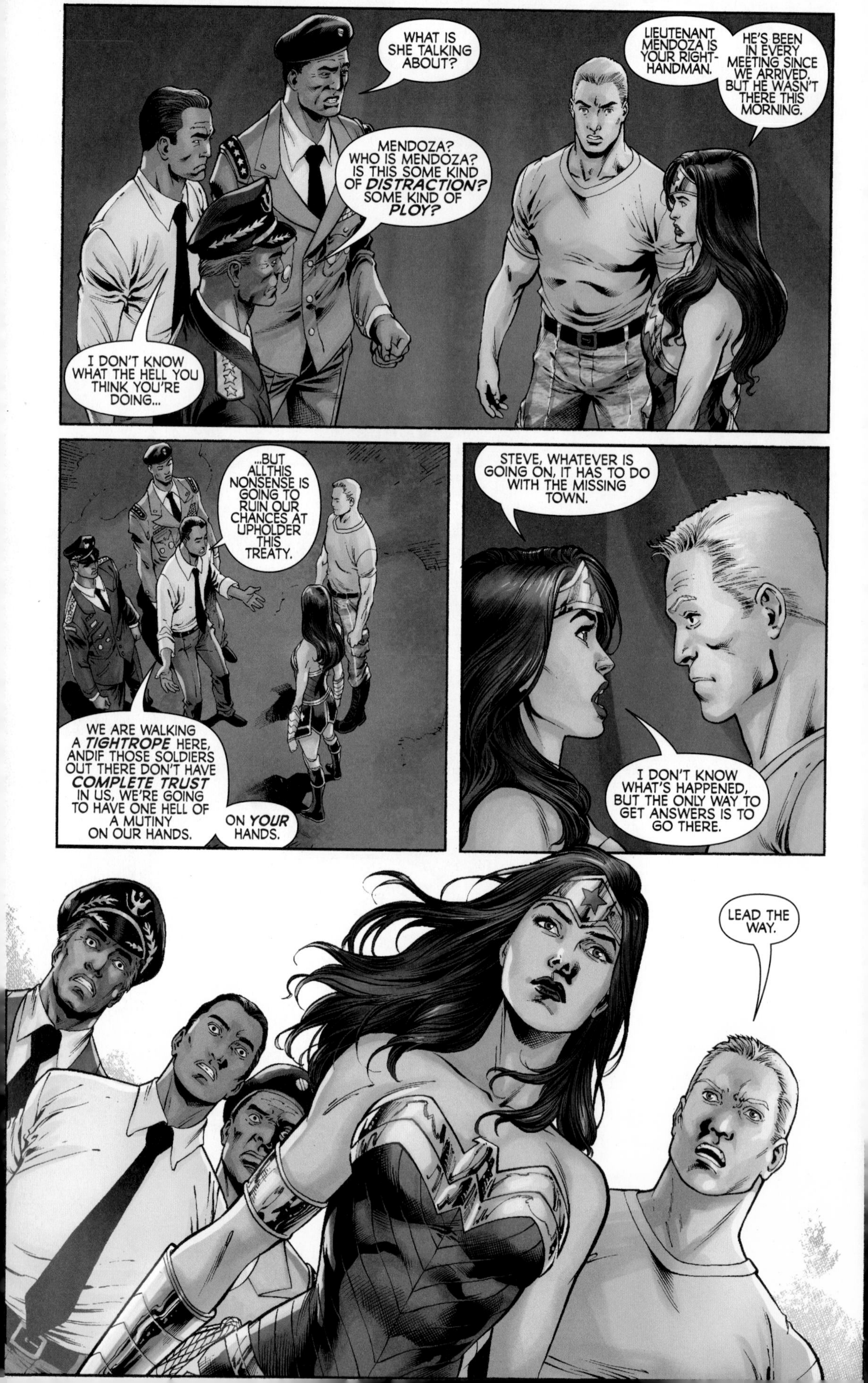

WHAT IS SHE TALKING ABOUT?
LIEUTENANT MENDOZA IS YOUR RIGHT-HANDMAN.
HE'S BEEN IN EVERY MEETING SINCE WE ARRIVED, BUT HE WASN'T THERE THIS MORNING.
MENDOZA? WHO IS MENDOZA? IS THIS SOME KIND OF DISTRACTION? SOME KIND OF PLOY?
I DON'T KNOW WHAT THE HELL YOU THINK YOU'RE DOING...
...BUT ALLTHIS NONSENSE IS GOING TO RUIN OUR CHANCES AT UPHOLDER THIS TREATY.
WE ARE WALKING A TIGHTROPE HERE, ANDIF THOSE SOLDIERS OUT THERE DON'T HAVE COMPLETE TRUST IN US, WE'RE GOING TO HAVE ONE HELL OF A MUTINY ON OUR HANDS.
ON YOUR HANDS.
STEVE, WHATEVER IS GOING ON, IT HAS TO DO WITH THE MISSING TOWN.
I DON'T KNOW WHAT'S HAPPENED, BUT THE ONLY WAY TO GET ANSWERS IS TO GO THERE.
LEAD THE WAY.

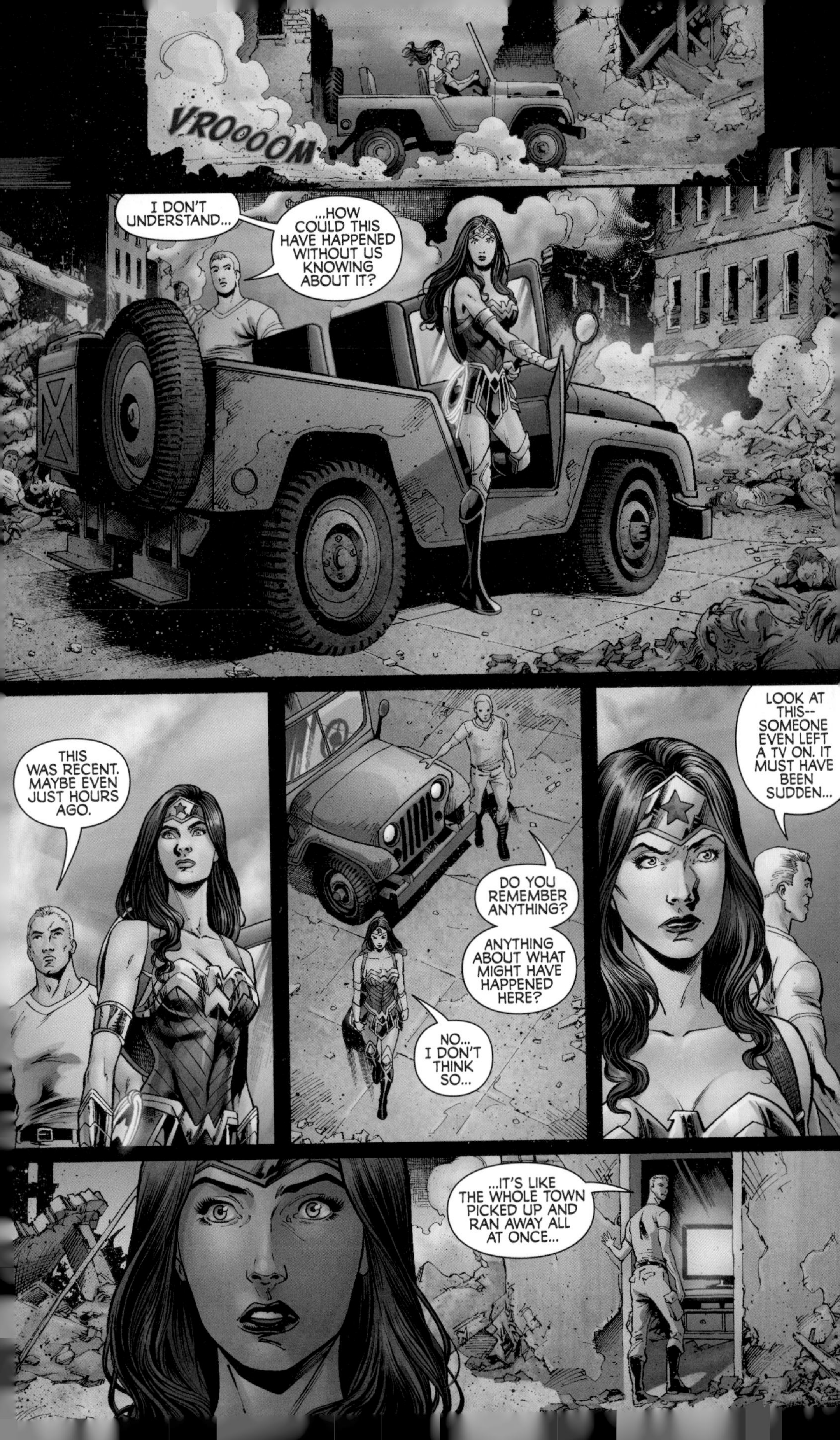
VROOOOM
I DON'T UNDERSTAND...
...HOW COULD THIS HAVE HAPPENED WITHOUT US KNOWING ABOUT IT?
THIS WAS RECENT. MAYBE EVEN JUST HOURS AGO.
DO YOU REMEMBER ANYTHING?
ANYTHING ABOUT WHAT MIGHT HAVE HAPPENED HERE?
NO... I DON'T THINK SO...
LOOK AT THIS-- SOMEONE EVEN LEFT A TV ON. IT MUST HAVE BEEN SUDDEN...
...IT'S LIKE THE WHOLE TOWN PICKED UP AND RAN AWAY ALL AT ONCE...

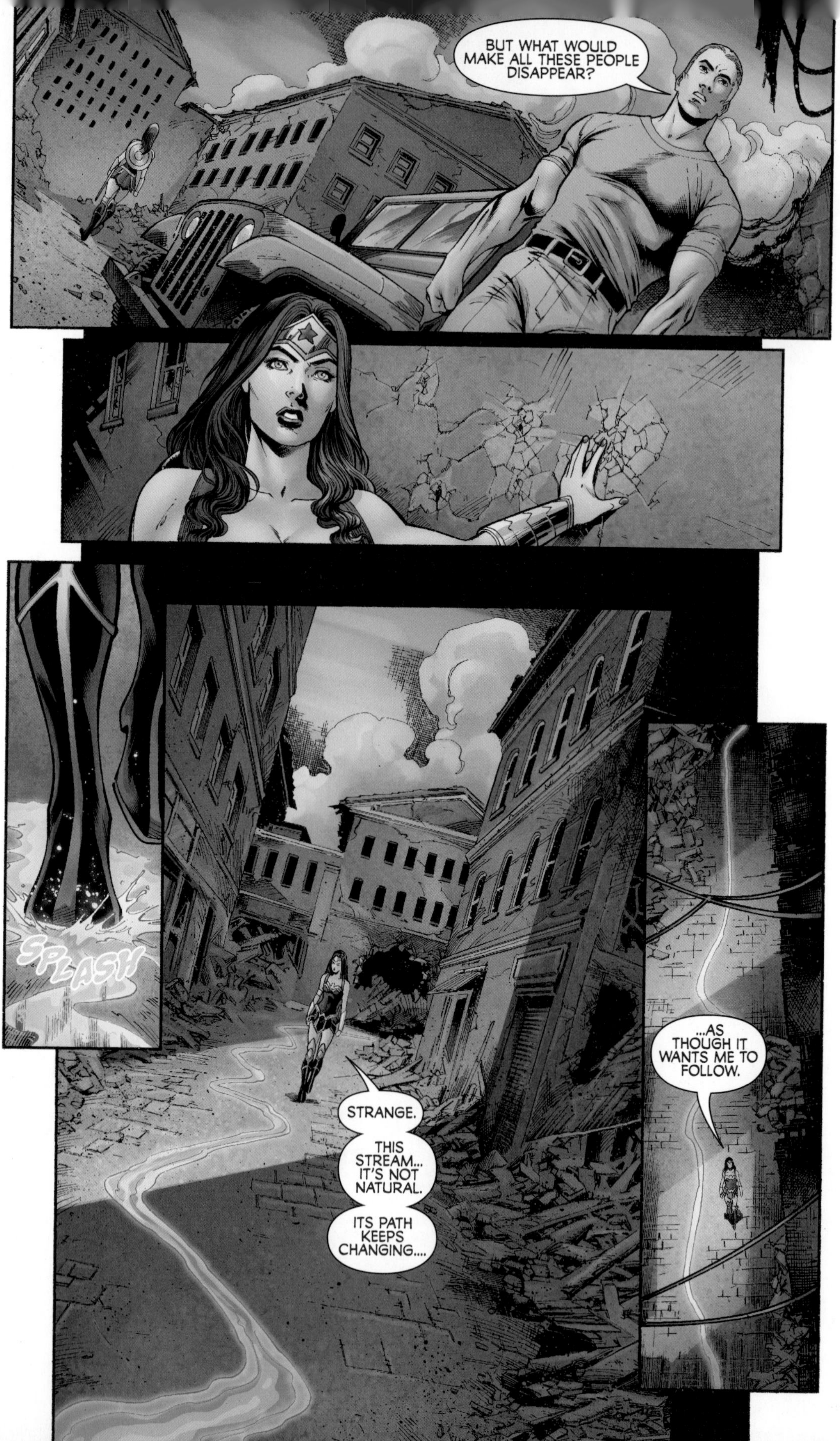
BUT WHAT WOULD MAKE ALL THESE PEOPLE DISAPPEAR?
SPLASH
STRANGE.
THIS STREAM... IT'S NOT NATURAL.
ITS PATH KEEPS CHANGING....
...AS THOUGH IT WANTS ME TO FOLLOW.

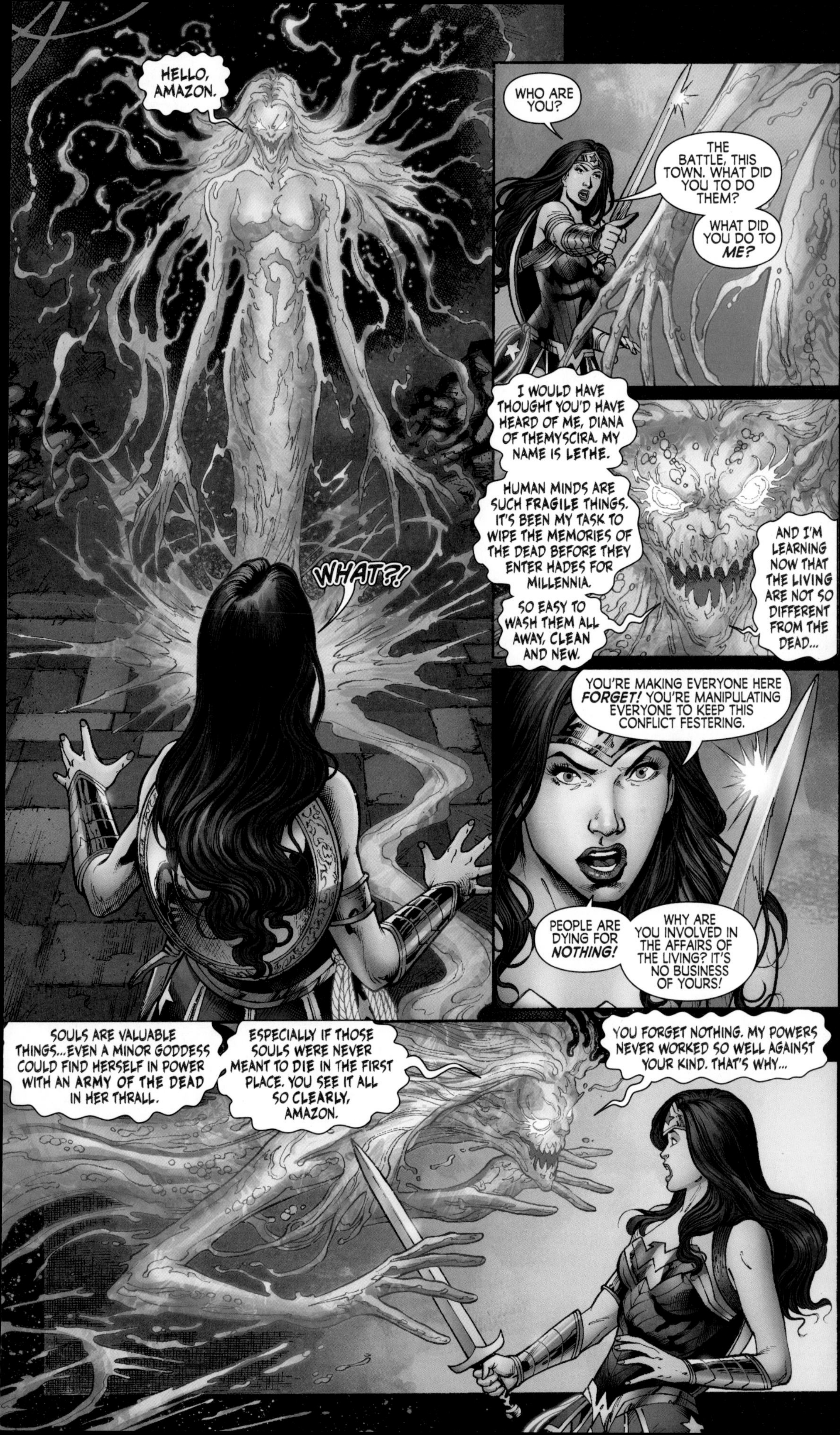
HELLO, AMAZON.
WHAT?!
WHO ARE YOU?
THE BATTLE, THIS TOWN. WHAT DID YOU TO DO THEM?
WHAT DID YOU DO TO ME?
I WOULD HAVE THOUGHT YOU'D HAVE HEARD OF ME, DIANA OF THEMYSCIRA. MY NAME IS LETHE.
HUMAN MINDS ARE SUCH FRAGILE THINGS. IT'S BEEN MY TASK TO WIPE THE MEMORIES OF THE DEAD BEFORE THEY ENTER HADES FOR MILLENNIA.
SO EASY TO WASH THEM ALL AWAY, CLEAN AND NEW.
AND I'M LEARNING NOW THAT THE LIVING ARE NOT SO DIFFERENT FROM THE DEAD...
YOU'RE MAKING EVERYONE HERE FORGET! YOU'RE MANIPULATING EVERYONE TO KEEP THIS CONFLICT FESTERING.
PEOPLE ARE DYING FOR NOTHING!
WHY ARE YOU INVOLVED IN THE AFFAIRS OF THE LIVING? IT'S NO BUSINESS OF YOURS!
SOULS ARE VALUABLE THINGS...EVEN A MINOR GODDESS COULD FIND HERSELF IN POWER WITH AN ARMY OF THE DEAD IN HER THRALL.
ESPECIALLY IF THOSE SOULS WERE NEVER MEANT TO DIE IN THE FIRST PLACE. YOU SEE IT ALL SO CLEARLY, AMAZON.
YOU FORGET NOTHING. MY POWERS NEVER WORKED SO WELL AGAINST YOUR KIND. THAT'S WHY...

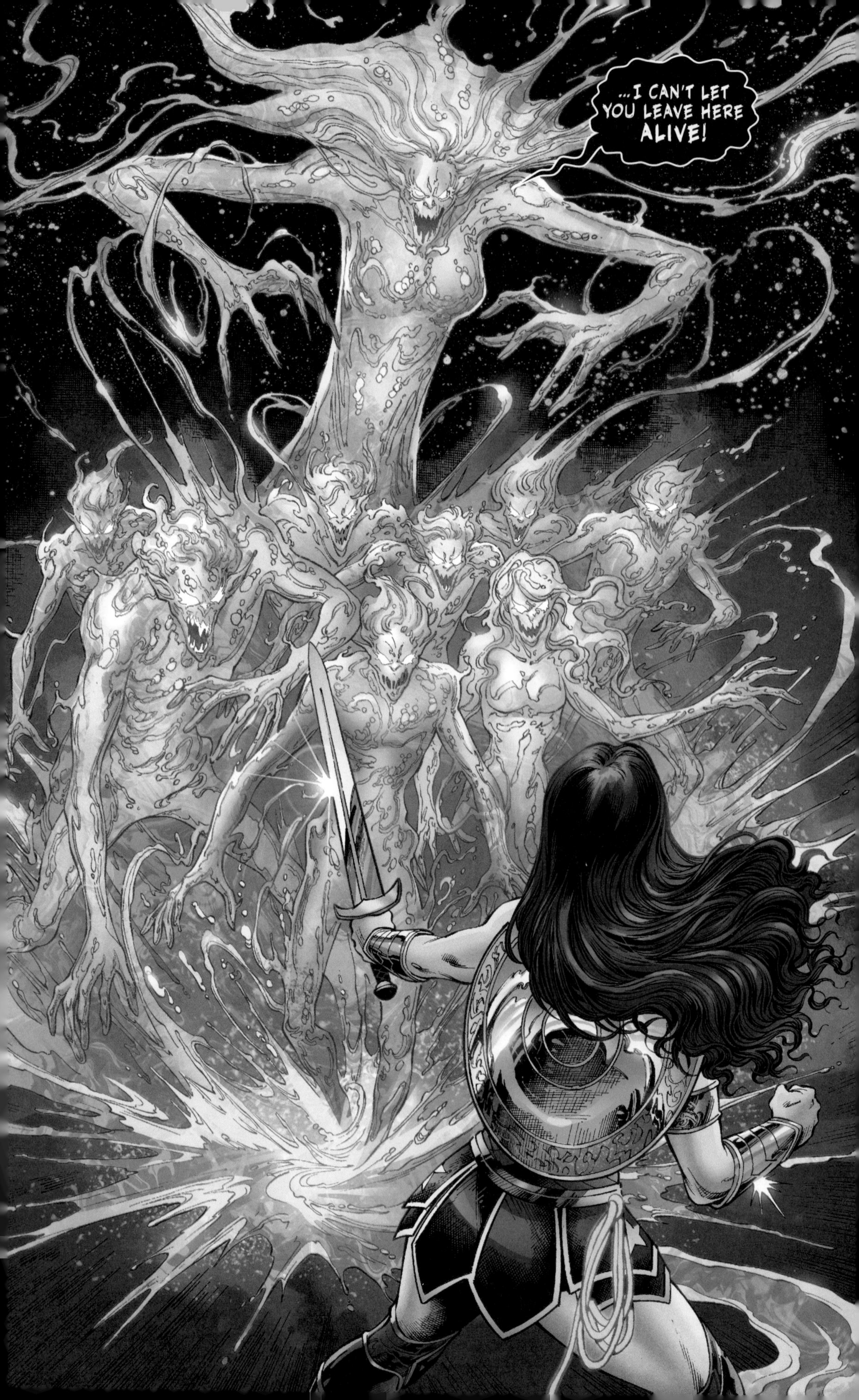
...I CAN'T LET YOU LEAVE HERE ALIVE!

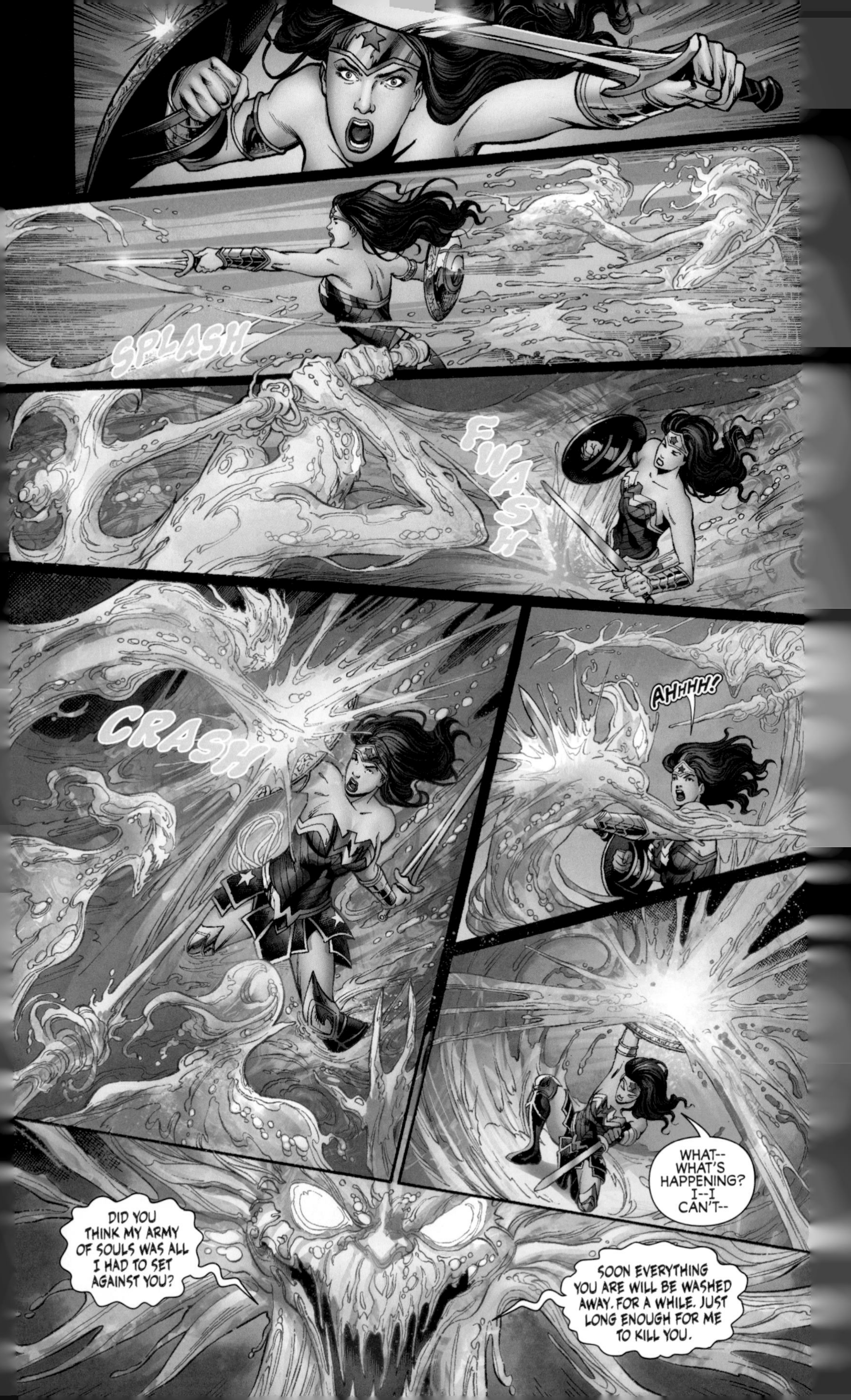
SPLASH
FWASH
CRASH
AHHHH!
WHAT-- WHAT'S HAPPENING? I--I CAN'T--
DID YOU THINK MY ARMY OF SOULS WAS ALL I HAD TO SET AGAINST YOU?
SOON EVERYTHING YOU ARE WILL BE WASHED AWAY. FOR A WHILE. JUST LONG ENOUGH FOR ME TO KILL YOU.

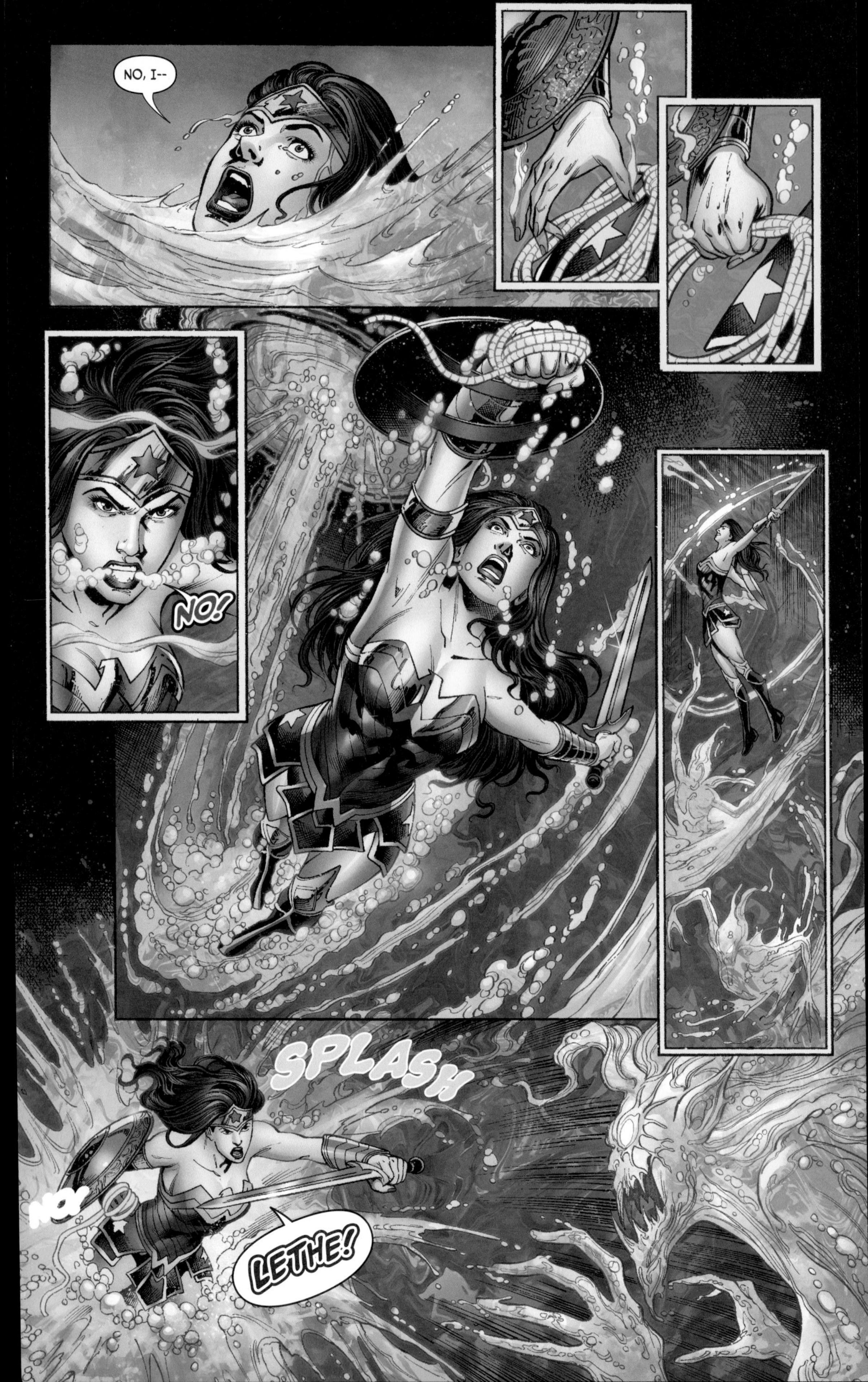
NO, I--
NO!
SPLASH
NO!
LETHE!

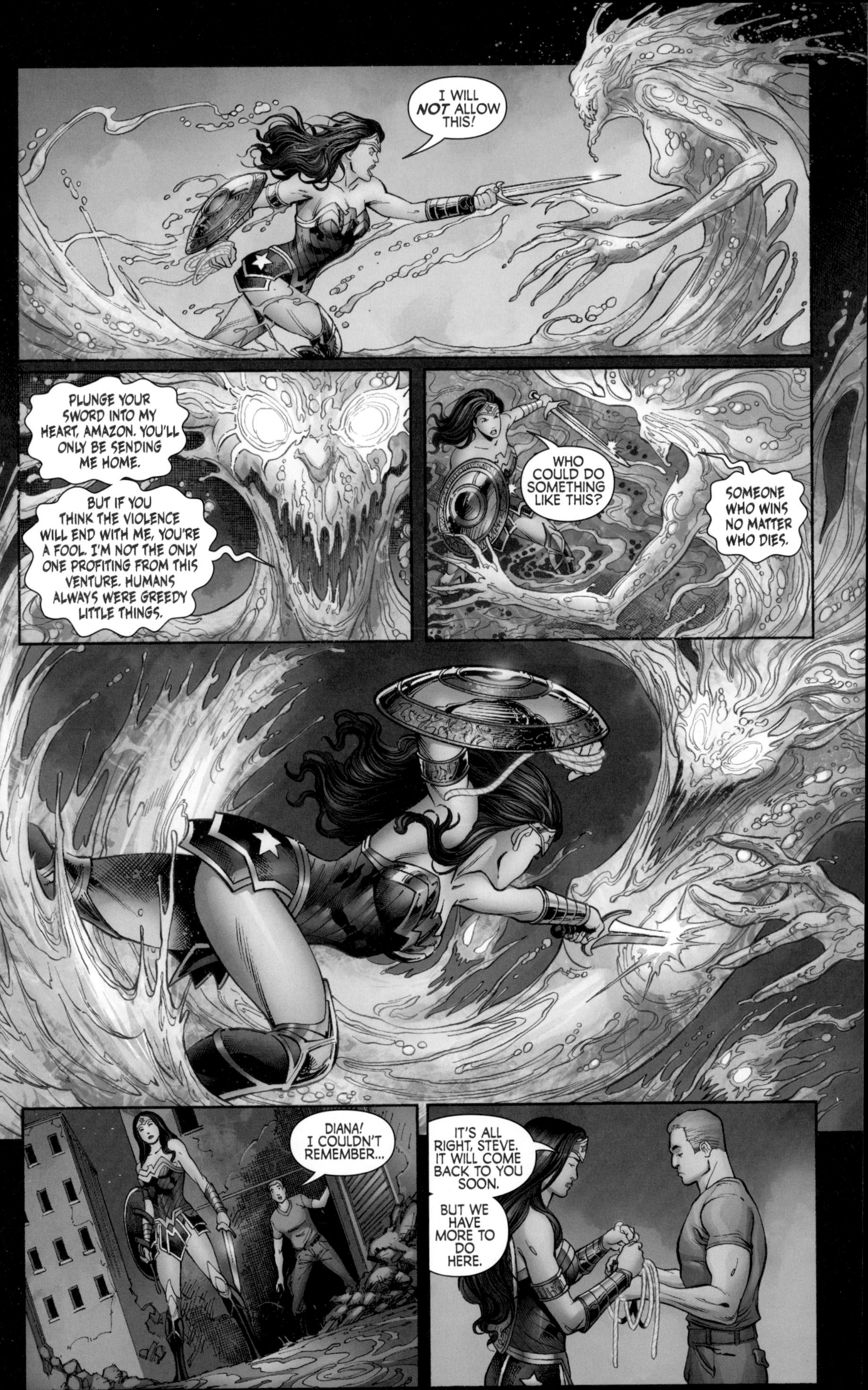
I WILL *NOT* ALLOW THIS!
PLUNGE YOUR SWORD INTO MY HEART, AMAZON. YOU'LL ONLY BE SENDING ME HOME.
BUT IF YOU THINK THE VIOLENCE WILL END WITH ME, YOU'RE A FOOL. I'M NOT THE ONLY ONE PROFITING FROM THIS VENTURE. HUMANS ALWAYS WERE GREEDY LITTLE THINGS.
WHO COULD DO SOMETHING LIKE THIS?
SOMEONE WHO WINS NO MATTER WHO DIES.
DIANA! I COULDN'T REMEMBER...
IT'S ALL RIGHT, STEVE. IT WILL COME BACK TO YOU SOON.
BUT WE HAVE MORE TO DO HERE.

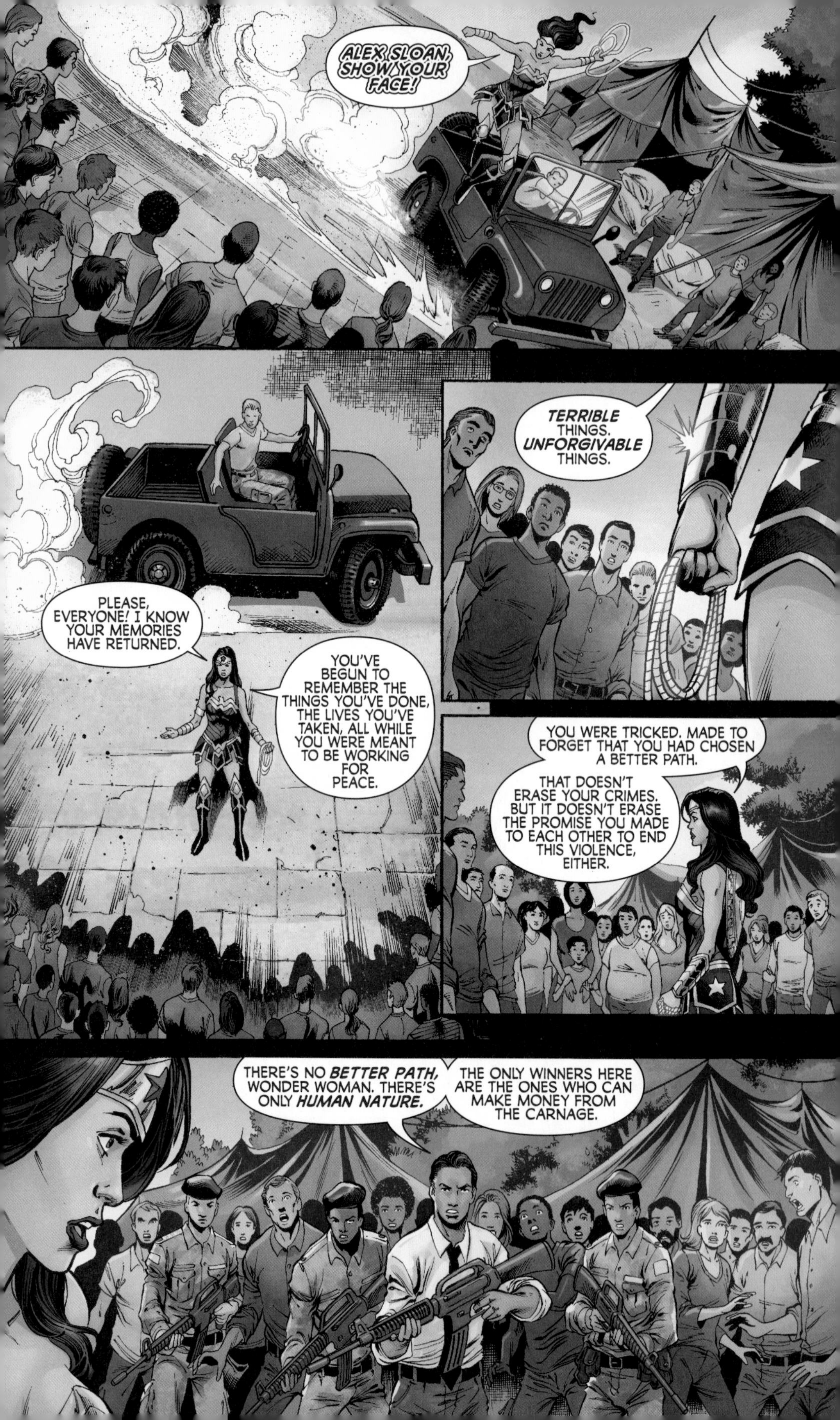
ALEX SLOAN, SHOW YOUR FACE!
PLEASE, EVERYONE! I KNOW YOUR MEMORIES HAVE RETURNED.
YOU'VE BEGUN TO REMEMBER THE THINGS YOU'VE DONE, THE LIVES YOU'VE TAKEN, ALL WHILE YOU WERE MEANT TO BE WORKING FOR PEACE.
TERRIBLE THINGS. UNFORGIVABLE THINGS.
YOU WERE TRICKED. MADE TO FORGET THAT YOU HAD CHOSEN A BETTER PATH.
THAT DOESN'T ERASE YOUR CRIMES. BUT IT DOESN'T ERASE THE PROMISE YOU MADE TO EACH OTHER TO END THIS VIOLENCE, EITHER.
THERE'S NO BETTER PATH, WONDER WOMAN. THERE'S ONLY HUMAN NATURE.
THE ONLY WINNERS HERE ARE THE ONES WHO CAN MAKE MONEY FROM THE CARNAGE.

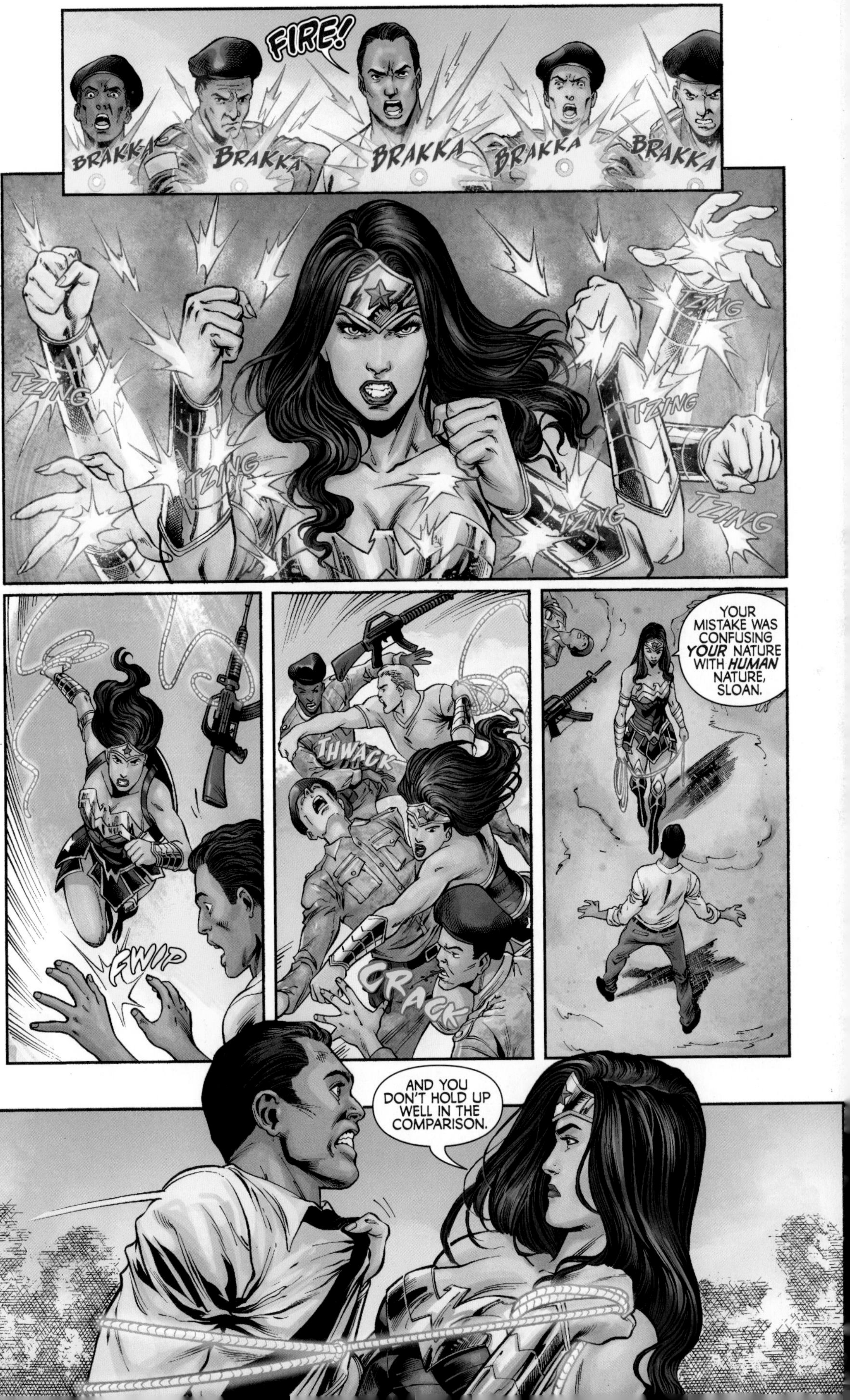
FIRE!
BRAKKA
BRAKKA
BRAKKA
BRAKKA
BRAKKA
TZING
TZING
TZING
TZING
TZING
FWIP
THWACK
CRACK
YOUR MISTAKE WAS CONFUSING ***YOUR*** NATURE WITH ***HUMAN*** NATURE, SLOAN.
AND YOU DON'T HOLD UP WELL IN THE COMPARISON.

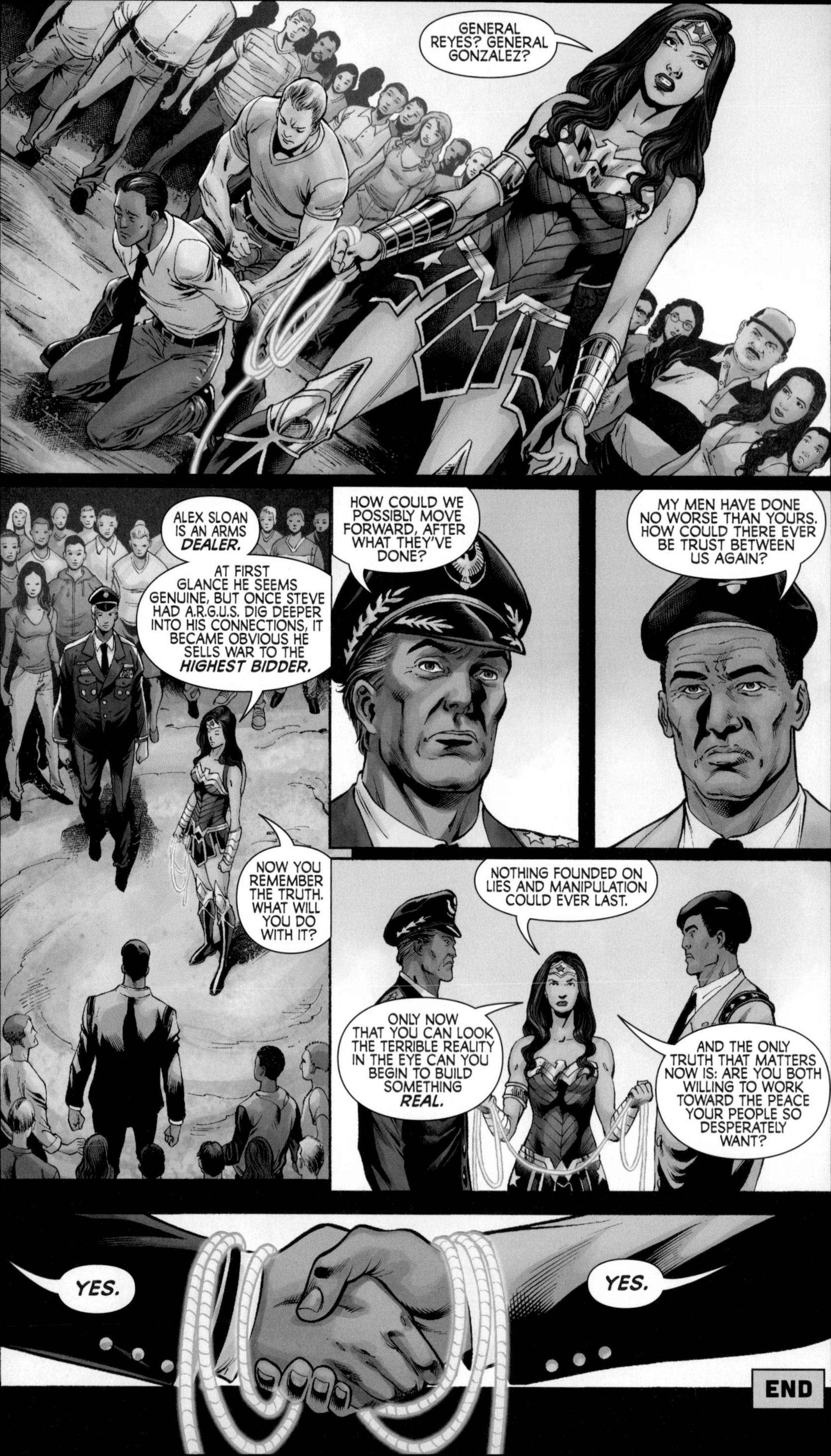
GENERAL REYES? GENERAL GONZALEZ?
ALEX SLOAN IS AN ARMS DEALER.
AT FIRST GLANCE HE SEEMS GENUINE, BUT ONCE STEVE HAD A.R.G.U.S. DIG DEEPER INTO HIS CONNECTIONS, IT BECAME OBVIOUS HE SELLS WAR TO THE HIGHEST BIDDER.
NOW YOU REMEMBER THE TRUTH. WHAT WILL YOU DO WITH IT?
HOW COULD WE POSSIBLY MOVE FORWARD, AFTER WHAT THEY'VE DONE?
MY MEN HAVE DONE NO WORSE THAN YOURS. HOW COULD THERE EVER BE TRUST BETWEEN US AGAIN?
NOTHING FOUNDED ON LIES AND MANIPULATION COULD EVER LAST.
ONLY NOW THAT YOU CAN LOOK THE TERRIBLE REALITY IN THE EYE CAN YOU BEGIN TO BUILD SOMETHING REAL.
AND THE ONLY TRUTH THAT MATTERS NOW IS: ARE YOU BOTH WILLING TO WORK TOWARD THE PEACE YOUR PEOPLE SO DESPERATELY WANT?
YES.
YES.
END

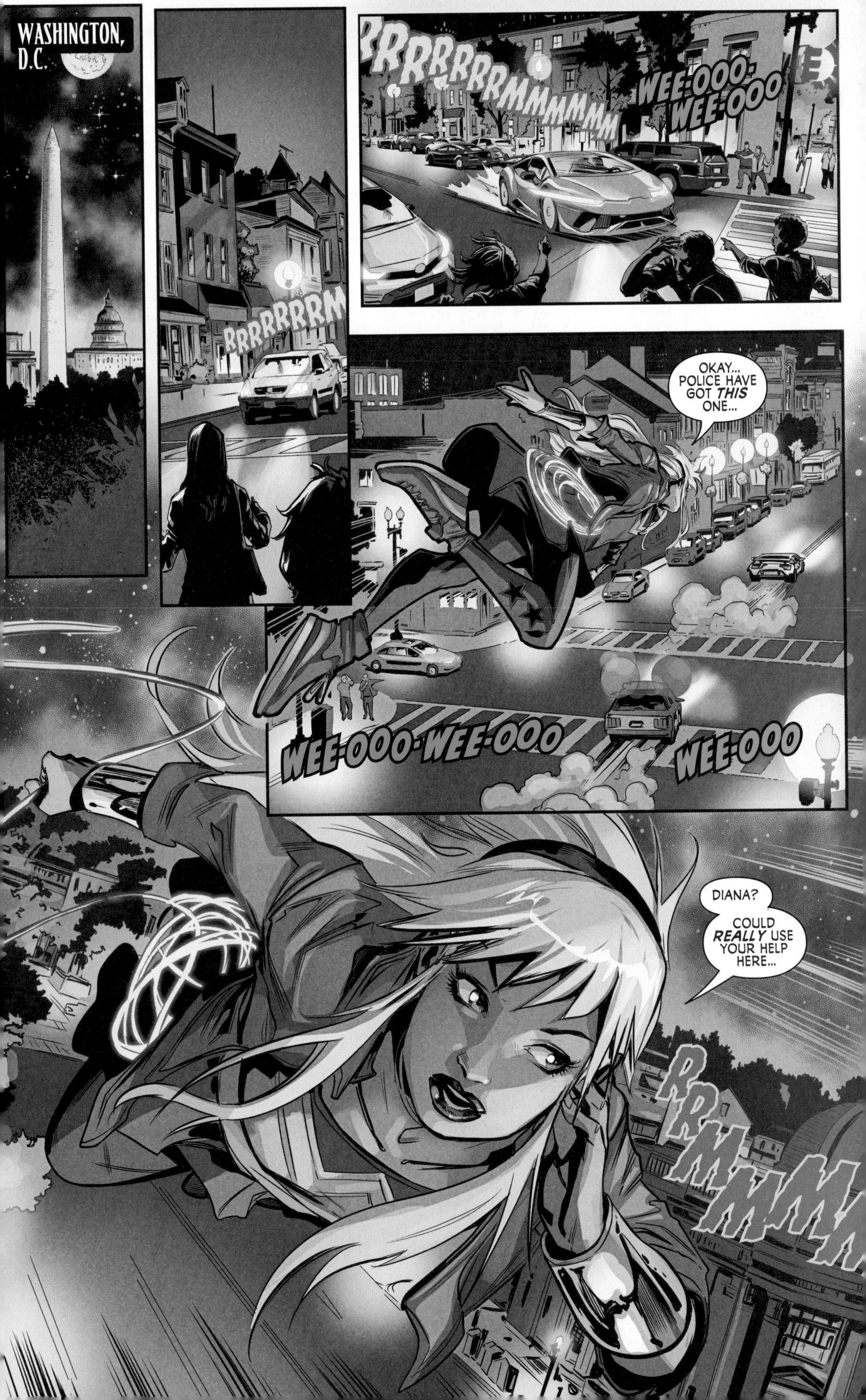
WASHINGTON, D.C.
RRRRRRRM
RRRRRRRRMMMMMMM
WEE-OOO-
WEE-OOO
OKAY... POLICE HAVE GOT THIS ONE...
WEE-OOO-WEE-OOO
WEE-OOO
DIANA?
COULD REALLY USE YOUR HELP HERE...
RRMMM

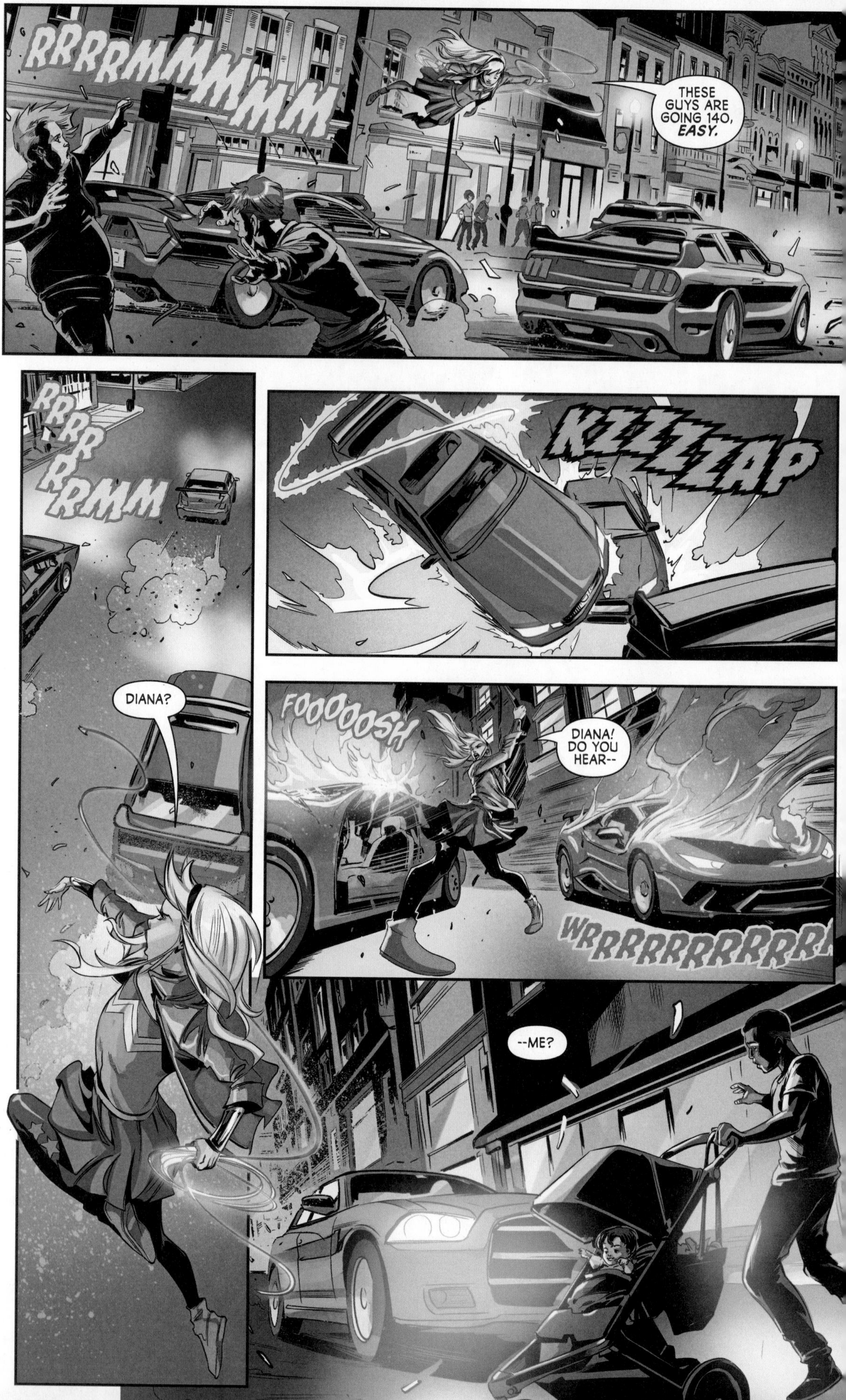
RRRRMMMMMMM
THESE GUYS ARE GOING 140, *EASY.*
RRRRRMM
KZZZZZAP
DIANA?
FOOOOOSH
DIANA! DO YOU HEAR--
WRRRRRRRRRRR
--ME?

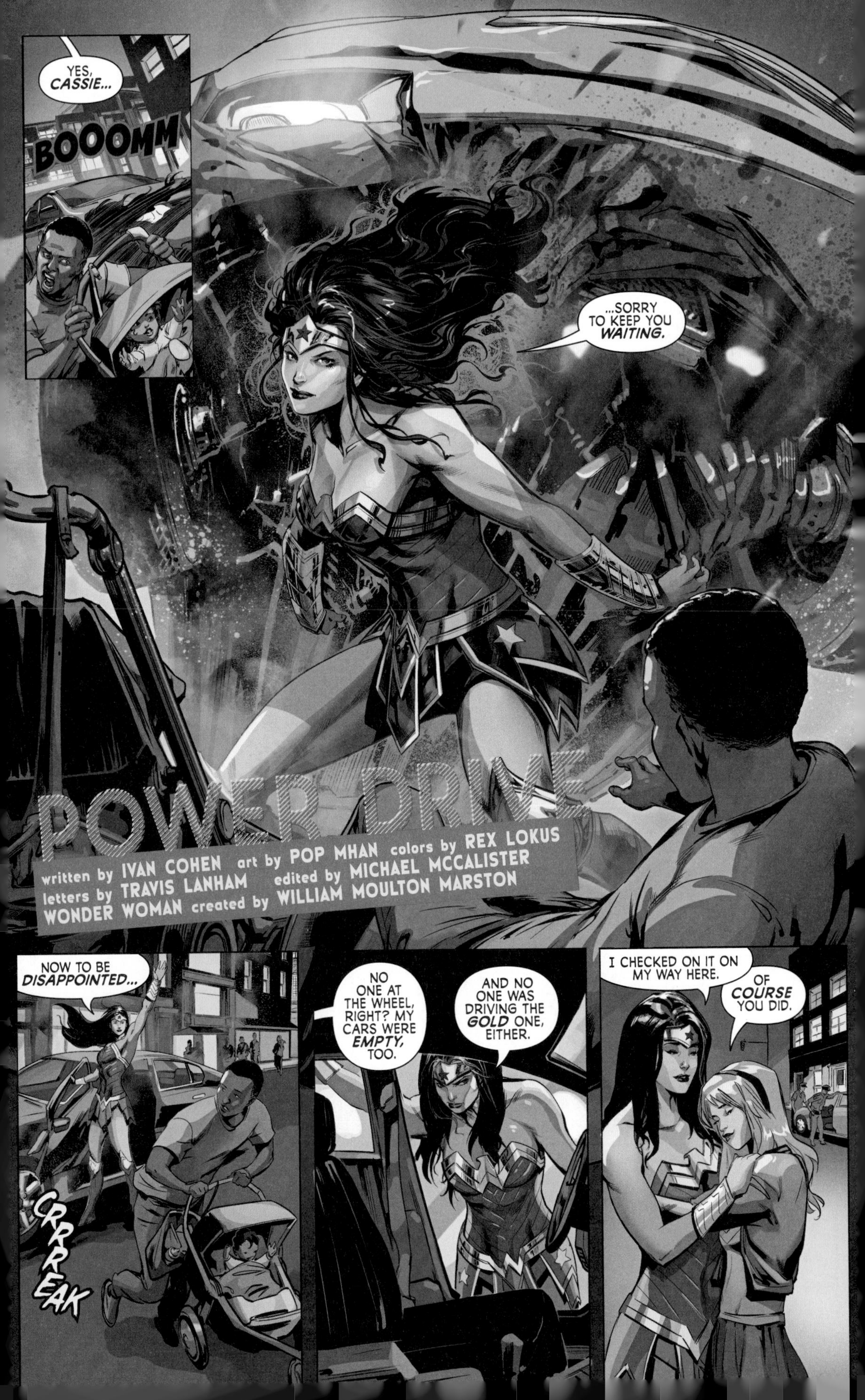
YES, CASSIE...
BOOOMM
...SORRY TO KEEP YOU WAITING.
POWER DRIVE
written by IVAN COHEN art by POP MHAN colors by REX LOKUS
letters by TRAVIS LANHAM edited by MICHAEL MCCALISTER
WONDER WOMAN created by WILLIAM MOULTON MARSTON
NOW TO BE DISAPPOINTED...
CRRREAK
NO ONE AT THE WHEEL, RIGHT? MY CARS WERE EMPTY, TOO.
AND NO ONE WAS DRIVING THE GOLD ONE, EITHER.
I CHECKED ON IT ON MY WAY HERE.
OF COURSE YOU DID.

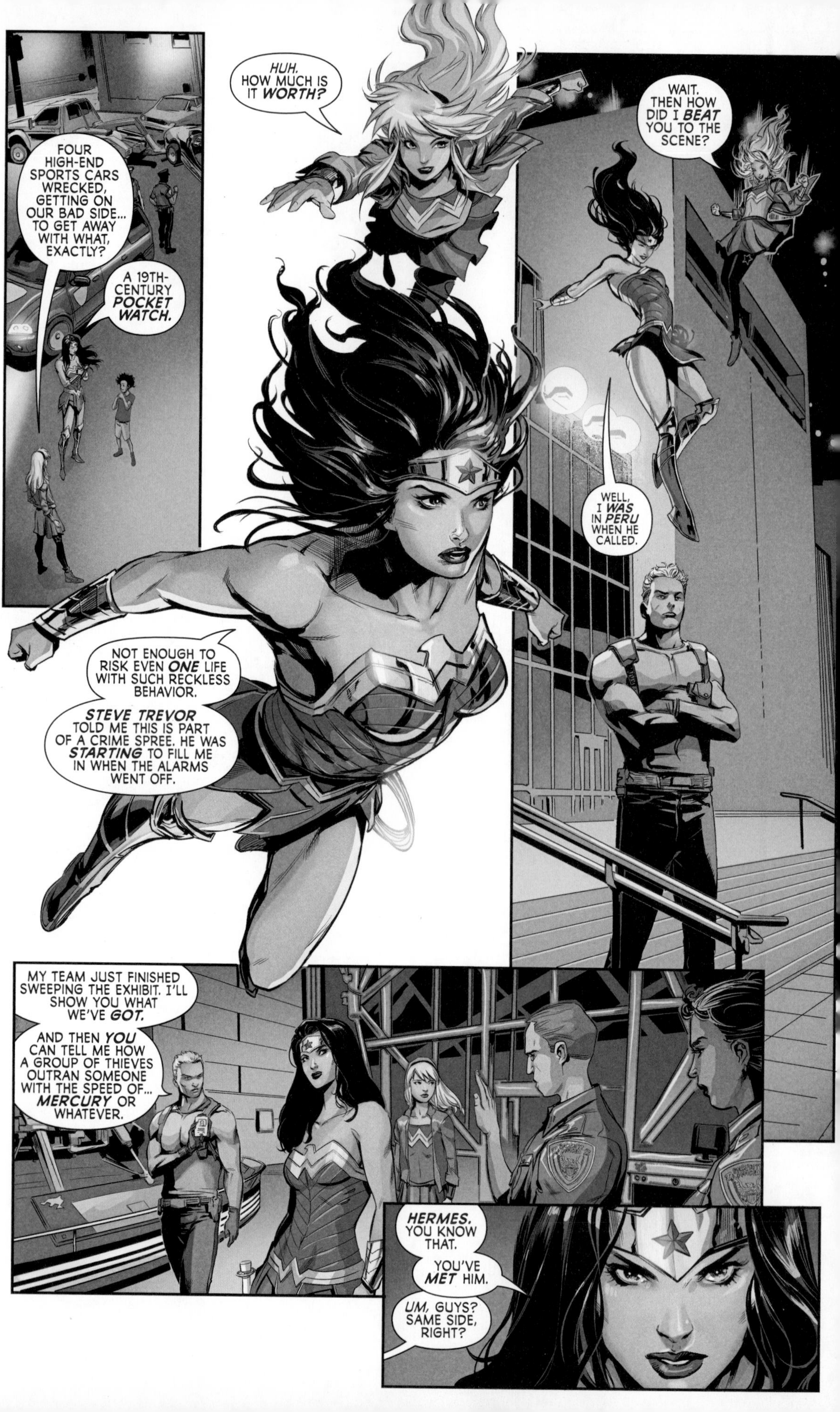

FOUR HIGH-END SPORTS CARS WRECKED, GETTING ON OUR BAD SIDE... TO GET AWAY WITH WHAT, EXACTLY?
A 19TH-CENTURY POCKET WATCH.
HUH. HOW MUCH IS IT WORTH?
NOT ENOUGH TO RISK EVEN ONE LIFE WITH SUCH RECKLESS BEHAVIOR.
STEVE TREVOR TOLD ME THIS IS PART OF A CRIME SPREE. HE WAS STARTING TO FILL ME IN WHEN THE ALARMS WENT OFF.
WAIT. THEN HOW DID I BEAT YOU TO THE SCENE?
WELL, I WAS IN PERU WHEN HE CALLED.
MY TEAM JUST FINISHED SWEEPING THE EXHIBIT. I'LL SHOW YOU WHAT WE'VE GOT.
AND THEN YOU CAN TELL ME HOW A GROUP OF THIEVES OUTRAN SOMEONE WITH THE SPEED OF... MERCURY OR WHATEVER.
HERMES. YOU KNOW THAT.
YOU'VE MET HIM.
UM, GUYS? SAME SIDE, RIGHT?

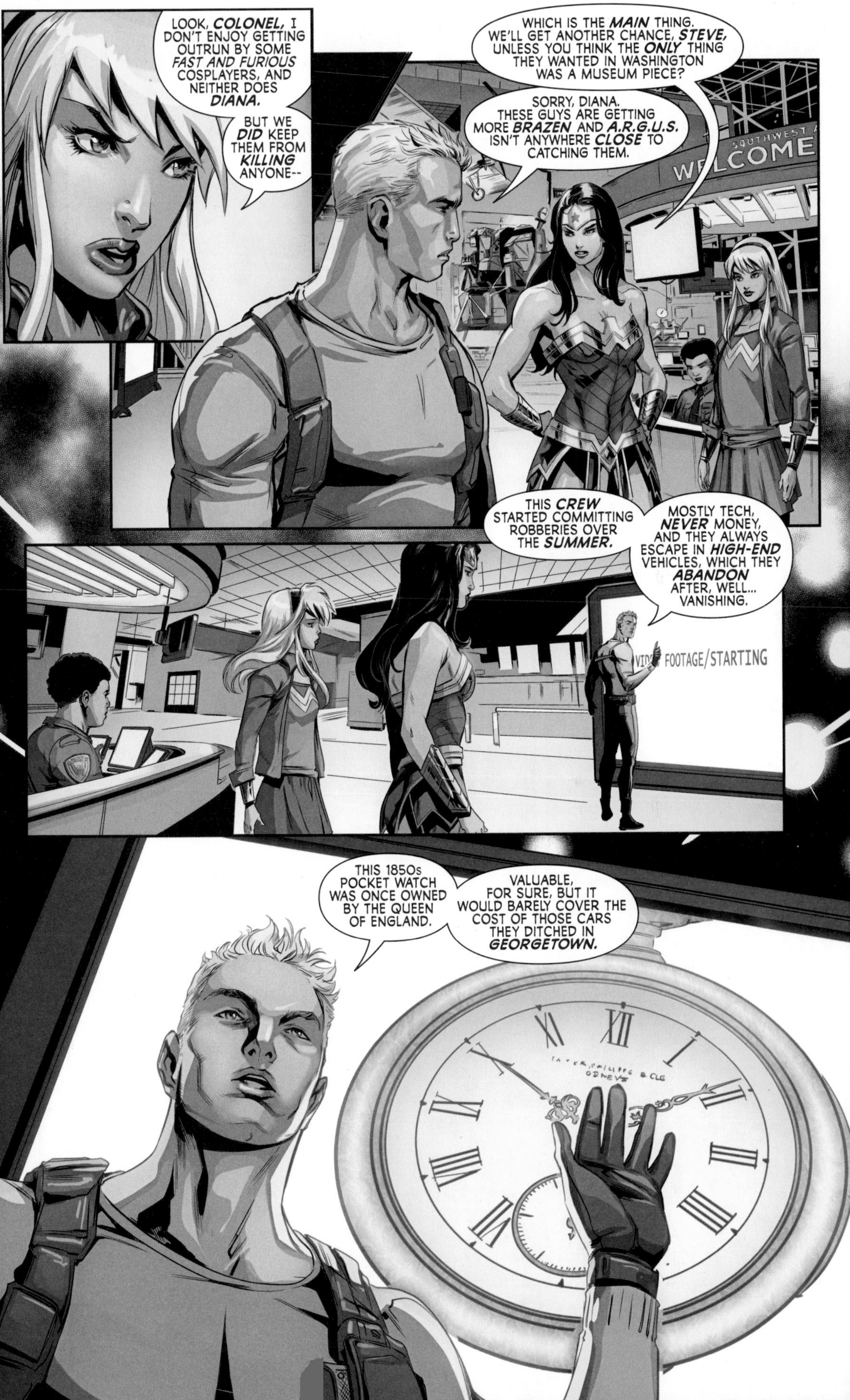
LOOK, COLONEL, I DON'T ENJOY GETTING OUTRUN BY SOME FAST AND FURIOUS COSPLAYERS, AND NEITHER DOES DIANA.
BUT WE DID KEEP THEM FROM KILLING ANYONE--
WHICH IS THE MAIN THING. WE'LL GET ANOTHER CHANCE, STEVE, UNLESS YOU THINK THE ONLY THING THEY WANTED IN WASHINGTON WAS A MUSEUM PIECE?
SORRY, DIANA. THESE GUYS ARE GETTING MORE BRAZEN AND A.R.G.U.S. ISN'T ANYWHERE CLOSE TO CATCHING THEM.
SOUTHWEST A
WELCOME
THIS CREW STARTED COMMITTING ROBBERIES OVER THE SUMMER.
MOSTLY TECH, NEVER MONEY, AND THEY ALWAYS ESCAPE IN HIGH-END VEHICLES, WHICH THEY ABANDON AFTER, WELL... VANISHING.
FOOTAGE/STARTING
THIS 1850s POCKET WATCH WAS ONCE OWNED BY THE QUEEN OF ENGLAND.
VALUABLE, FOR SURE, BUT IT WOULD BARELY COVER THE COST OF THOSE CARS THEY DITCHED IN GEORGETOWN.

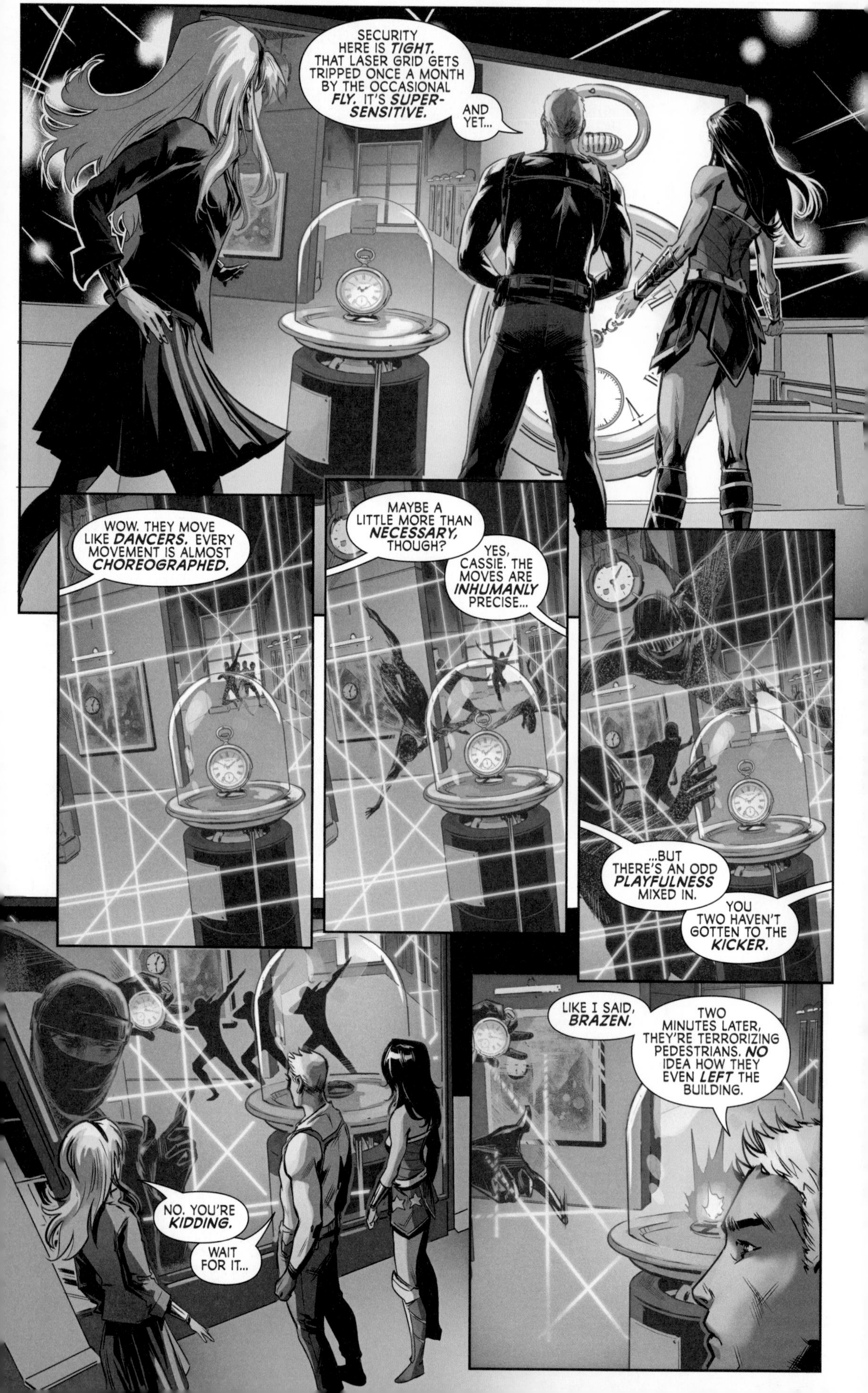

SECURITY HERE IS TIGHT. THAT LASER GRID GETS TRIPPED ONCE A MONTH BY THE OCCASIONAL FLY. IT'S SUPER-SENSITIVE.
AND YET...
WOW. THEY MOVE LIKE DANCERS. EVERY MOVEMENT IS ALMOST CHOREOGRAPHED.
MAYBE A LITTLE MORE THAN NECESSARY, THOUGH?
YES, CASSIE. THE MOVES ARE INHUMANLY PRECISE...
...BUT THERE'S AN ODD PLAYFULNESS MIXED IN.
YOU TWO HAVEN'T GOTTEN TO THE KICKER.
NO. YOU'RE KIDDING.
WAIT FOR IT...
LIKE I SAID, BRAZEN.
TWO MINUTES LATER, THEY'RE TERRORIZING PEDESTRIANS. NO IDEA HOW THEY EVEN LEFT THE BUILDING.

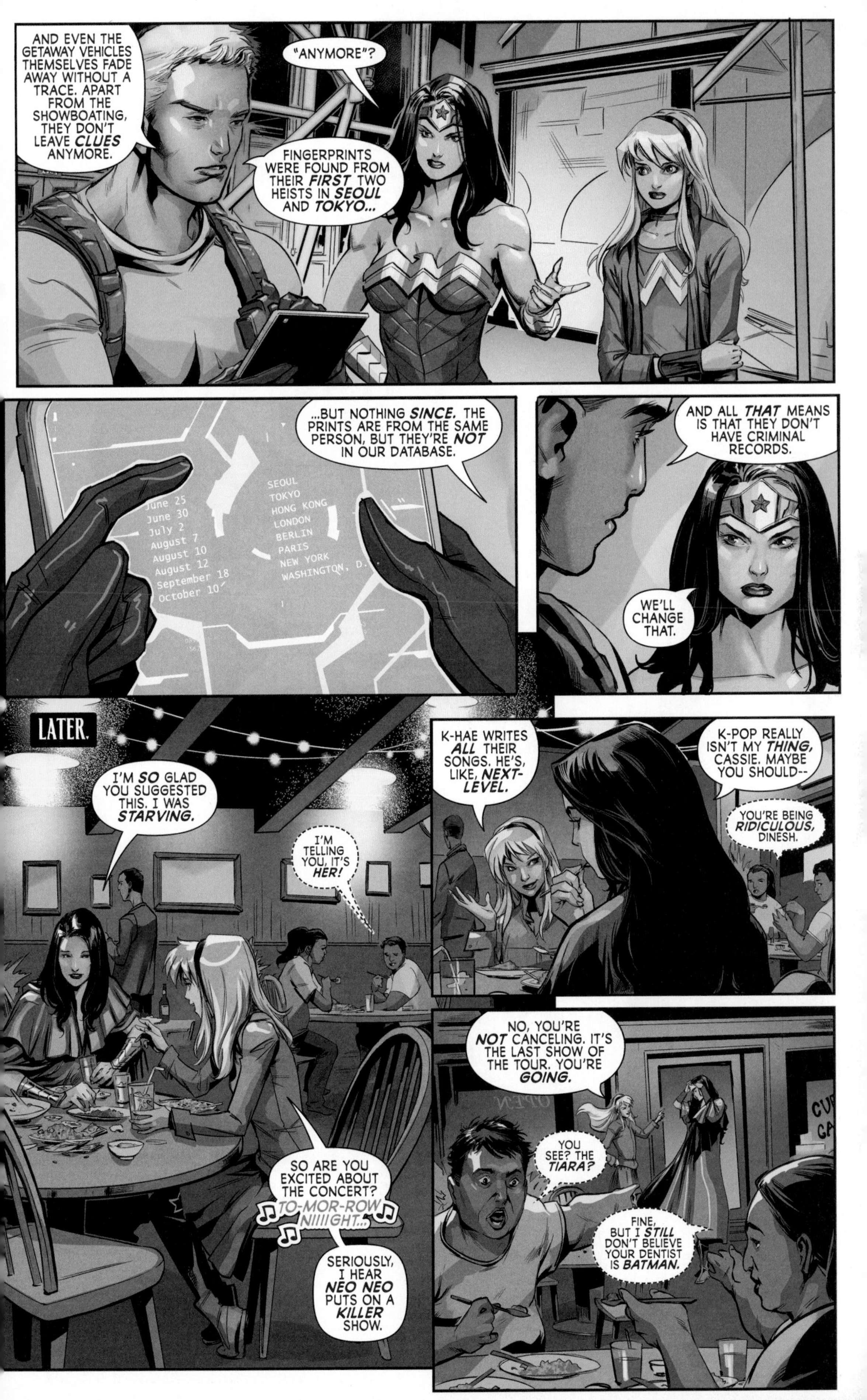
AND EVEN THE GETAWAY VEHICLES THEMSELVES FADE AWAY WITHOUT A TRACE. APART FROM THE SHOWBOATING, THEY DON'T LEAVE *CLUES* ANYMORE.
"ANYMORE"?
FINGERPRINTS WERE FOUND FROM THEIR *FIRST* TWO HEISTS IN *SEOUL* AND *TOKYO...*
June 25
June 30
July 2
August 7
August 10
August 12
September 18
October 10
SEOUL
TOKYO
HONG KONG
LONDON
BERLIN
PARIS
NEW YORK
WASHINGTON, D.
...BUT NOTHING *SINCE.* THE PRINTS ARE FROM THE SAME PERSON, BUT THEY'RE *NOT* IN OUR DATABASE.
AND ALL *THAT* MEANS IS THAT THEY DON'T HAVE CRIMINAL RECORDS.
WE'LL CHANGE THAT.
LATER.
I'M *SO* GLAD YOU SUGGESTED THIS. I WAS *STARVING.*
I'M TELLING YOU, IT'S *HER!*
SO ARE YOU EXCITED ABOUT THE CONCERT?
TO-MOR-ROW NIIIIGHT...
SERIOUSLY, I HEAR *NEO NEO* PUTS ON A *KILLER* SHOW.
K-HAE WRITES *ALL* THEIR SONGS. HE'S, LIKE, *NEXT-LEVEL.*
K-POP REALLY ISN'T MY *THING,* CASSIE. MAYBE YOU SHOULD--
YOU'RE BEING *RIDICULOUS,* DINESH.
NO, YOU'RE *NOT* CANCELING. IT'S THE LAST SHOW OF THE TOUR. YOU'RE *GOING.*
YOU SEE? THE *TIARA?*
FINE, BUT I *STILL* DON'T BELIEVE YOUR DENTIST IS *BATMAN.*

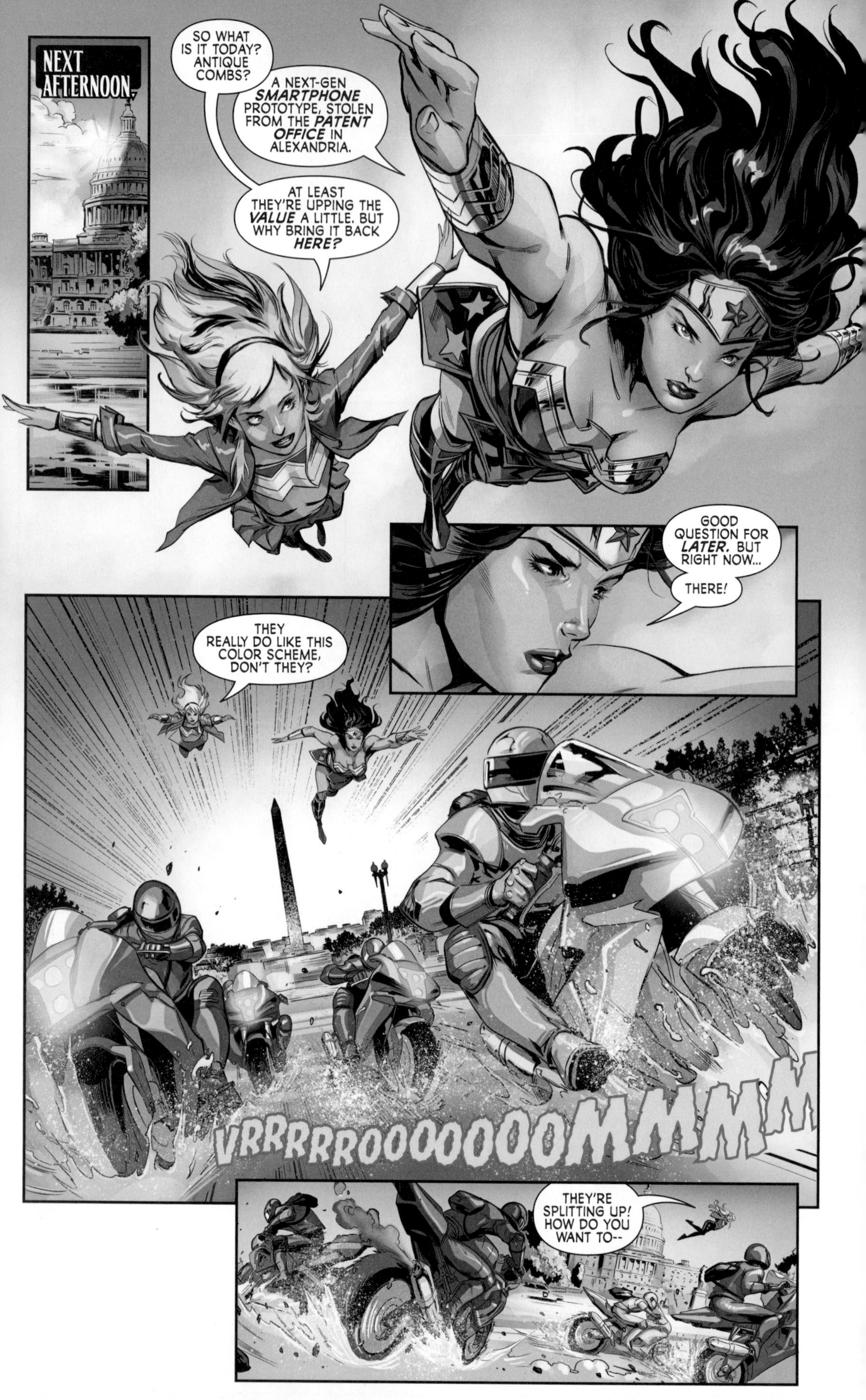
NEXT AFTERNOON.
SO WHAT IS IT TODAY? ANTIQUE COMBS?
A NEXT-GEN SMARTPHONE PROTOTYPE, STOLEN FROM THE PATENT OFFICE IN ALEXANDRIA.
AT LEAST THEY'RE UPPING THE VALUE A LITTLE. BUT WHY BRING IT BACK HERE?
GOOD QUESTION FOR LATER. BUT RIGHT NOW...
THERE!
THEY REALLY DO LIKE THIS COLOR SCHEME, DON'T THEY?
VRRRRROOOOOOOOMMMM
THEY'RE SPLITTING UP! HOW DO YOU WANT TO--

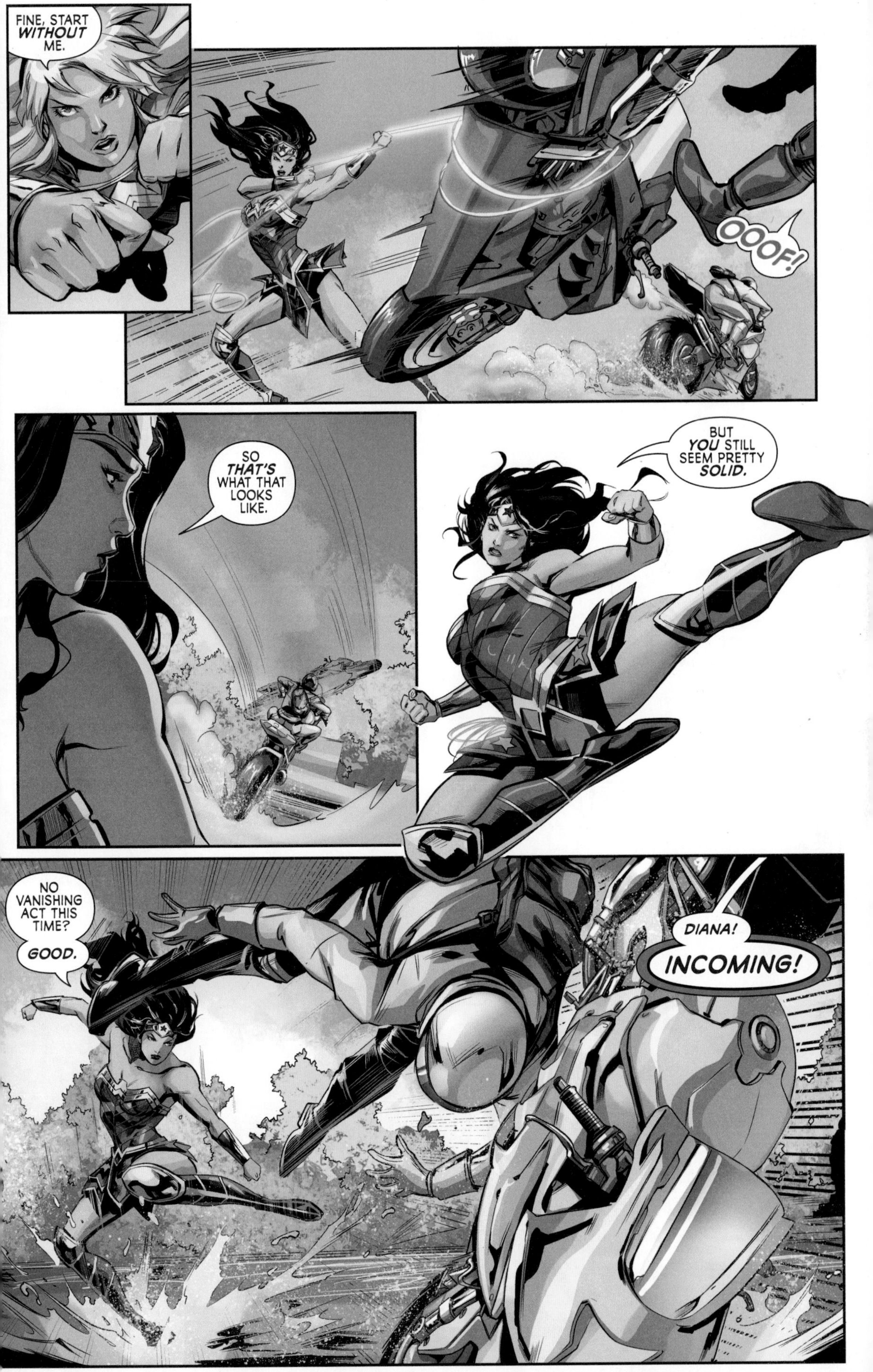
FINE, START *WITHOUT* ME.
OOOF!
SO *THAT'S* WHAT THAT LOOKS LIKE.
BUT *YOU* STILL SEEM PRETTY *SOLID.*
NO VANISHING ACT THIS TIME? *GOOD.*
DIANA! **INCOMING!**

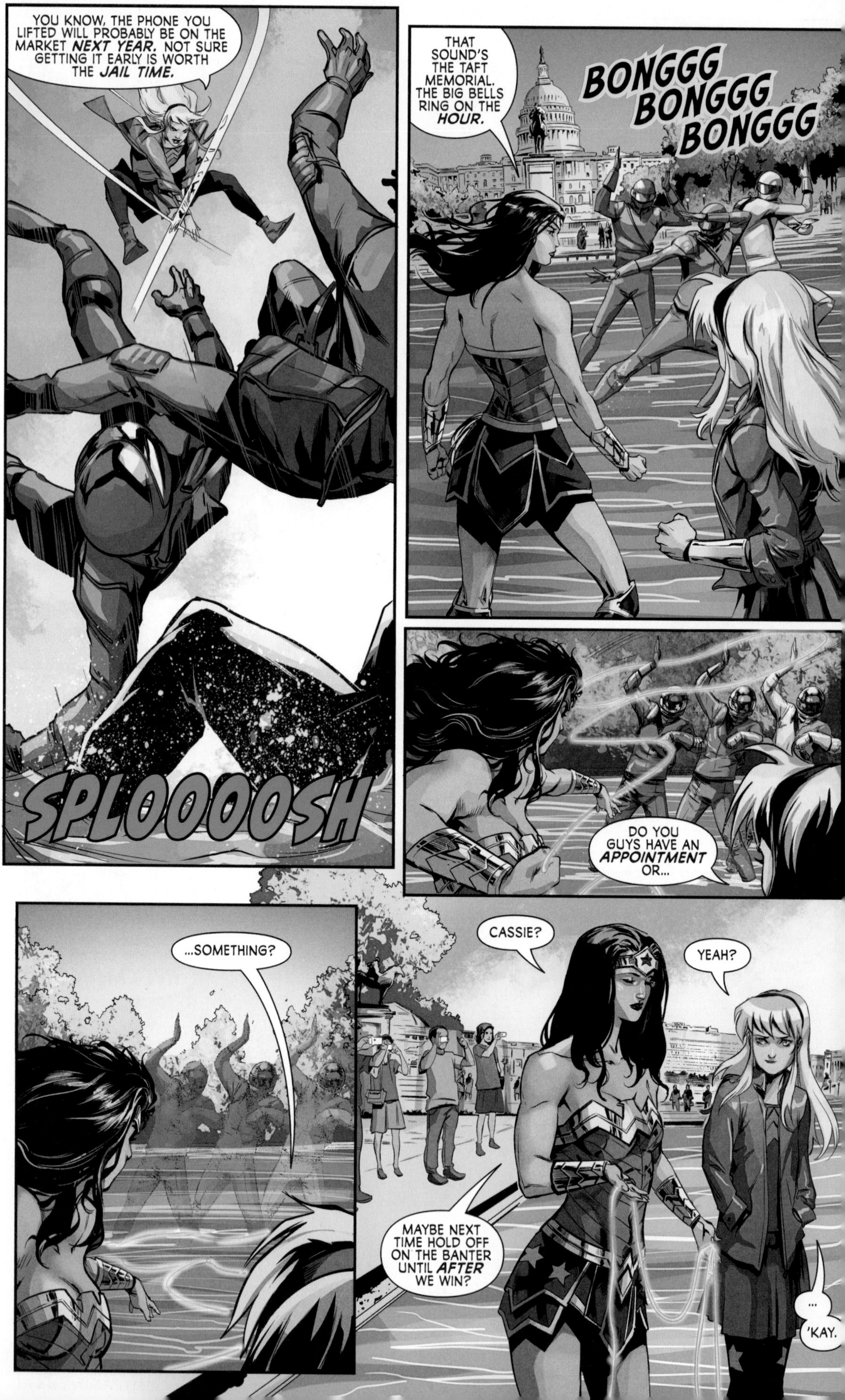
YOU KNOW, THE PHONE YOU LIFTED WILL PROBABLY BE ON THE MARKET NEXT YEAR. NOT SURE GETTING IT EARLY IS WORTH THE JAIL TIME.
SPLOOOOSH
THAT SOUND'S THE TAFT MEMORIAL. THE BIG BELLS RING ON THE HOUR.
BONGGG BONGGG BONGGG
DO YOU GUYS HAVE AN APPOINTMENT OR...
...SOMETHING?
CASSIE?
YEAH?
MAYBE NEXT TIME HOLD OFF ON THE BANTER UNTIL AFTER WE WIN?
...
'KAY.

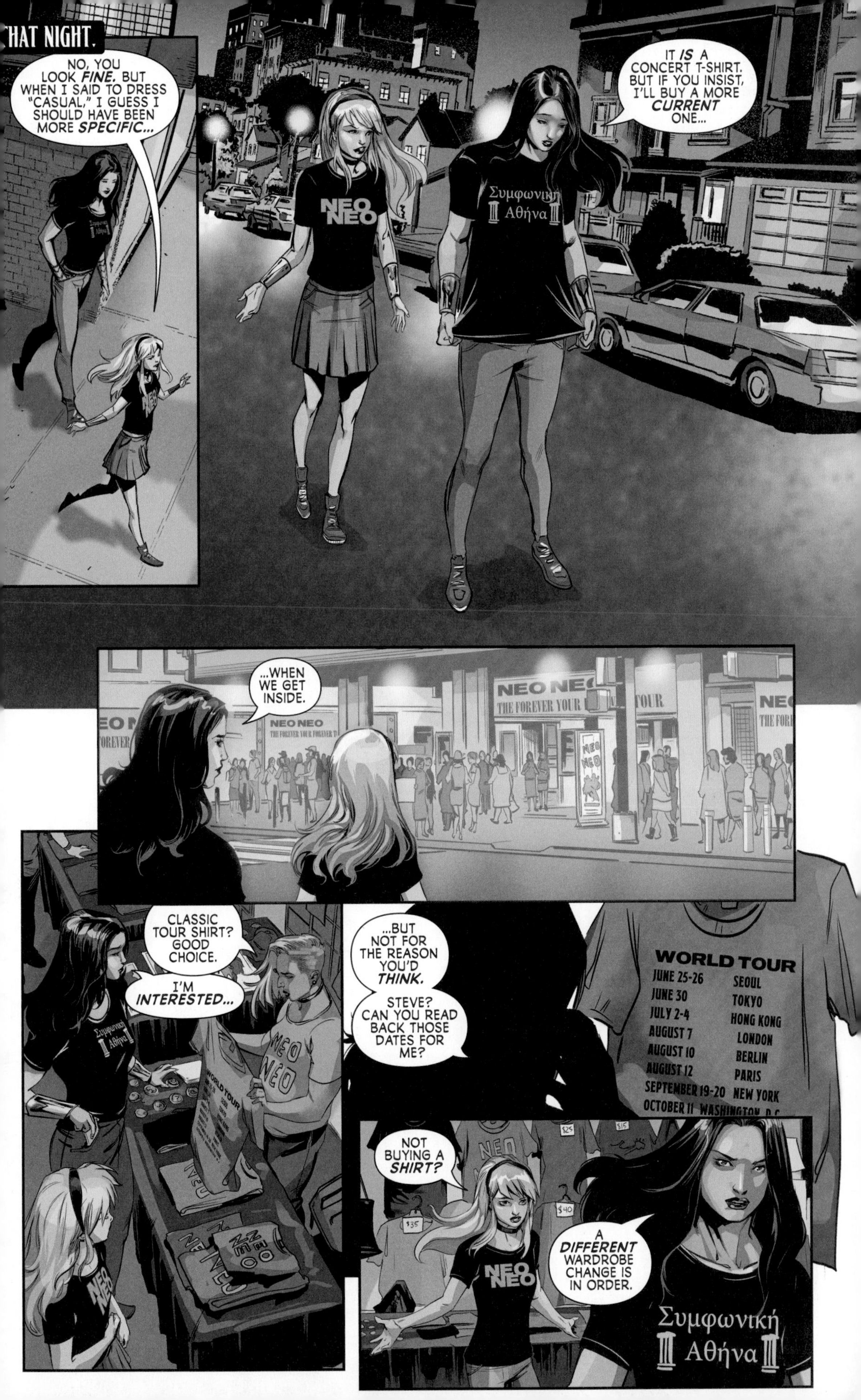
HAT NIGHT.
NO, YOU LOOK FINE. BUT WHEN I SAID TO DRESS "CASUAL," I GUESS I SHOULD HAVE BEEN MORE SPECIFIC...
IT IS A CONCERT T-SHIRT. BUT IF YOU INSIST, I'LL BUY A MORE CURRENT ONE...
NEO NEO
Συμφωνική Αθήνα
...WHEN WE GET INSIDE.
NEO NEO
THE FOREVER YOUR
TOUR
CLASSIC TOUR SHIRT? GOOD CHOICE.
I'M INTERESTED...
...BUT NOT FOR THE REASON YOU'D THINK.
STEVE? CAN YOU READ BACK THOSE DATES FOR ME?
WORLD TOUR
JUNE 25-26 SEOUL
JUNE 30 TOKYO
JULY 2-4 HONG KONG
AUGUST 7 LONDON
AUGUST 10 BERLIN
AUGUST 12 PARIS
SEPTEMBER 19-20 NEW YORK
NOT BUYING A SHIRT?
A DIFFERENT WARDROBE CHANGE IS IN ORDER.
Συμφωνική Αθήνα

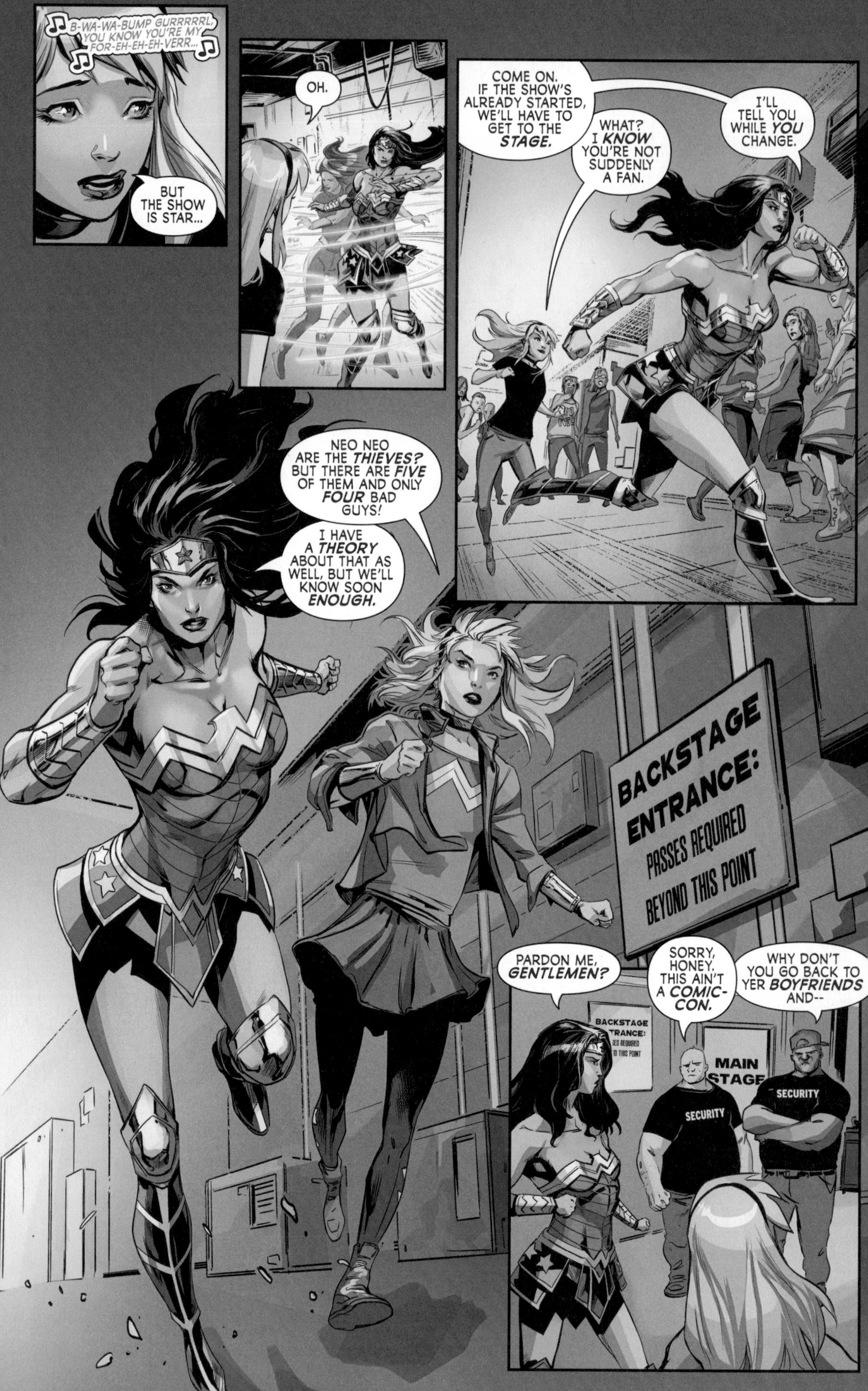
B-WA-WA-BUMP GURRRRRL, YOU KNOW YOU'RE MY FOR-EH-EH-EH-VERR...
BUT THE SHOW IS STAR...
OH.
COME ON. IF THE SHOW'S ALREADY STARTED, WE'LL HAVE TO GET TO THE STAGE.
WHAT? I KNOW YOU'RE NOT SUDDENLY A FAN.
I'LL TELL YOU WHILE YOU CHANGE.
NEO NEO ARE THE THIEVES? BUT THERE ARE FIVE OF THEM AND ONLY FOUR BAD GUYS!
I HAVE A THEORY ABOUT THAT AS WELL, BUT WE'LL KNOW SOON ENOUGH.
BACKSTAGE ENTRANCE: PASSES REQUIRED BEYOND THIS POINT
PARDON ME, GENTLEMEN?
SORRY, HONEY. THIS AIN'T A COMIC-CON.
WHY DON'T YOU GO BACK TO YER BOYFRIENDS AND--
MAIN STAGE
SECURITY
SECURITY

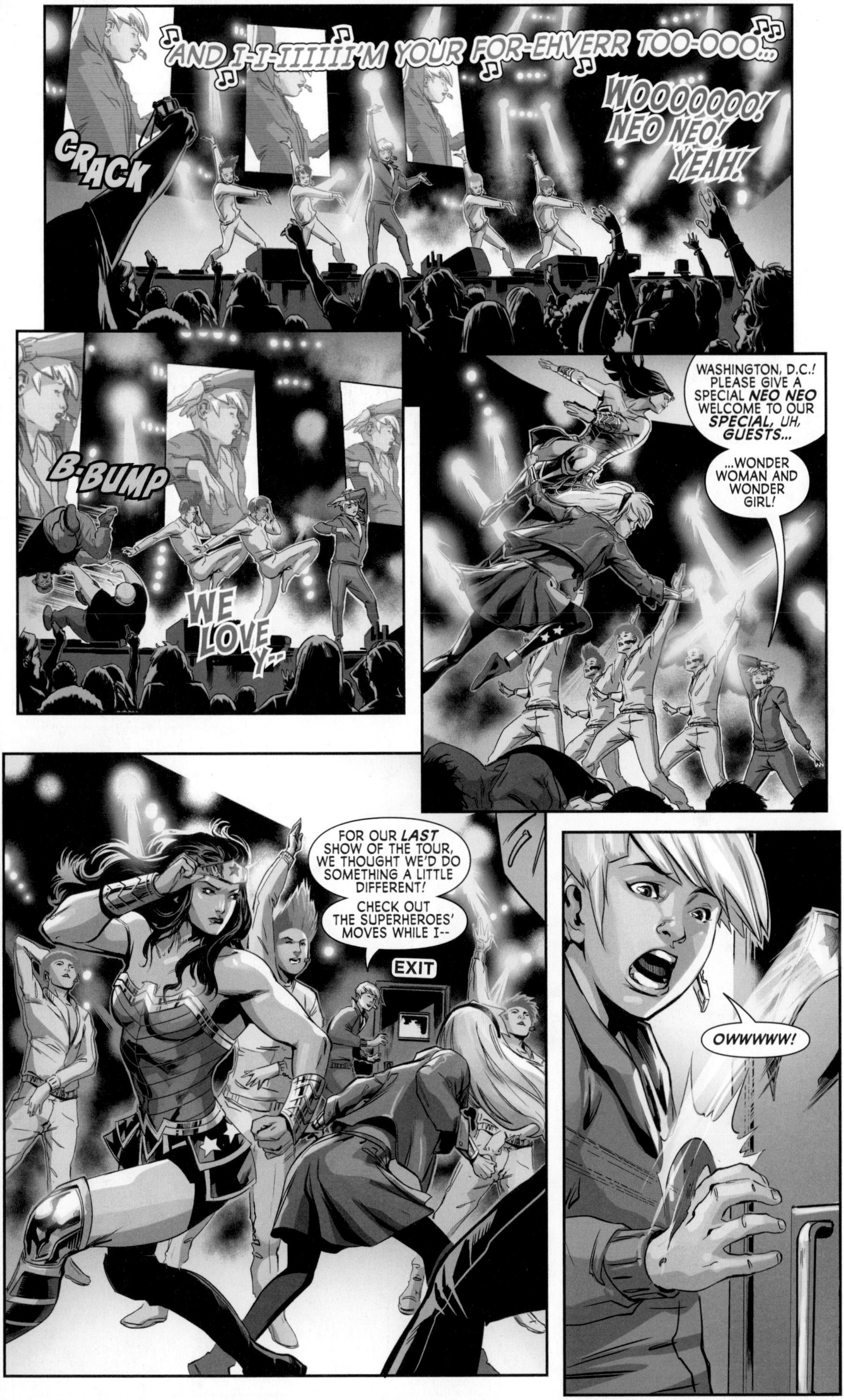

AND I-I-IIIIII'M YOUR FOR-EHVERR TOO-OOO...
CRACK
WOOOOOOO! NEO NEO! YEAH!
B-BUMP
WE LOVE Y--
WASHINGTON, D.C.! PLEASE GIVE A SPECIAL NEO NEO WELCOME TO OUR SPECIAL, UH, GUESTS...
...WONDER WOMAN AND WONDER GIRL!
FOR OUR LAST SHOW OF THE TOUR, WE THOUGHT WE'D DO SOMETHING A LITTLE DIFFERENT!
CHECK OUT THE SUPERHEROES' MOVES WHILE I--
EXIT
OWWWWW!

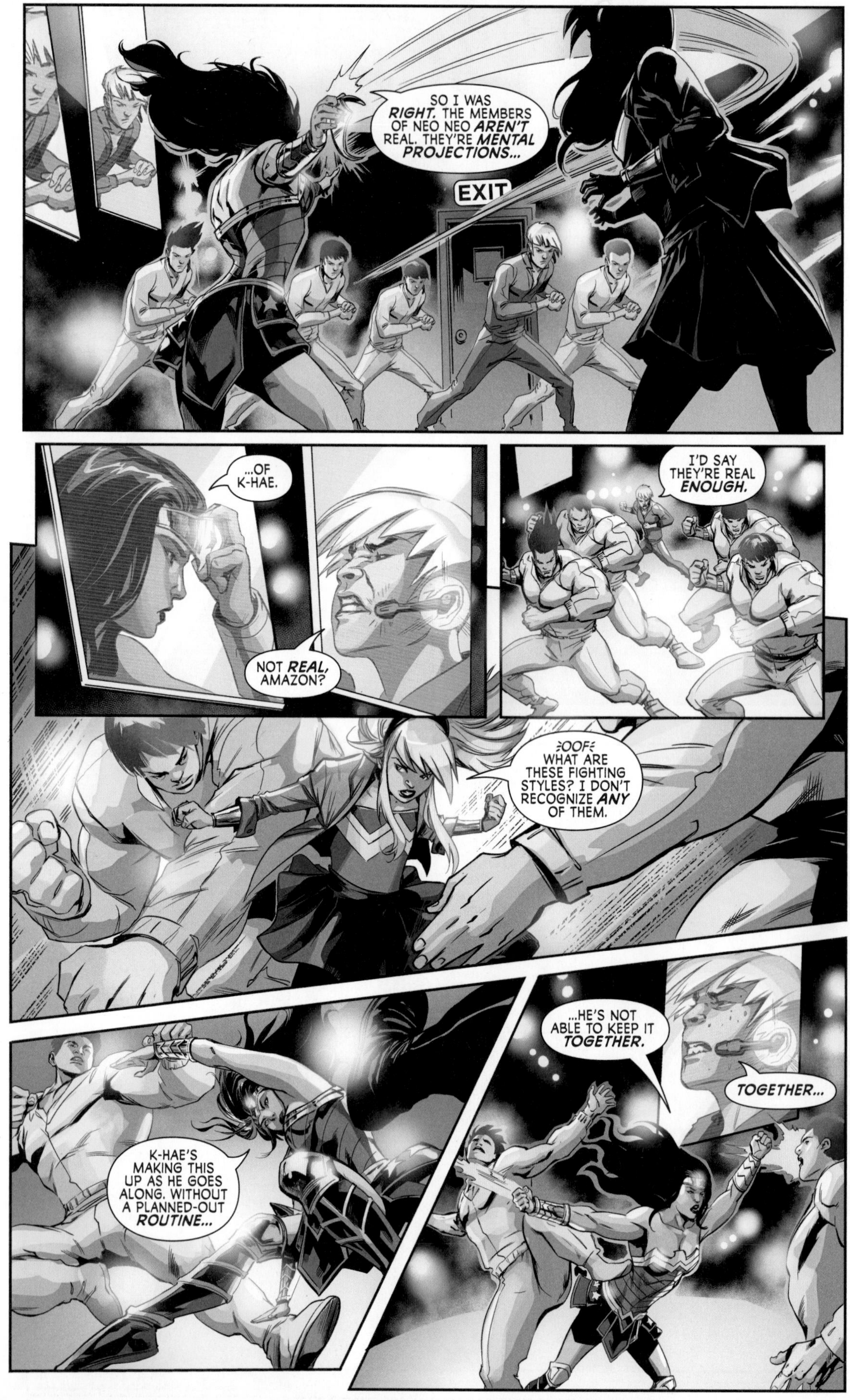
SO I WAS RIGHT. THE MEMBERS OF NEO NEO AREN'T REAL. THEY'RE MENTAL PROJECTIONS...
EXIT
...OF K-HAE.
NOT REAL, AMAZON?
I'D SAY THEY'RE REAL ENOUGH.
OOF WHAT ARE THESE FIGHTING STYLES? I DON'T RECOGNIZE ANY OF THEM.
K-HAE'S MAKING THIS UP AS HE GOES ALONG. WITHOUT A PLANNED-OUT ROUTINE...
...HE'S NOT ABLE TO KEEP IT TOGETHER.
TOGETHER...

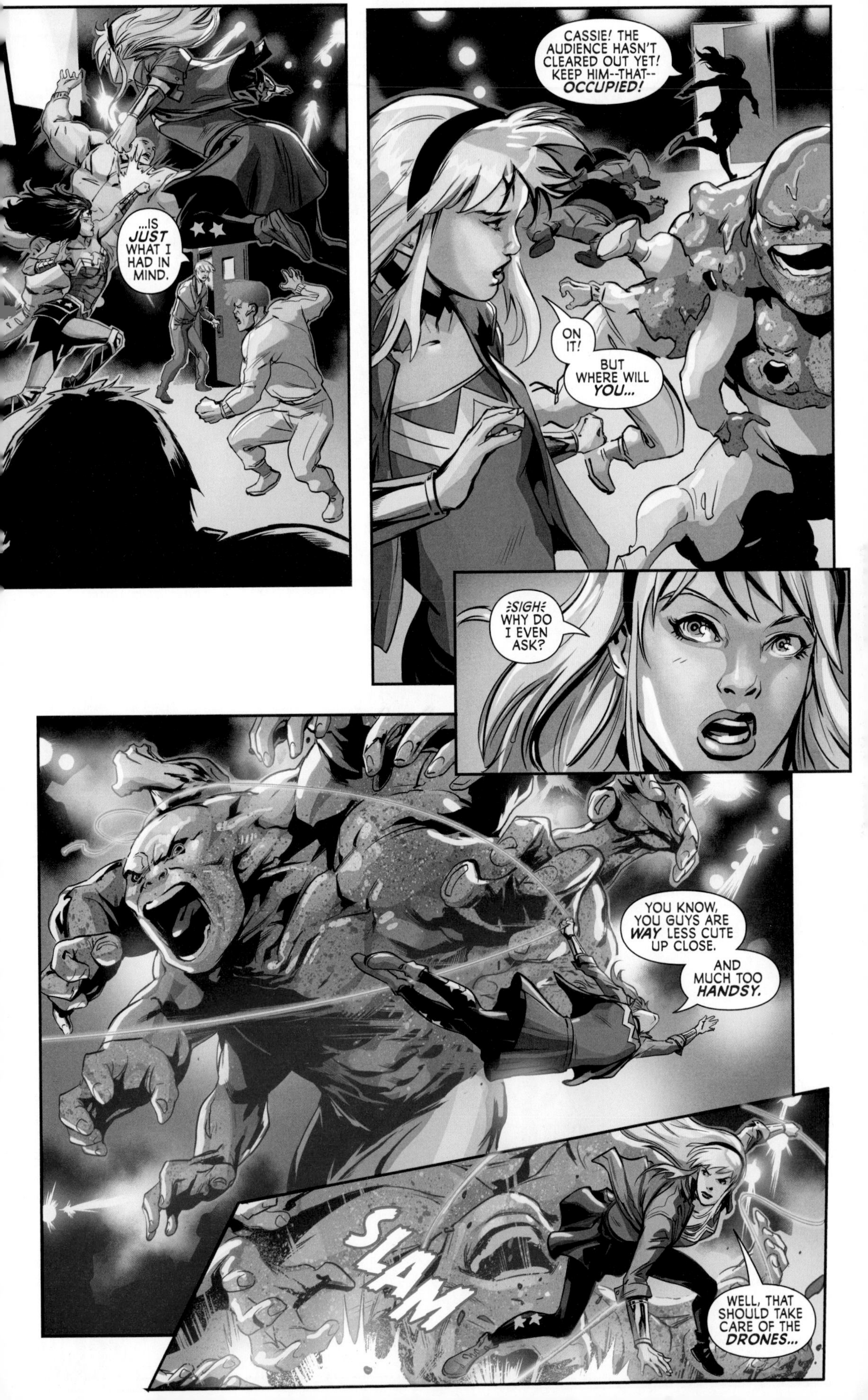
...IS JUST WHAT I HAD IN MIND.
CASSIE! THE AUDIENCE HASN'T CLEARED OUT YET! KEEP HIM--THAT--OCCUPIED!
ON IT!
BUT WHERE WILL YOU...
≥SIGH≤ WHY DO I EVEN ASK?
YOU KNOW, YOU GUYS ARE WAY LESS CUTE UP CLOSE.
AND MUCH TOO HANDSY.
SLAM
WELL, THAT SHOULD TAKE CARE OF THE DRONES...

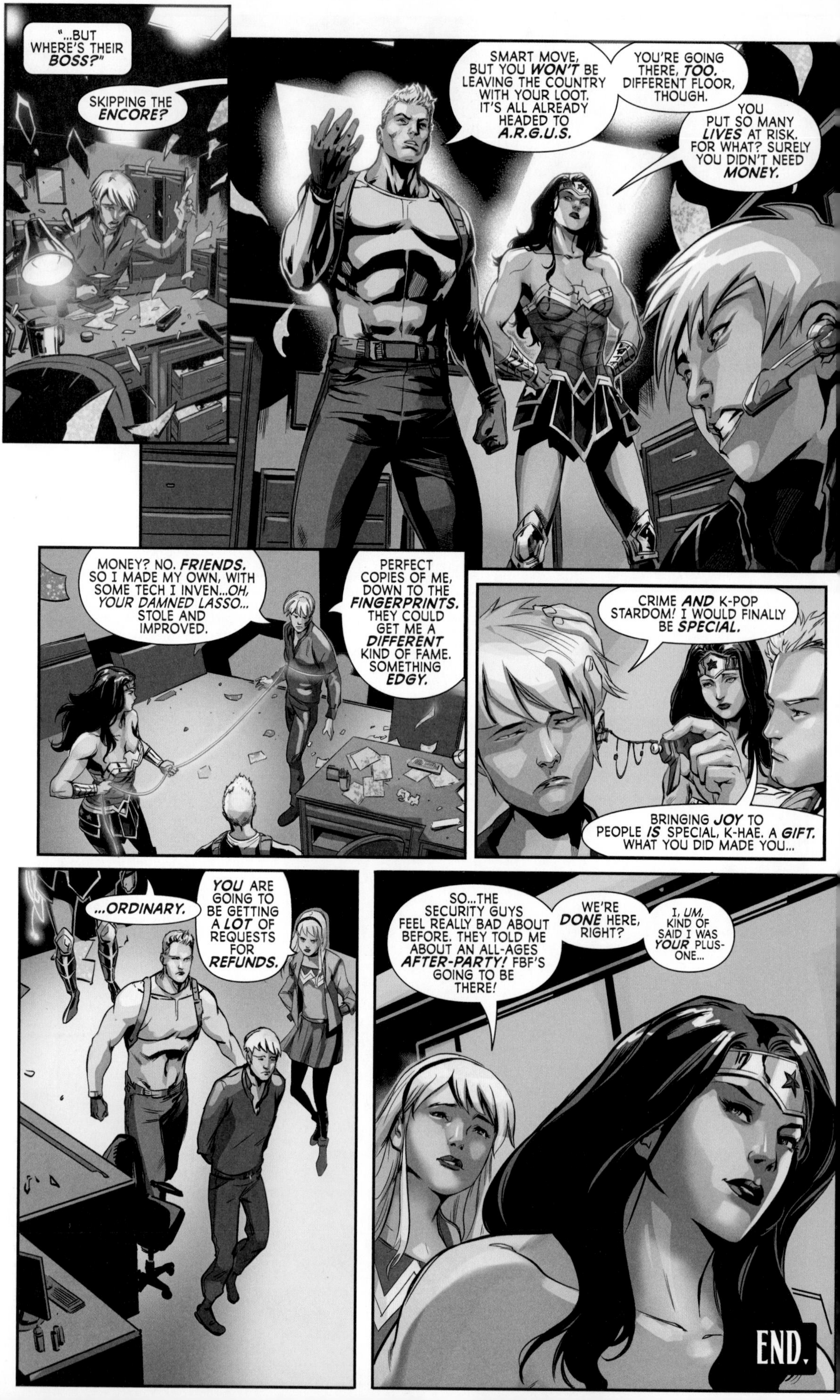
"...BUT WHERE'S THEIR BOSS?"
SKIPPING THE ENCORE?
SMART MOVE, BUT YOU WON'T BE LEAVING THE COUNTRY WITH YOUR LOOT. IT'S ALL ALREADY HEADED TO A.R.G.U.S.
YOU'RE GOING THERE, TOO. DIFFERENT FLOOR, THOUGH.
YOU PUT SO MANY LIVES AT RISK. FOR WHAT? SURELY YOU DIDN'T NEED MONEY.
MONEY? NO. FRIENDS. SO I MADE MY OWN, WITH SOME TECH I INVEN...OH, YOUR DAMNED LASSO... STOLE AND IMPROVED.
PERFECT COPIES OF ME, DOWN TO THE FINGERPRINTS. THEY COULD GET ME A DIFFERENT KIND OF FAME. SOMETHING EDGY.
CRIME AND K-POP STARDOM! I WOULD FINALLY BE SPECIAL.
BRINGING JOY TO PEOPLE IS SPECIAL, K-HAE. A GIFT. WHAT YOU DID MADE YOU...
...ORDINARY.
YOU ARE GOING TO BE GETTING A LOT OF REQUESTS FOR REFUNDS.
SO...THE SECURITY GUYS FEEL REALLY BAD ABOUT BEFORE. THEY TOLD ME ABOUT AN ALL-AGES AFTER-PARTY! FBF'S GOING TO BE THERE!
WE'RE DONE HERE, RIGHT?
I, UM, KIND OF SAID I WAS YOUR PLUS-ONE...
END.

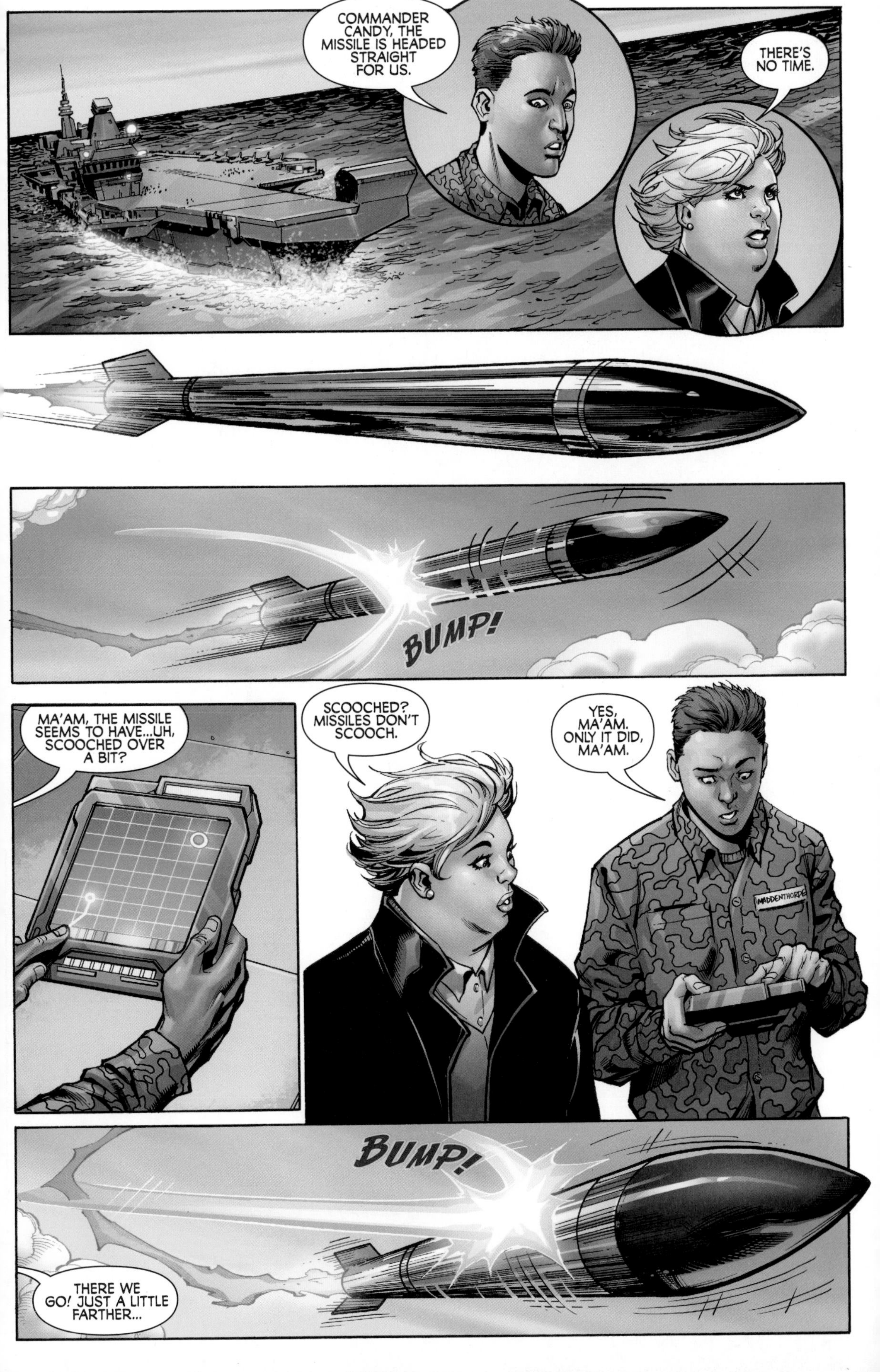
COMMANDER CANDY, THE MISSILE IS HEADED STRAIGHT FOR US.
THERE'S NO TIME.
BUMP!
MA'AM, THE MISSILE SEEMS TO HAVE...UH, SCOOCHED OVER A BIT?
SCOOCHED? MISSILES DON'T SCOOCH.
YES, MA'AM. ONLY IT DID, MA'AM.
MADDENTHORPE
BUMP!
THERE WE GO! JUST A LITTLE FARTHER...

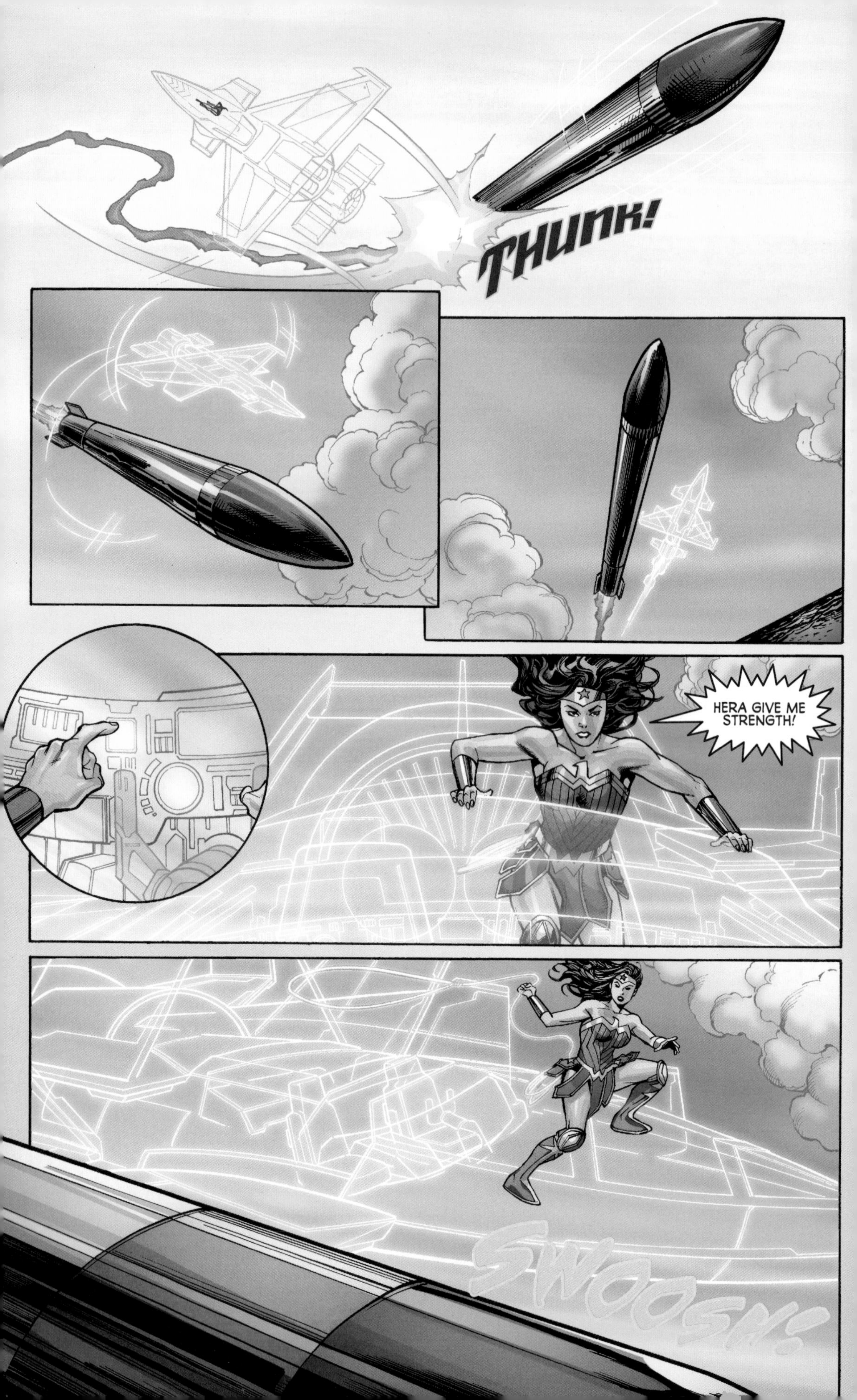
THUNK!
HERA GIVE ME STRENGTH!
SWOOSH!

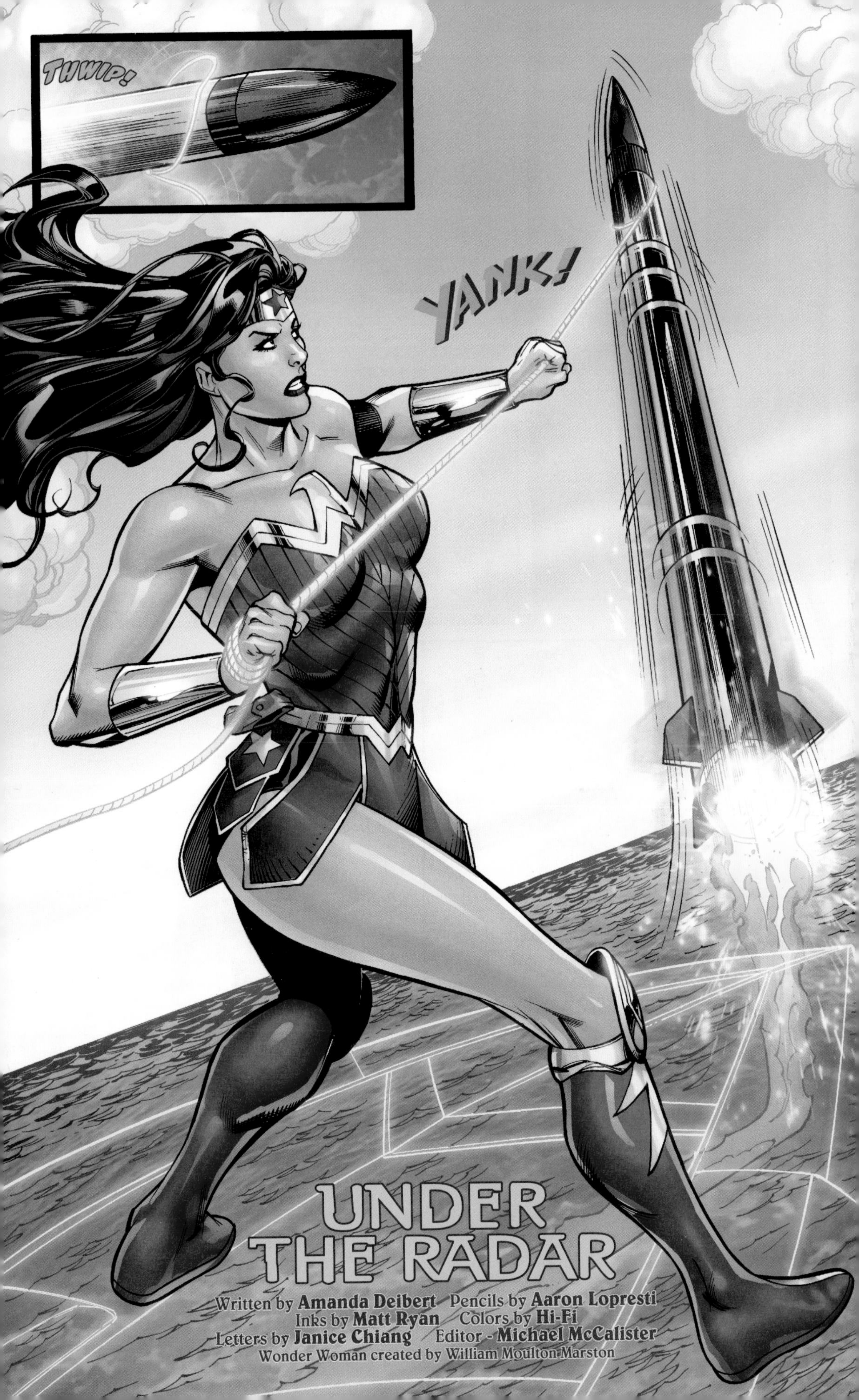
THWIP!
YANK!
UNDER THE RADAR
Written by Amanda Deibert Pencils by Aaron Lopresti
Inks by Matt Ryan Colors by Hi-Fi
Letters by Janice Chiang Editor - Michael McCalister
Wonder Woman created by William Moulton Marston

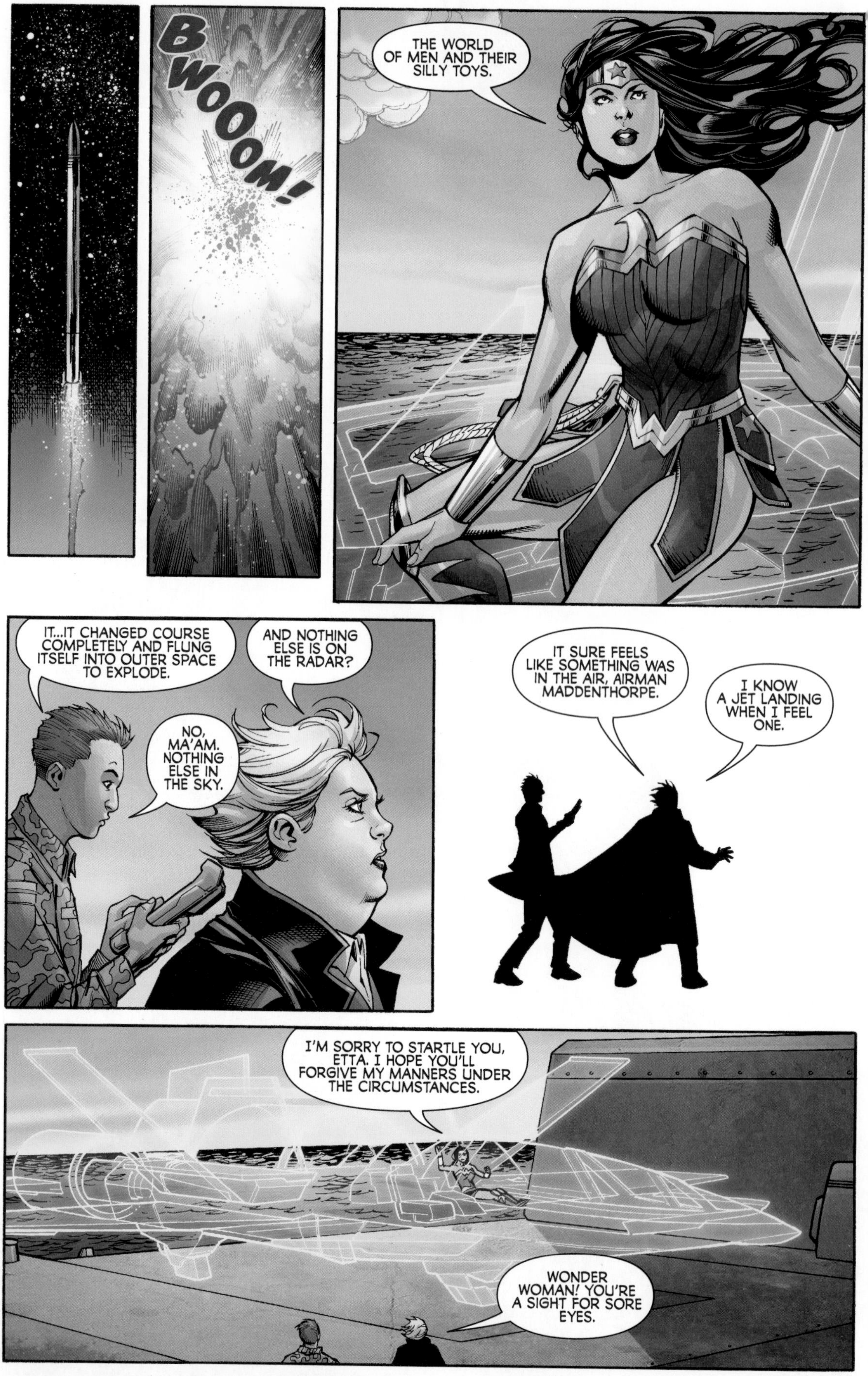
BWOOOM!
THE WORLD OF MEN AND THEIR SILLY TOYS.
IT...IT CHANGED COURSE COMPLETELY AND FLUNG ITSELF INTO OUTER SPACE TO EXPLODE.
AND NOTHING ELSE IS ON THE RADAR?
NO, MA'AM. NOTHING ELSE IN THE SKY.
IT SURE FEELS LIKE SOMETHING WAS IN THE AIR, AIRMAN MADDENTHORPE.
I KNOW A JET LANDING WHEN I FEEL ONE.
I'M SORRY TO STARTLE YOU, ETTA. I HOPE YOU'LL FORGIVE MY MANNERS UNDER THE CIRCUMSTANCES.
WONDER WOMAN! YOU'RE A SIGHT FOR SORE EYES.

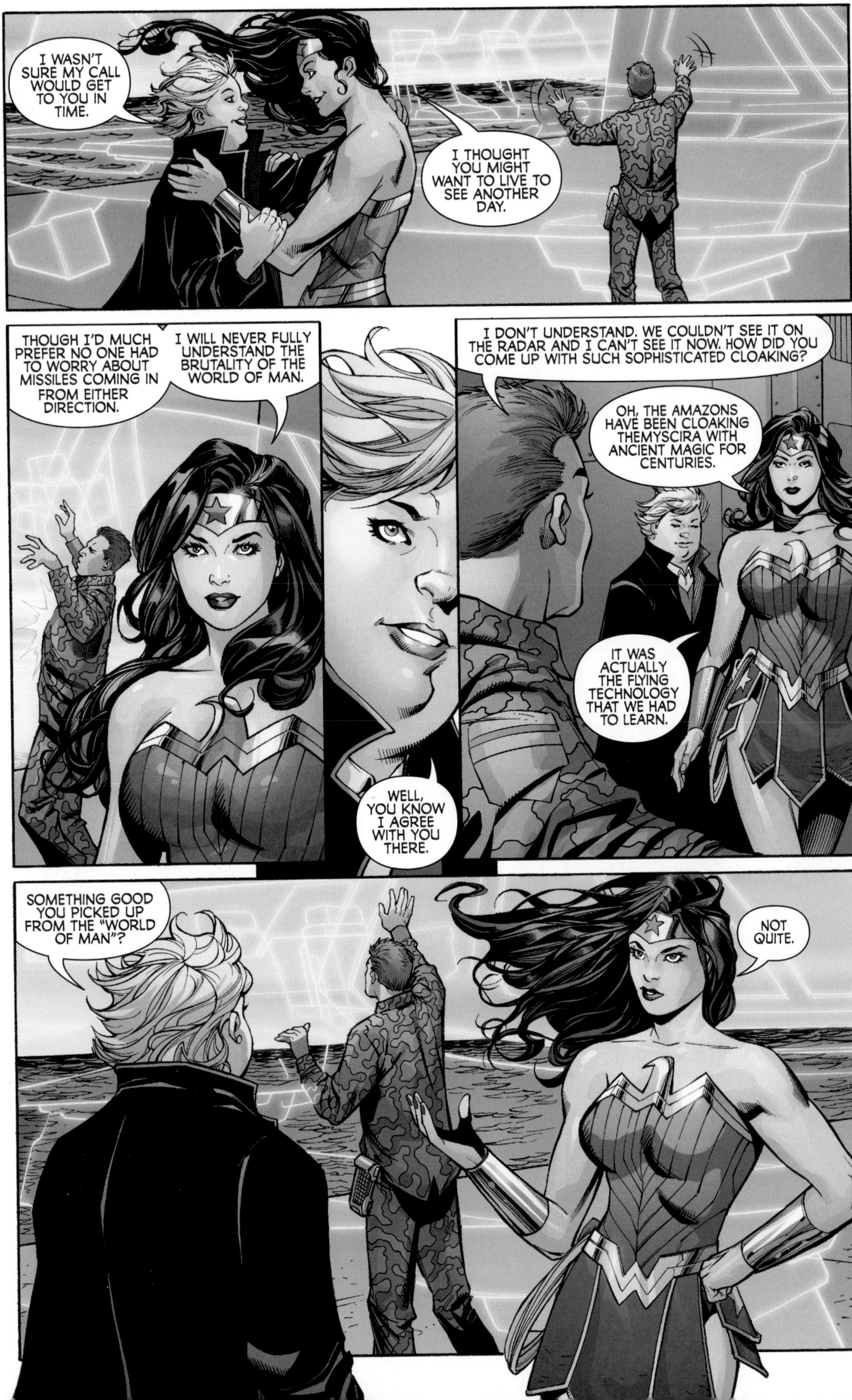
I WASN'T SURE MY CALL WOULD GET TO YOU IN TIME.
I THOUGHT YOU MIGHT WANT TO LIVE TO SEE ANOTHER DAY.
THOUGH I'D MUCH PREFER NO ONE HAD TO WORRY ABOUT MISSILES COMING IN FROM EITHER DIRECTION.
I WILL NEVER FULLY UNDERSTAND THE BRUTALITY OF THE WORLD OF MAN.
WELL, YOU KNOW I AGREE WITH YOU THERE.
I DON'T UNDERSTAND. WE COULDN'T SEE IT ON THE RADAR AND I CAN'T SEE IT NOW. HOW DID YOU COME UP WITH SUCH SOPHISTICATED CLOAKING?
OH, THE AMAZONS HAVE BEEN CLOAKING THEMYSCIRA WITH ANCIENT MAGIC FOR CENTURIES.
IT WAS ACTUALLY THE FLYING TECHNOLOGY THAT WE HAD TO LEARN.
SOMETHING GOOD YOU PICKED UP FROM THE "WORLD OF MAN"?
NOT QUITE.

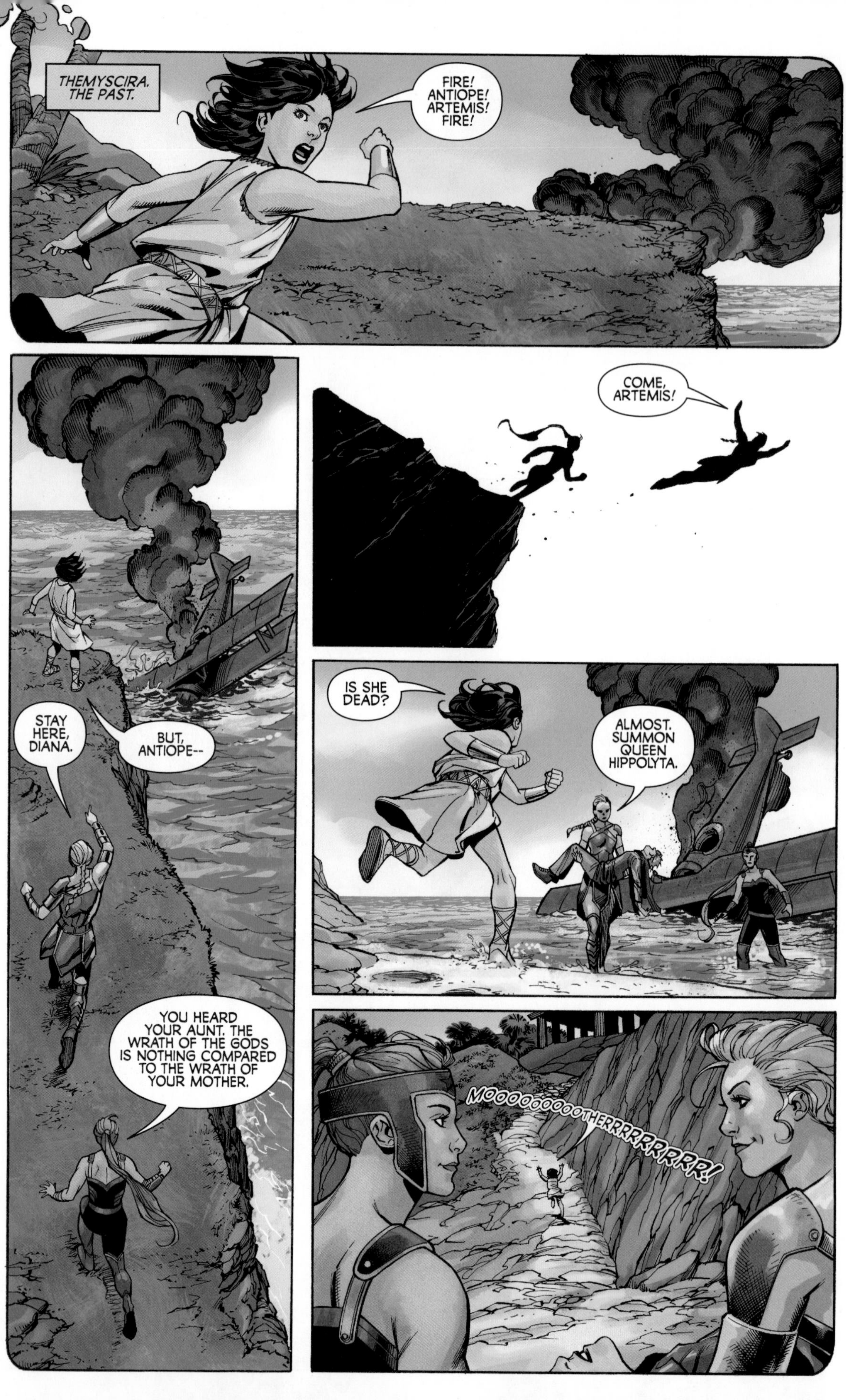
THEMYSCIRA. THE PAST.
FIRE! ANTIOPE! ARTEMIS! FIRE!
STAY HERE, DIANA.
BUT, ANTIOPE--
YOU HEARD YOUR AUNT. THE WRATH OF THE GODS IS NOTHING COMPARED TO THE WRATH OF YOUR MOTHER.
COME, ARTEMIS!
IS SHE DEAD?
ALMOST. SUMMON QUEEN HIPPOLYTA.
MOOOOOOOOOTHERRRRRRRRR!

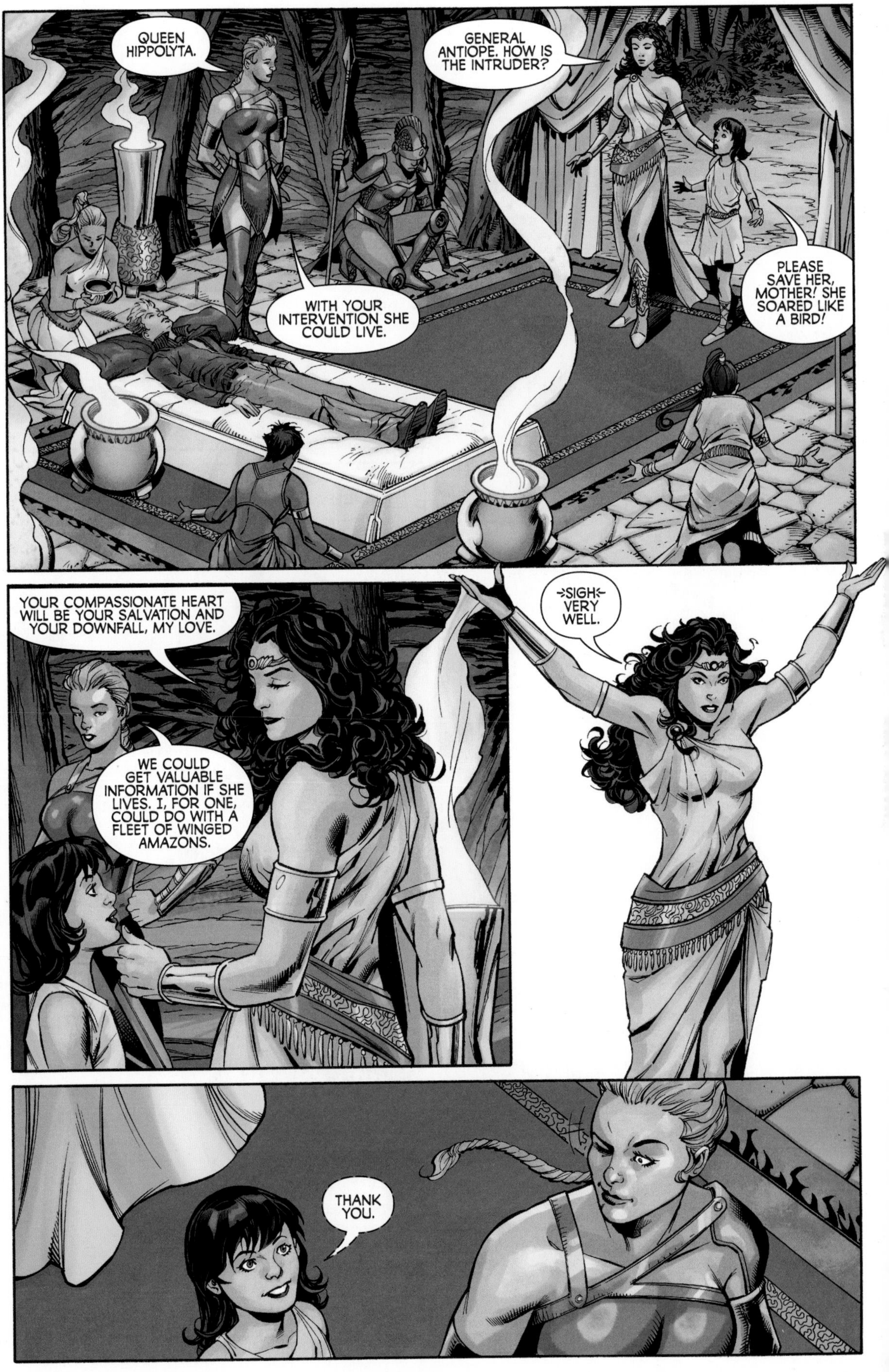
QUEEN HIPPOLYTA.
GENERAL ANTIOPE. HOW IS THE INTRUDER?
WITH YOUR INTERVENTION SHE COULD LIVE.
PLEASE SAVE HER, MOTHER! SHE SOARED LIKE A BIRD!
YOUR COMPASSIONATE HEART WILL BE YOUR SALVATION AND YOUR DOWNFALL, MY LOVE.
WE COULD GET VALUABLE INFORMATION IF SHE LIVES. I, FOR ONE, COULD DO WITH A FLEET OF WINGED AMAZONS.
SIGH VERY WELL.
THANK YOU.

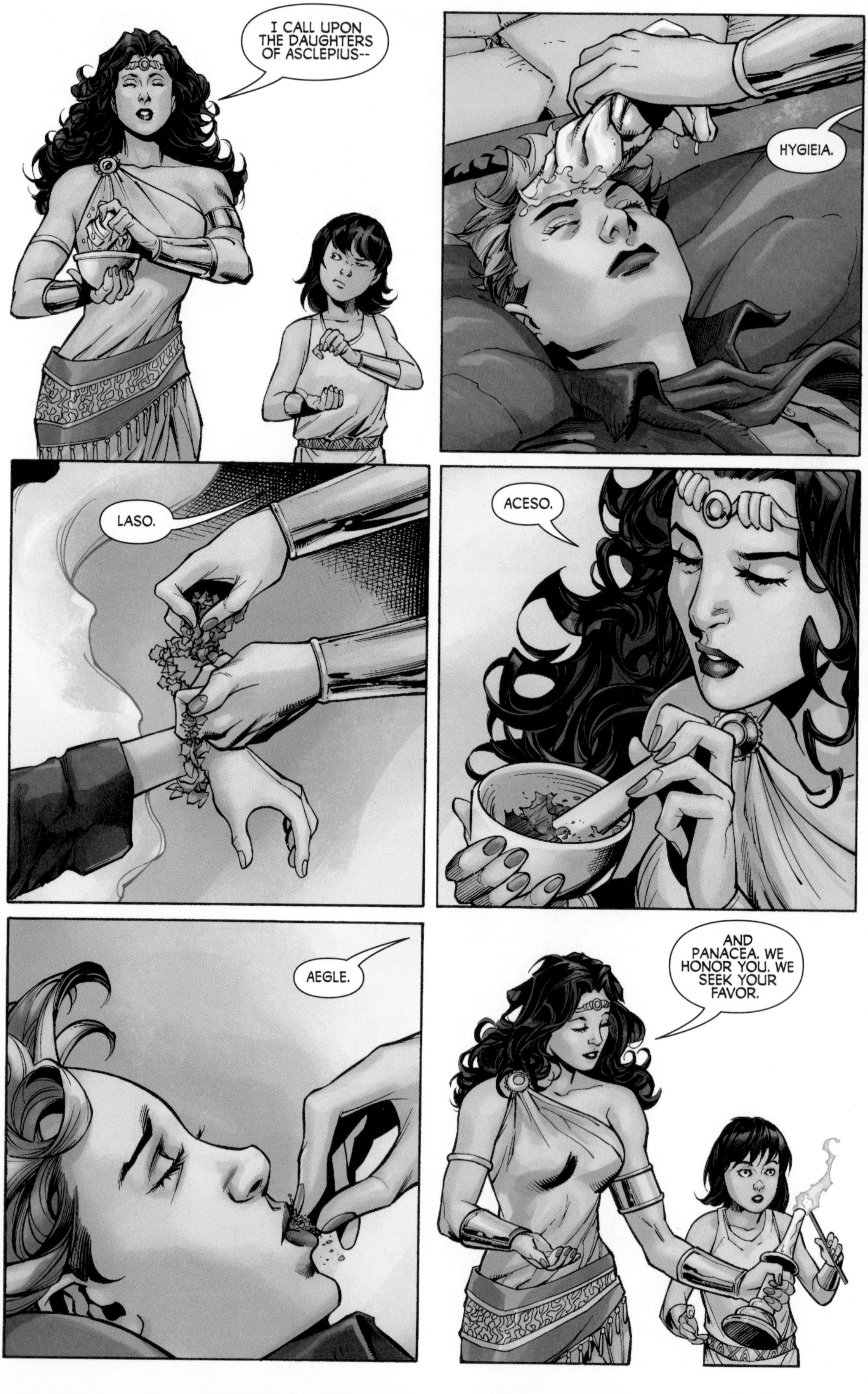
I CALL UPON THE DAUGHTERS OF ASCLEPIUS--
HYGIEIA.
LASO.
ACESO.
AEGLE.
AND PANACEA. WE HONOR YOU. WE SEEK YOUR FAVOR.

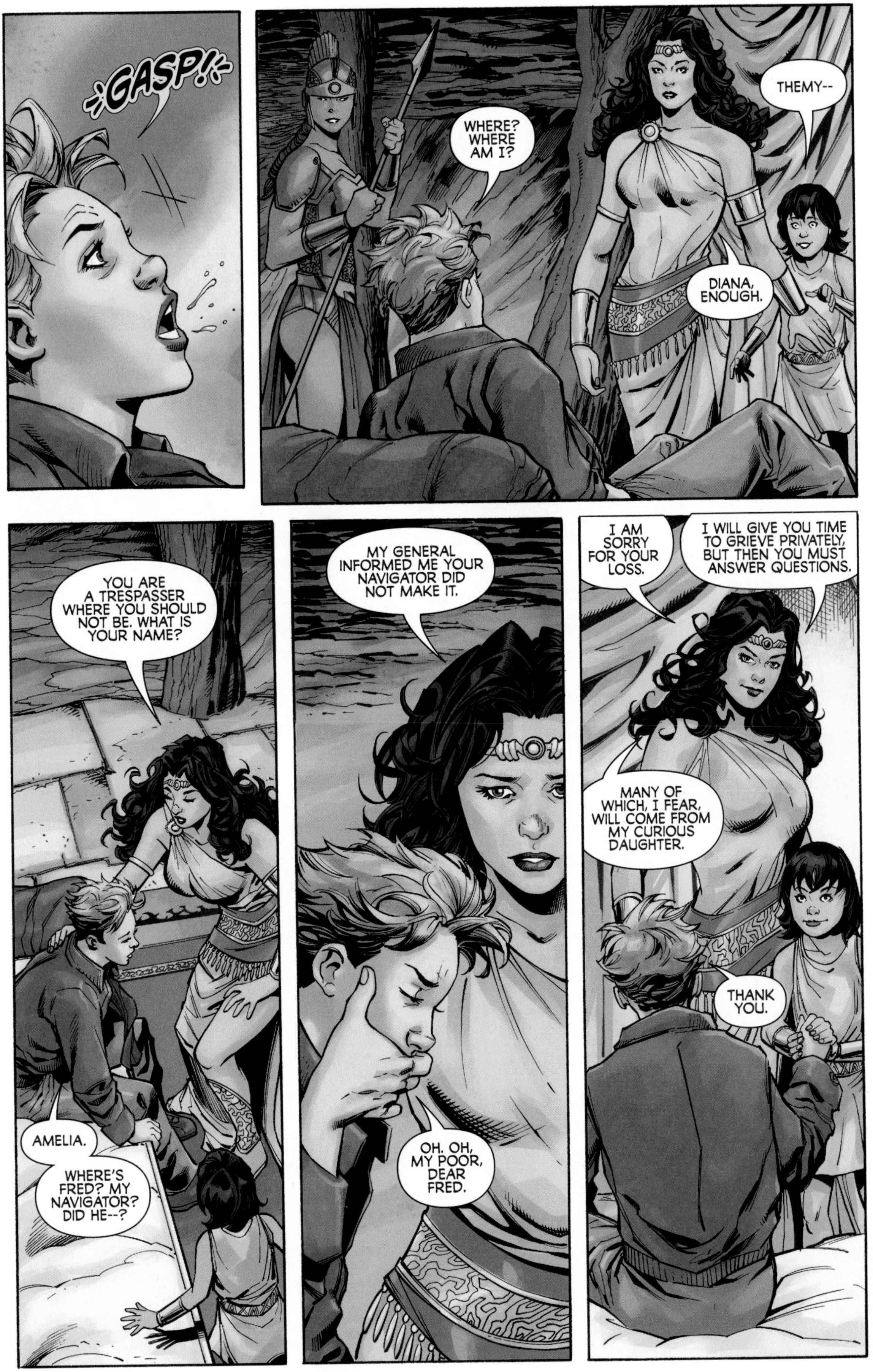
GASP!
WHERE? WHERE AM I?
THEMY--
DIANA, ENOUGH.
YOU ARE A TRESPASSER WHERE YOU SHOULD NOT BE. WHAT IS YOUR NAME?
AMELIA.
WHERE'S FRED? MY NAVIGATOR? DID HE--?
MY GENERAL INFORMED ME YOUR NAVIGATOR DID NOT MAKE IT.
OH. OH, MY POOR, DEAR FRED.
I AM SORRY FOR YOUR LOSS.
I WILL GIVE YOU TIME TO GRIEVE PRIVATELY, BUT THEN YOU MUST ANSWER QUESTIONS.
MANY OF WHICH, I FEAR, WILL COME FROM MY CURIOUS DAUGHTER.
THANK YOU.

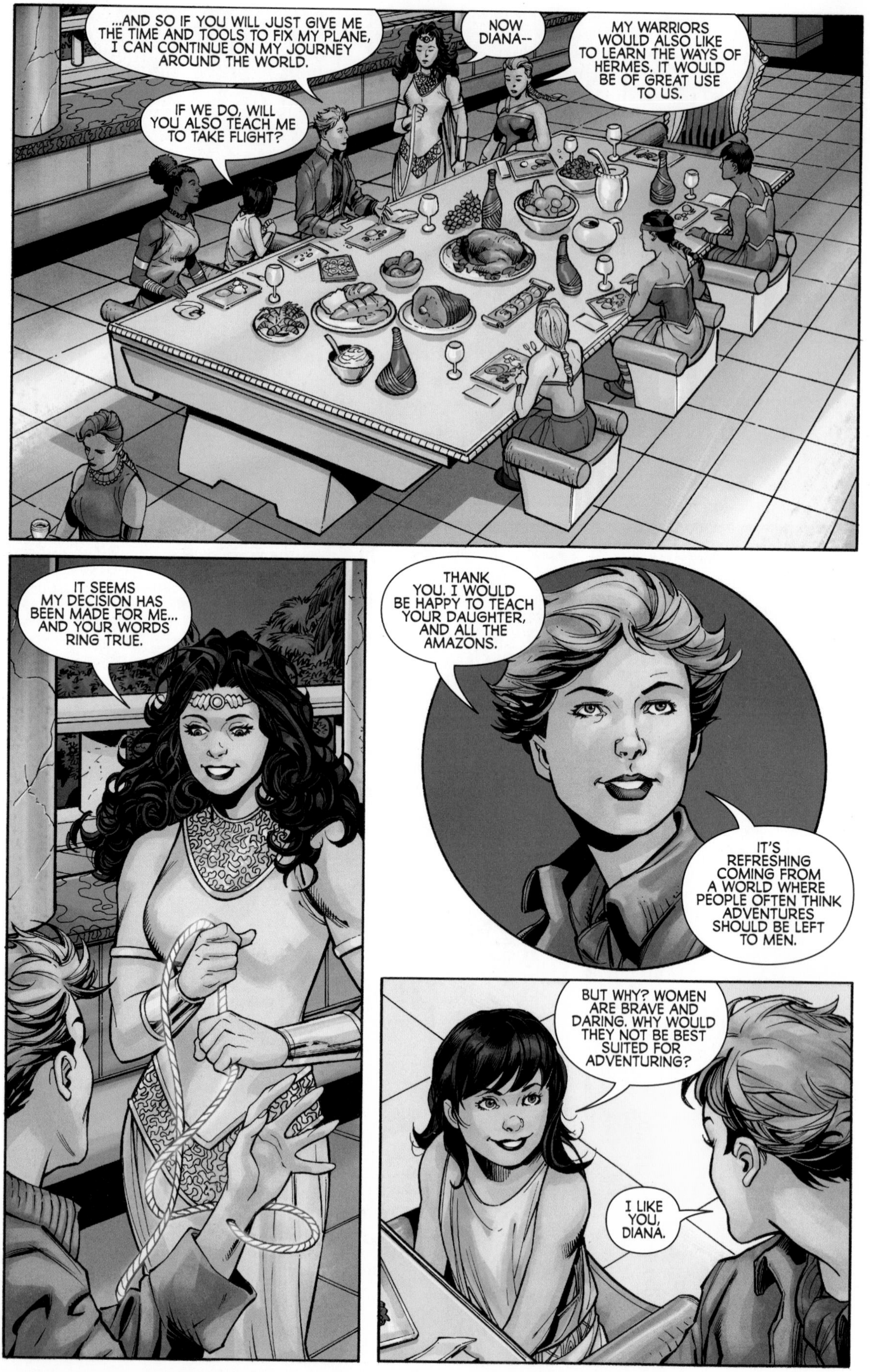
...AND SO IF YOU WILL JUST GIVE ME THE TIME AND TOOLS TO FIX MY PLANE, I CAN CONTINUE ON MY JOURNEY AROUND THE WORLD.
IF WE DO, WILL YOU ALSO TEACH ME TO TAKE FLIGHT?
NOW DIANA--
MY WARRIORS WOULD ALSO LIKE TO LEARN THE WAYS OF HERMES. IT WOULD BE OF GREAT USE TO US.
IT SEEMS MY DECISION HAS BEEN MADE FOR ME... AND YOUR WORDS RING TRUE.
THANK YOU. I WOULD BE HAPPY TO TEACH YOUR DAUGHTER, AND ALL THE AMAZONS.
IT'S REFRESHING COMING FROM A WORLD WHERE PEOPLE OFTEN THINK ADVENTURES SHOULD BE LEFT TO MEN.
BUT WHY? WOMEN ARE BRAVE AND DARING. WHY WOULD THEY NOT BE BEST SUITED FOR ADVENTURING?
I LIKE YOU, DIANA.

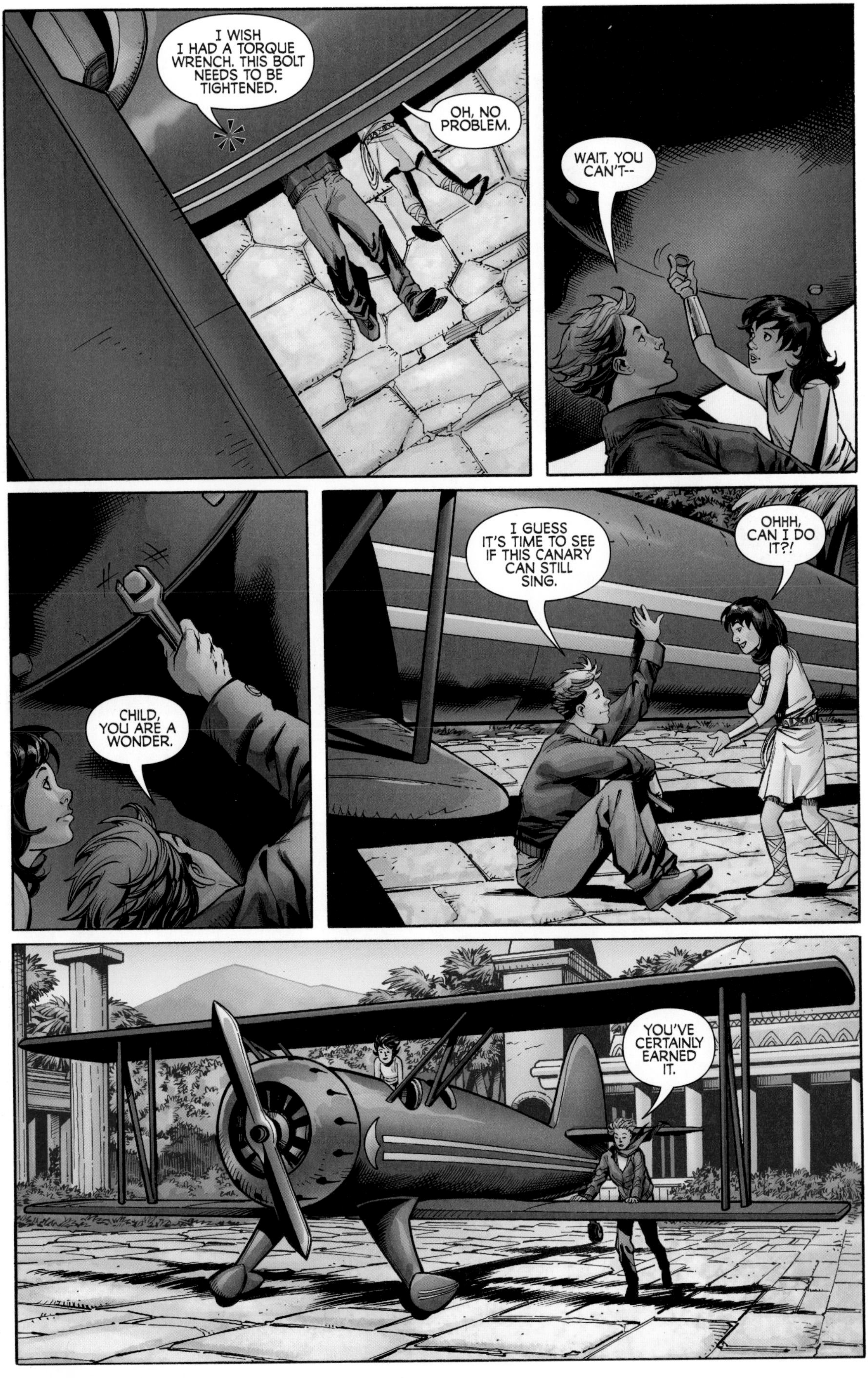
I WISH I HAD A TORQUE WRENCH. THIS BOLT NEEDS TO BE TIGHTENED.
OH, NO PROBLEM.
WAIT, YOU CAN'T--
CHILD, YOU ARE A WONDER.
I GUESS IT'S TIME TO SEE IF THIS CANARY CAN STILL SING.
OHHH, CAN I DO IT?!
YOU'VE CERTAINLY EARNED IT.

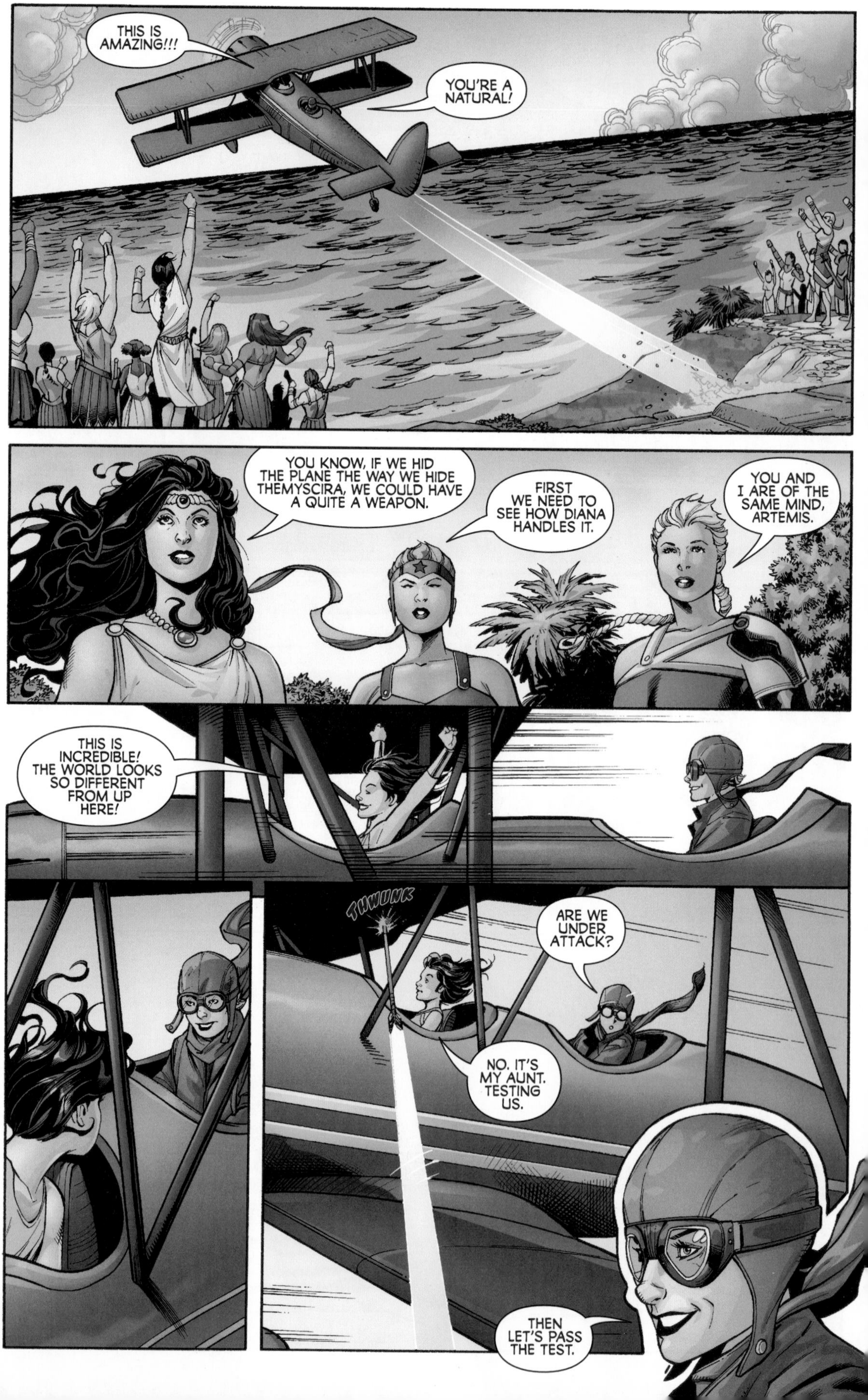
THIS IS AMAZING!!!
YOU'RE A NATURAL!
YOU KNOW, IF WE HID THE PLANE THE WAY WE HIDE THEMYSCIRA, WE COULD HAVE A QUITE A WEAPON.
FIRST WE NEED TO SEE HOW DIANA HANDLES IT.
YOU AND I ARE OF THE SAME MIND, ARTEMIS.
THIS IS INCREDIBLE! THE WORLD LOOKS SO DIFFERENT FROM UP HERE!
THWUNK
ARE WE UNDER ATTACK?
NO. IT'S MY AUNT. TESTING US.
THEN LET'S PASS THE TEST.

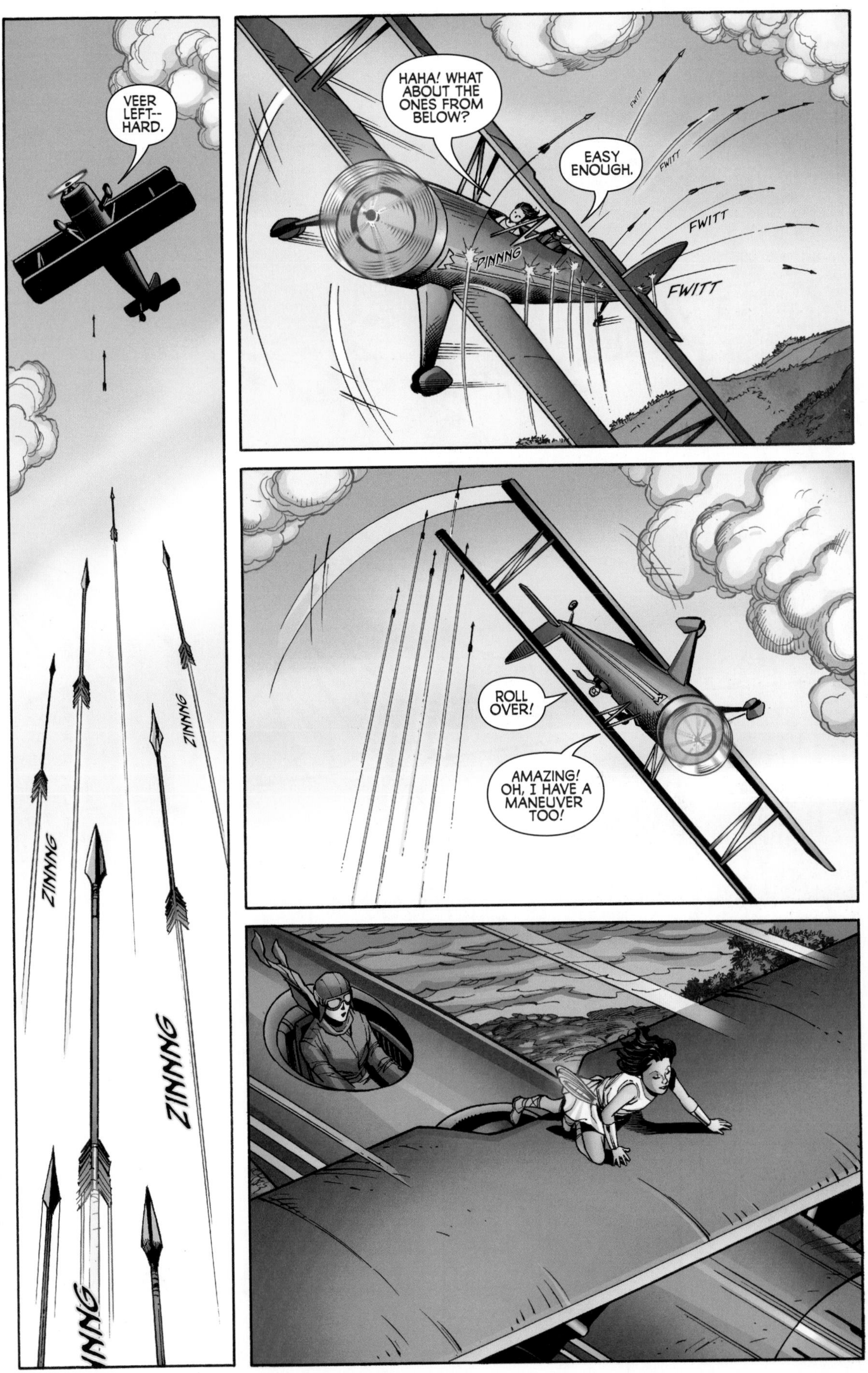
VEER LEFT-- HARD.
ZINNNG
ZINNNG
ZINNNG
HAHA! WHAT ABOUT THE ONES FROM BELOW?
EASY ENOUGH.
FWITT
FWITT
FWITT
FWITT
ZINNNG
ROLL OVER!
AMAZING! OH, I HAVE A MANEUVER TOO!

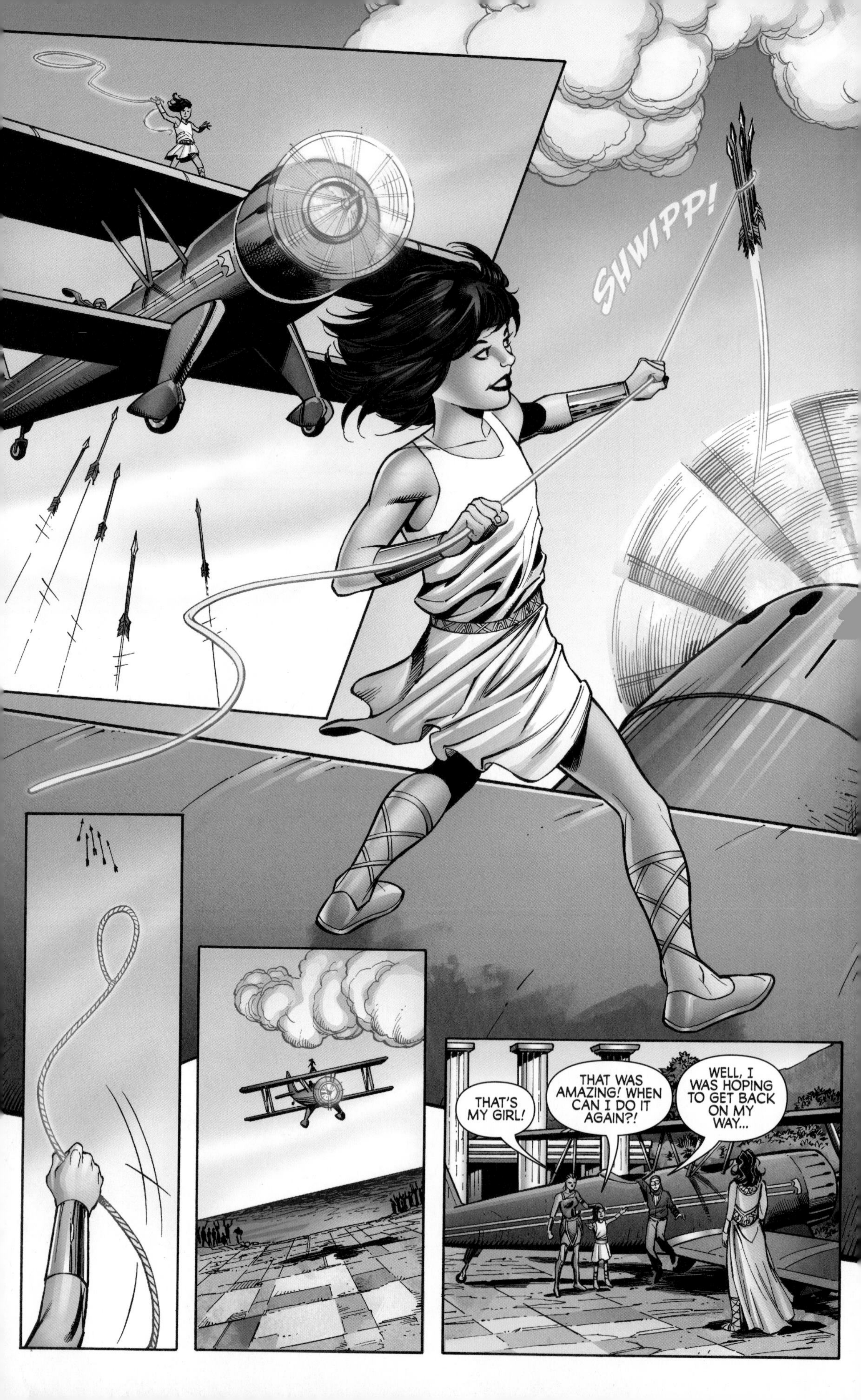
SHWIPP!
THAT'S MY GIRL!
THAT WAS AMAZING! WHEN CAN I DO IT AGAIN?!
WELL, I WAS HOPING TO GET BACK ON MY WAY...

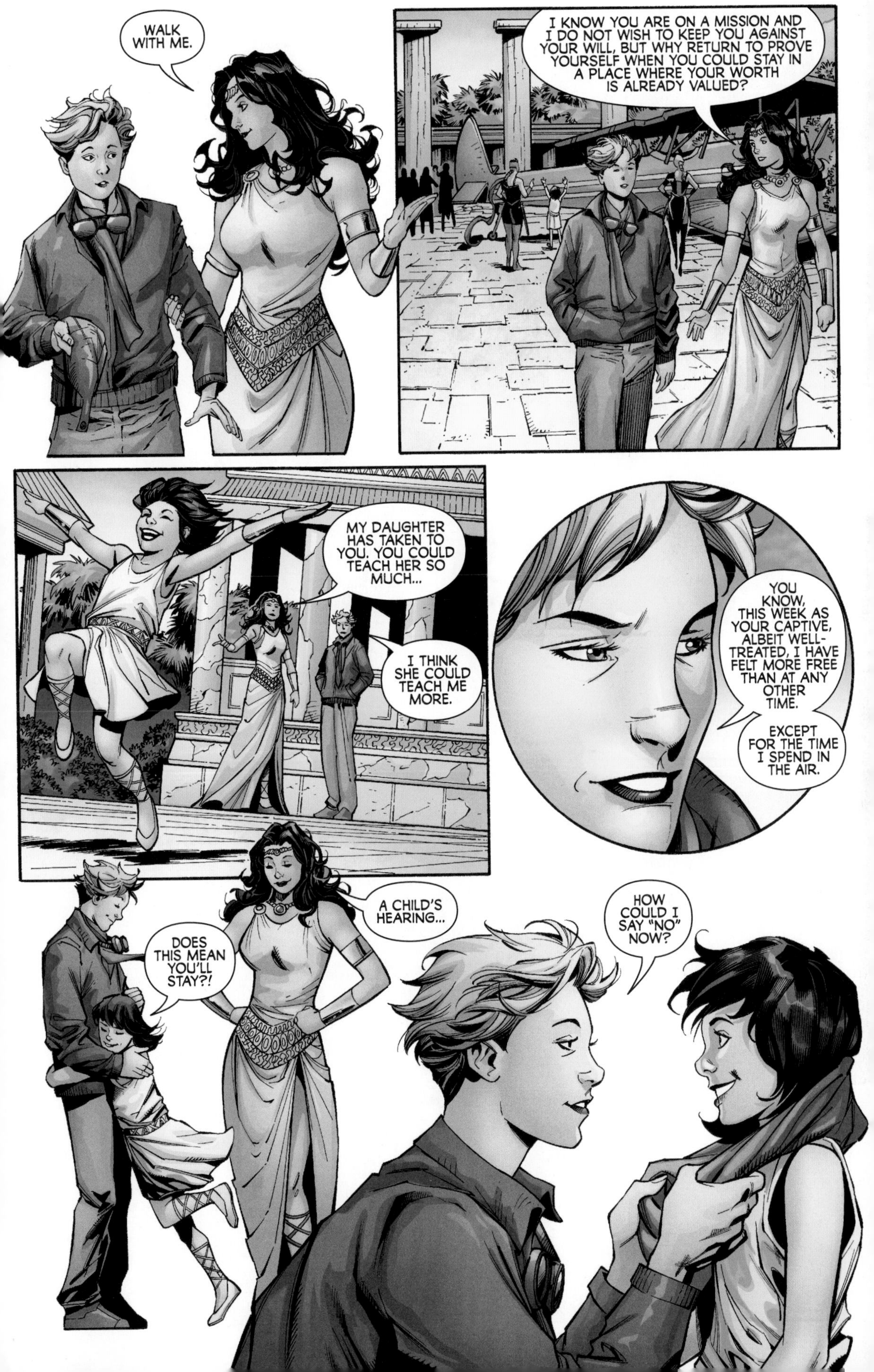
WALK WITH ME.
I KNOW YOU ARE ON A MISSION AND I DO NOT WISH TO KEEP YOU AGAINST YOUR WILL, BUT WHY RETURN TO PROVE YOURSELF WHEN YOU COULD STAY IN A PLACE WHERE YOUR WORTH IS ALREADY VALUED?
MY DAUGHTER HAS TAKEN TO YOU. YOU COULD TEACH HER SO MUCH...
I THINK SHE COULD TEACH ME MORE.
YOU KNOW, THIS WEEK AS YOUR CAPTIVE, ALBEIT WELL-TREATED, I HAVE FELT MORE FREE THAN AT ANY OTHER TIME.
EXCEPT FOR THE TIME I SPEND IN THE AIR.
A CHILD'S HEARING...
DOES THIS MEAN YOU'LL STAY?!
HOW COULD I SAY "NO" NOW?

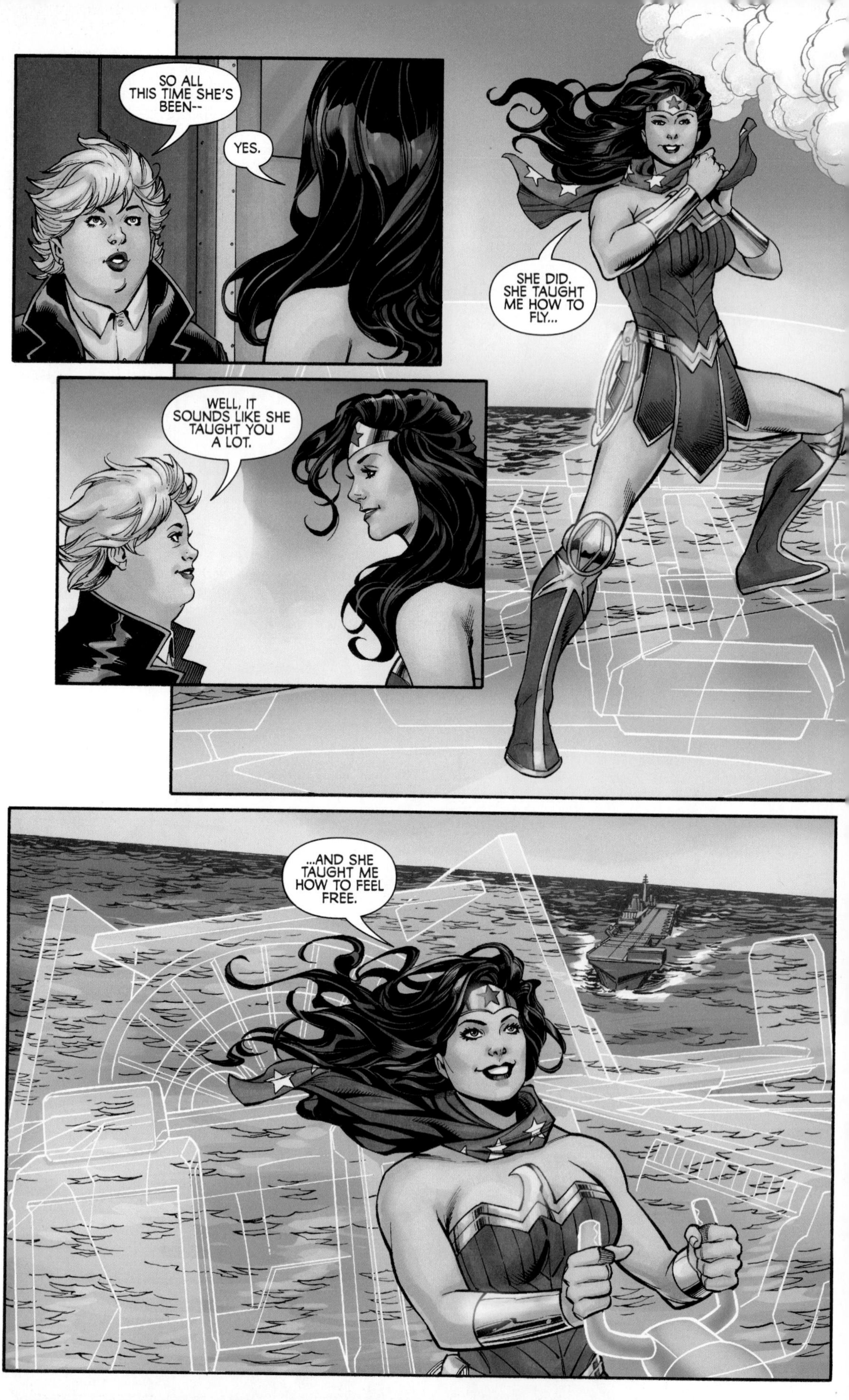
SO ALL THIS TIME SHE'S BEEN--
YES.
SHE DID. SHE TAUGHT ME HOW TO FLY...
WELL, IT SOUNDS LIKE SHE TAUGHT YOU A LOT.
...AND SHE TAUGHT ME HOW TO FEEL FREE.

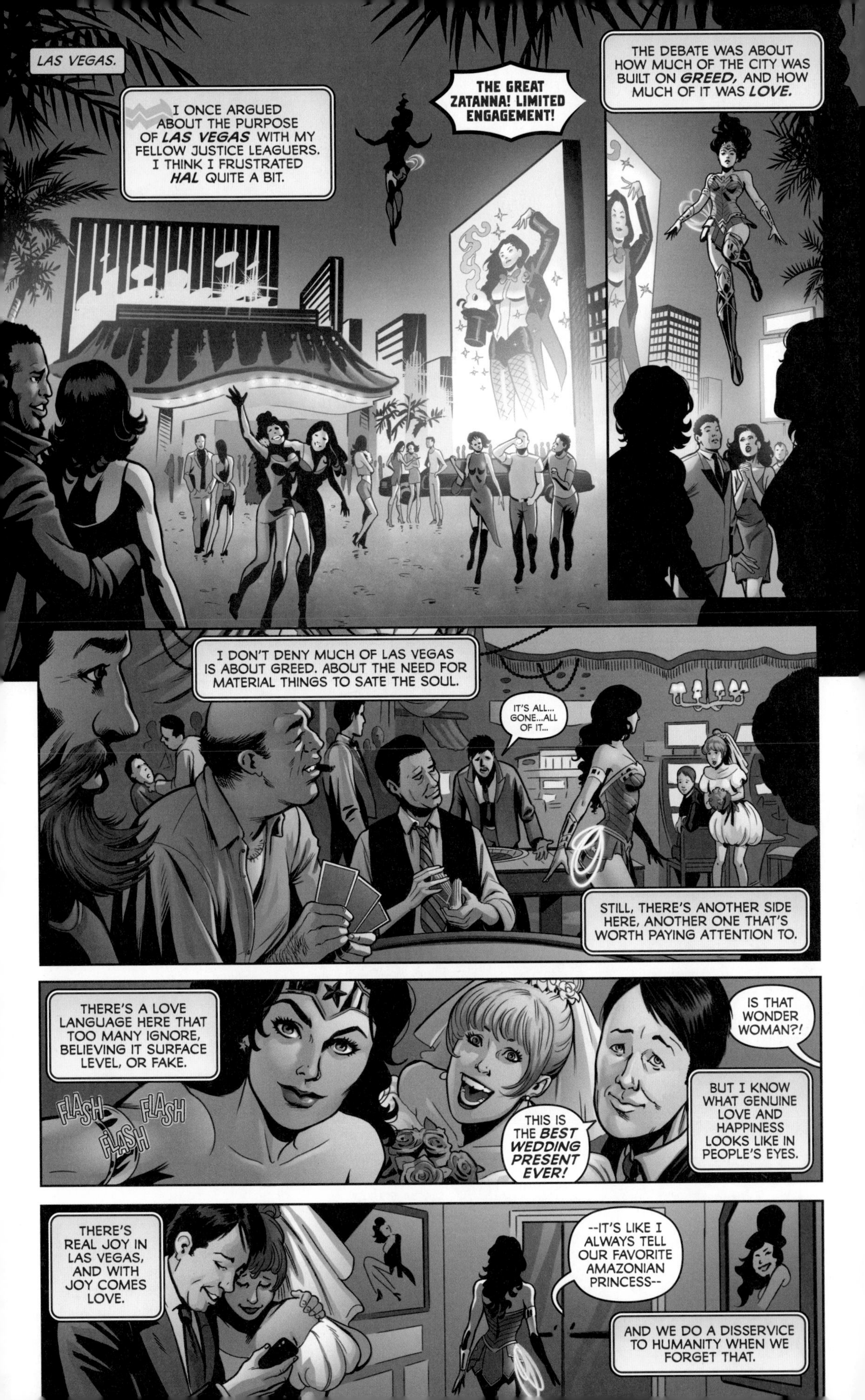
LAS VEGAS.
I ONCE ARGUED ABOUT THE PURPOSE OF LAS VEGAS WITH MY FELLOW JUSTICE LEAGUERS. I THINK I FRUSTRATED HAL QUITE A BIT.
THE GREAT ZATANNA! LIMITED ENGAGEMENT!
THE DEBATE WAS ABOUT HOW MUCH OF THE CITY WAS BUILT ON GREED, AND HOW MUCH OF IT WAS LOVE.
I DON'T DENY MUCH OF LAS VEGAS IS ABOUT GREED. ABOUT THE NEED FOR MATERIAL THINGS TO SATE THE SOUL.
IT'S ALL... GONE...ALL OF IT...
STILL, THERE'S ANOTHER SIDE HERE, ANOTHER ONE THAT'S WORTH PAYING ATTENTION TO.
THERE'S A LOVE LANGUAGE HERE THAT TOO MANY IGNORE, BELIEVING IT SURFACE LEVEL, OR FAKE.
FLASH
FLASH
FLASH
THIS IS THE BEST WEDDING PRESENT EVER!
IS THAT WONDER WOMAN?!
BUT I KNOW WHAT GENUINE LOVE AND HAPPINESS LOOKS LIKE IN PEOPLE'S EYES.
THERE'S REAL JOY IN LAS VEGAS, AND WITH JOY COMES LOVE.
--IT'S LIKE I ALWAYS TELL OUR FAVORITE AMAZONIAN PRINCESS--
AND WE DO A DISSERVICE TO HUMANITY WHEN WE FORGET THAT.

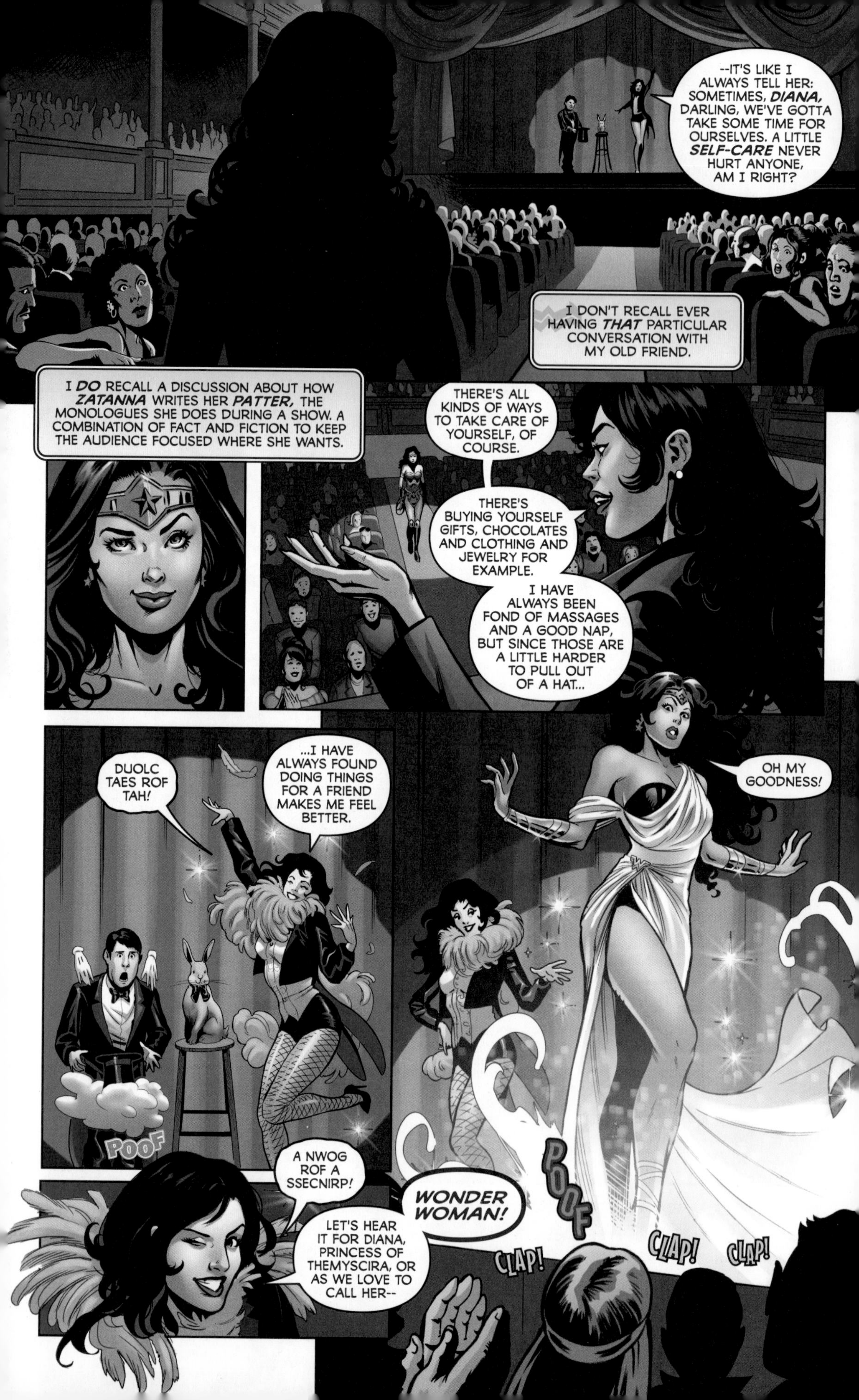
--IT'S LIKE I ALWAYS TELL HER: SOMETIMES, DIANA, DARLING, WE'VE GOTTA TAKE SOME TIME FOR OURSELVES. A LITTLE SELF-CARE NEVER HURT ANYONE, AM I RIGHT?
I DON'T RECALL EVER HAVING THAT PARTICULAR CONVERSATION WITH MY OLD FRIEND.
I DO RECALL A DISCUSSION ABOUT HOW ZATANNA WRITES HER PATTER, THE MONOLOGUES SHE DOES DURING A SHOW. A COMBINATION OF FACT AND FICTION TO KEEP THE AUDIENCE FOCUSED WHERE SHE WANTS.
THERE'S ALL KINDS OF WAYS TO TAKE CARE OF YOURSELF, OF COURSE.
THERE'S BUYING YOURSELF GIFTS, CHOCOLATES AND CLOTHING AND JEWELRY FOR EXAMPLE.
I HAVE ALWAYS BEEN FOND OF MASSAGES AND A GOOD NAP, BUT SINCE THOSE ARE A LITTLE HARDER TO PULL OUT OF A HAT...
DUOLC TAES ROF TAH!
...I HAVE ALWAYS FOUND DOING THINGS FOR A FRIEND MAKES ME FEEL BETTER.
POOF
OH MY GOODNESS!
A NWOG ROF A SSECNIRP!
WONDER WOMAN!
LET'S HEAR IT FOR DIANA, PRINCESS OF THEMYSCIRA, OR AS WE LOVE TO CALL HER--
POOF
CLAP!
CLAP!
CLAP!

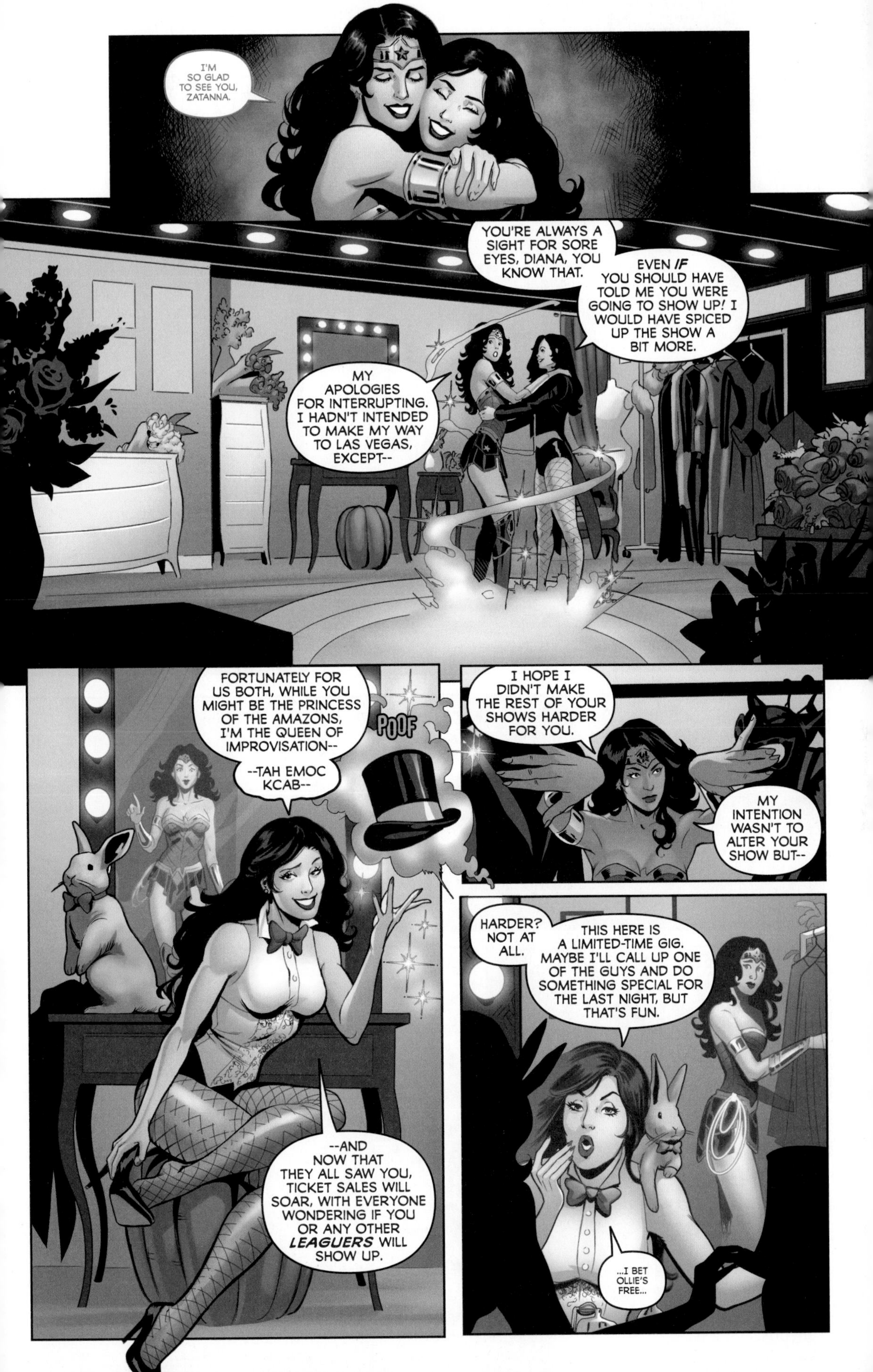
I'M SO GLAD TO SEE YOU, ZATANNA.
YOU'RE ALWAYS A SIGHT FOR SORE EYES, DIANA, YOU KNOW THAT.
EVEN *IF* YOU SHOULD HAVE TOLD ME YOU WERE GOING TO SHOW UP! I WOULD HAVE SPICED UP THE SHOW A BIT MORE.
MY APOLOGIES FOR INTERRUPTING. I HADN'T INTENDED TO MAKE MY WAY TO LAS VEGAS, EXCEPT--
FORTUNATELY FOR US BOTH, WHILE YOU MIGHT BE THE PRINCESS OF THE AMAZONS, I'M THE QUEEN OF IMPROVISATION--
--TAH EMOC KCAB--
POOF
--AND NOW THAT THEY ALL SAW YOU, TICKET SALES WILL SOAR, WITH EVERYONE WONDERING IF YOU OR ANY OTHER *LEAGUERS* WILL SHOW UP.
I HOPE I DIDN'T MAKE THE REST OF YOUR SHOWS HARDER FOR YOU.
MY INTENTION WASN'T TO ALTER YOUR SHOW BUT--
HARDER? NOT AT ALL.
THIS HERE IS A LIMITED-TIME GIG. MAYBE I'LL CALL UP ONE OF THE GUYS AND DO SOMETHING SPECIAL FOR THE LAST NIGHT, BUT THAT'S FUN.
...I BET OLLIE'S FREE...

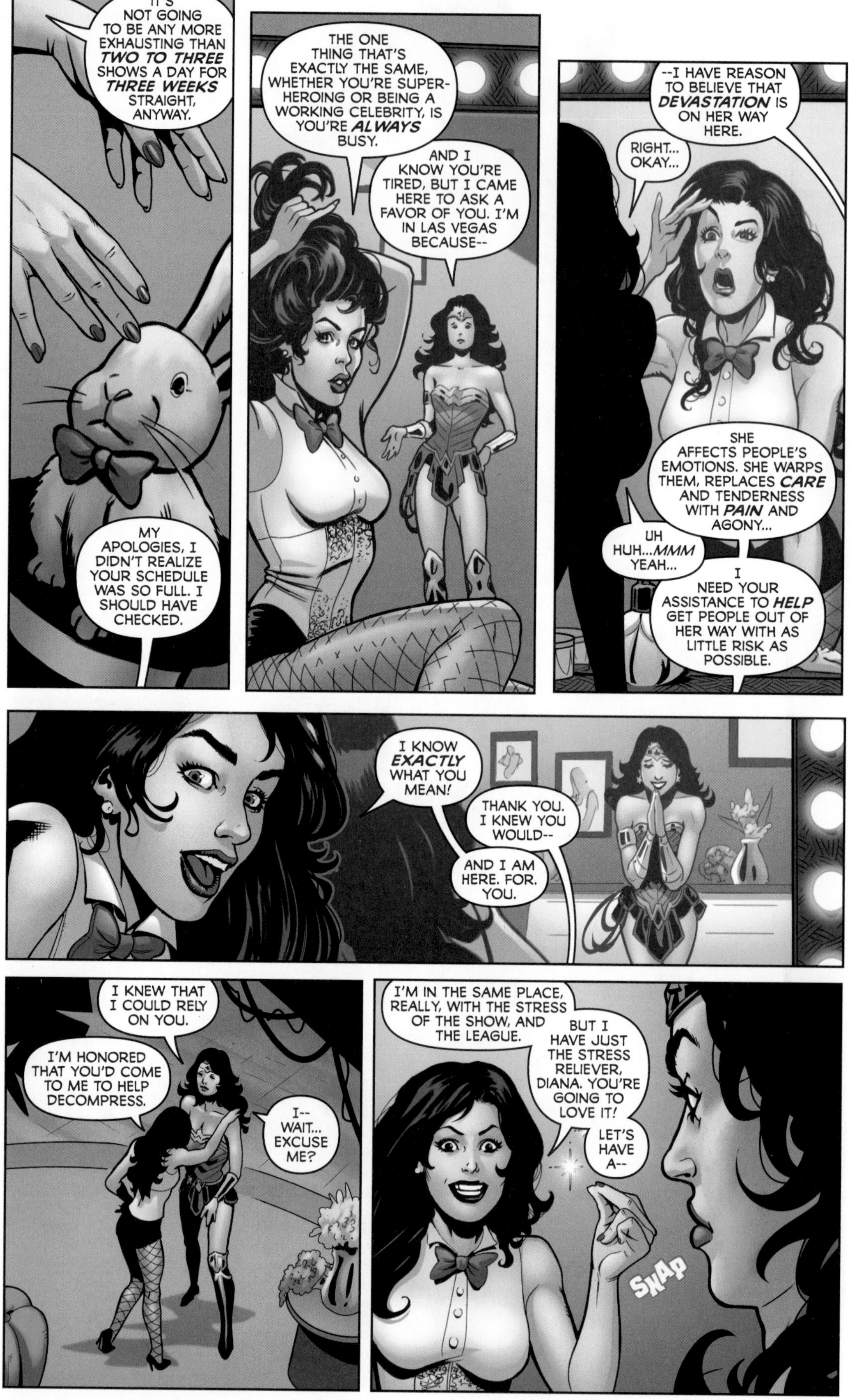
IT'S NOT GOING TO BE ANY MORE EXHAUSTING THAN TWO TO THREE SHOWS A DAY FOR THREE WEEKS STRAIGHT, ANYWAY.
MY APOLOGIES, I DIDN'T REALIZE YOUR SCHEDULE WAS SO FULL. I SHOULD HAVE CHECKED.
THE ONE THING THAT'S EXACTLY THE SAME, WHETHER YOU'RE SUPER-HEROING OR BEING A WORKING CELEBRITY, IS YOU'RE ALWAYS BUSY.
AND I KNOW YOU'RE TIRED, BUT I CAME HERE TO ASK A FAVOR OF YOU. I'M IN LAS VEGAS BECAUSE--
--I HAVE REASON TO BELIEVE THAT DEVASTATION IS ON HER WAY HERE.
RIGHT... OKAY...
SHE AFFECTS PEOPLE'S EMOTIONS. SHE WARPS THEM, REPLACES CARE AND TENDERNESS WITH PAIN AND AGONY...
UH HUH...MMM YEAH...
I NEED YOUR ASSISTANCE TO HELP GET PEOPLE OUT OF HER WAY WITH AS LITTLE RISK AS POSSIBLE.
I KNOW EXACTLY WHAT YOU MEAN!
THANK YOU. I KNEW YOU WOULD--
AND I AM HERE. FOR. YOU.
I KNEW THAT I COULD RELY ON YOU.
I'M HONORED THAT YOU'D COME TO ME TO HELP DECOMPRESS.
I-- WAIT... EXCUSE ME?
I'M IN THE SAME PLACE, REALLY, WITH THE STRESS OF THE SHOW, AND THE LEAGUE.
BUT I HAVE JUST THE STRESS RELIEVER, DIANA. YOU'RE GOING TO LOVE IT!
LET'S HAVE A--
SNAP

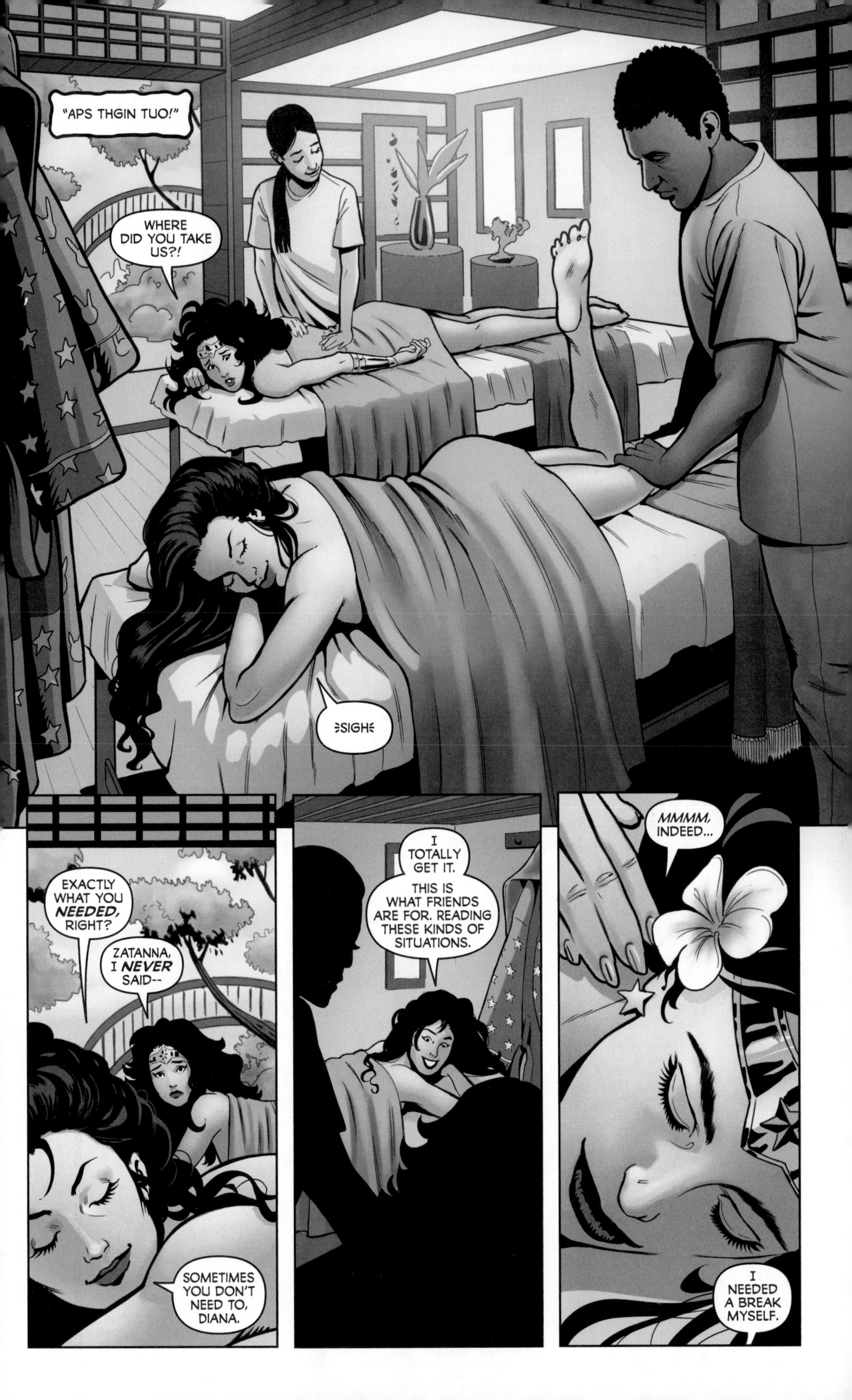
"APS THGIN TUO!"
WHERE DID YOU TAKE US?!
SIGH
EXACTLY WHAT YOU *NEEDED,* RIGHT?
ZATANNA, I *NEVER* SAID--
SOMETIMES YOU DON'T NEED TO, DIANA.
I TOTALLY GET IT.
THIS IS WHAT FRIENDS ARE FOR. READING THESE KINDS OF SITUATIONS.
MMMM, INDEED...
I NEEDED A BREAK MYSELF.

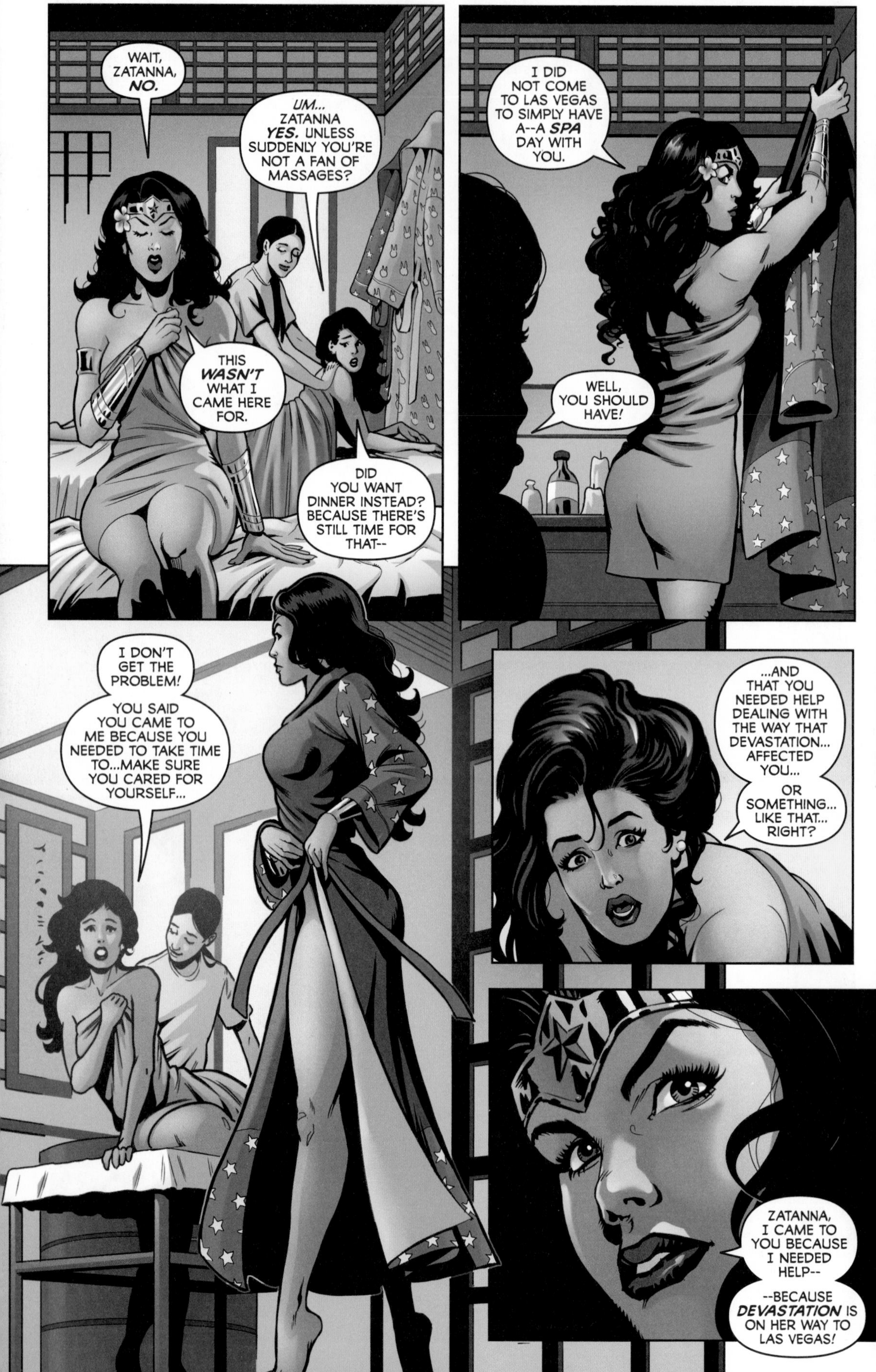
WAIT, ZATANNA, NO.
UM... ZATANNA YES. UNLESS SUDDENLY YOU'RE NOT A FAN OF MASSAGES?
THIS WASN'T WHAT I CAME HERE FOR.
DID YOU WANT DINNER INSTEAD? BECAUSE THERE'S STILL TIME FOR THAT--
I DID NOT COME TO LAS VEGAS TO SIMPLY HAVE A--A SPA DAY WITH YOU.
WELL, YOU SHOULD HAVE!
I DON'T GET THE PROBLEM!
YOU SAID YOU CAME TO ME BECAUSE YOU NEEDED TO TAKE TIME TO...MAKE SURE YOU CARED FOR YOURSELF...
...AND THAT YOU NEEDED HELP DEALING WITH THE WAY THAT DEVASTATION... AFFECTED YOU...
OR SOMETHING... LIKE THAT... RIGHT?
ZATANNA, I CAME TO YOU BECAUSE I NEEDED HELP--
--BECAUSE DEVASTATION IS ON HER WAY TO LAS VEGAS!

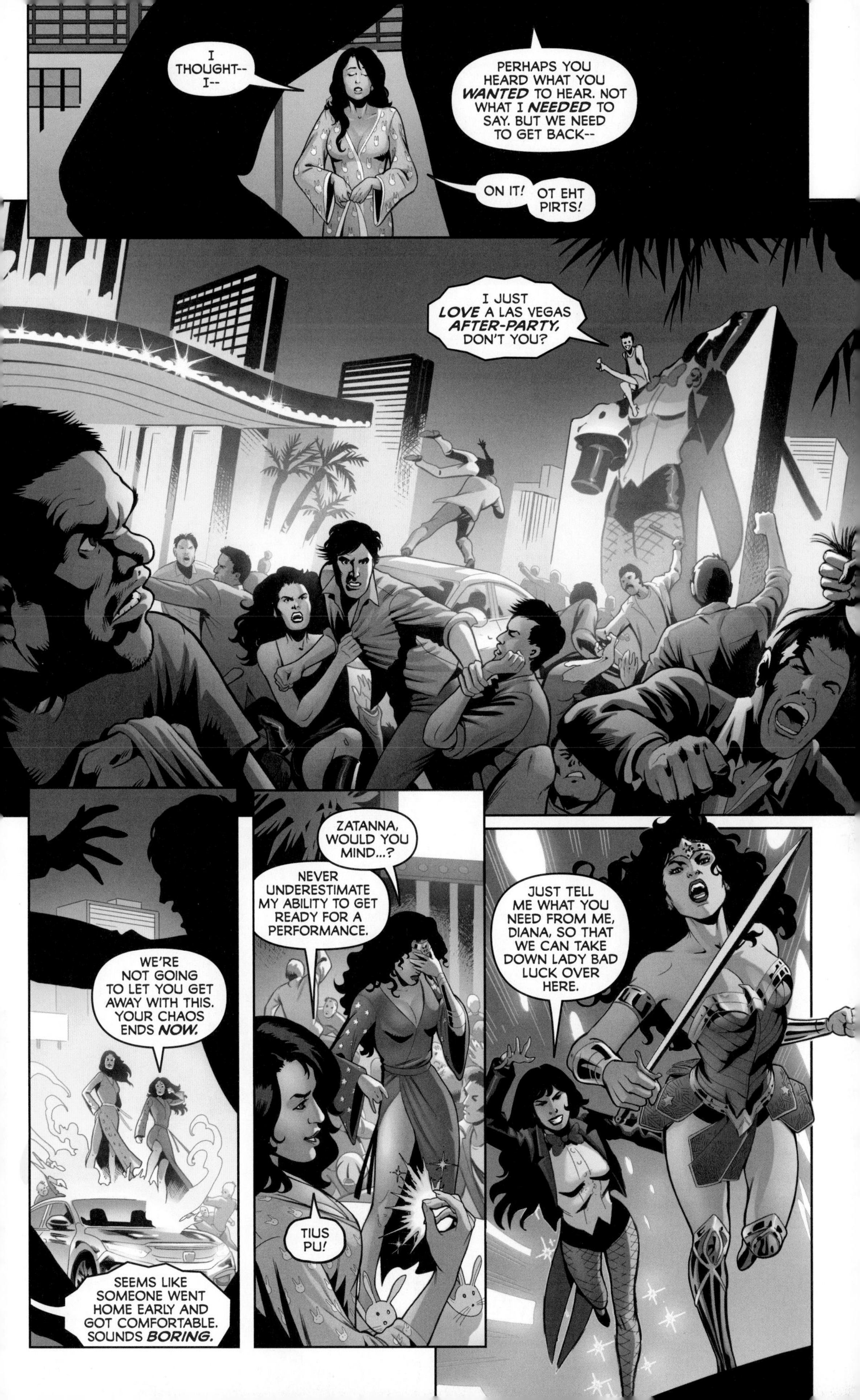
I THOUGHT-- I--
PERHAPS YOU HEARD WHAT YOU WANTED TO HEAR. NOT WHAT I NEEDED TO SAY. BUT WE NEED TO GET BACK--
ON IT!
OT EHT PIRTS!
I JUST LOVE A LAS VEGAS AFTER-PARTY, DON'T YOU?
WE'RE NOT GOING TO LET YOU GET AWAY WITH THIS. YOUR CHAOS ENDS NOW.
SEEMS LIKE SOMEONE WENT HOME EARLY AND GOT COMFORTABLE. SOUNDS BORING.
ZATANNA, WOULD YOU MIND...?
NEVER UNDERESTIMATE MY ABILITY TO GET READY FOR A PERFORMANCE.
TIUS PU!
JUST TELL ME WHAT YOU NEED FROM ME, DIANA, SO THAT WE CAN TAKE DOWN LADY BAD LUCK OVER HERE.

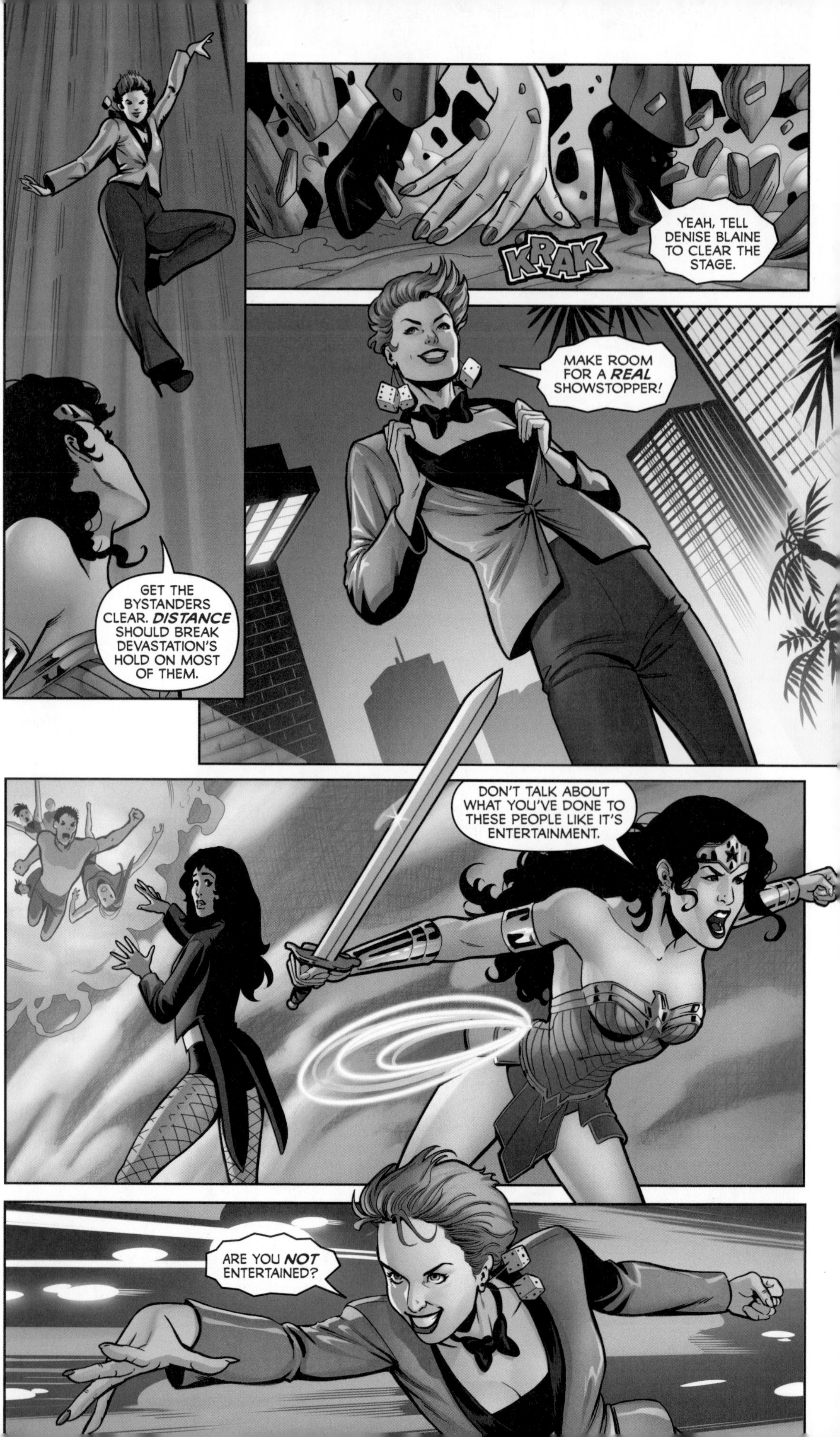
KRAK
YEAH, TELL DENISE BLAINE TO CLEAR THE STAGE.
GET THE BYSTANDERS CLEAR. ***DISTANCE*** SHOULD BREAK DEVASTATION'S HOLD ON MOST OF THEM.
MAKE ROOM FOR A ***REAL*** SHOWSTOPPER!
DON'T TALK ABOUT WHAT YOU'VE DONE TO THESE PEOPLE LIKE IT'S ENTERTAINMENT.
ARE YOU ***NOT*** ENTERTAINED?

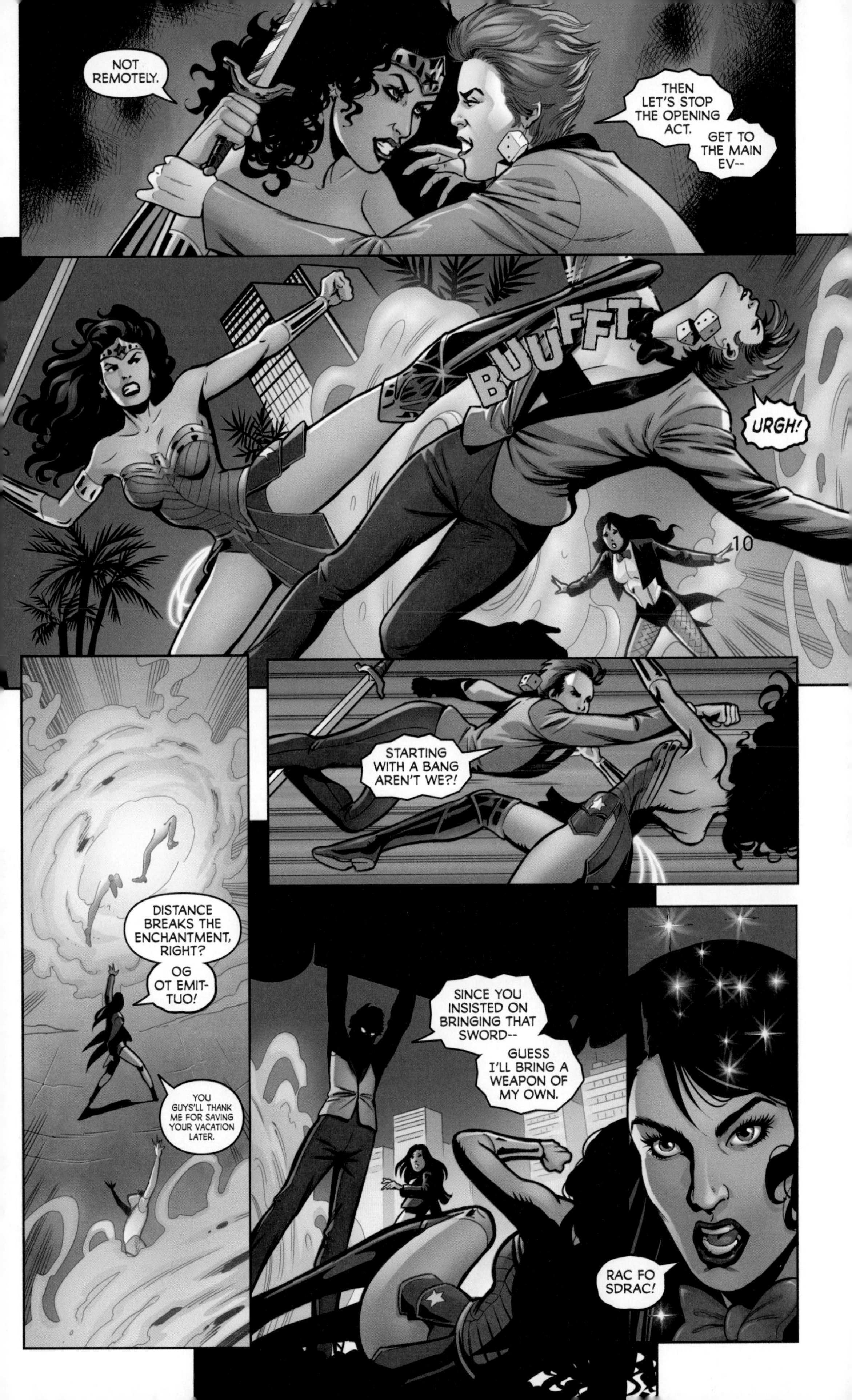
NOT REMOTELY.
THEN LET'S STOP THE OPENING ACT.
GET TO THE MAIN EV--
BUUFFT
URGH!
10
STARTING WITH A BANG AREN'T WE?!
DISTANCE BREAKS THE ENCHANTMENT, RIGHT?
OG OT EMIT-TUO!
YOU GUYS'LL THANK ME FOR SAVING YOUR VACATION LATER.
SINCE YOU INSISTED ON BRINGING THAT SWORD--
GUESS I'LL BRING A WEAPON OF MY OWN.
RAC FO SDRAC!

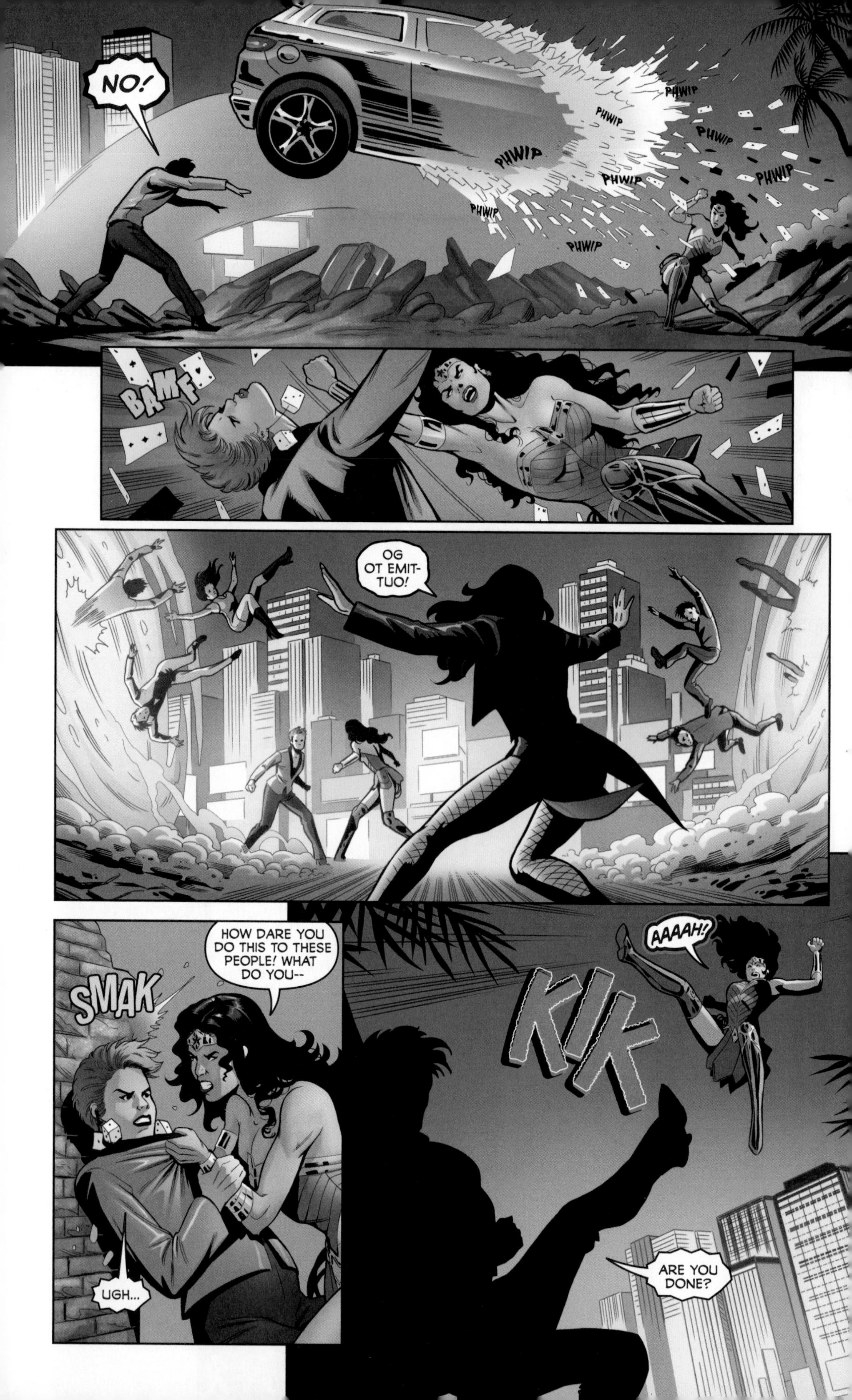
NO!
PHWIP
PHWIP
PHWIP
PHWIP
PHWIP
PHWIP
PHWIP
BAMF
OG OT EMIT-TUO!
SMAK
HOW DARE YOU DO THIS TO THESE PEOPLE! WHAT DO YOU--
UGH...
AAAAH!
KIK
ARE YOU DONE?

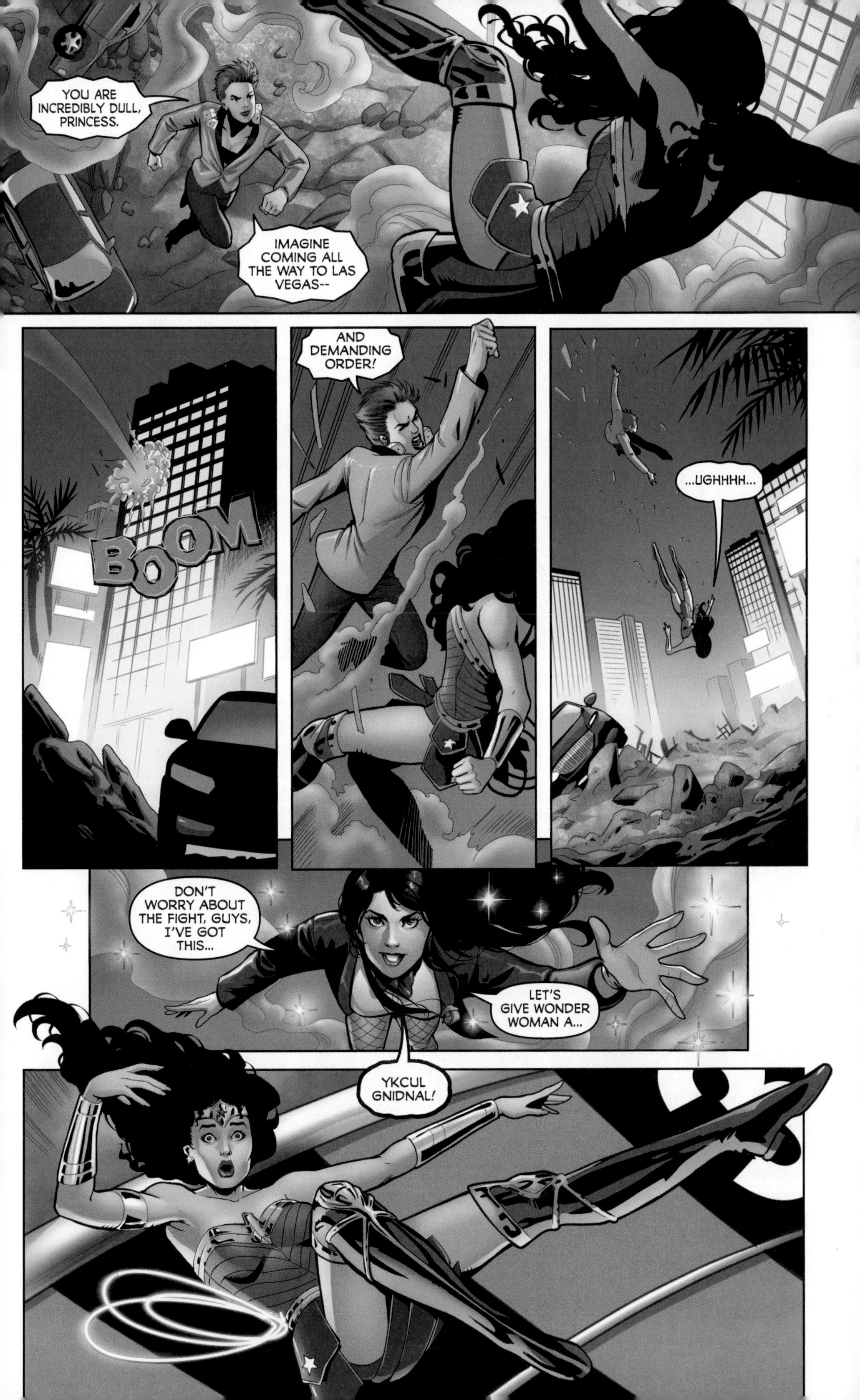
YOU ARE INCREDIBLY DULL, PRINCESS.
IMAGINE COMING ALL THE WAY TO LAS VEGAS--
BOOM
AND DEMANDING ORDER!
...UGHHHH...
DON'T WORRY ABOUT THE FIGHT, GUYS, I'VE GOT THIS...
LET'S GIVE WONDER WOMAN A...
YKCUL GNIDNAL!

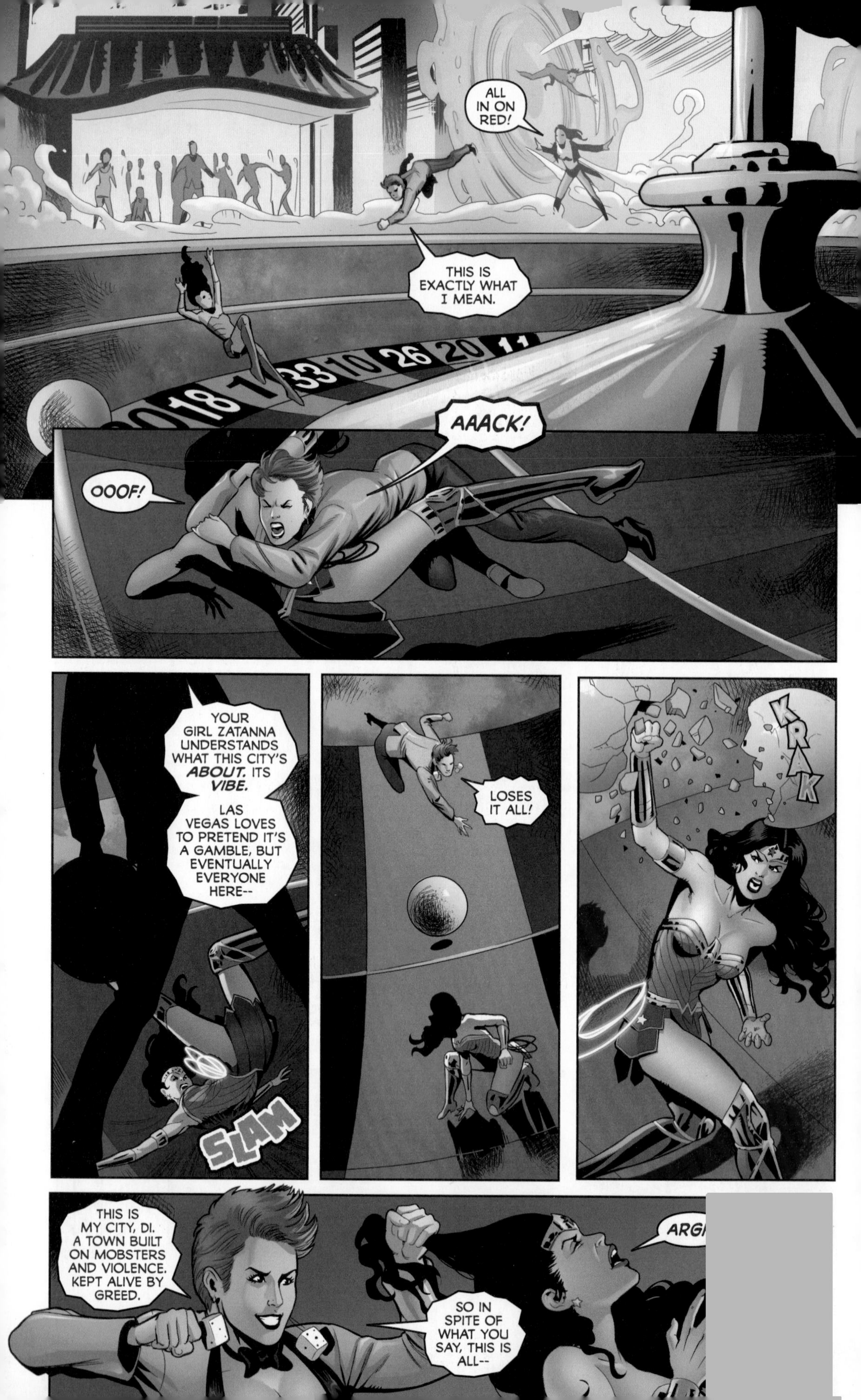
ALL IN ON RED!
THIS IS EXACTLY WHAT I MEAN.
AAACK!
OOOF!
YOUR GIRL ZATANNA UNDERSTANDS WHAT THIS CITY'S ABOUT. ITS VIBE.
LAS VEGAS LOVES TO PRETEND IT'S A GAMBLE, BUT EVENTUALLY EVERYONE HERE--
SLAM
LOSES IT ALL!
KRAK
THIS IS MY CITY, DI. A TOWN BUILT ON MOBSTERS AND VIOLENCE. KEPT ALIVE BY GREED.
SO IN SPITE OF WHAT YOU SAY, THIS IS ALL--

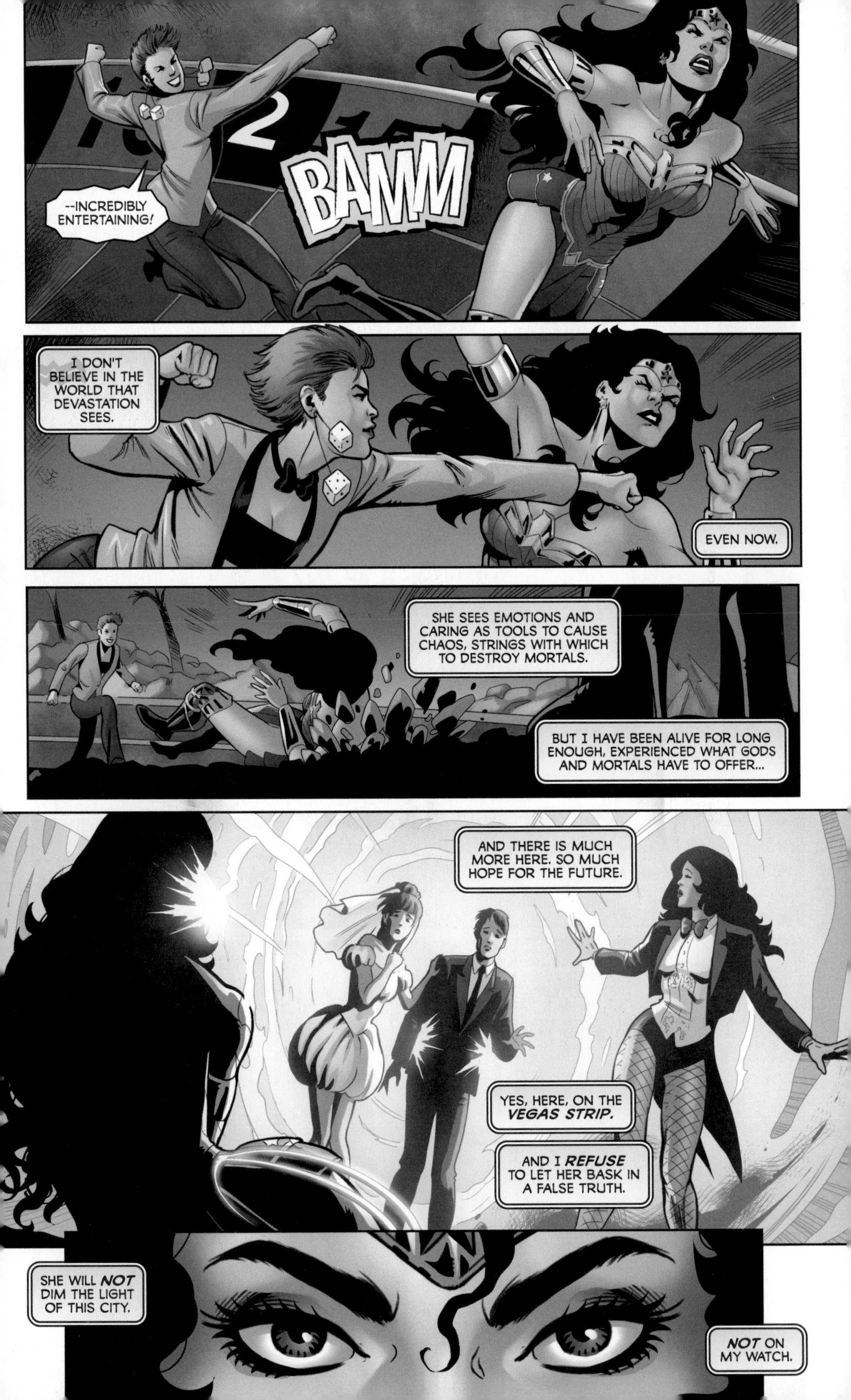

--INCREDIBLY ENTERTAINING!
BAMM
I DON'T BELIEVE IN THE WORLD THAT DEVASTATION SEES.
EVEN NOW.
SHE SEES EMOTIONS AND CARING AS TOOLS TO CAUSE CHAOS, STRINGS WITH WHICH TO DESTROY MORTALS.
BUT I HAVE BEEN ALIVE FOR LONG ENOUGH, EXPERIENCED WHAT GODS AND MORTALS HAVE TO OFFER...
AND THERE IS MUCH MORE HERE. SO MUCH HOPE FOR THE FUTURE.
YES, HERE, ON THE *VEGAS STRIP.*
AND I *REFUSE* TO LET HER BASK IN A FALSE TRUTH.
SHE WILL *NOT* DIM THE LIGHT OF THIS CITY.
NOT ON MY WATCH.

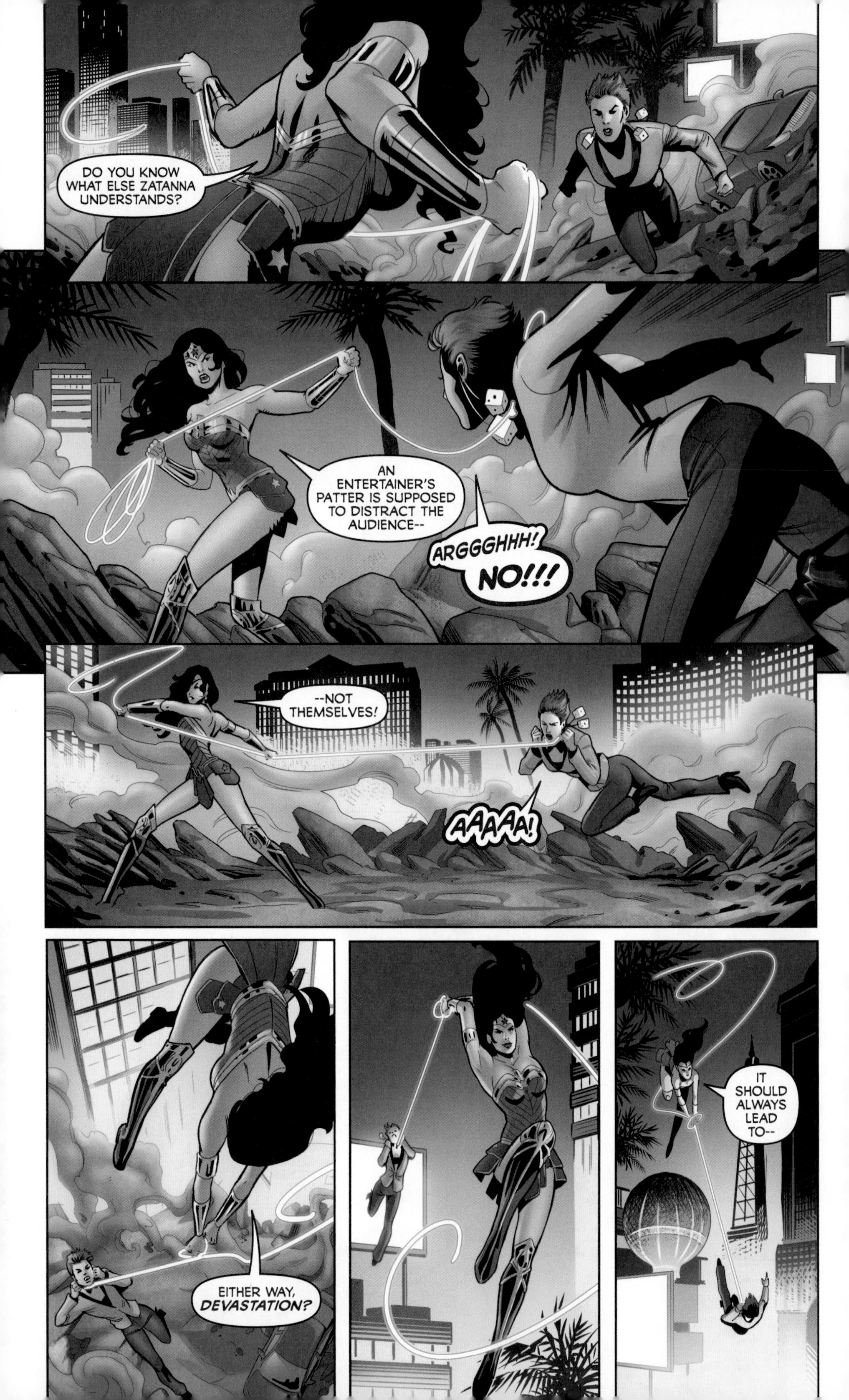
DO YOU KNOW WHAT ELSE ZATANNA UNDERSTANDS?
AN ENTERTAINER'S PATTER IS SUPPOSED TO DISTRACT THE AUDIENCE--
ARGGGHHH! NO!!!
--NOT THEMSELVES!
AAAAA!
EITHER WAY, DEVASTATION?
IT SHOULD ALWAYS LEAD TO--

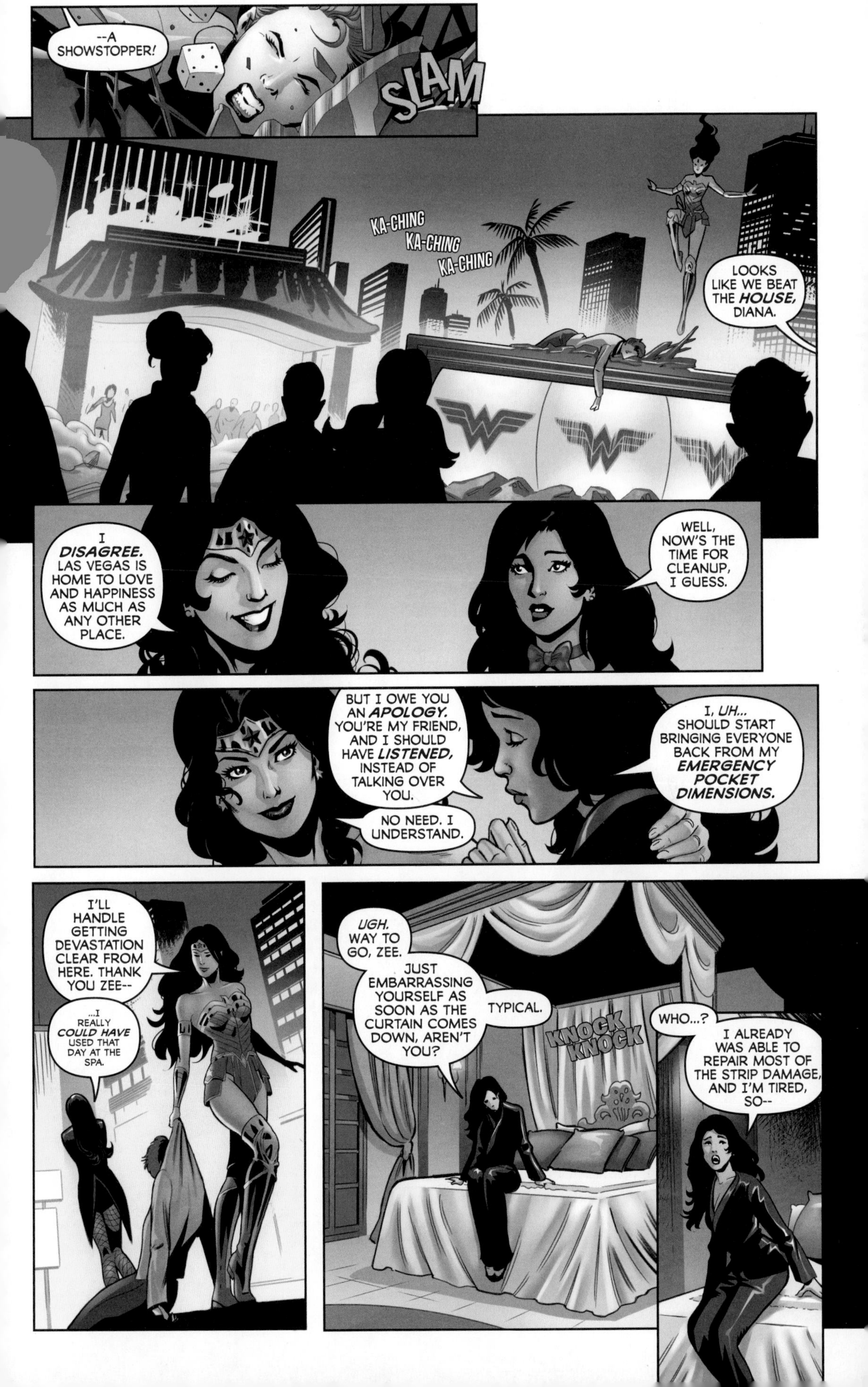
--A SHOWSTOPPER!
SLAM
KA-CHING
KA-CHING
KA-CHING
LOOKS LIKE WE BEAT THE HOUSE, DIANA.
I DISAGREE. LAS VEGAS IS HOME TO LOVE AND HAPPINESS AS MUCH AS ANY OTHER PLACE.
WELL, NOW'S THE TIME FOR CLEANUP, I GUESS.
BUT I OWE YOU AN APOLOGY. YOU'RE MY FRIEND, AND I SHOULD HAVE LISTENED, INSTEAD OF TALKING OVER YOU.
NO NEED. I UNDERSTAND.
I, UH... SHOULD START BRINGING EVERYONE BACK FROM MY EMERGENCY POCKET DIMENSIONS.
I'LL HANDLE GETTING DEVASTATION CLEAR FROM HERE. THANK YOU ZEE--
...I REALLY COULD HAVE USED THAT DAY AT THE SPA.
UGH. WAY TO GO, ZEE.
JUST EMBARRASSING YOURSELF AS SOON AS THE CURTAIN COMES DOWN, AREN'T YOU?
TYPICAL.
KNOCK KNOCK
WHO...?
I ALREADY WAS ABLE TO REPAIR MOST OF THE STRIP DAMAGE, AND I'M TIRED, SO--

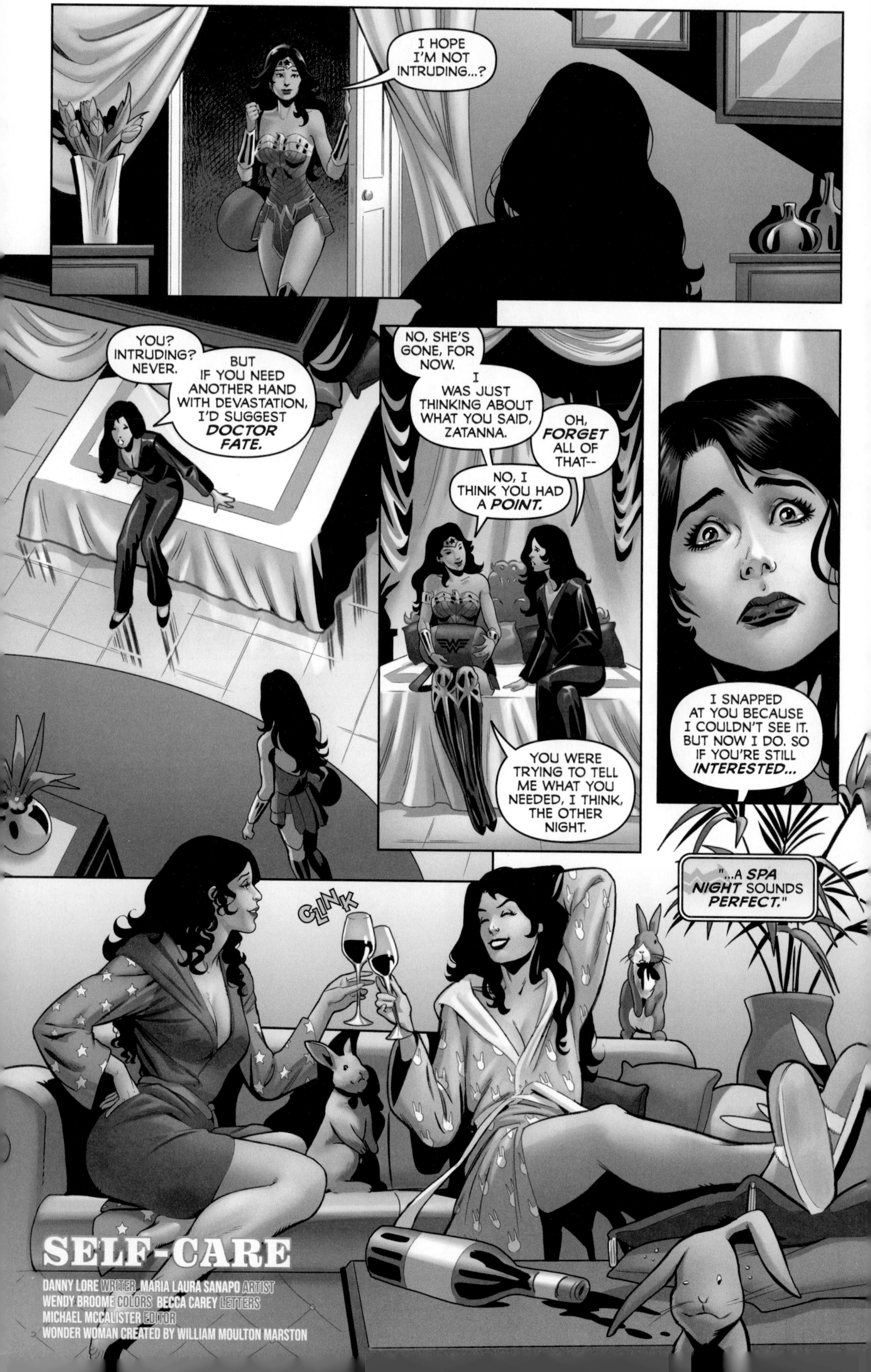
I HOPE I'M NOT INTRUDING...?
YOU? INTRUDING? NEVER.
BUT IF YOU NEED ANOTHER HAND WITH DEVASTATION, I'D SUGGEST DOCTOR FATE.
NO, SHE'S GONE, FOR NOW.
I WAS JUST THINKING ABOUT WHAT YOU SAID, ZATANNA.
OH, FORGET ALL OF THAT--
NO, I THINK YOU HAD A POINT.
YOU WERE TRYING TO TELL ME WHAT YOU NEEDED, I THINK, THE OTHER NIGHT.
I SNAPPED AT YOU BECAUSE I COULDN'T SEE IT. BUT NOW I DO. SO IF YOU'RE STILL INTERESTED...
"...A SPA NIGHT SOUNDS PERFECT."
CLINK
SELF-CARE
DANNY LORE WRITER MARIA LAURA SANAPO ARTIST
WENDY BROOME COLORS BECCA CAREY LETTERS
MICHAEL MCCALISTER EDITOR
WONDER WOMAN CREATED BY WILLIAM MOULTON MARSTON

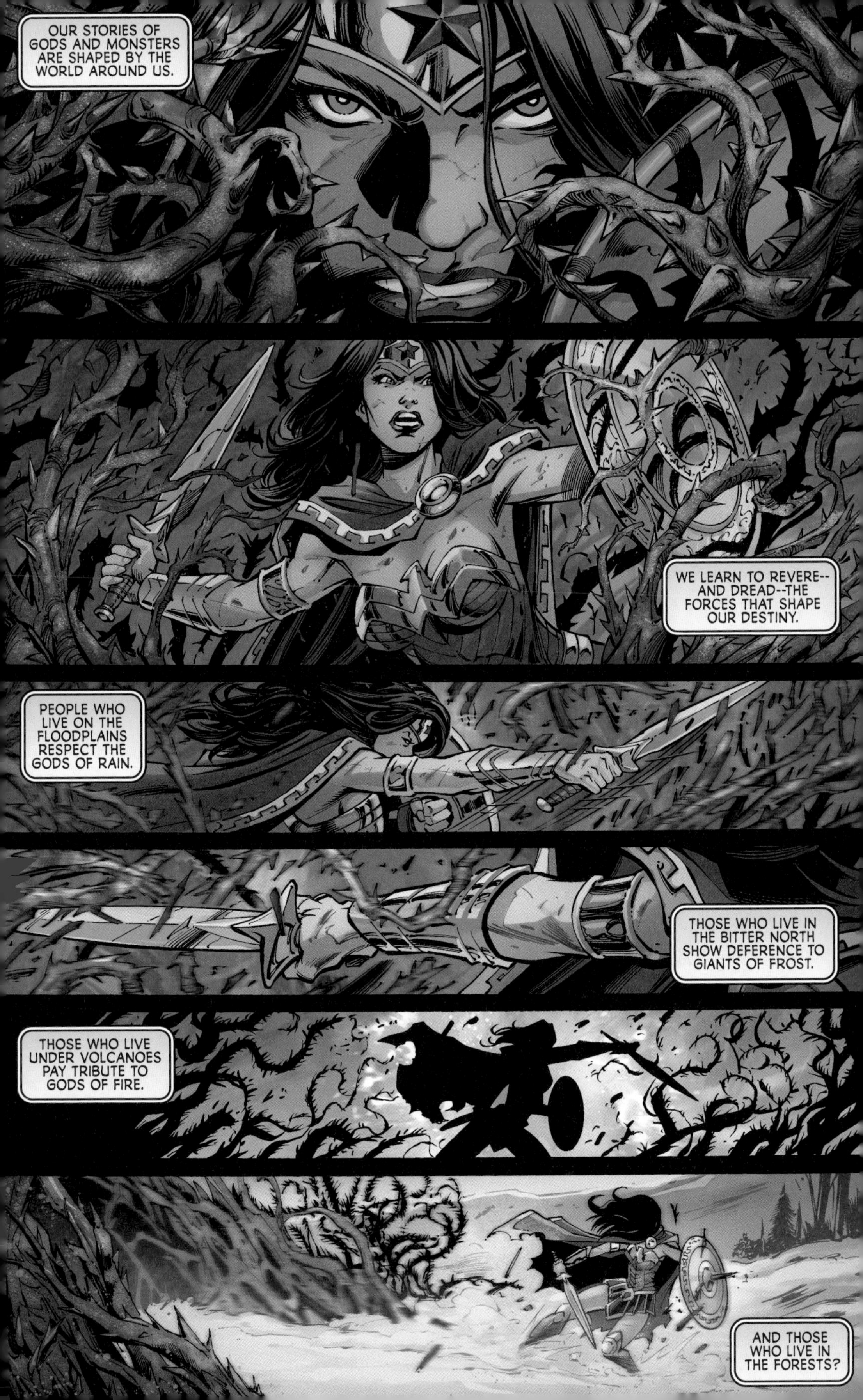
OUR STORIES OF GODS AND MONSTERS ARE SHAPED BY THE WORLD AROUND US.
WE LEARN TO REVERE--AND DREAD--THE FORCES THAT SHAPE OUR DESTINY.
PEOPLE WHO LIVE ON THE FLOODPLAINS RESPECT THE GODS OF RAIN.
THOSE WHO LIVE IN THE BITTER NORTH SHOW DEFERENCE TO GIANTS OF FROST.
THOSE WHO LIVE UNDER VOLCANOES PAY TRIBUTE TO GODS OF FIRE.
AND THOSE WHO LIVE IN THE FORESTS?

FEAR THE
DARK.

FEAR the DARK

ANDREW
WHEELER
writer

PAUL
PELLETIER
penciller

NORM
RAPMUND
inker

ADRIAN
LUCAS
colorist

TRAVIS LANHAM • letterer   MICHAEL McCALISTER • ed

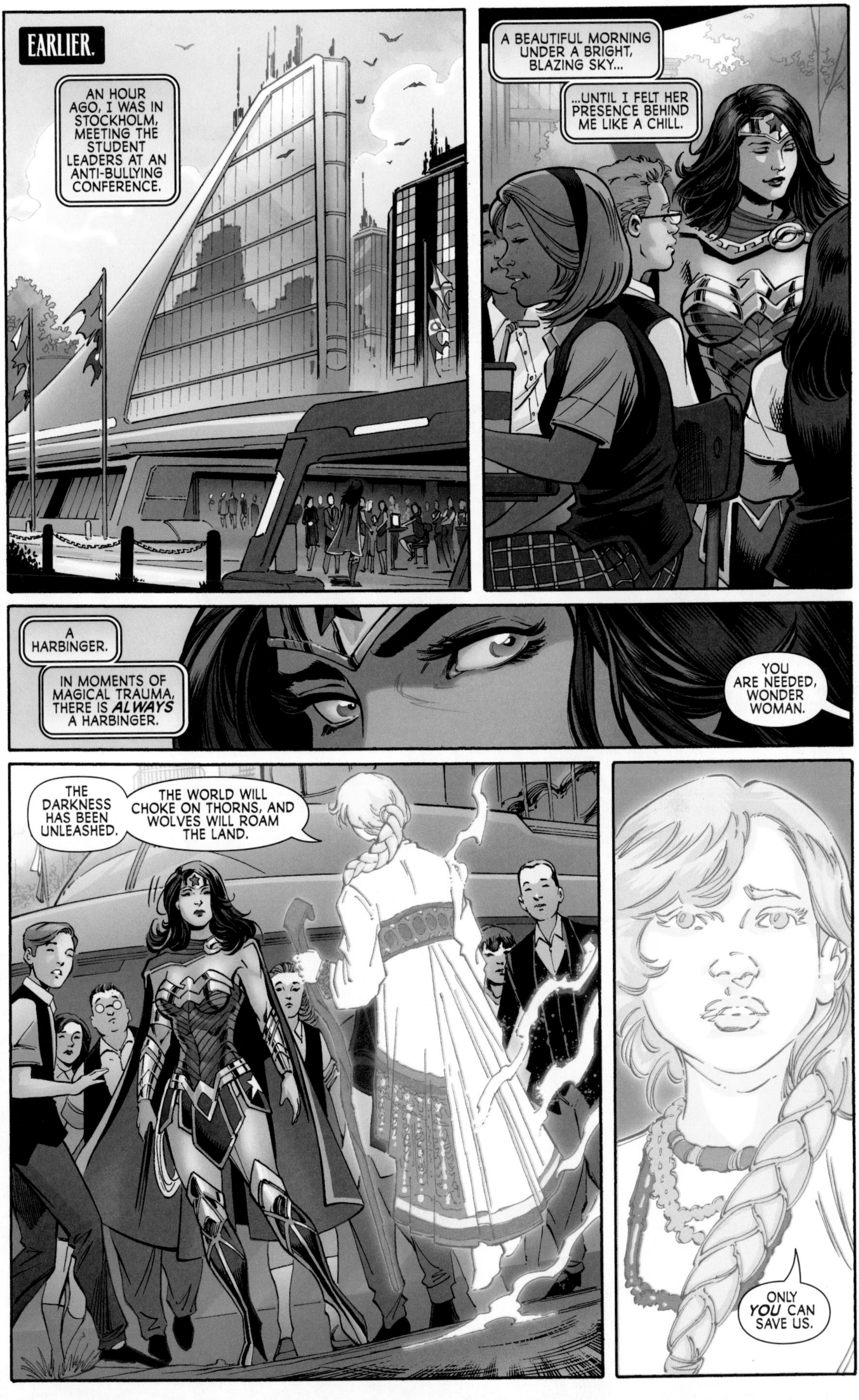
EARLIER.
AN HOUR AGO, I WAS IN STOCKHOLM, MEETING THE STUDENT LEADERS AT AN ANTI-BULLYING CONFERENCE.
A BEAUTIFUL MORNING UNDER A BRIGHT, BLAZING SKY...
...UNTIL I FELT HER PRESENCE BEHIND ME LIKE A CHILL.
A HARBINGER.
IN MOMENTS OF MAGICAL TRAUMA, THERE IS *ALWAYS* A HARBINGER.
YOU ARE NEEDED, WONDER WOMAN.
THE DARKNESS HAS BEEN UNLEASHED.
THE WORLD WILL CHOKE ON THORNS, AND WOLVES WILL ROAM THE LAND.
ONLY *YOU* CAN SAVE US.

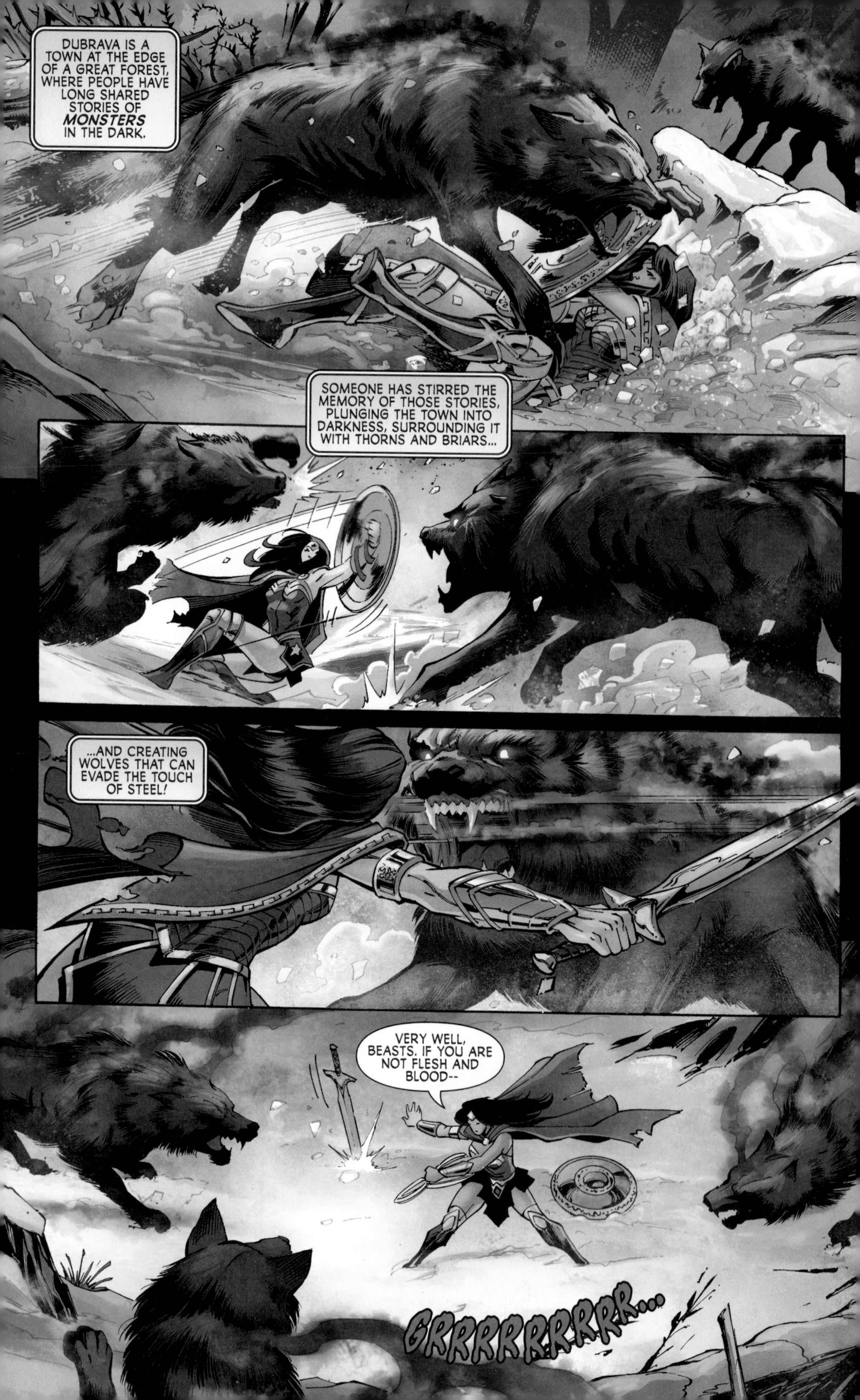
DUBRAVA IS A TOWN AT THE EDGE OF A GREAT FOREST, WHERE PEOPLE HAVE LONG SHARED STORIES OF *MONSTERS* IN THE DARK.
SOMEONE HAS STIRRED THE MEMORY OF THOSE STORIES, PLUNGING THE TOWN INTO DARKNESS, SURROUNDING IT WITH THORNS AND BRIARS...
...AND CREATING WOLVES THAT CAN EVADE THE TOUCH OF STEEL!
VERY WELL, BEASTS. IF YOU ARE NOT FLESH AND BLOOD--
GRRRRRRRRR...

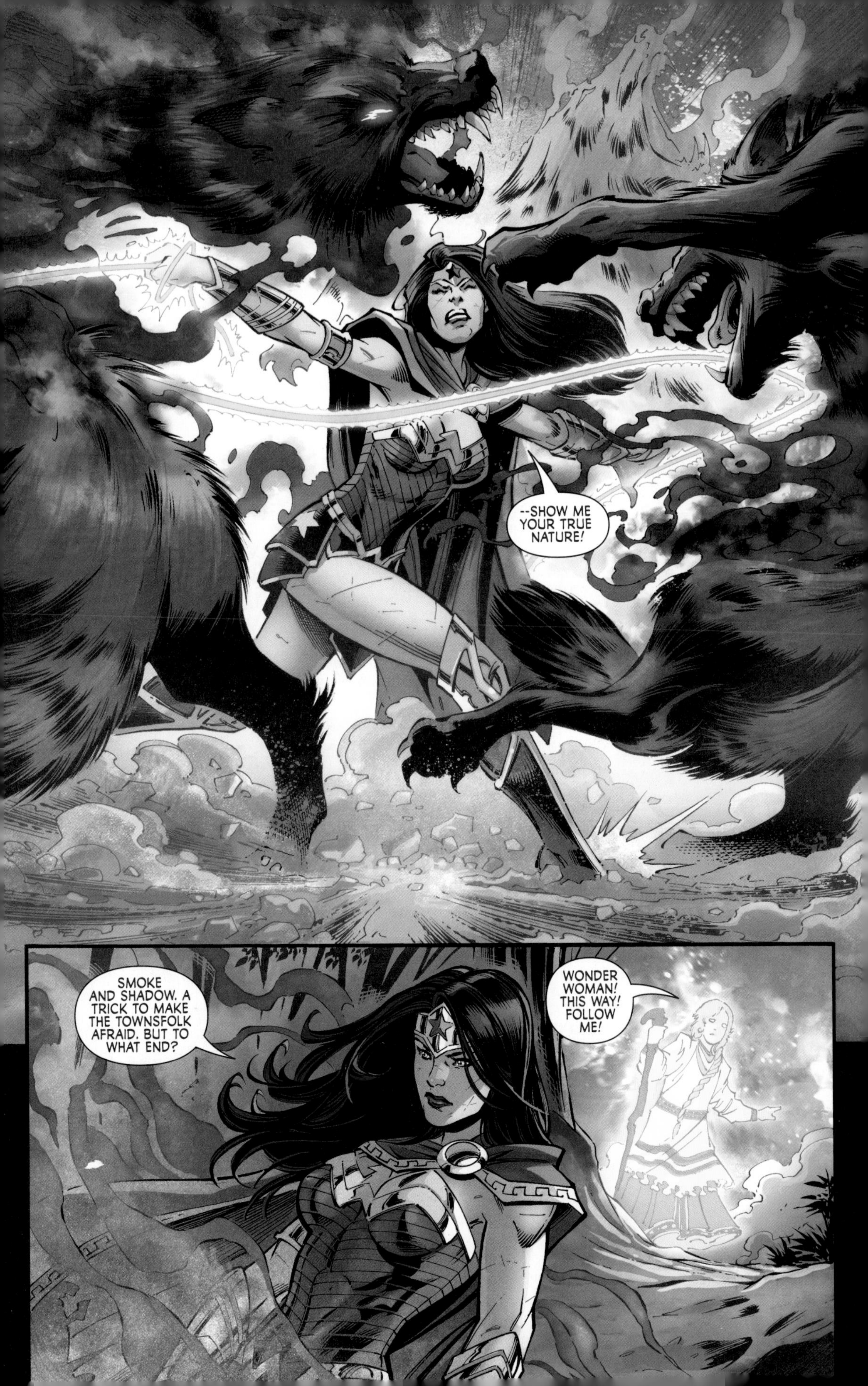
--SHOW ME YOUR TRUE NATURE!
SMOKE AND SHADOW. A TRICK TO MAKE THE TOWNSFOLK AFRAID. BUT TO WHAT END?
WONDER WOMAN! THIS WAY! FOLLOW ME!

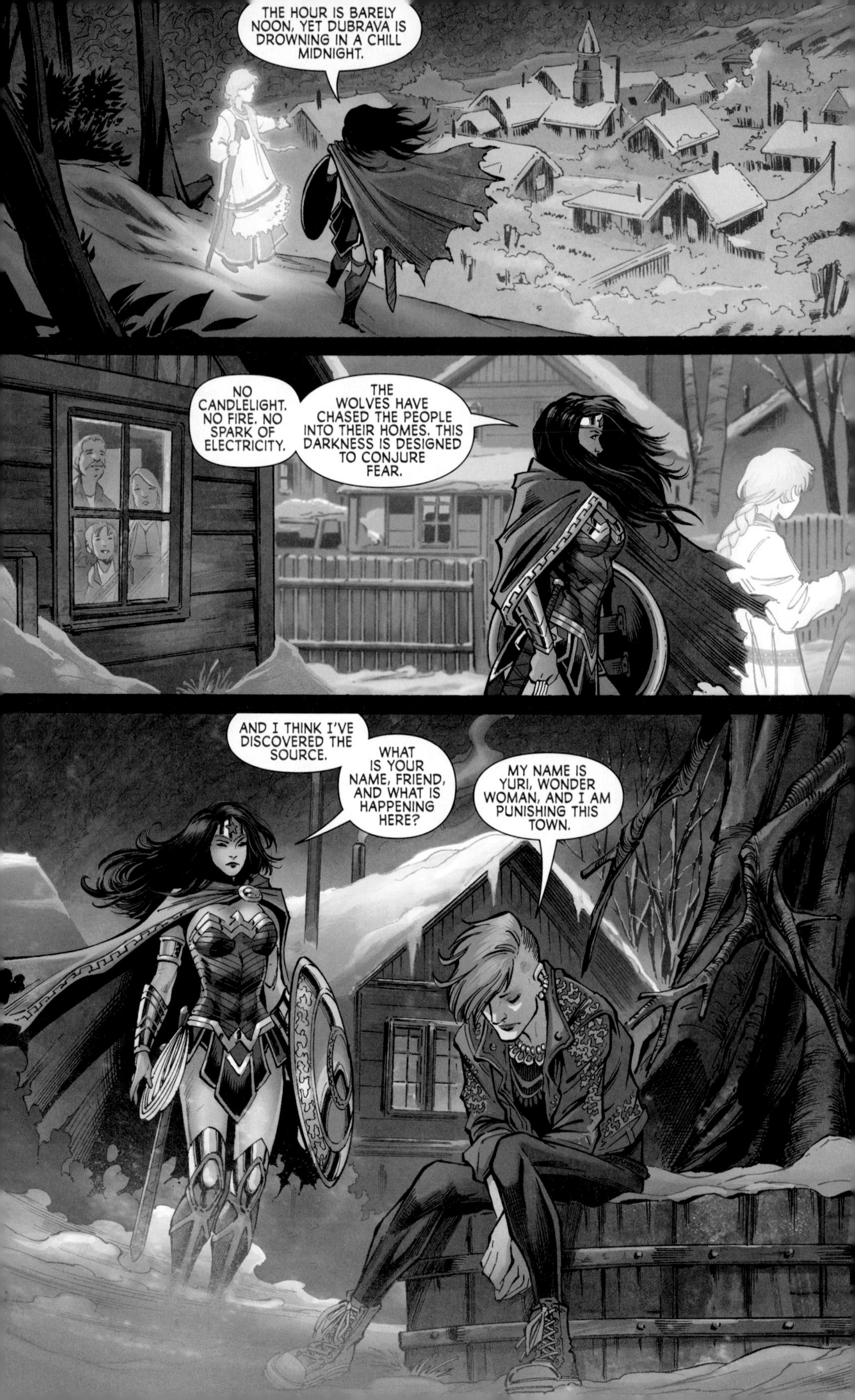
THE HOUR IS BARELY NOON, YET DUBRAVA IS DROWNING IN A CHILL MIDNIGHT.
NO CANDLELIGHT. NO FIRE. NO SPARK OF ELECTRICITY.
THE WOLVES HAVE CHASED THE PEOPLE INTO THEIR HOMES. THIS DARKNESS IS DESIGNED TO CONJURE FEAR.
AND I THINK I'VE DISCOVERED THE SOURCE.
WHAT IS YOUR NAME, FRIEND, AND WHAT IS HAPPENING HERE?
MY NAME IS YURI, WONDER WOMAN, AND I AM PUNISHING THIS TOWN.

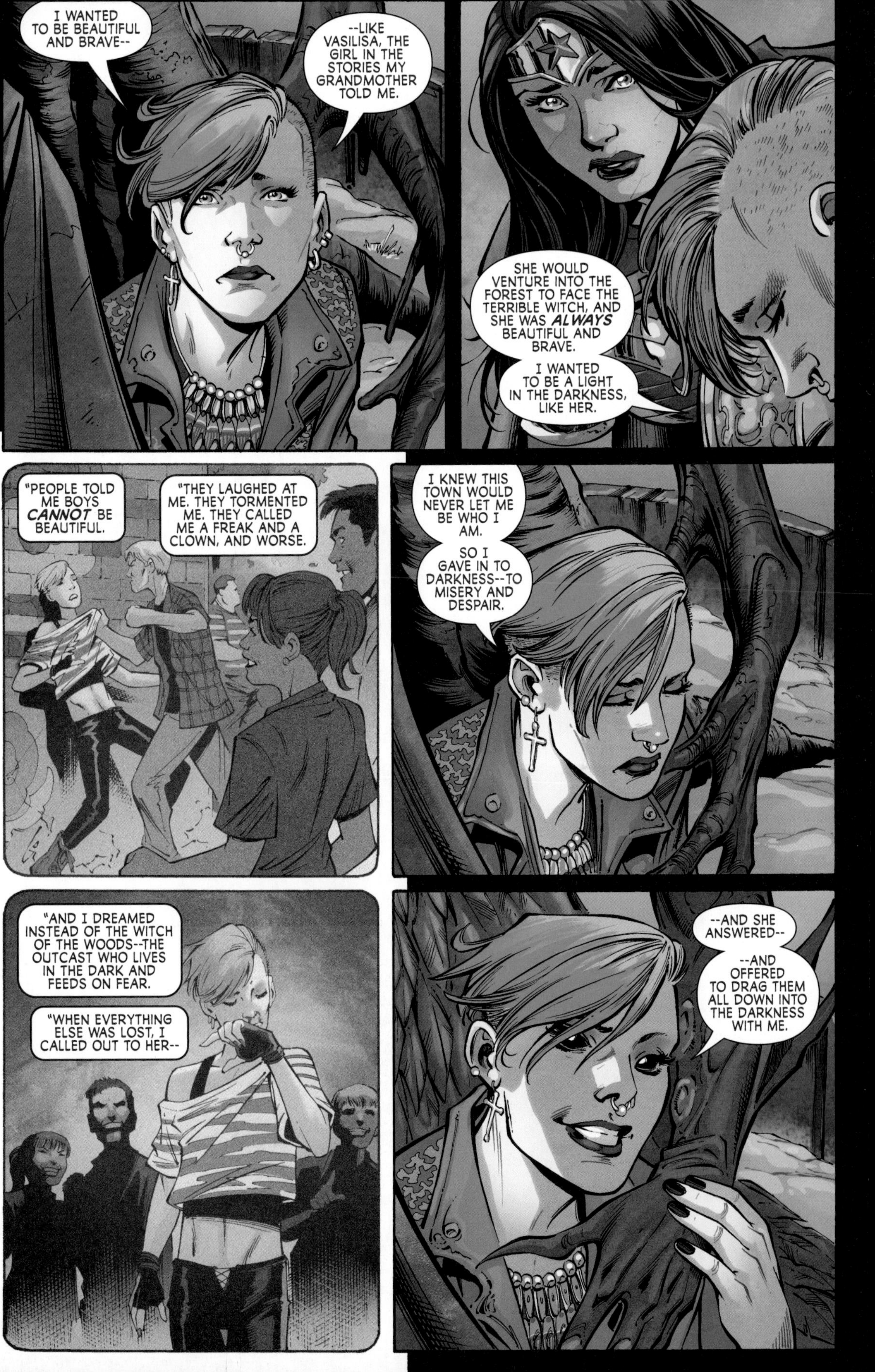
I WANTED TO BE BEAUTIFUL AND BRAVE--
--LIKE VASILISA, THE GIRL IN THE STORIES MY GRANDMOTHER TOLD ME.
SHE WOULD VENTURE INTO THE FOREST TO FACE THE TERRIBLE WITCH, AND SHE WAS *ALWAYS* BEAUTIFUL AND BRAVE.
I WANTED TO BE A LIGHT IN THE DARKNESS, LIKE HER.
"PEOPLE TOLD ME BOYS *CANNOT* BE BEAUTIFUL.
"THEY LAUGHED AT ME. THEY TORMENTED ME. THEY CALLED ME A FREAK AND A CLOWN, AND WORSE.
I KNEW THIS TOWN WOULD NEVER LET ME BE WHO I AM.
SO I GAVE IN TO DARKNESS--TO MISERY AND DESPAIR.
"AND I DREAMED INSTEAD OF THE WITCH OF THE WOODS--THE OUTCAST WHO LIVES IN THE DARK AND FEEDS ON FEAR.
"WHEN EVERYTHING ELSE WAS LOST, I CALLED OUT TO HER--
--AND SHE ANSWERED--
--AND OFFERED TO DRAG THEM ALL DOWN INTO THE DARKNESS WITH ME.

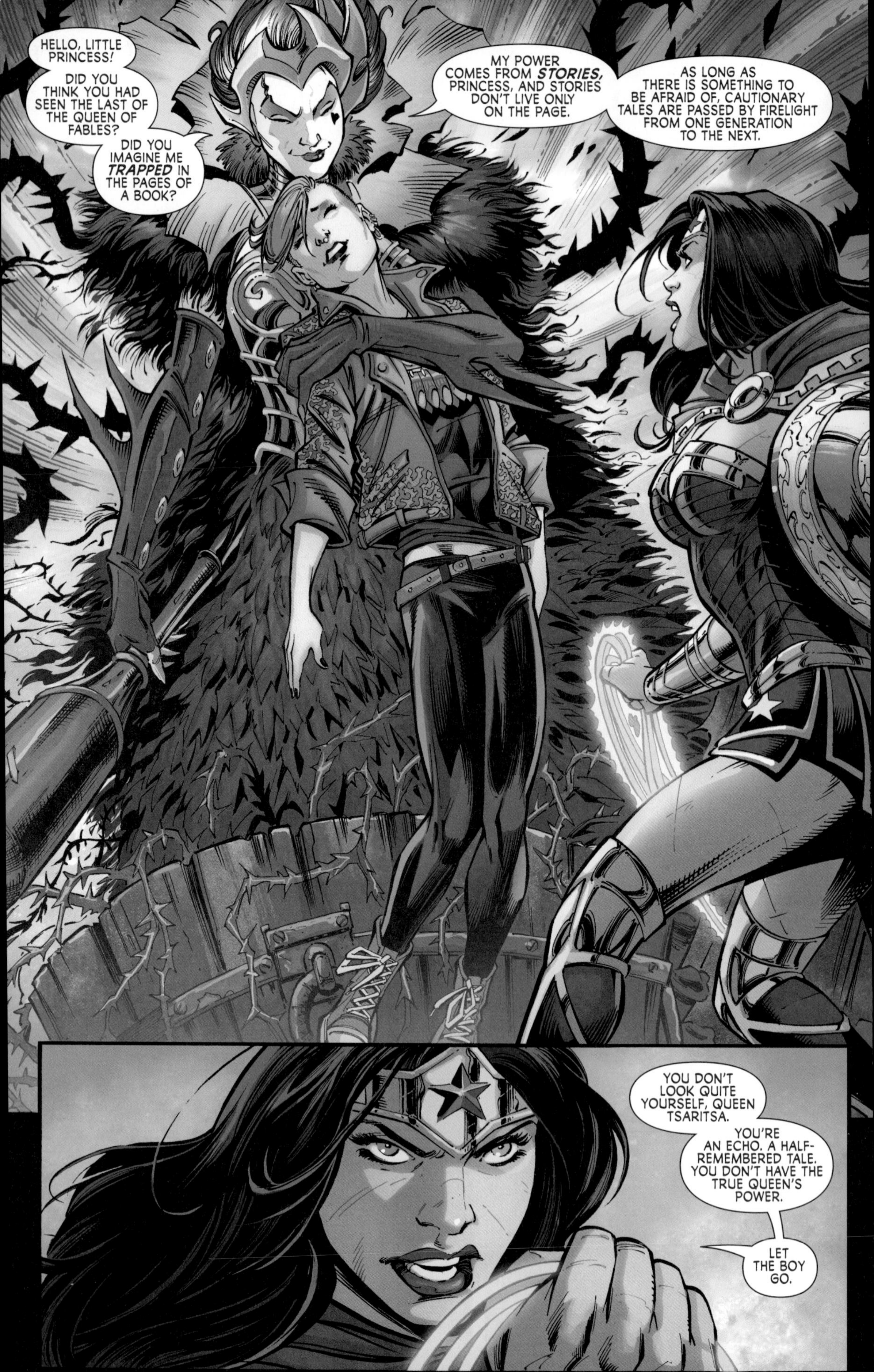
HELLO, LITTLE PRINCESS!
DID YOU THINK YOU HAD SEEN THE LAST OF THE QUEEN OF FABLES?
DID YOU IMAGINE ME TRAPPED IN THE PAGES OF A BOOK?
MY POWER COMES FROM STORIES, PRINCESS, AND STORIES DON'T LIVE ONLY ON THE PAGE.
AS LONG AS THERE IS SOMETHING TO BE AFRAID OF, CAUTIONARY TALES ARE PASSED BY FIRELIGHT FROM ONE GENERATION TO THE NEXT.
YOU DON'T LOOK QUITE YOURSELF, QUEEN TSARITSA.
YOU'RE AN ECHO. A HALF-REMEMBERED TALE. YOU DON'T HAVE THE TRUE QUEEN'S POWER.
LET THE BOY GO.

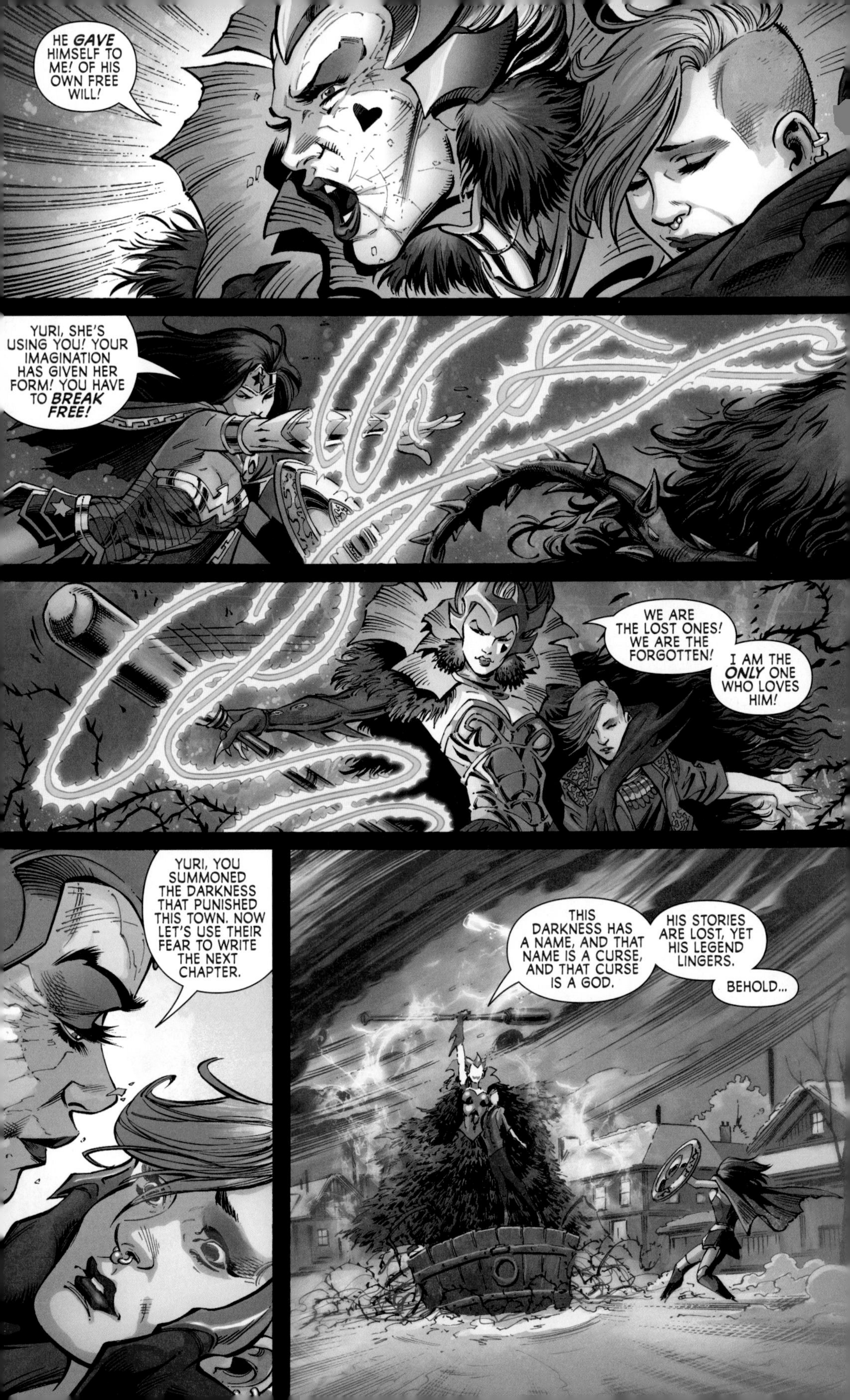
HE GAVE HIMSELF TO ME! OF HIS OWN FREE WILL!
YURI, SHE'S USING YOU! YOUR IMAGINATION HAS GIVEN HER FORM! YOU HAVE TO BREAK FREE!
WE ARE THE LOST ONES! WE ARE THE FORGOTTEN!
I AM THE ONLY ONE WHO LOVES HIM!
YURI, YOU SUMMONED THE DARKNESS THAT PUNISHED THIS TOWN. NOW LET'S USE THEIR FEAR TO WRITE THE NEXT CHAPTER.
THIS DARKNESS HAS A NAME, AND THAT NAME IS A CURSE, AND THAT CURSE IS A GOD.
HIS STORIES ARE LOST, YET HIS LEGEND LINGERS.
BEHOLD...

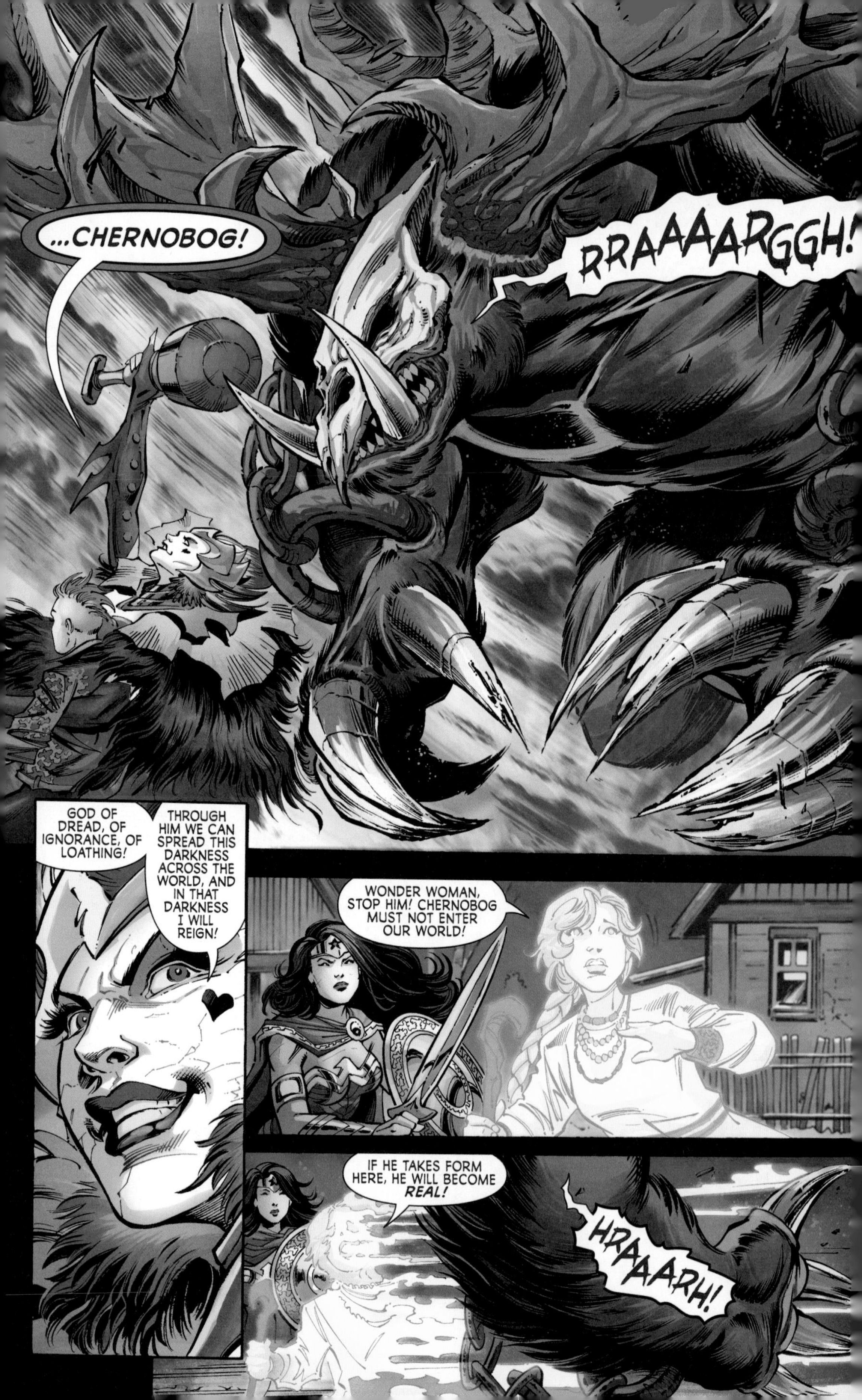
...CHERNOBOG!
DRAAAARGGH!
GOD OF DREAD, OF IGNORANCE, OF LOATHING!
THROUGH HIM WE CAN SPREAD THIS DARKNESS ACROSS THE WORLD, AND IN THAT DARKNESS I WILL REIGN!
WONDER WOMAN, STOP HIM! CHERNOBOG MUST NOT ENTER OUR WORLD!
IF HE TAKES FORM HERE, HE WILL BECOME REAL!
HRAAARH!

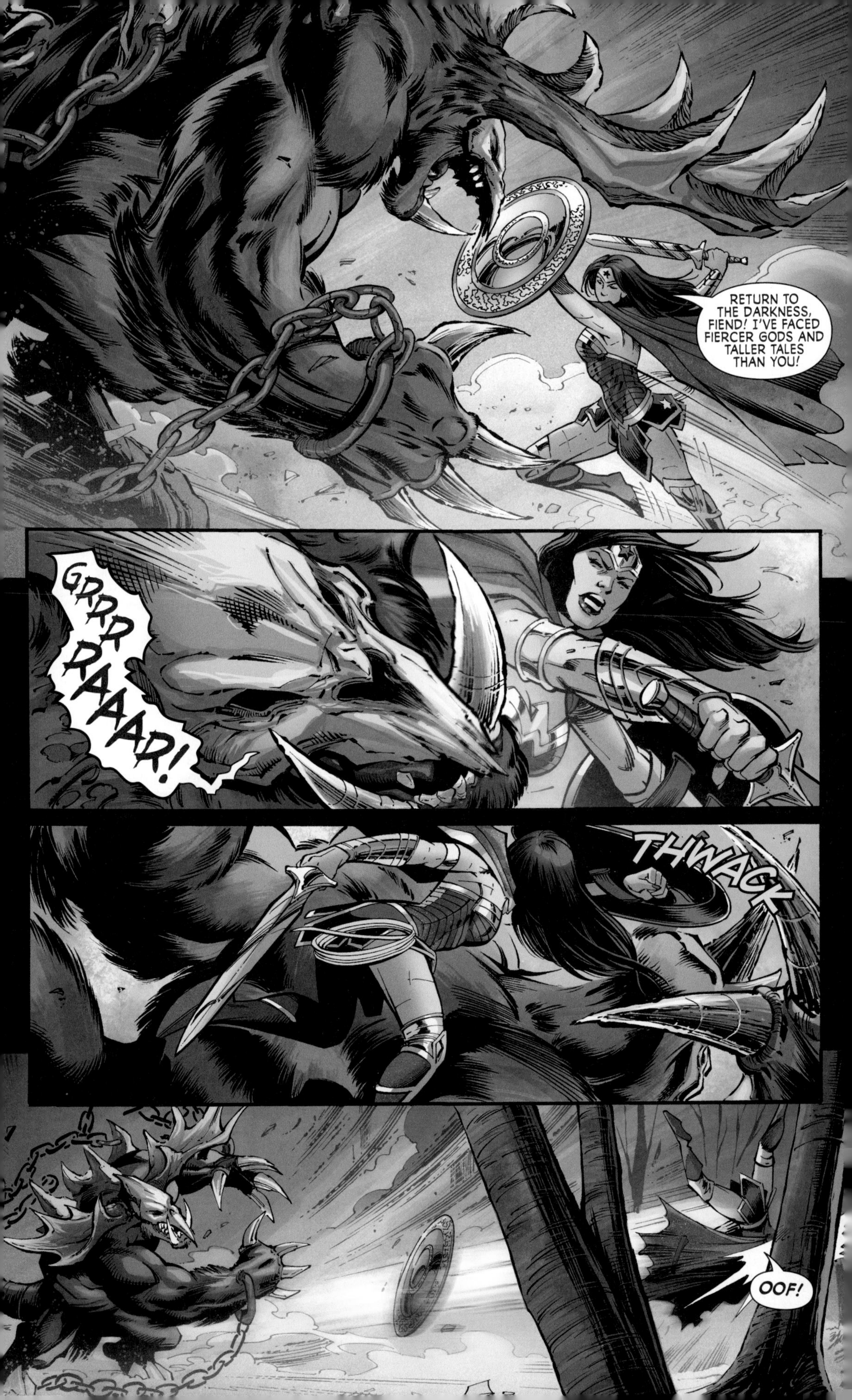
RETURN TO THE DARKNESS, FIEND! I'VE FACED FIERCER GODS AND TALLER TALES THAN YOU!
GRRRR RAAAR!
THWACK
OOF!

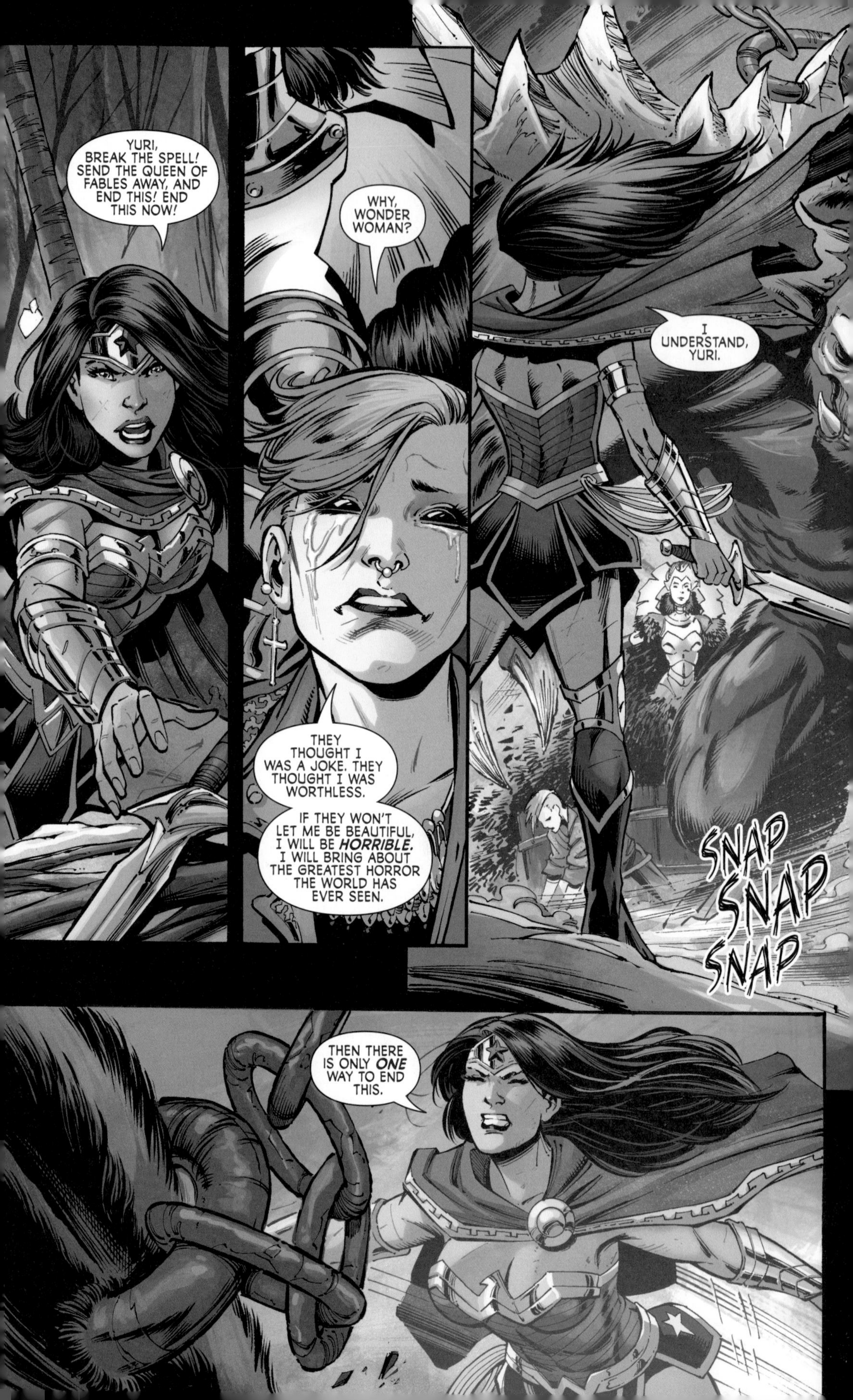
YURI, BREAK THE SPELL! SEND THE QUEEN OF FABLES AWAY, AND END THIS! END THIS NOW!
WHY, WONDER WOMAN?
THEY THOUGHT I WAS A JOKE. THEY THOUGHT I WAS WORTHLESS.
IF THEY WON'T LET ME BE BEAUTIFUL, I WILL BE *HORRIBLE.* I WILL BRING ABOUT THE GREATEST HORROR THE WORLD HAS EVER SEEN.
I UNDERSTAND, YURI.
SNAP SNAP SNAP
THEN THERE IS ONLY *ONE* WAY TO END THIS.

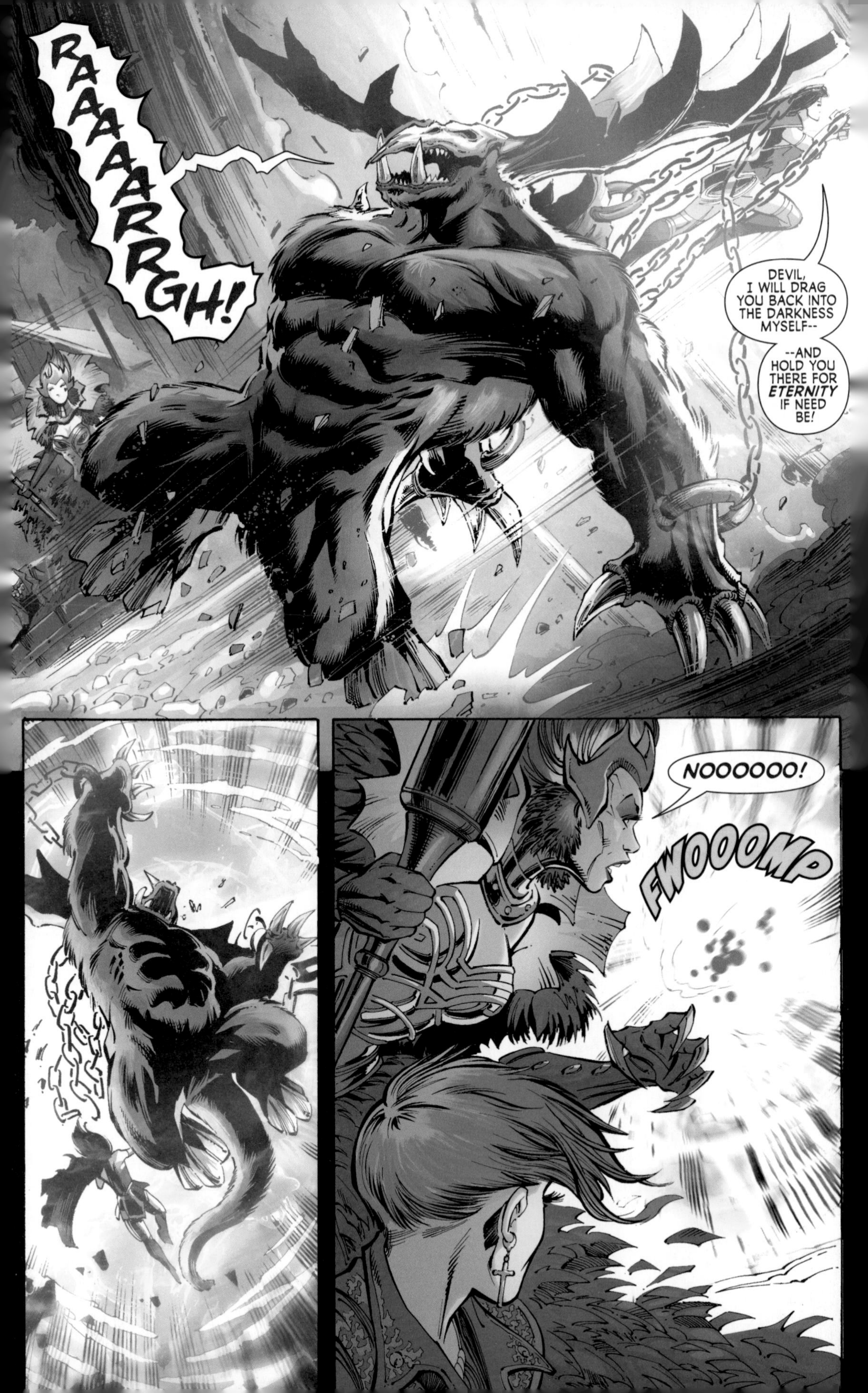
RAAAAARRRGH!
DEVIL, I WILL DRAG YOU BACK INTO THE DARKNESS MYSELF--
--AND HOLD YOU THERE FOR ETERNITY IF NEED BE!
NOOOOOO!
FWOOOMP

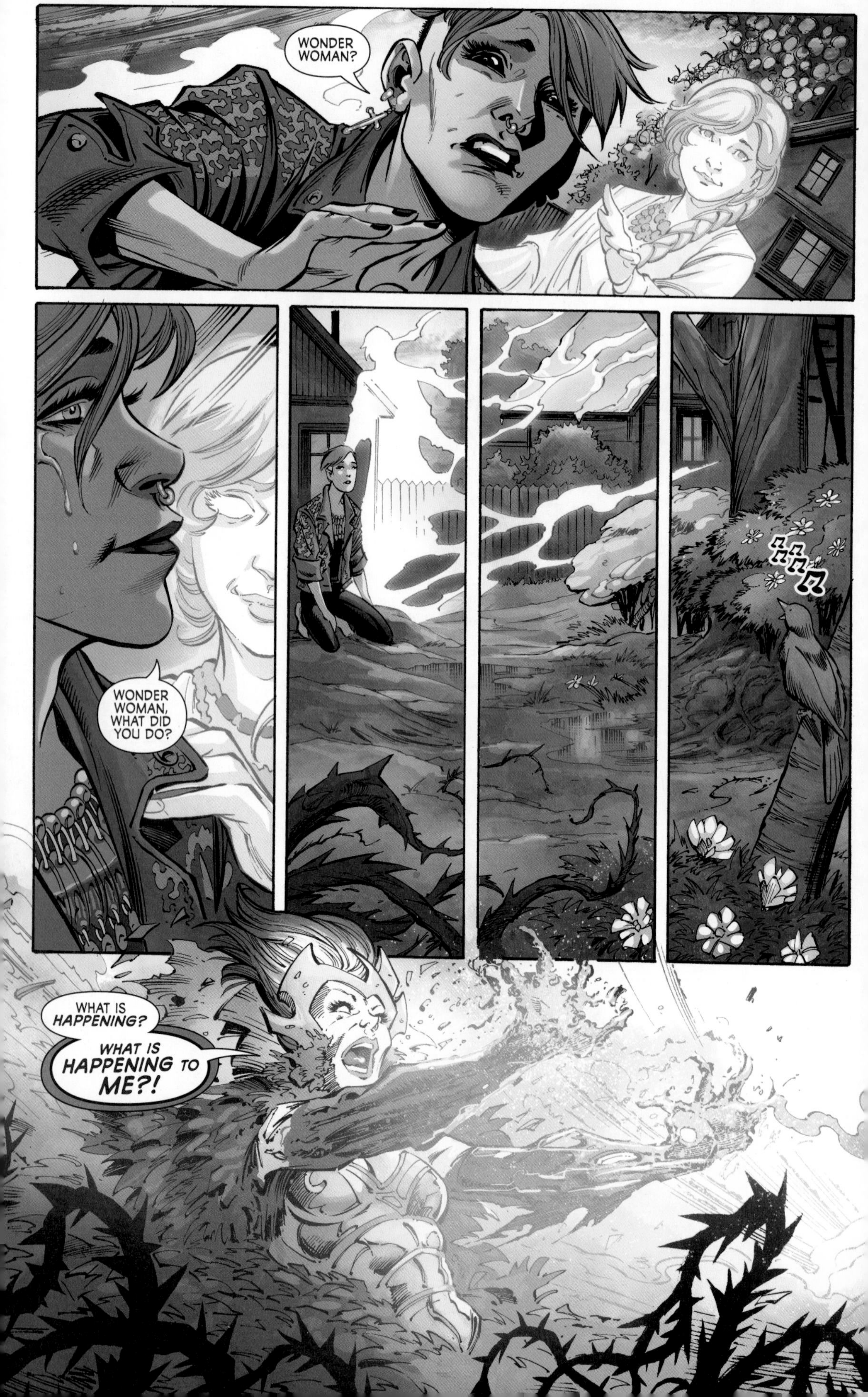
WONDER WOMAN?
WONDER WOMAN, WHAT DID YOU DO?
WHAT IS HAPPENING?
WHAT IS HAPPENING TO ME?!

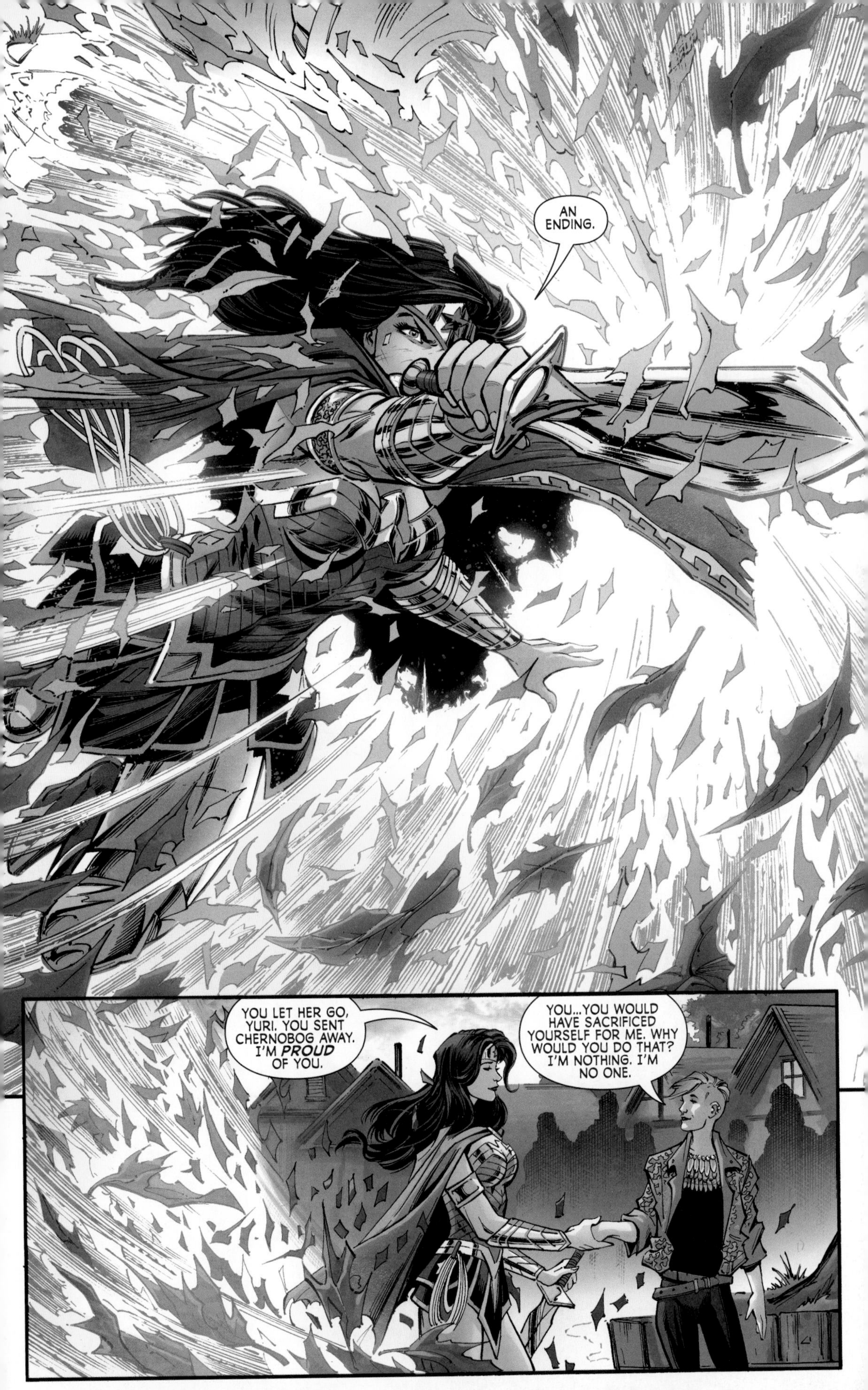
AN ENDING.
YOU LET HER GO, YURI. YOU SENT CHERNOBOG AWAY. I'M *PROUD* OF YOU.
YOU...YOU WOULD HAVE SACRIFICED YOURSELF FOR ME. WHY WOULD YOU DO THAT? I'M NOTHING. I'M NO ONE.

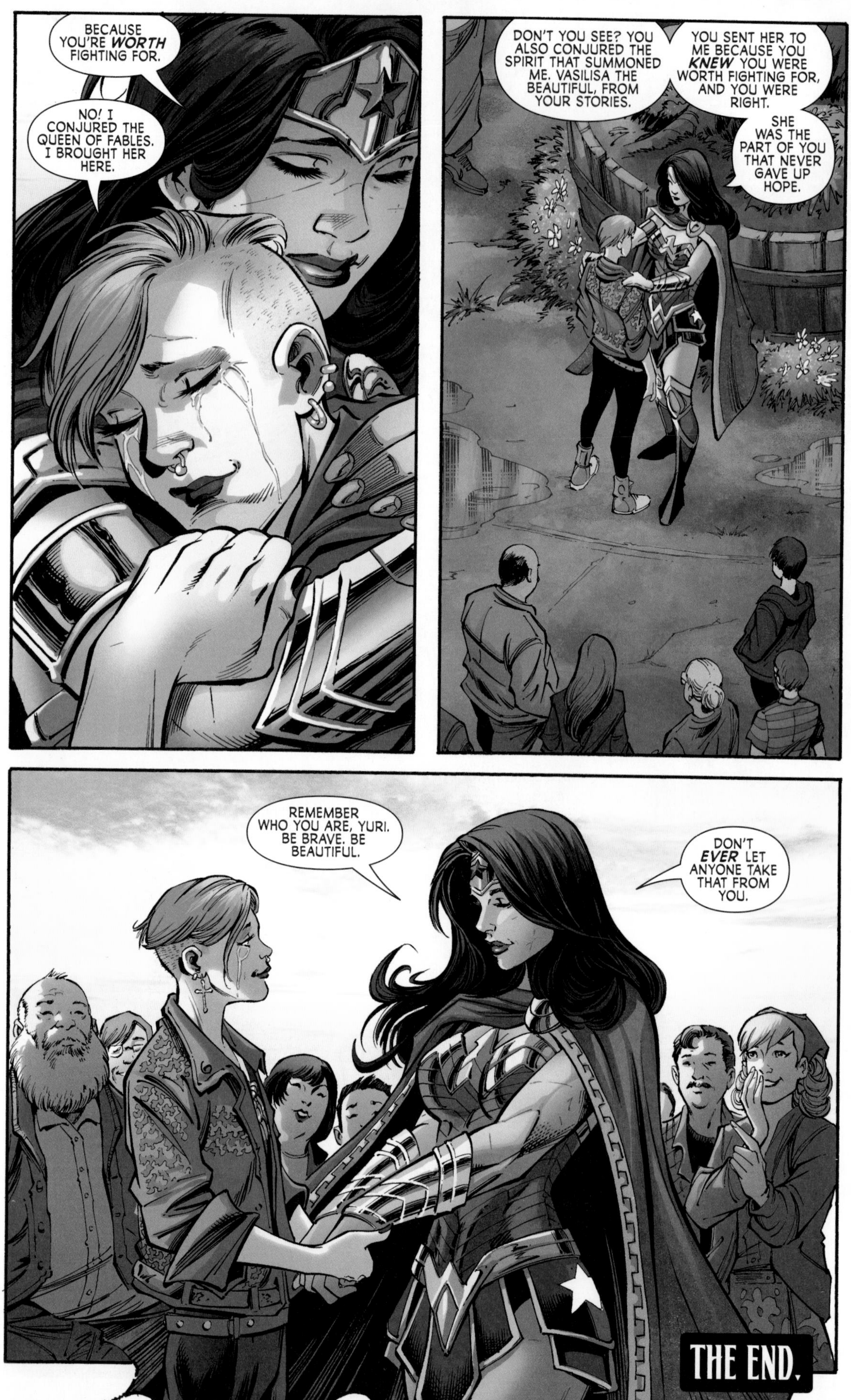
BECAUSE YOU'RE **WORTH** FIGHTING FOR.
NO! I CONJURED THE QUEEN OF FABLES. I BROUGHT HER HERE.
DON'T YOU SEE? YOU ALSO CONJURED THE SPIRIT THAT SUMMONED ME. VASILISA THE BEAUTIFUL, FROM YOUR STORIES.
YOU SENT HER TO ME BECAUSE YOU **KNEW** YOU WERE WORTH FIGHTING FOR, AND YOU WERE RIGHT.
SHE WAS THE PART OF YOU THAT NEVER GAVE UP HOPE.
REMEMBER WHO YOU ARE, YURI. BE BRAVE. BE BEAUTIFUL.
DON'T **EVER** LET ANYONE TAKE THAT FROM YOU.
THE END.

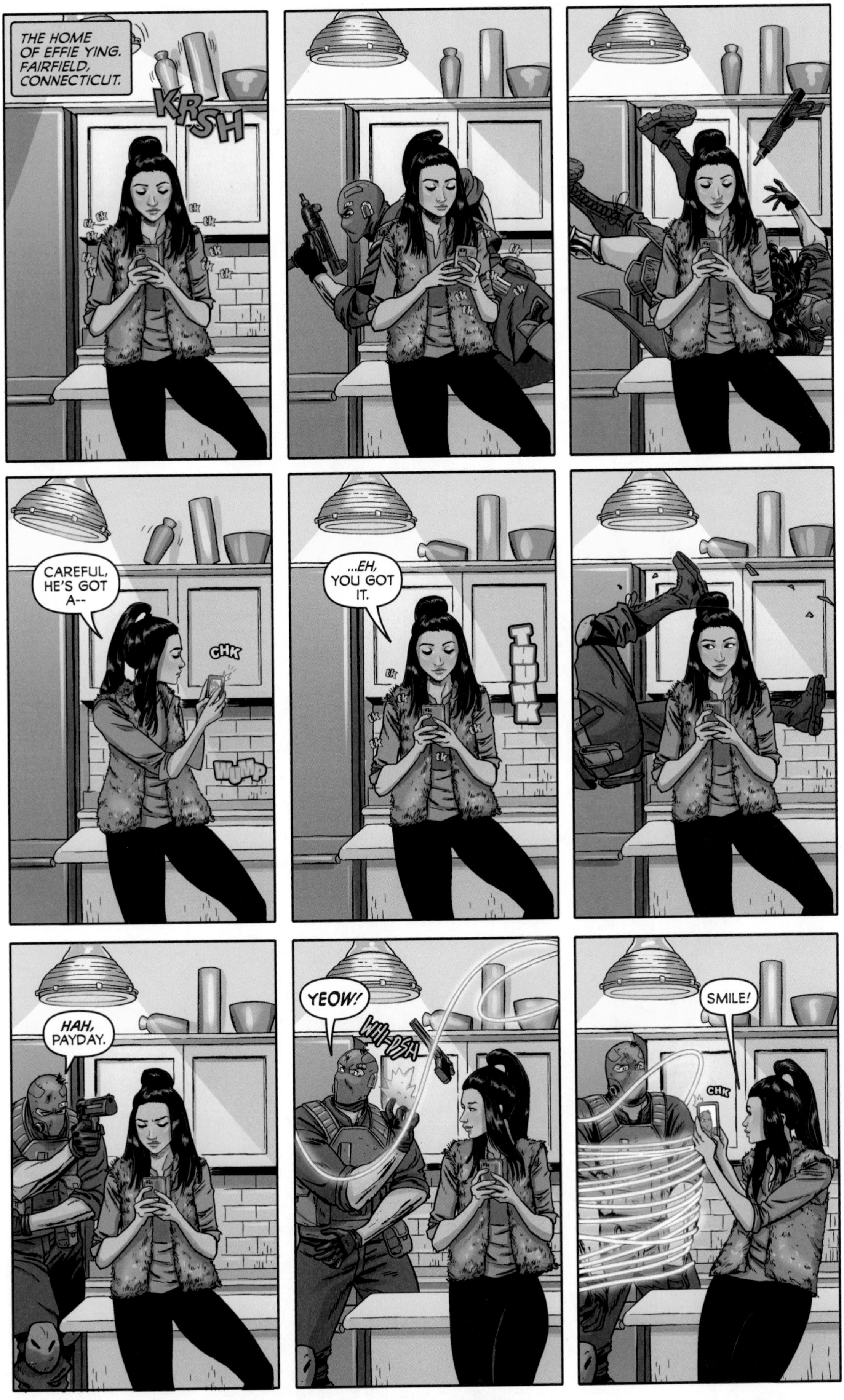
THE HOME OF EFFIE YING. FAIRFIELD, CONNECTICUT.
KRSH
tk
CAREFUL, HE'S GOT A--
CHK
WUMP
...EH, YOU GOT IT.
THUNK
HAH, PAYDAY.
YEOW!
WH-DSH
SMILE!
CHK

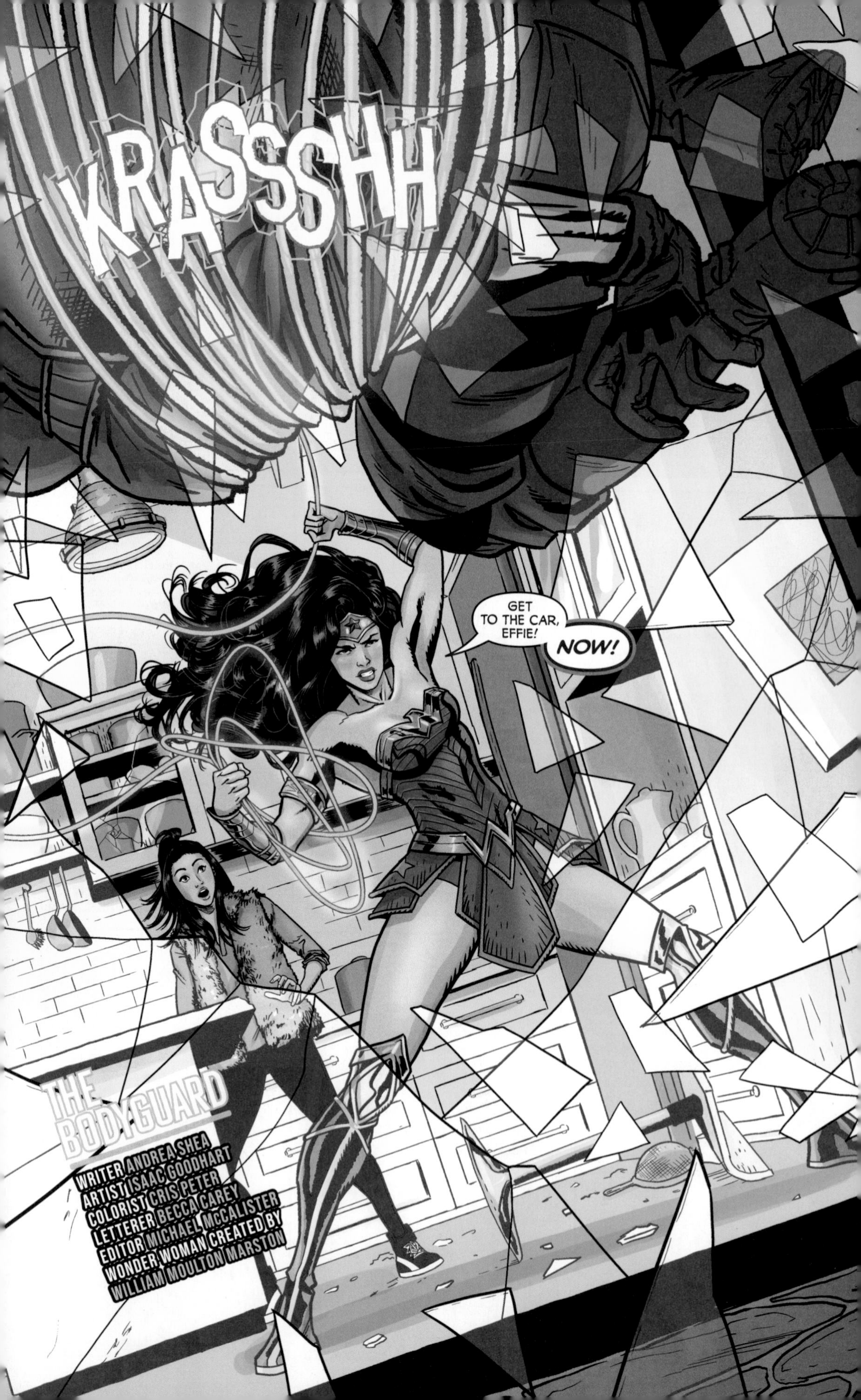
KRASSHH
GET TO THE CAR, EFFIE!
NOW!
THE BODYGUARD
WRITER ANDREA SHEA
ARTIST ISAAC GOODHART
COLORIST CRIS PETER
LETTERER BECCA CAREY
EDITOR MICHAEL McCALISTER
WONDER WOMAN CREATED BY
WILLIAM MOULTON MARSTON

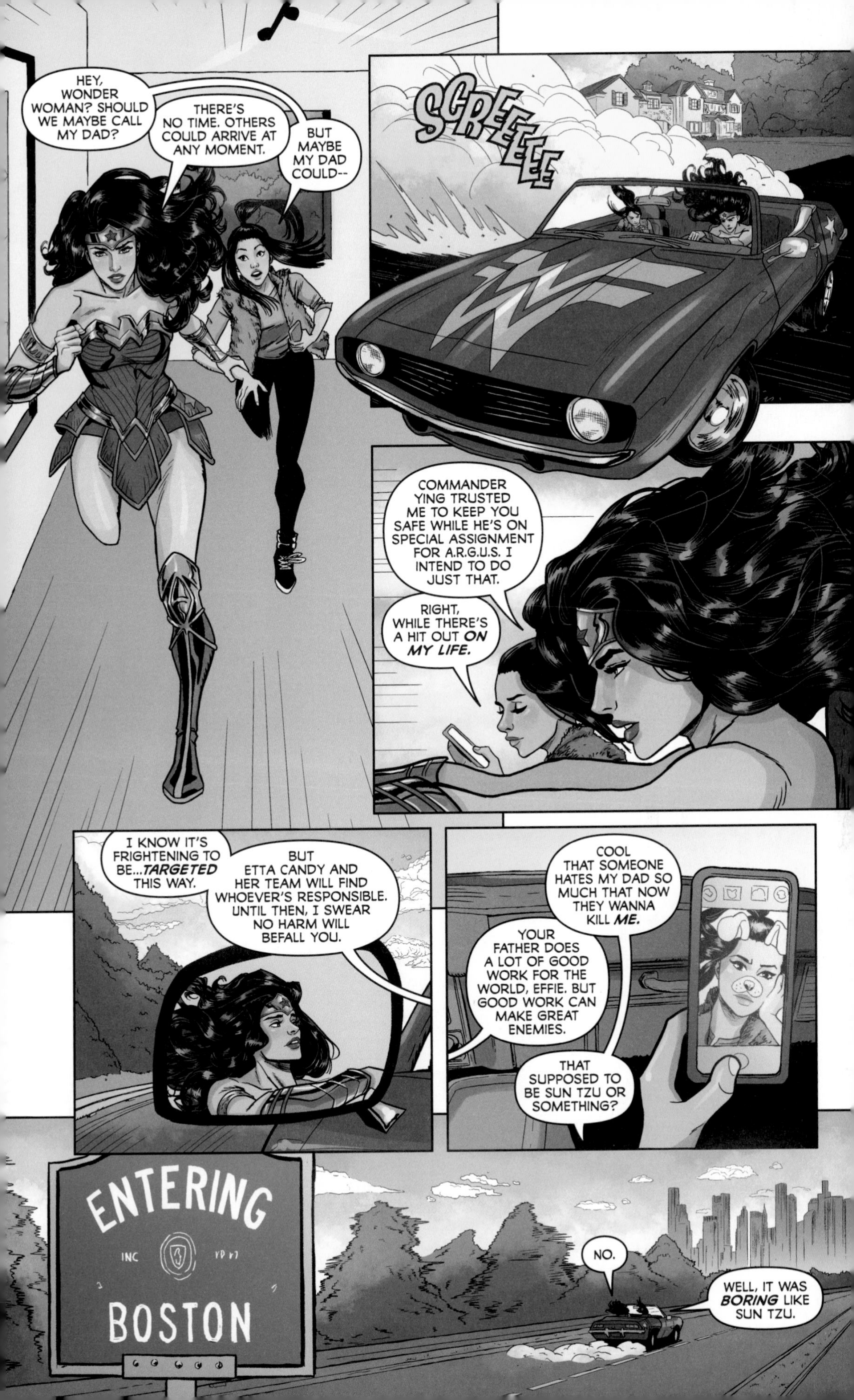

HEY, WONDER WOMAN? SHOULD WE MAYBE CALL MY DAD?
THERE'S NO TIME. OTHERS COULD ARRIVE AT ANY MOMENT.
BUT MAYBE MY DAD COULD--
SCREEEEE
COMMANDER YING TRUSTED ME TO KEEP YOU SAFE WHILE HE'S ON SPECIAL ASSIGNMENT FOR A.R.G.U.S. I INTEND TO DO JUST THAT.
RIGHT, WHILE THERE'S A HIT OUT ON MY LIFE.
I KNOW IT'S FRIGHTENING TO BE...TARGETED THIS WAY.
BUT ETTA CANDY AND HER TEAM WILL FIND WHOEVER'S RESPONSIBLE. UNTIL THEN, I SWEAR NO HARM WILL BEFALL YOU.
COOL THAT SOMEONE HATES MY DAD SO MUCH THAT NOW THEY WANNA KILL ME.
YOUR FATHER DOES A LOT OF GOOD WORK FOR THE WORLD, EFFIE. BUT GOOD WORK CAN MAKE GREAT ENEMIES.
THAT SUPPOSED TO BE SUN TZU OR SOMETHING?
ENTERING
INC
BOSTON
NO.
WELL, IT WAS BORING LIKE SUN TZU.

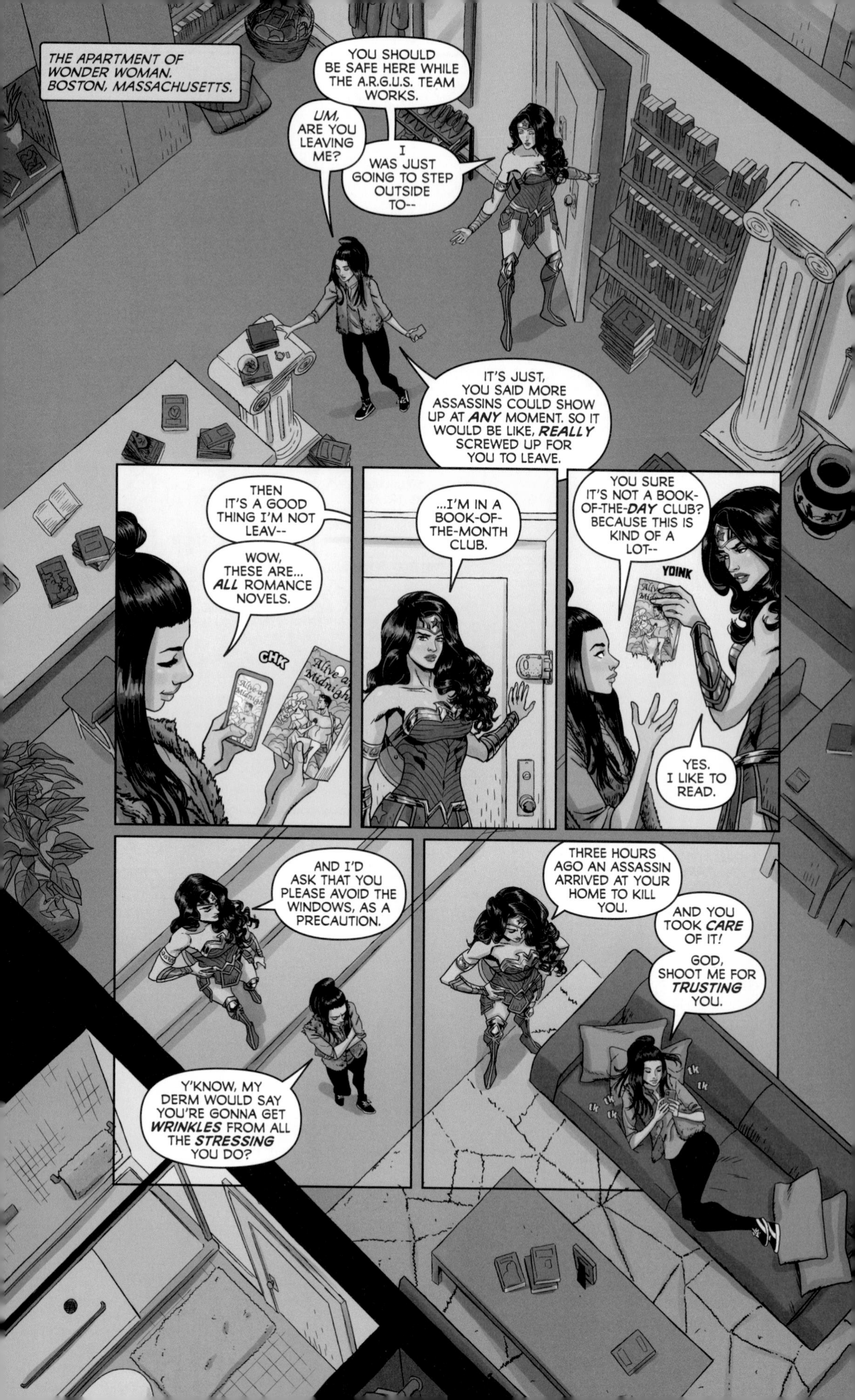
THE APARTMENT OF WONDER WOMAN. BOSTON, MASSACHUSETTS.
YOU SHOULD BE SAFE HERE WHILE THE A.R.G.U.S. TEAM WORKS.
UM, ARE YOU LEAVING ME?
I WAS JUST GOING TO STEP OUTSIDE TO--
IT'S JUST, YOU SAID MORE ASSASSINS COULD SHOW UP AT ANY MOMENT. SO IT WOULD BE LIKE, REALLY SCREWED UP FOR YOU TO LEAVE.
THEN IT'S A GOOD THING I'M NOT LEAV--
WOW, THESE ARE... ALL ROMANCE NOVELS.
CHK
Alive at Midnight
...I'M IN A BOOK-OF-THE-MONTH CLUB.
YOU SURE IT'S NOT A BOOK-OF-THE-DAY CLUB? BECAUSE THIS IS KIND OF A LOT--
YOINK
YES. I LIKE TO READ.
AND I'D ASK THAT YOU PLEASE AVOID THE WINDOWS, AS A PRECAUTION.
Y'KNOW, MY DERM WOULD SAY YOU'RE GONNA GET WRINKLES FROM ALL THE STRESSING YOU DO?
THREE HOURS AGO AN ASSASSIN ARRIVED AT YOUR HOME TO KILL YOU.
AND YOU TOOK CARE OF IT!
GOD, SHOOT ME FOR TRUSTING YOU.
tk tk tk tk

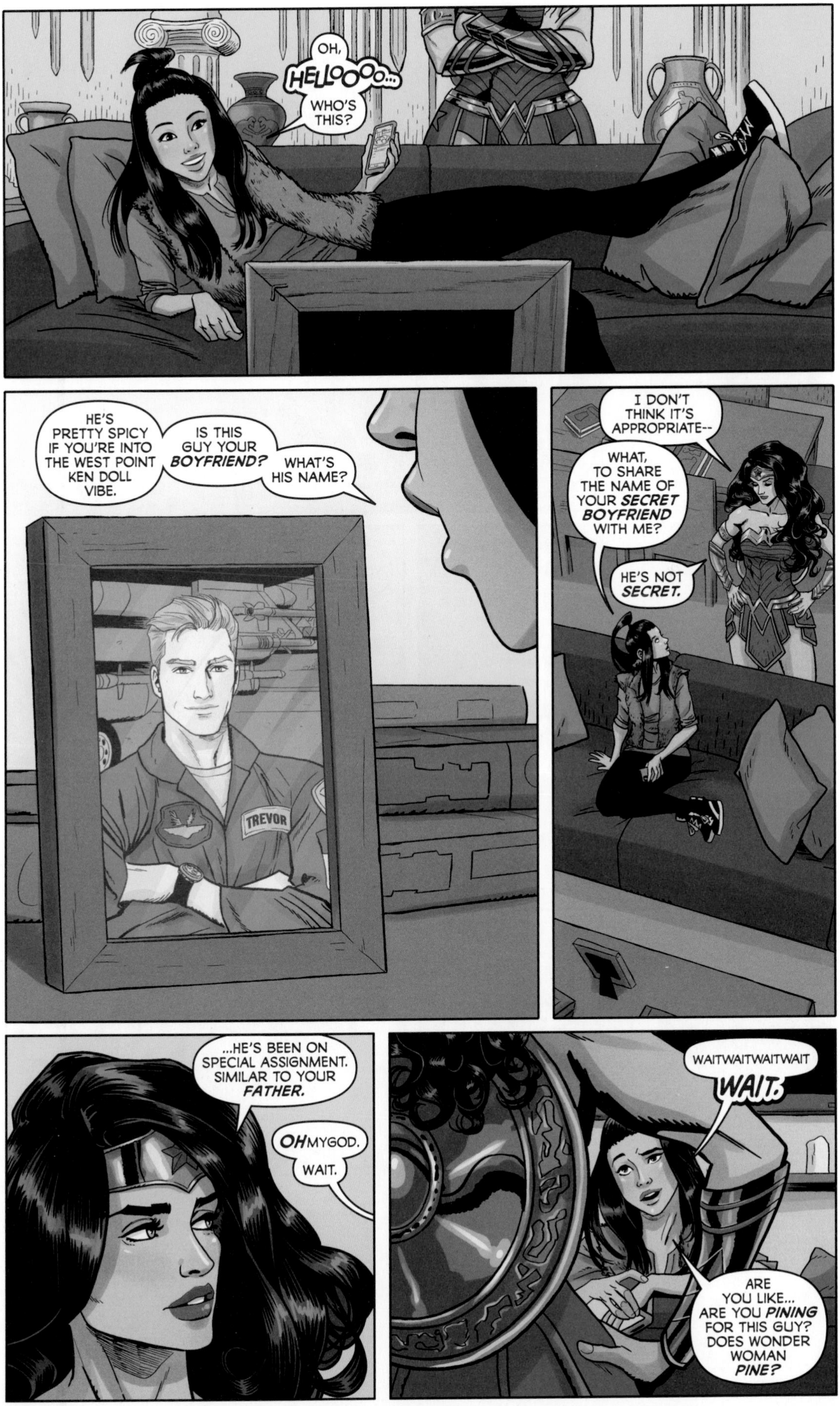
OH, HELLOOOO... WHO'S THIS?
HE'S PRETTY SPICY IF YOU'RE INTO THE WEST POINT KEN DOLL VIBE.
IS THIS GUY YOUR BOYFRIEND?
WHAT'S HIS NAME?
TREVOR
I DON'T THINK IT'S APPROPRIATE--
WHAT, TO SHARE THE NAME OF YOUR SECRET BOYFRIEND WITH ME?
HE'S NOT SECRET.
...HE'S BEEN ON SPECIAL ASSIGNMENT. SIMILAR TO YOUR FATHER.
OHMYGOD.
WAIT.
WAITWAITWAITWAIT
WAIT.
ARE YOU LIKE... ARE YOU PINING FOR THIS GUY? DOES WONDER WOMAN PINE?

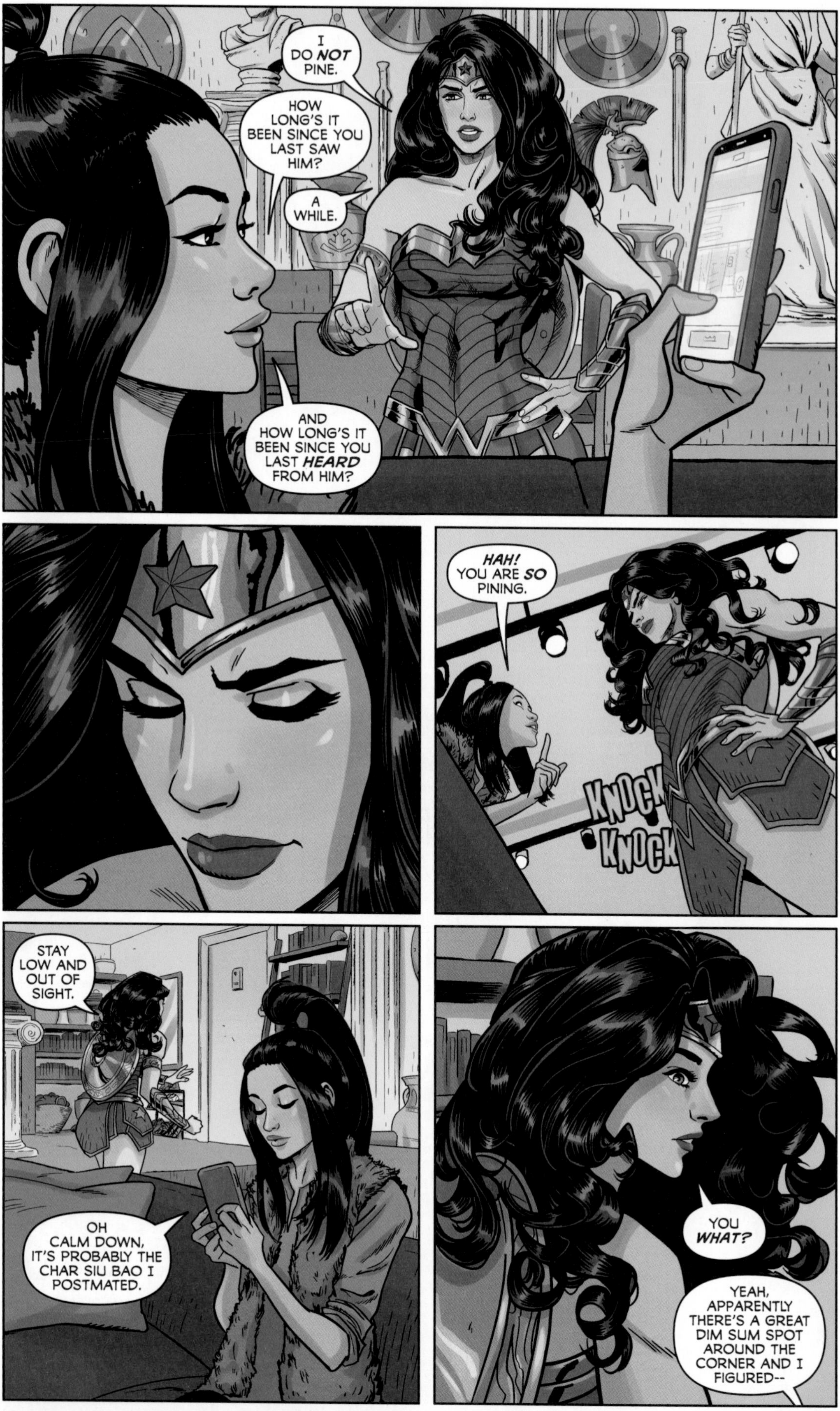
I DO NOT PINE.
HOW LONG'S IT BEEN SINCE YOU LAST SAW HIM?
A WHILE.
AND HOW LONG'S IT BEEN SINCE YOU LAST HEARD FROM HIM?
HAH! YOU ARE SO PINING.
KNOCK
KNOCK
STAY LOW AND OUT OF SIGHT.
OH CALM DOWN, IT'S PROBABLY THE CHAR SIU BAO I POSTMATED.
YOU WHAT?
YEAH, APPARENTLY THERE'S A GREAT DIM SUM SPOT AROUND THE CORNER AND I FIGURED--

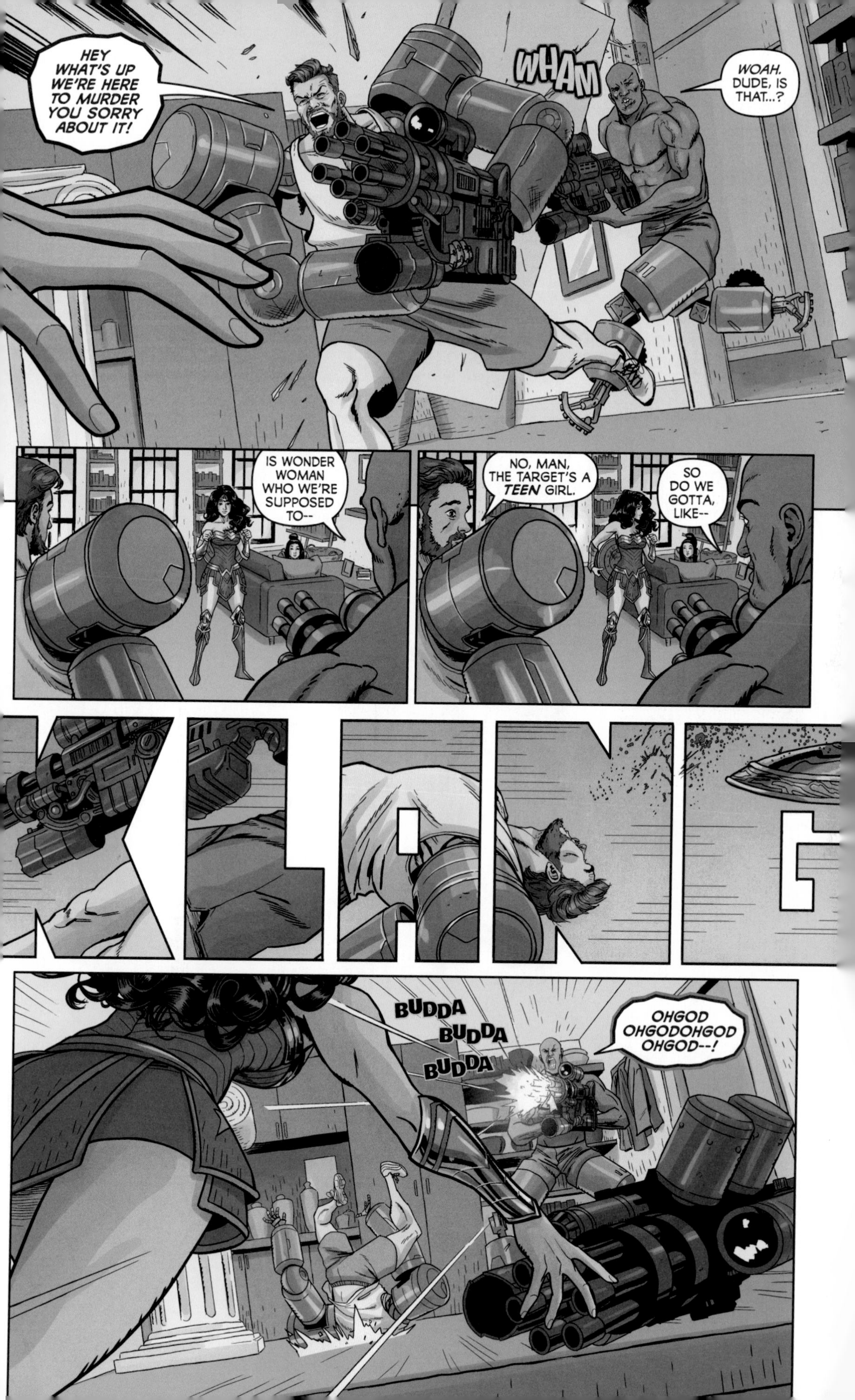

HEY WHAT'S UP WE'RE HERE TO MURDER YOU SORRY ABOUT IT!
WHAM
WOAH. DUDE, IS THAT...?
IS WONDER WOMAN WHO WE'RE SUPPOSED TO--
NO, MAN, THE TARGET'S A TEEN GIRL.
SO DO WE GOTTA, LIKE--
KLANG
BUDDA
BUDDA
BUDDA
OHGOD OHGODOHGOD OHGOD--!

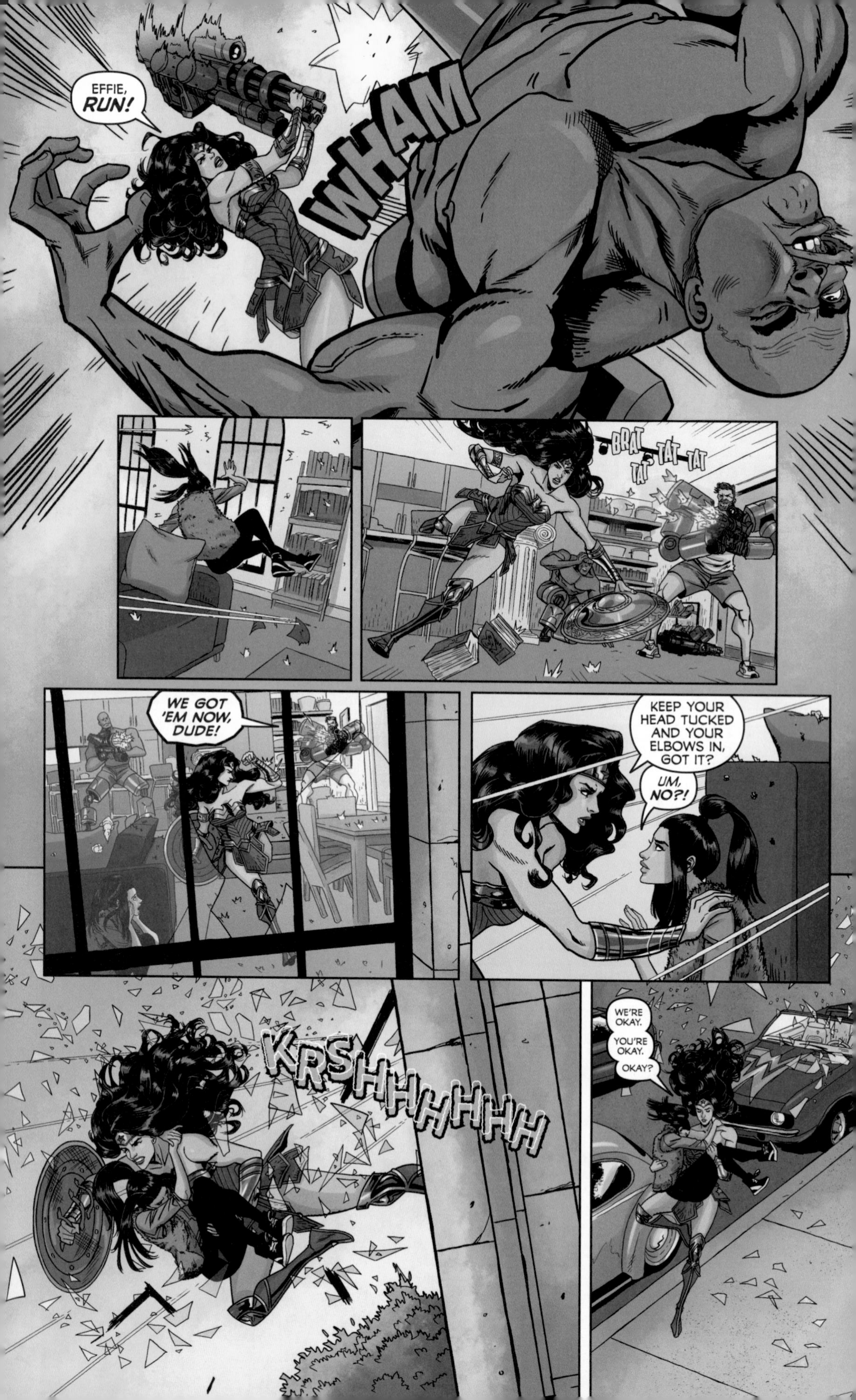
EFFIE, RUN!
WHAM
BRAT TAT TAT TAT
WE GOT 'EM NOW, DUDE!
KEEP YOUR HEAD TUCKED AND YOUR ELBOWS IN, GOT IT?
UM, NO?!
KRSHHHHHHH
WE'RE OKAY.
YOU'RE OKAY.
OKAY?

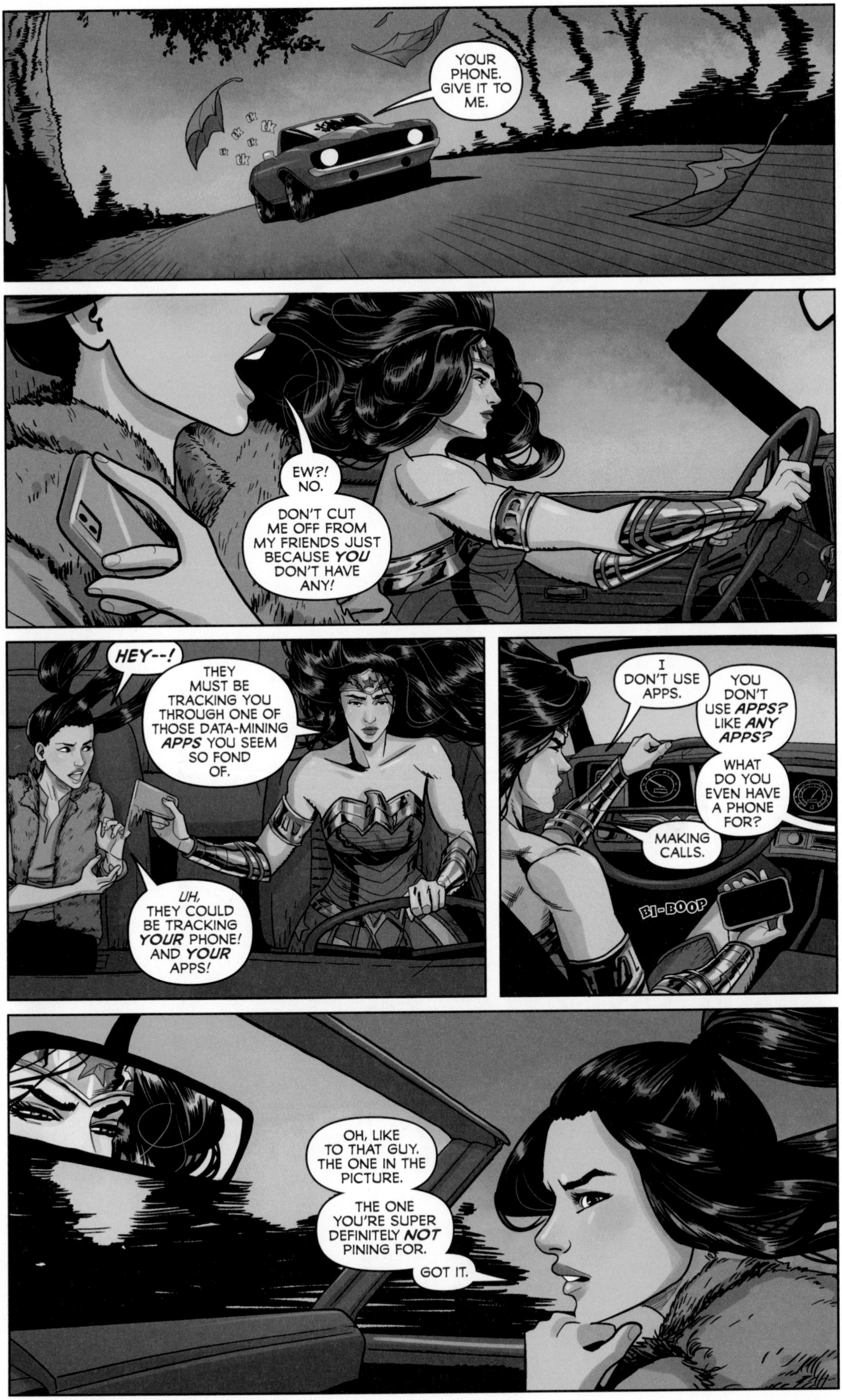

YOUR PHONE. GIVE IT TO ME.
EW?! NO.
DON'T CUT ME OFF FROM MY FRIENDS JUST BECAUSE *YOU* DON'T HAVE ANY!
HEY--!
THEY MUST BE TRACKING YOU THROUGH ONE OF THOSE DATA-MINING *APPS* YOU SEEM SO FOND OF.
UH, THEY COULD BE TRACKING *YOUR* PHONE! AND *YOUR* APPS!
I DON'T USE APPS.
YOU DON'T USE *APPS?* LIKE *ANY APPS?*
WHAT DO YOU EVEN HAVE A PHONE FOR?
MAKING CALLS.
BI-BOOP
OH, LIKE TO THAT GUY. THE ONE IN THE PICTURE.
THE ONE YOU'RE SUPER DEFINITELY *NOT* PINING FOR.
GOT IT.

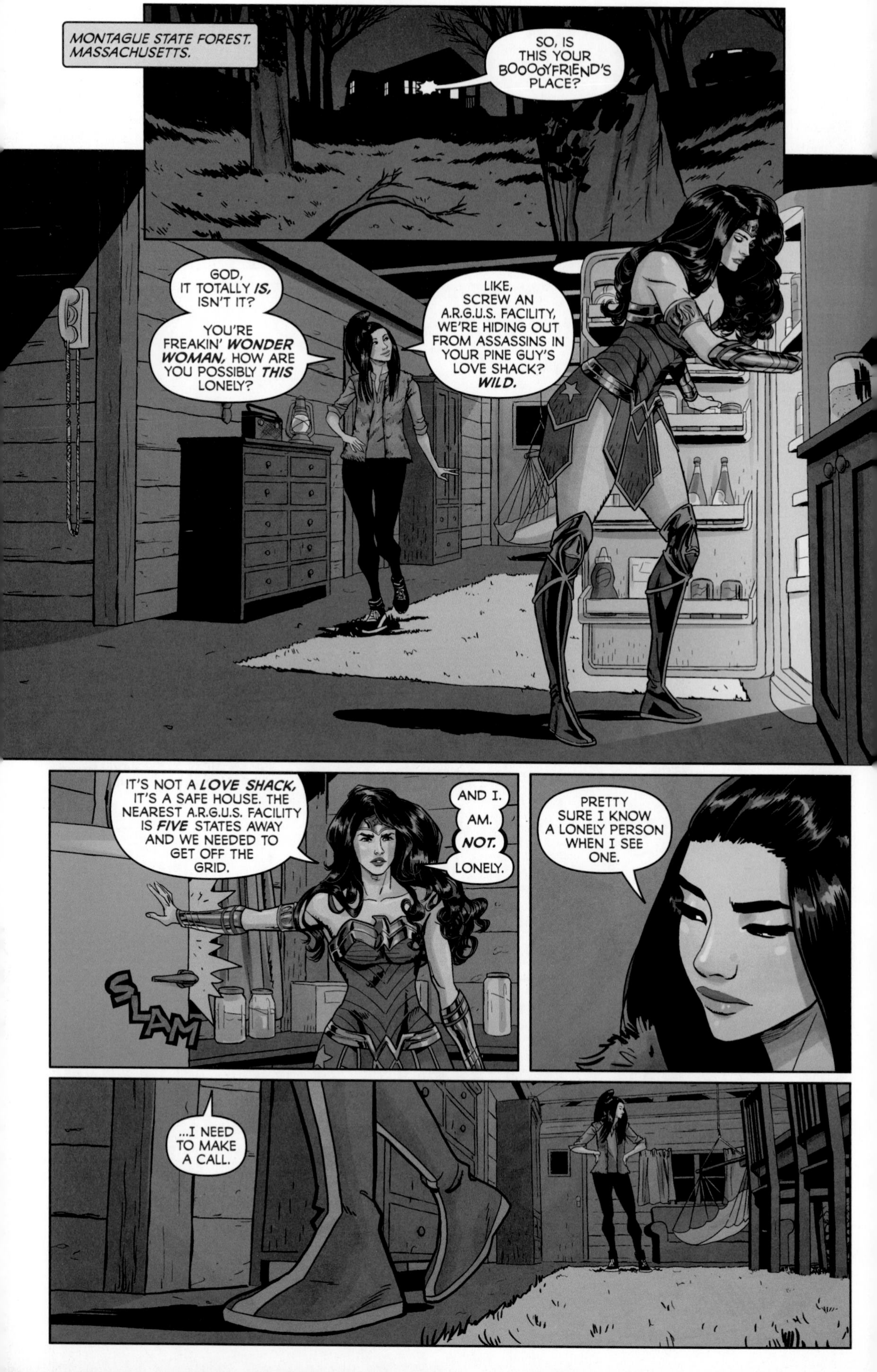
MONTAGUE STATE FOREST. MASSACHUSETTS.
SO, IS THIS YOUR BOOOOYFRIEND'S PLACE?
GOD, IT TOTALLY IS, ISN'T IT?
YOU'RE FREAKIN' WONDER WOMAN, HOW ARE YOU POSSIBLY THIS LONELY?
LIKE, SCREW AN A.R.G.U.S. FACILITY, WE'RE HIDING OUT FROM ASSASSINS IN YOUR PINE GUY'S LOVE SHACK? WILD.
IT'S NOT A LOVE SHACK, IT'S A SAFE HOUSE. THE NEAREST A.R.G.U.S. FACILITY IS FIVE STATES AWAY AND WE NEEDED TO GET OFF THE GRID.
AND I.
AM.
NOT.
LONELY.
SLAM
PRETTY SURE I KNOW A LONELY PERSON WHEN I SEE ONE.
...I NEED TO MAKE A CALL.

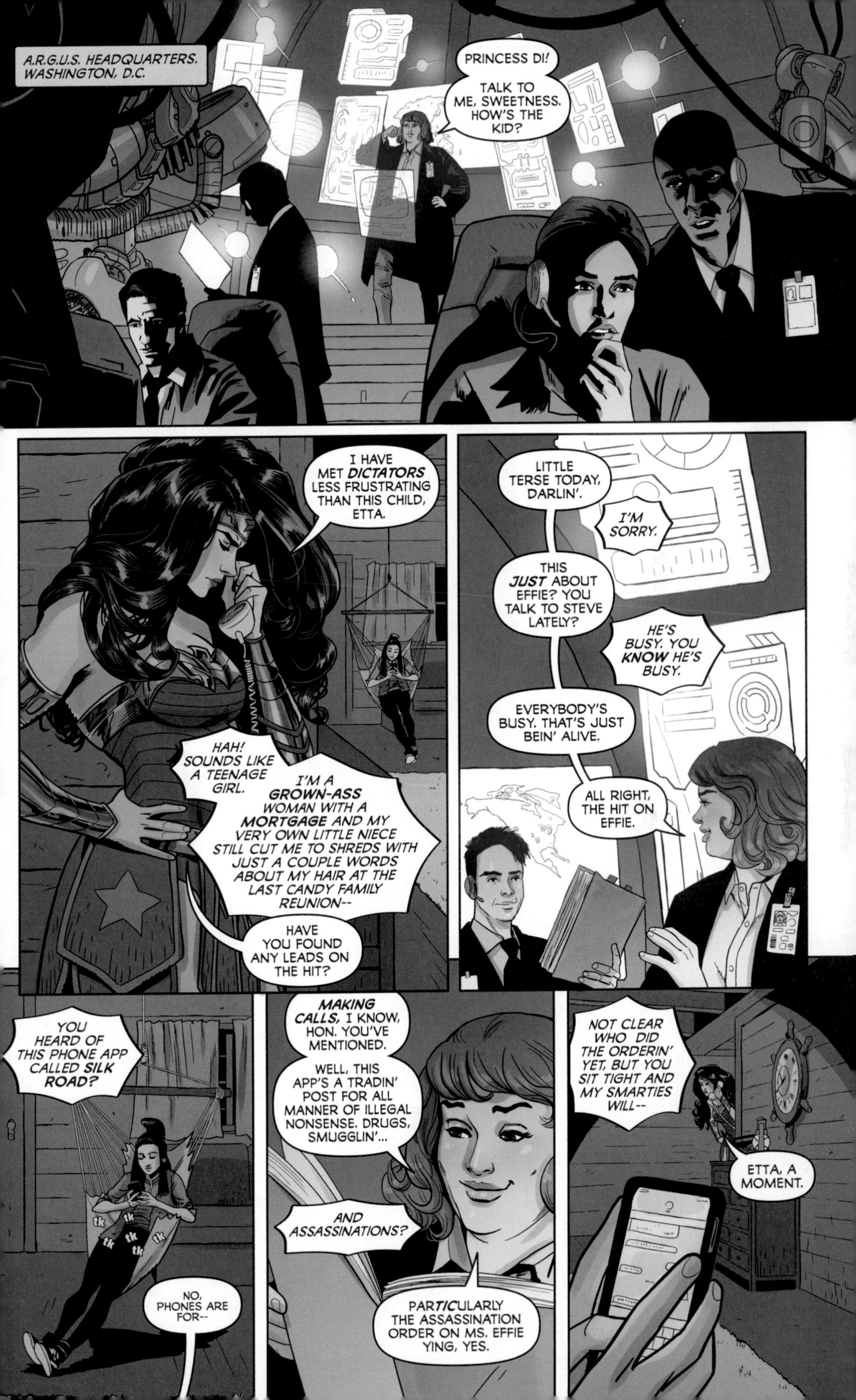
A.R.G.U.S. HEADQUARTERS. WASHINGTON, D.C.
PRINCESS DI!
TALK TO ME, SWEETNESS. HOW'S THE KID?
I HAVE MET DICTATORS LESS FRUSTRATING THAN THIS CHILD, ETTA.
HAH! SOUNDS LIKE A TEENAGE GIRL.
I'M A GROWN-ASS WOMAN WITH A MORTGAGE AND MY VERY OWN LITTLE NIECE STILL CUT ME TO SHREDS WITH JUST A COUPLE WORDS ABOUT MY HAIR AT THE LAST CANDY FAMILY REUNION--
HAVE YOU FOUND ANY LEADS ON THE HIT?
LITTLE TERSE TODAY, DARLIN'.
I'M SORRY.
THIS JUST ABOUT EFFIE? YOU TALK TO STEVE LATELY?
HE'S BUSY. YOU KNOW HE'S BUSY.
EVERYBODY'S BUSY. THAT'S JUST BEIN' ALIVE.
ALL RIGHT, THE HIT ON EFFIE.
YOU HEARD OF THIS PHONE APP CALLED SILK ROAD?
tk tk tk tk tk tk
NO, PHONES ARE FOR--
MAKING CALLS, I KNOW, HON. YOU'VE MENTIONED.
WELL, THIS APP'S A TRADIN' POST FOR ALL MANNER OF ILLEGAL NONSENSE. DRUGS, SMUGGLIN'...
AND ASSASSINATIONS?
PARTICULARLY THE ASSASSINATION ORDER ON MS. EFFIE YING, YES.
NOT CLEAR WHO DID THE ORDERIN' YET, BUT YOU SIT TIGHT AND MY SMARTIES WILL--
ETTA, A MOMENT.

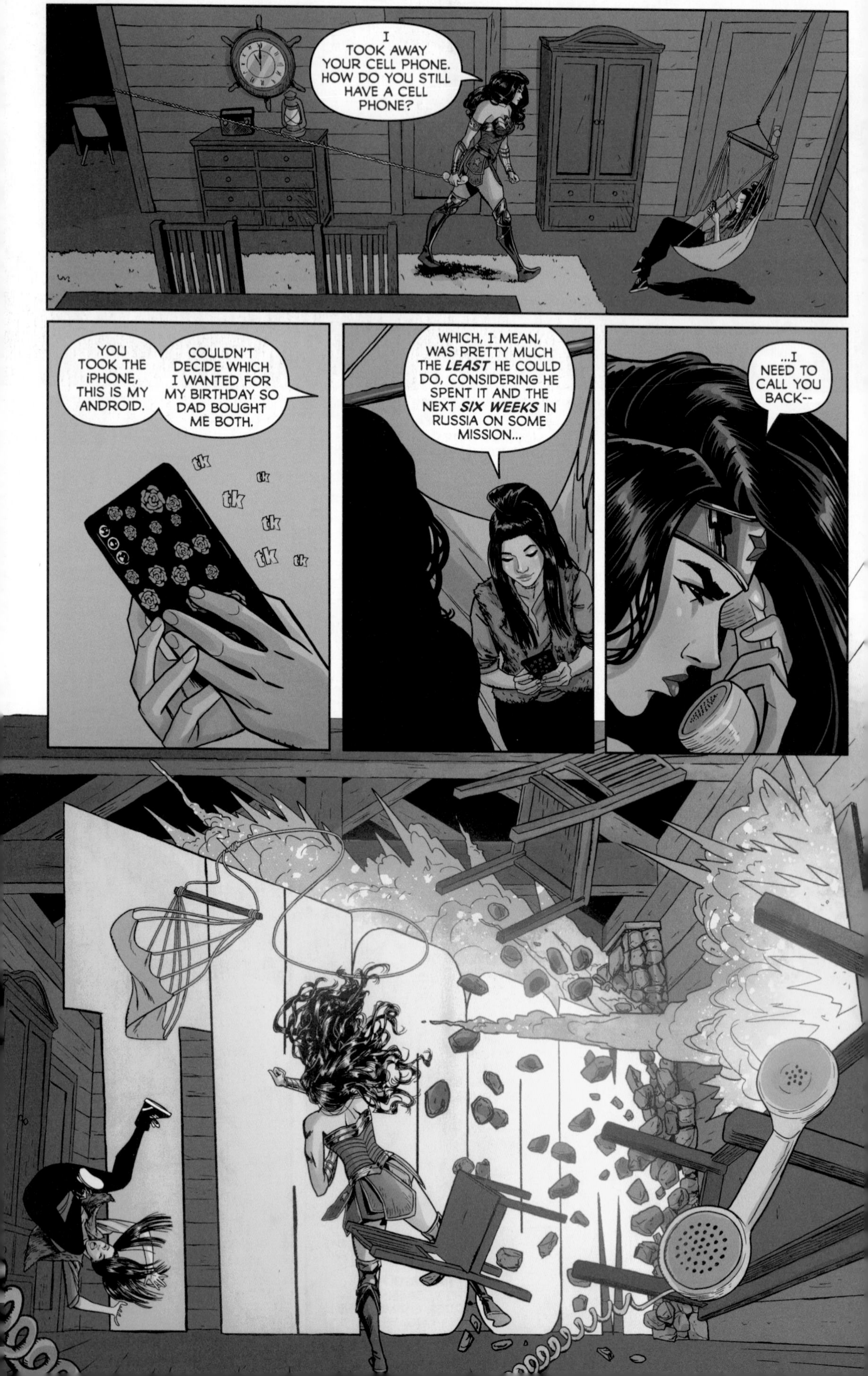
I TOOK AWAY YOUR CELL PHONE. HOW DO YOU STILL HAVE A CELL PHONE?
YOU TOOK THE iPHONE, THIS IS MY ANDROID.
COULDN'T DECIDE WHICH I WANTED FOR MY BIRTHDAY SO DAD BOUGHT ME BOTH.
tk tk tk tk tk tk
WHICH, I MEAN, WAS PRETTY MUCH THE LEAST HE COULD DO, CONSIDERING HE SPENT IT AND THE NEXT SIX WEEKS IN RUSSIA ON SOME MISSION...
...I NEED TO CALL YOU BACK--

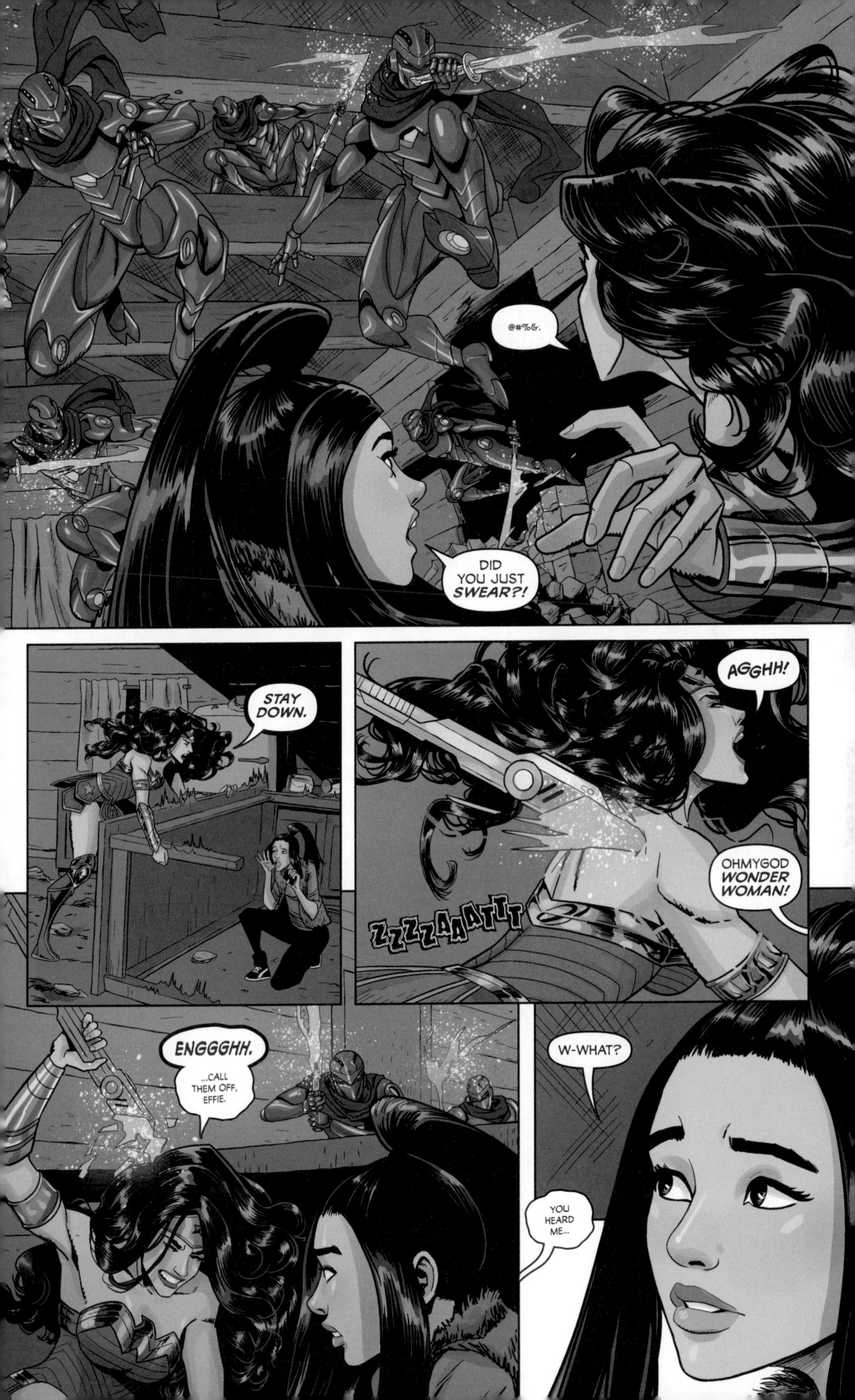
@#%&.
DID YOU JUST SWEAR?!
STAY DOWN.
AGGHH!
ZZZZAAATTT
OHMYGOD WONDER WOMAN!
ENGGGHH.
...CALL THEM OFF, EFFIE.
W-WHAT?
YOU HEARD ME...

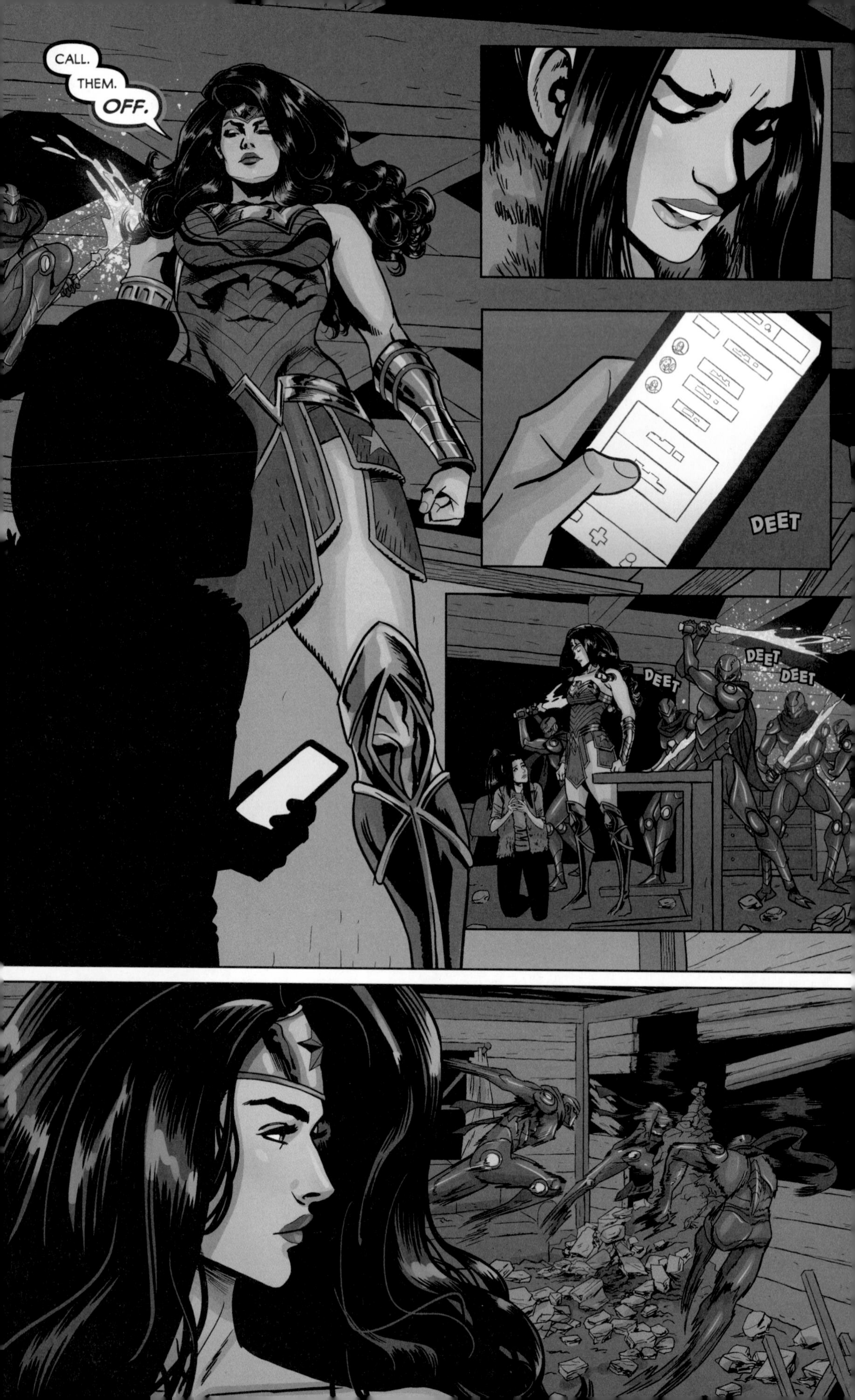
CALL. THEM. OFF.
DEET
DEET
DEET
DEET

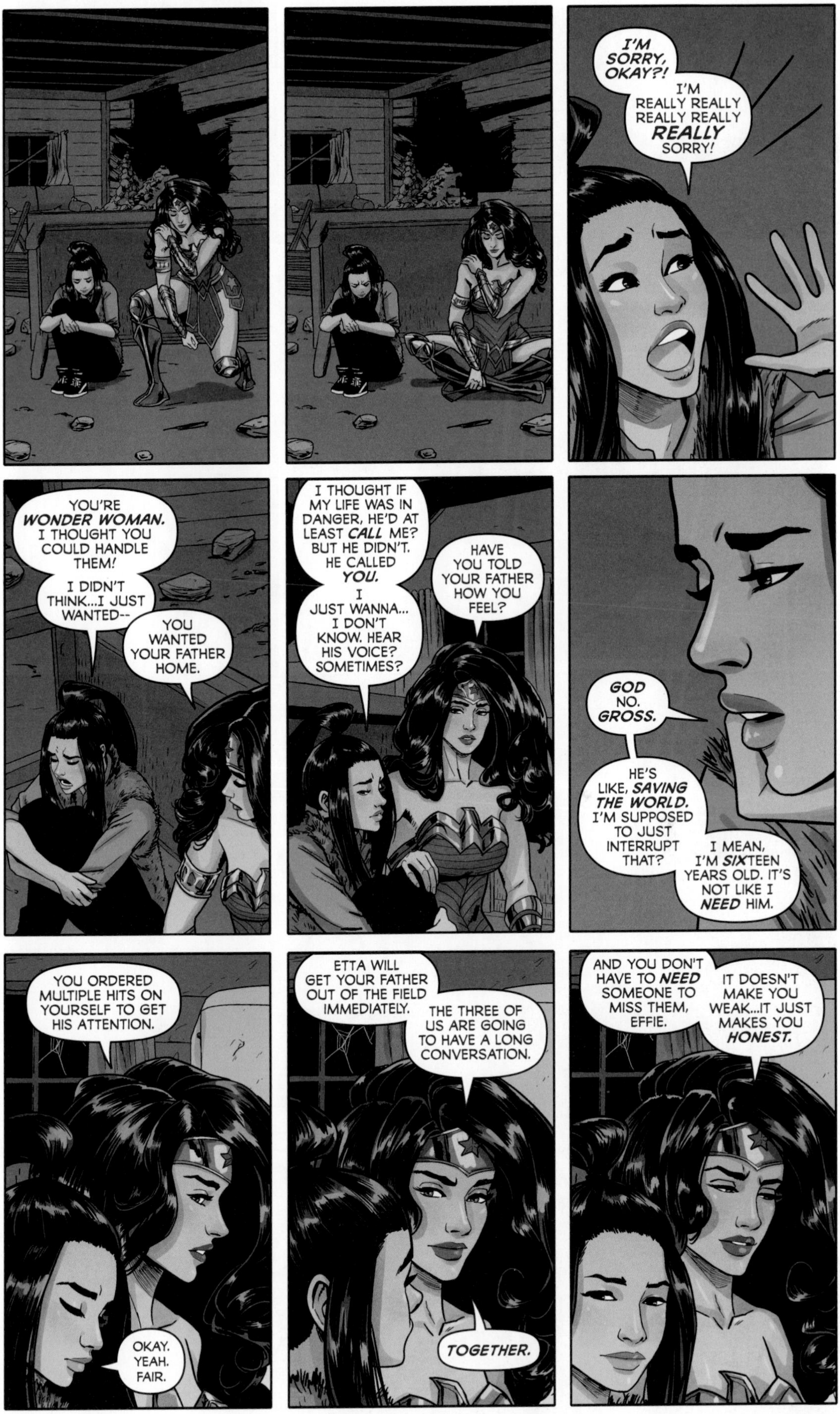
I'M SORRY, OKAY?!
I'M REALLY REALLY REALLY REALLY REALLY SORRY!
YOU'RE WONDER WOMAN. I THOUGHT YOU COULD HANDLE THEM!
I DIDN'T THINK...I JUST WANTED--
YOU WANTED YOUR FATHER HOME.
I THOUGHT IF MY LIFE WAS IN DANGER, HE'D AT LEAST CALL ME? BUT HE DIDN'T. HE CALLED YOU.
I JUST WANNA... I DON'T KNOW. HEAR HIS VOICE? SOMETIMES?
HAVE YOU TOLD YOUR FATHER HOW YOU FEEL?
GOD NO. GROSS.
HE'S LIKE, SAVING THE WORLD. I'M SUPPOSED TO JUST INTERRUPT THAT?
I MEAN, I'M SIXTEEN YEARS OLD. IT'S NOT LIKE I NEED HIM.
YOU ORDERED MULTIPLE HITS ON YOURSELF TO GET HIS ATTENTION.
OKAY. YEAH. FAIR.
ETTA WILL GET YOUR FATHER OUT OF THE FIELD IMMEDIATELY.
THE THREE OF US ARE GOING TO HAVE A LONG CONVERSATION.
TOGETHER.
AND YOU DON'T HAVE TO NEED SOMEONE TO MISS THEM, EFFIE.
IT DOESN'T MAKE YOU WEAK...IT JUST MAKES YOU HONEST.

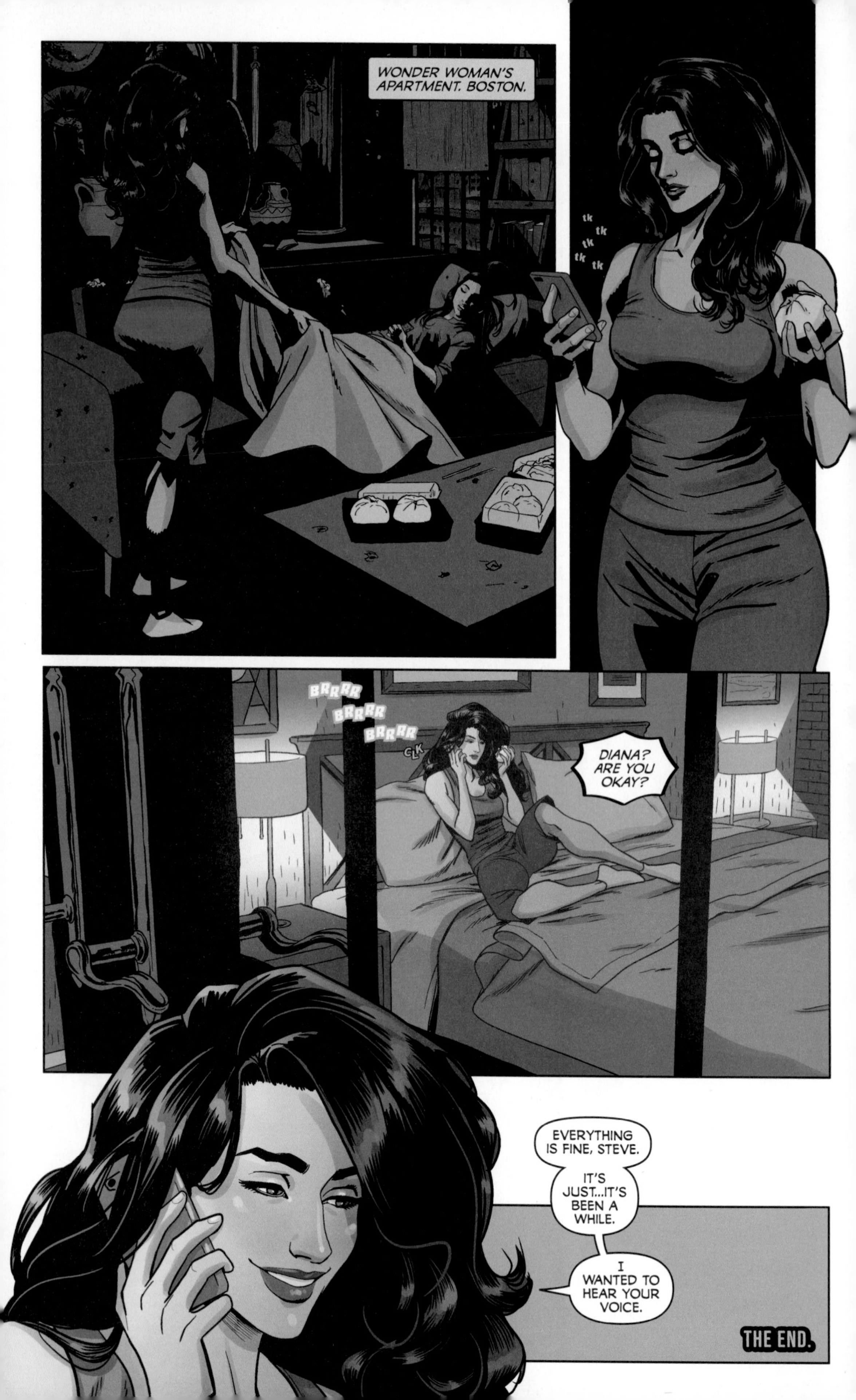
WONDER WOMAN'S APARTMENT. BOSTON.
tk tk tk tk tk
BRRRR BRRRR BRRRR
CLK
DIANA? ARE YOU OKAY?
EVERYTHING IS FINE, STEVE.
IT'S JUST...IT'S BEEN A WHILE.
I WANTED TO HEAR YOUR VOICE.
THE END.

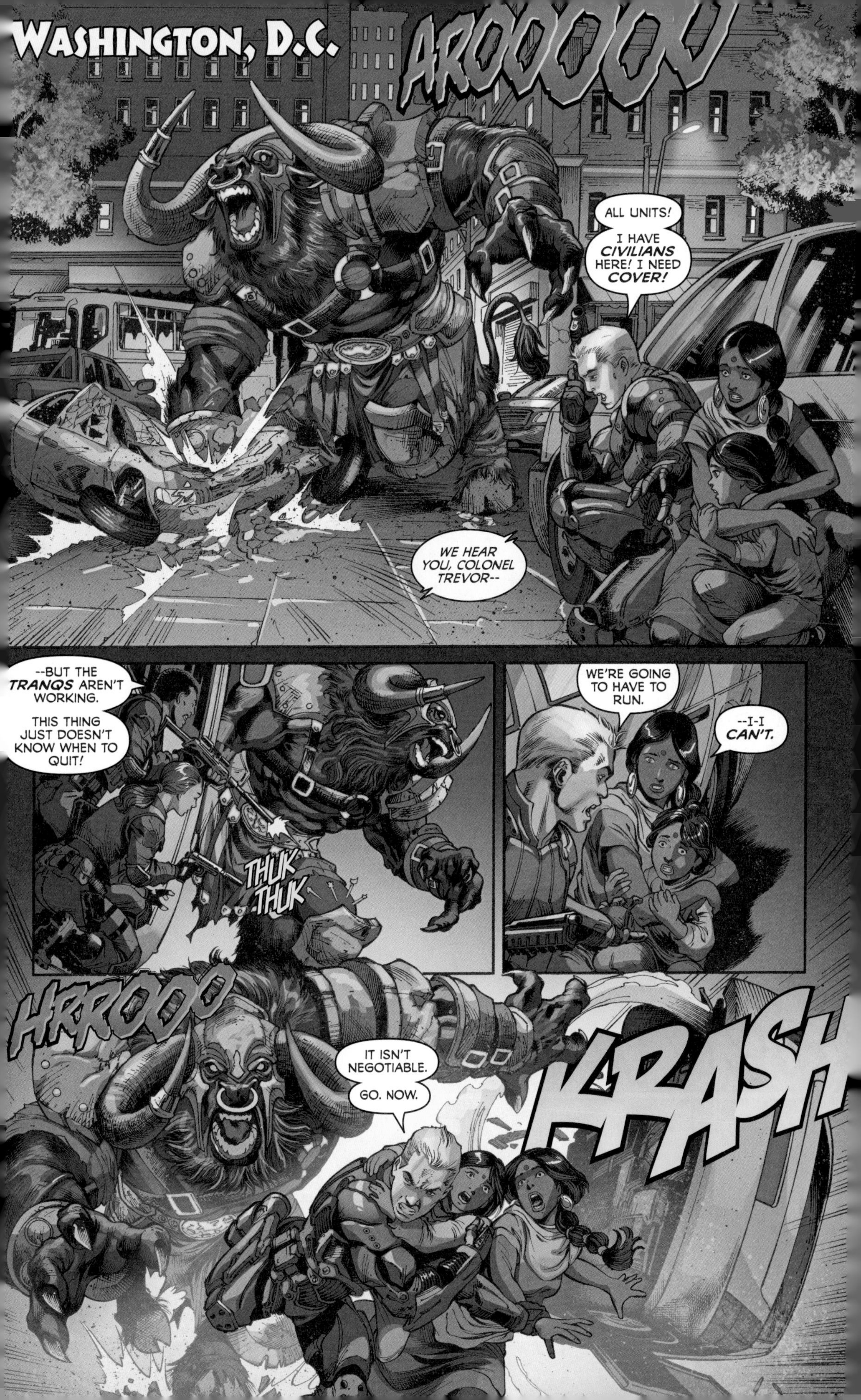
WASHINGTON, D.C.
AROOOOOU
ALL UNITS!
I HAVE CIVILIANS HERE! I NEED COVER!
WE HEAR YOU, COLONEL TREVOR--
--BUT THE TRANQS AREN'T WORKING.
THIS THING JUST DOESN'T KNOW WHEN TO QUIT!
THUK THUK
WE'RE GOING TO HAVE TO RUN.
--I-I CAN'T.
HRROOO
IT ISN'T NEGOTIABLE.
GO. NOW.
KRASH

FIGHT NIGHT

CAVAN SCOTT - SCRIPT JOSE LUIS - PENCILS JONAS TRINDADE - INKS
REX LOKUS - COLOR CARLOS M. MANGUAL - LETTERS MICHAEL McCALISTER - EDITOR

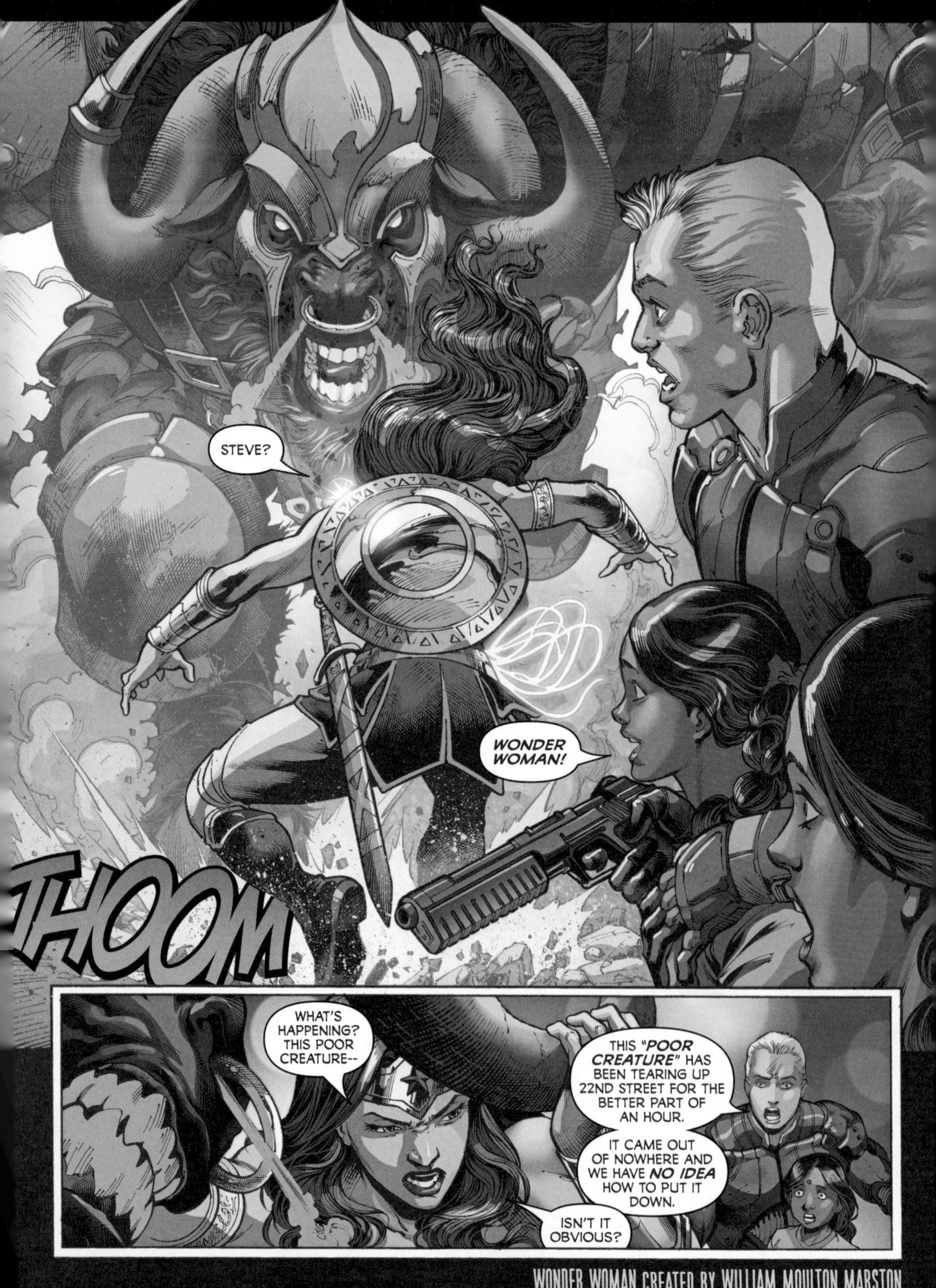
STEVE?
WONDER WOMAN!
THOOM
WHAT'S HAPPENING? THIS POOR CREATURE--
THIS "POOR CREATURE" HAS BEEN TEARING UP 22ND STREET FOR THE BETTER PART OF AN HOUR.
IT CAME OUT OF NOWHERE AND WE HAVE NO IDEA HOW TO PUT IT DOWN.
ISN'T IT OBVIOUS?

WONDER WOMAN CREATED BY WILLIAM MOULTON MARSTON

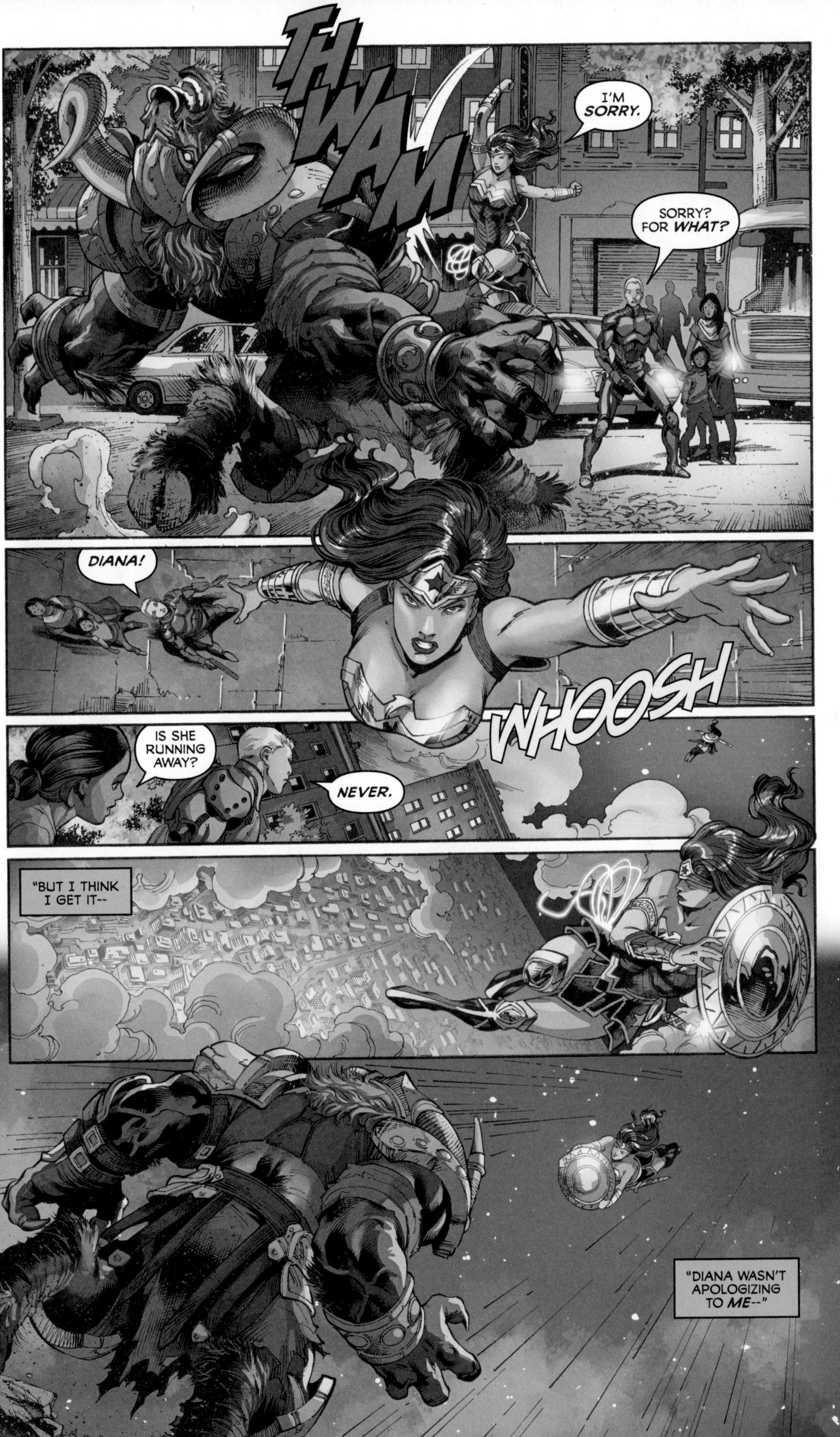
THWAM
I'M SORRY.
SORRY? FOR WHAT?
DIANA!
WHOOSH
IS SHE RUNNING AWAY?
NEVER.
"BUT I THINK I GET IT--
"DIANA WASN'T APOLOGIZING TO ME--"

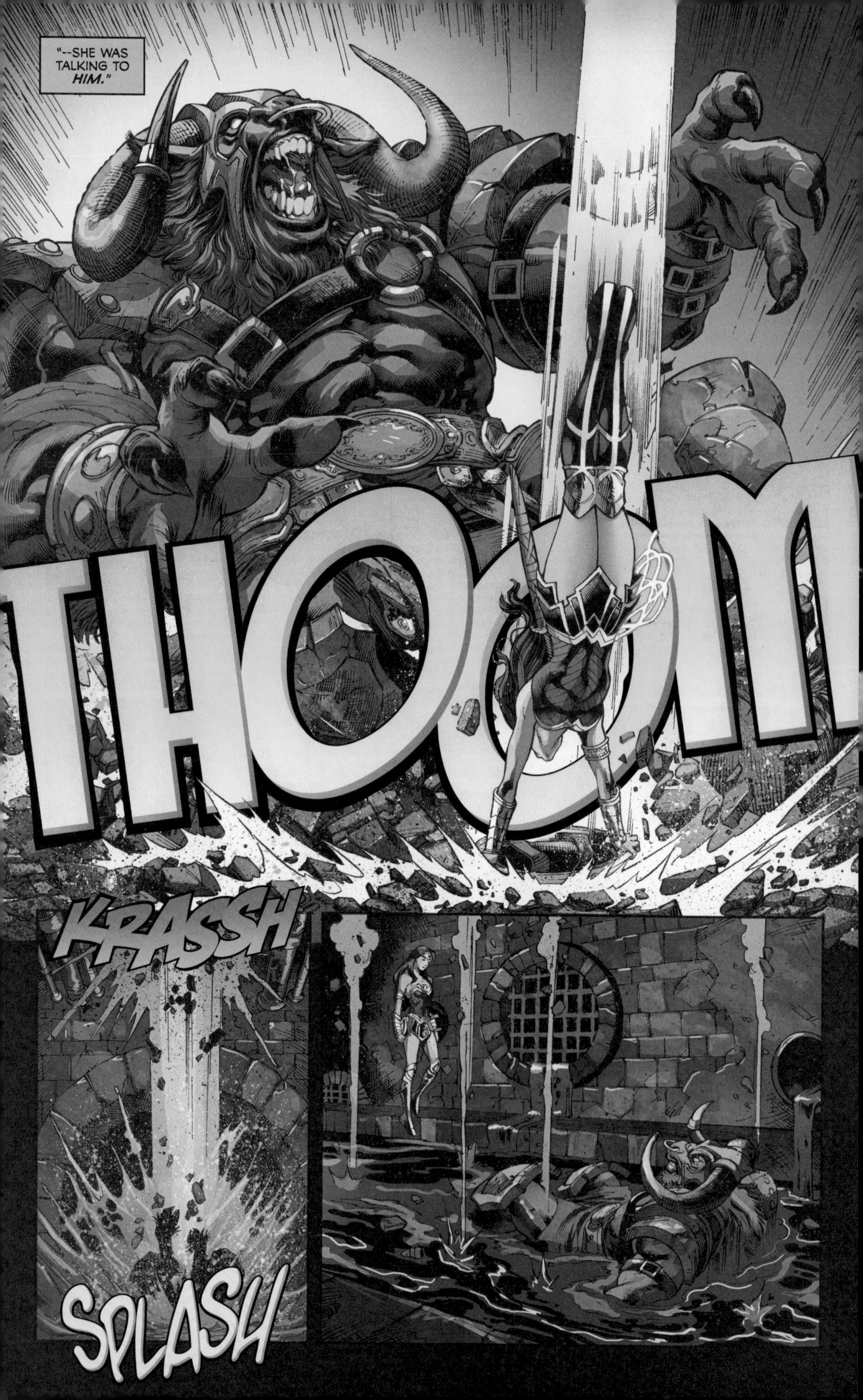
"--SHE WAS TALKING TO *HIM.*"
THOOM
KRASSH
SPLASH

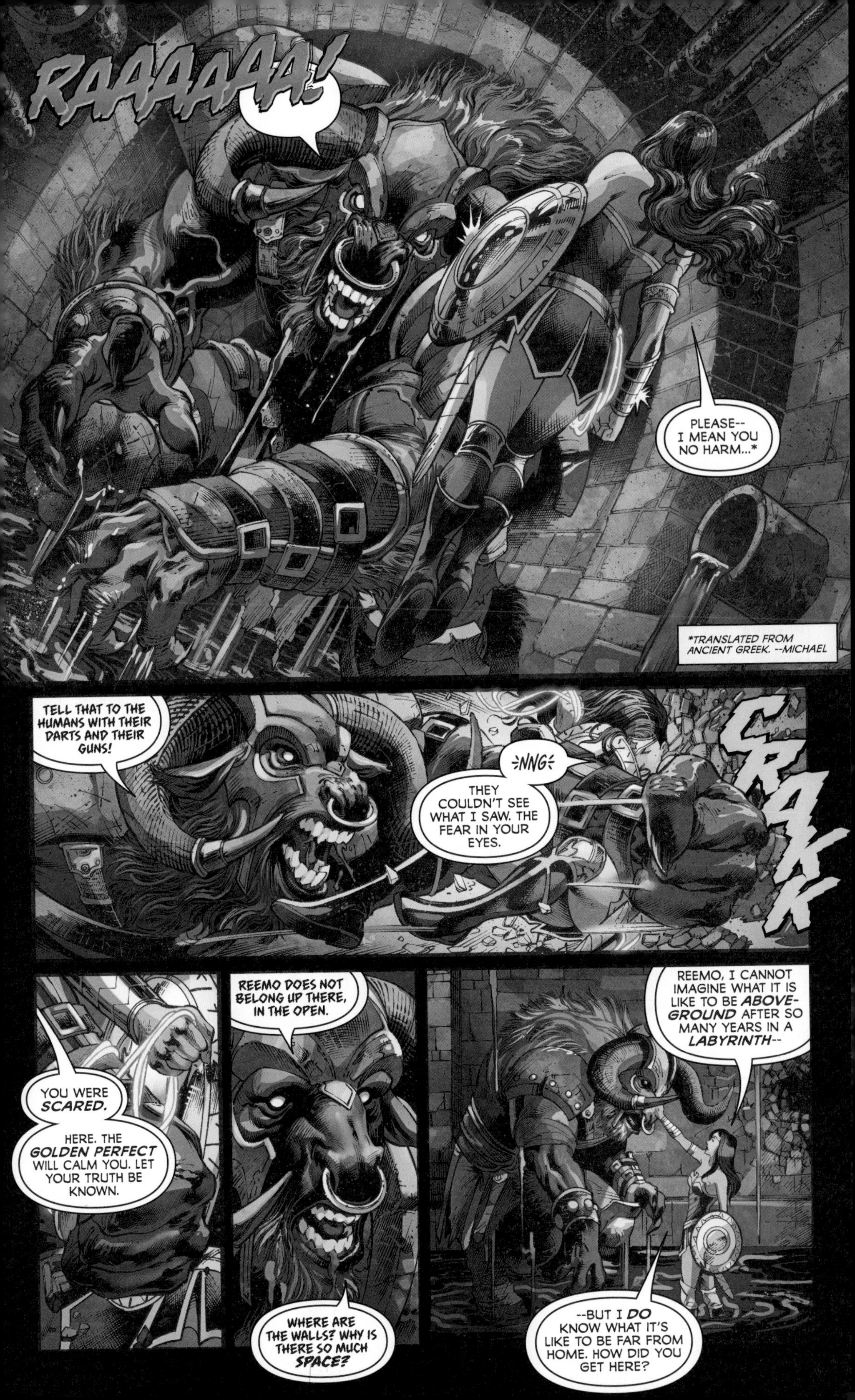
RAAAAAA!
PLEASE-- I MEAN YOU NO HARM...*
*TRANSLATED FROM ANCIENT GREEK. --MICHAEL
TELL THAT TO THE HUMANS WITH THEIR DARTS AND THEIR GUNS!
CRAKK
NNG
THEY COULDN'T SEE WHAT I SAW. THE FEAR IN YOUR EYES.
YOU WERE SCARED.
HERE. THE GOLDEN PERFECT WILL CALM YOU. LET YOUR TRUTH BE KNOWN.
REEMO DOES NOT BELONG UP THERE, IN THE OPEN.
WHERE ARE THE WALLS? WHY IS THERE SO MUCH SPACE?
REEMO, I CANNOT IMAGINE WHAT IT IS LIKE TO BE ABOVE-GROUND AFTER SO MANY YEARS IN A LABYRINTH--
--BUT I DO KNOW WHAT IT'S LIKE TO BE FAR FROM HOME. HOW DID YOU GET HERE?

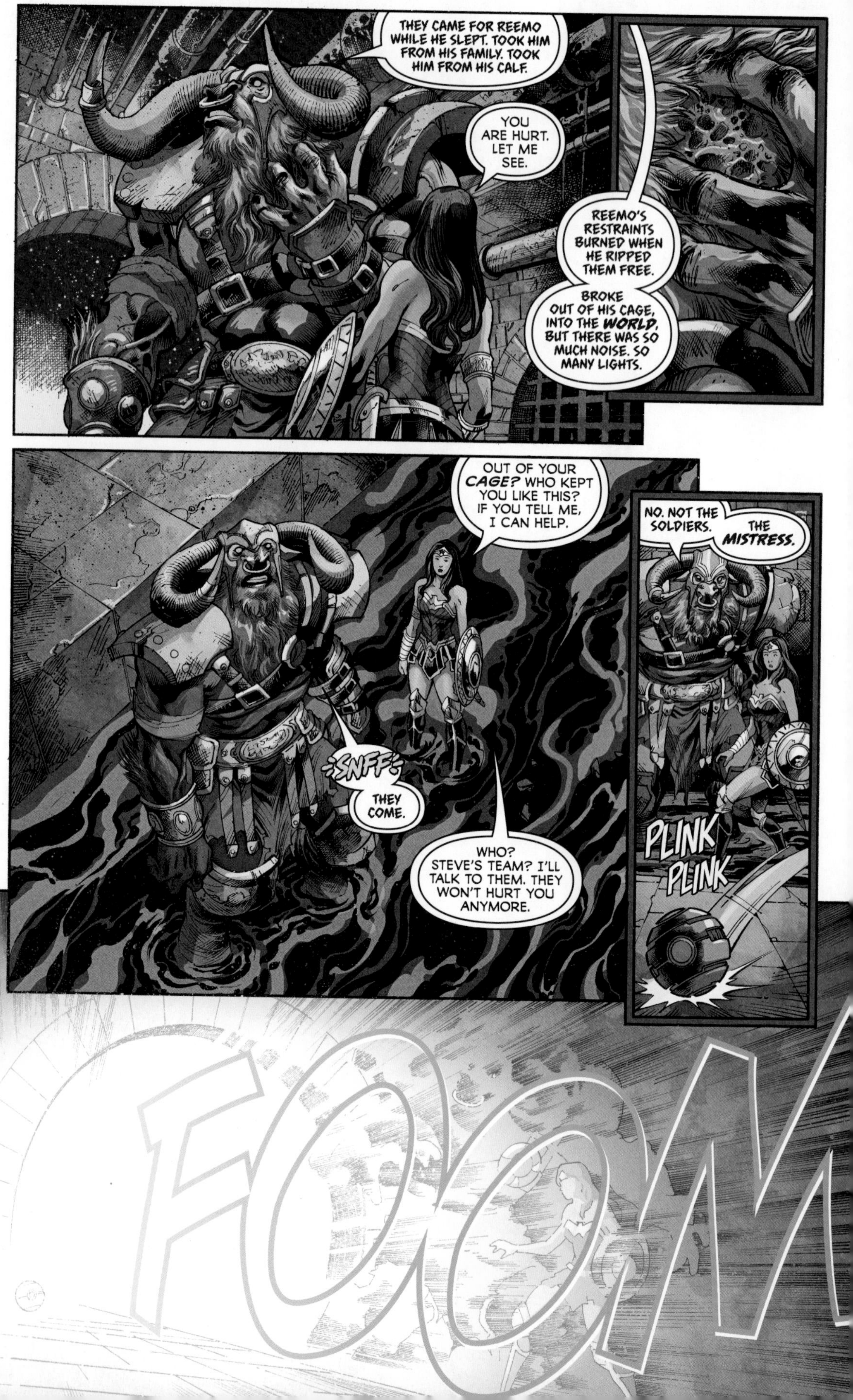
THEY CAME FOR REEMO WHILE HE SLEPT. TOOK HIM FROM HIS FAMILY. TOOK HIM FROM HIS CALF.
YOU ARE HURT. LET ME SEE.
REEMO'S RESTRAINTS BURNED WHEN HE RIPPED THEM FREE.
BROKE OUT OF HIS CAGE, INTO THE WORLD, BUT THERE WAS SO MUCH NOISE. SO MANY LIGHTS.
OUT OF YOUR CAGE? WHO KEPT YOU LIKE THIS? IF YOU TELL ME, I CAN HELP.
SNFF
THEY COME.
WHO? STEVE'S TEAM? I'LL TALK TO THEM. THEY WON'T HURT YOU ANYMORE.
NO. NOT THE SOLDIERS.
THE MISTRESS.
PLINK
PLINK
FOOM

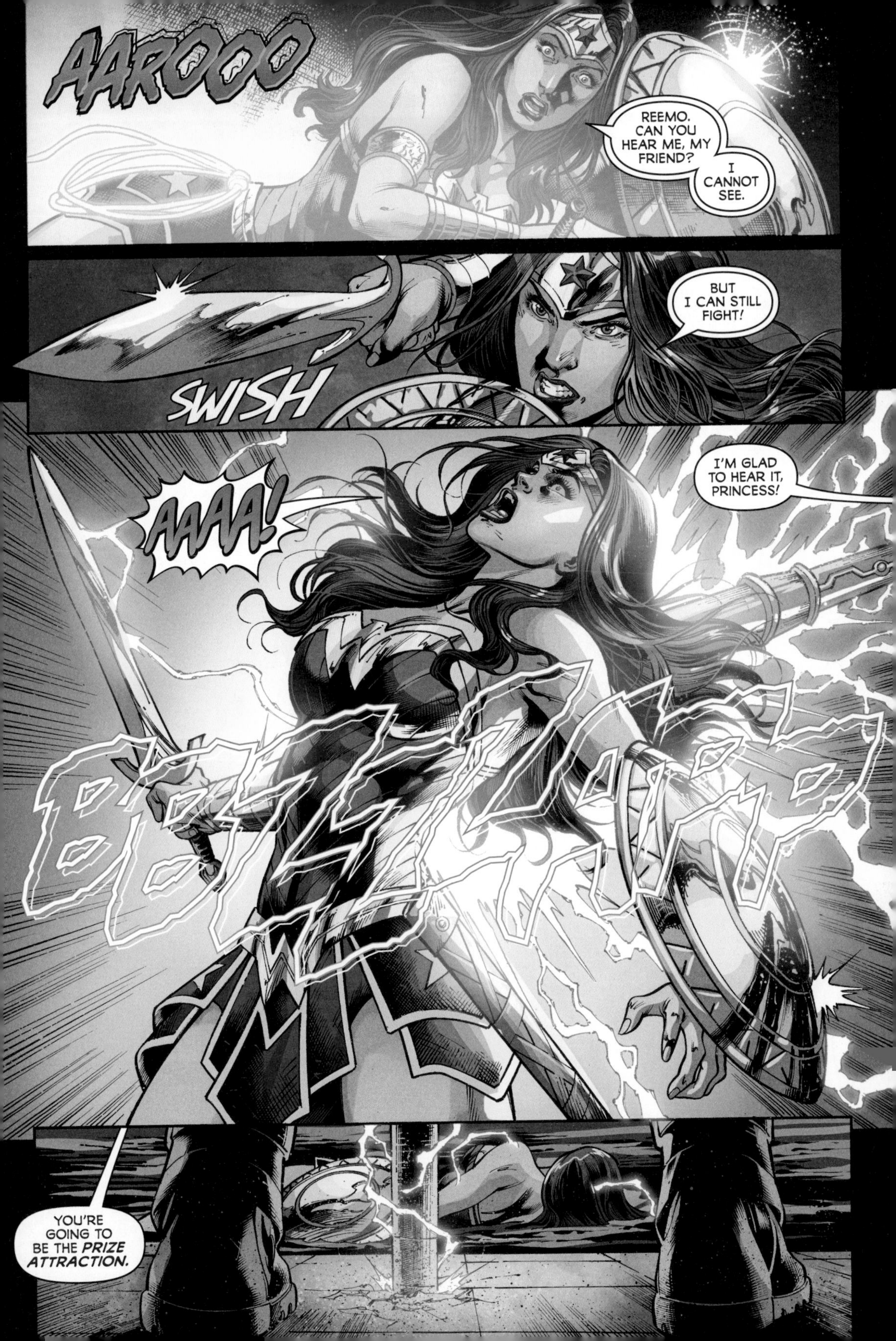
AAROOO
REEMO. CAN YOU HEAR ME, MY FRIEND?
I CANNOT SEE.
BUT I CAN STILL FIGHT!
SWISH
AAAA!
I'M GLAD TO HEAR IT, PRINCESS!
YOU'RE GOING TO BE THE *PRIZE ATTRACTION.*

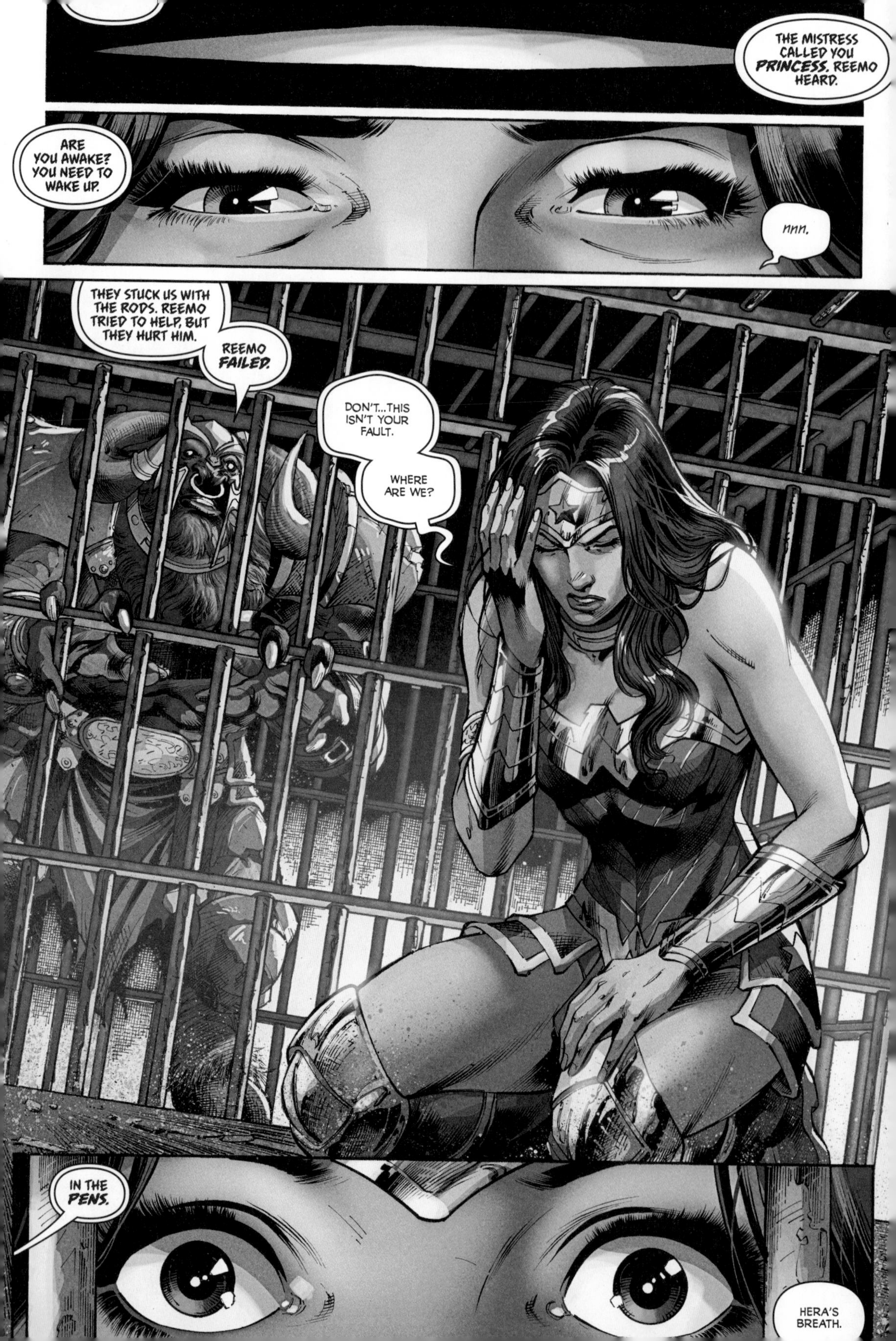
THE MISTRESS CALLED YOU PRINCESS. REEMO HEARD.
ARE YOU AWAKE? YOU NEED TO WAKE UP.
nnn.
THEY STUCK US WITH THE RODS. REEMO TRIED TO HELP, BUT THEY HURT HIM.
REEMO FAILED.
DON'T...THIS ISN'T YOUR FAULT.
WHERE ARE WE?
IN THE PENS.
HERA'S BREATH.

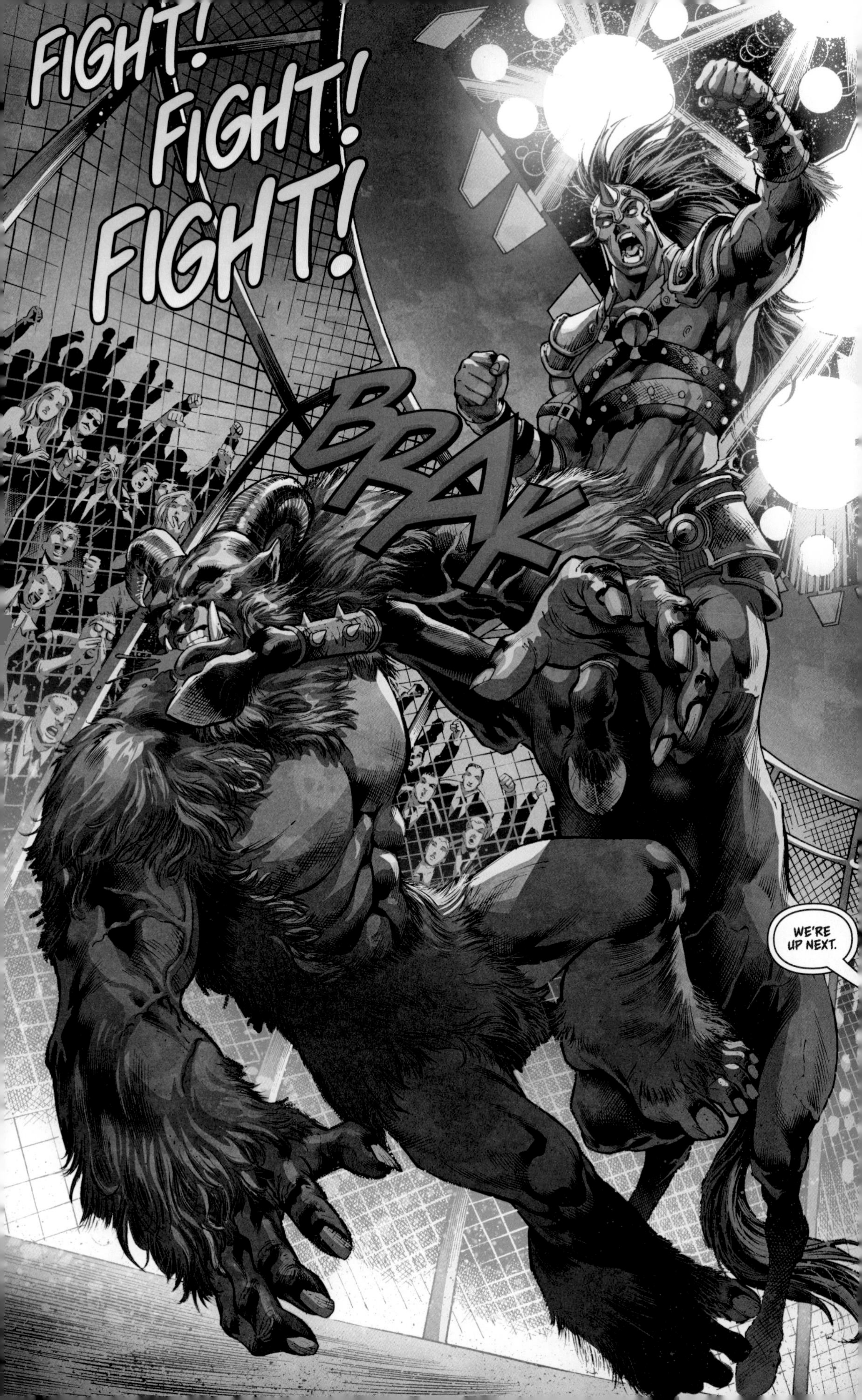
FIGHT! FIGHT! FIGHT!
BRAK
WE'RE UP NEXT.

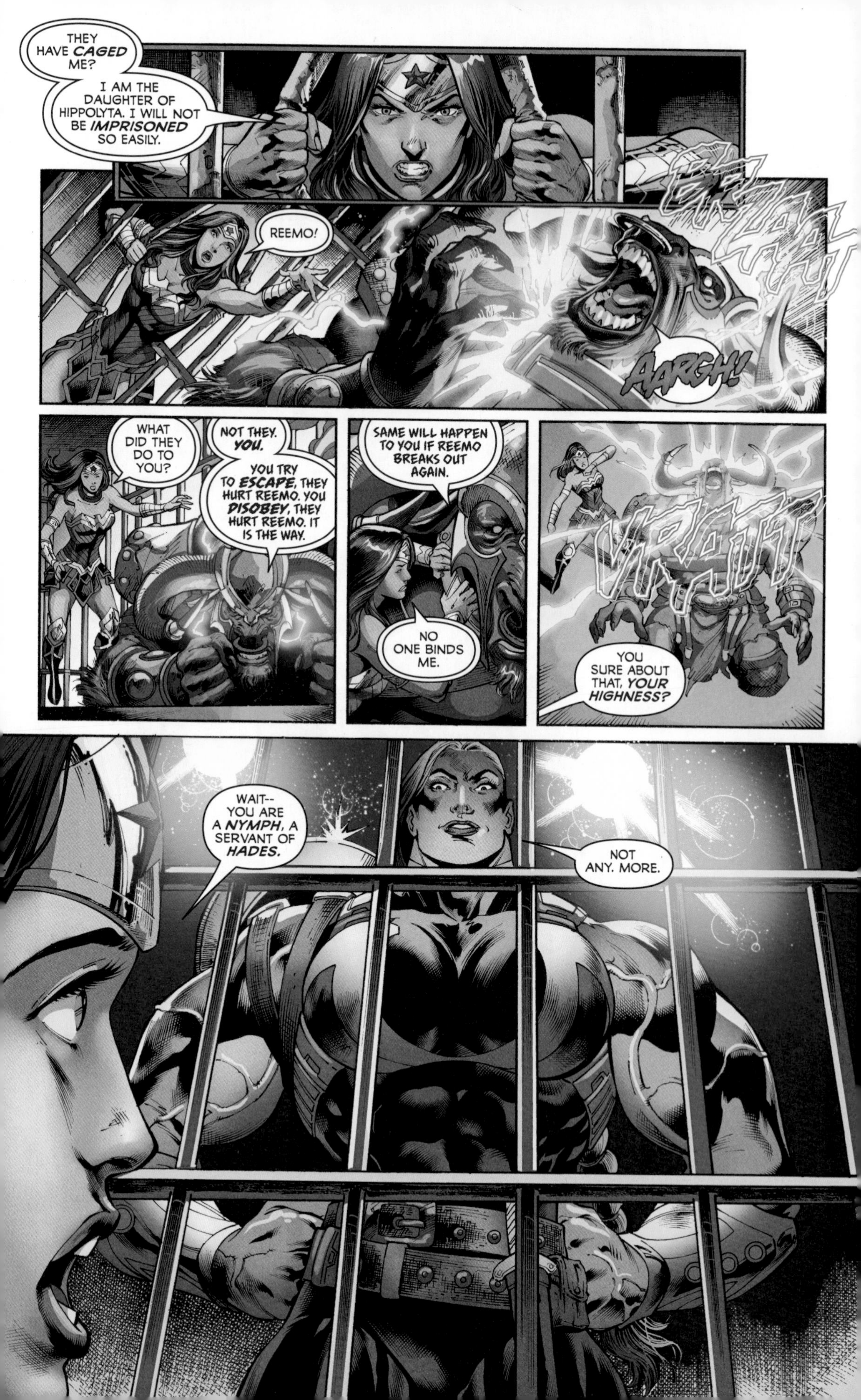
THEY HAVE CAGED ME?
I AM THE DAUGHTER OF HIPPOLYTA. I WILL NOT BE IMPRISONED SO EASILY.
ZZZAAAT
REEMO!
AARGH!
WHAT DID THEY DO TO YOU?
NOT THEY. YOU.
YOU TRY TO ESCAPE, THEY HURT REEMO. YOU DISOBEY, THEY HURT REEMO. IT IS THE WAY.
SAME WILL HAPPEN TO YOU IF REEMO BREAKS OUT AGAIN.
NO ONE BINDS ME.
VRASH
YOU SURE ABOUT THAT, YOUR HIGHNESS?
WAIT-- YOU ARE A NYMPH, A SERVANT OF HADES.
NOT ANY. MORE.

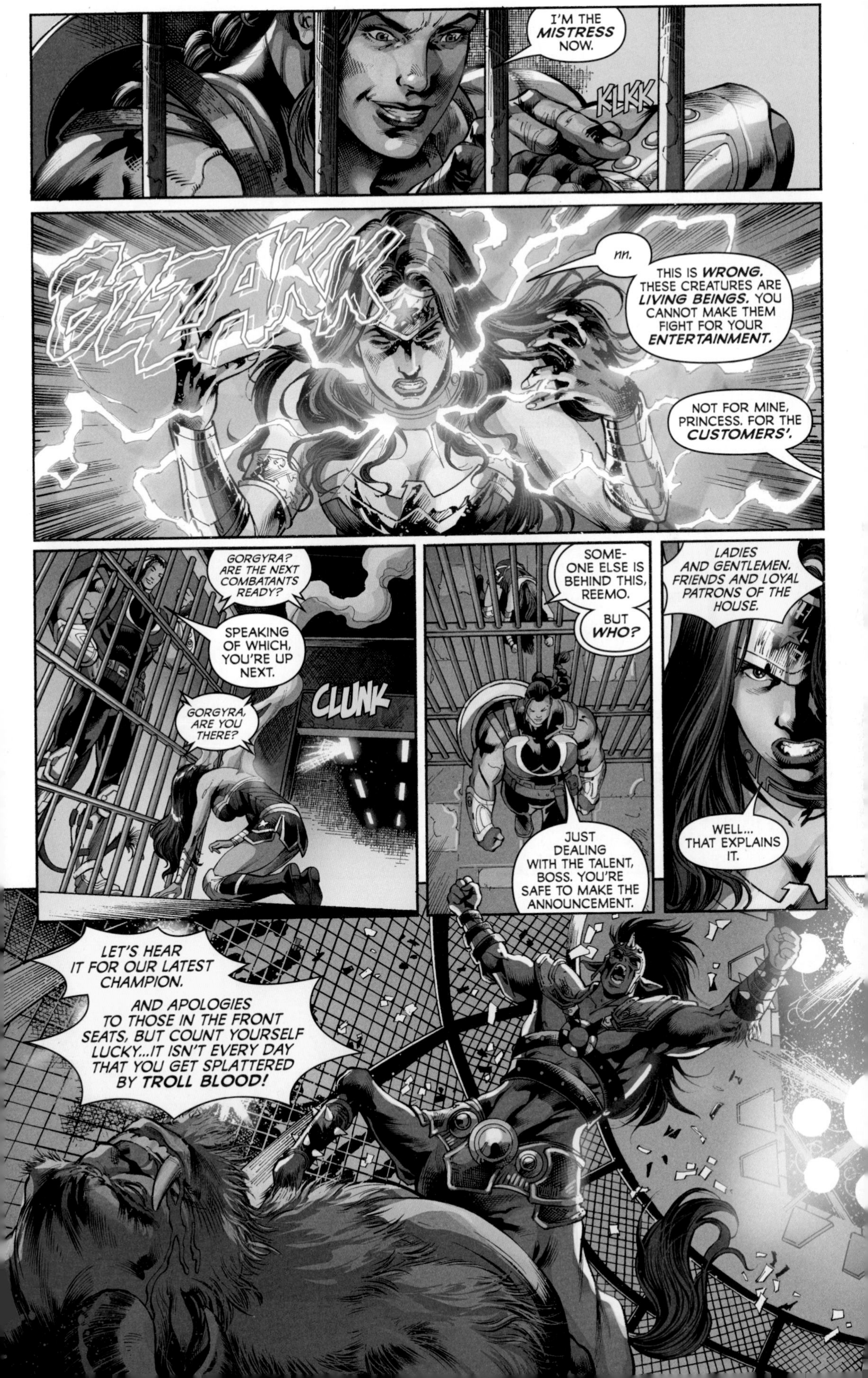
I'M THE MISTRESS NOW.
KLIKK
BZZAKK
nn.
THIS IS WRONG. THESE CREATURES ARE LIVING BEINGS. YOU CANNOT MAKE THEM FIGHT FOR YOUR ENTERTAINMENT.
NOT FOR MINE, PRINCESS. FOR THE CUSTOMERS'.
GORGYRA? ARE THE NEXT COMBATANTS READY?
SPEAKING OF WHICH, YOU'RE UP NEXT.
CLUNK
GORGYRA, ARE YOU THERE?
SOME-ONE ELSE IS BEHIND THIS, REEMO.
BUT WHO?
JUST DEALING WITH THE TALENT, BOSS. YOU'RE SAFE TO MAKE THE ANNOUNCEMENT.
LADIES AND GENTLEMEN. FRIENDS AND LOYAL PATRONS OF THE HOUSE.
WELL... THAT EXPLAINS IT.
LET'S HEAR IT FOR OUR LATEST CHAMPION.
AND APOLOGIES TO THOSE IN THE FRONT SEATS, BUT COUNT YOURSELF LUCKY...IT ISN'T EVERY DAY THAT YOU GET SPLATTERED BY TROLL BLOOD!

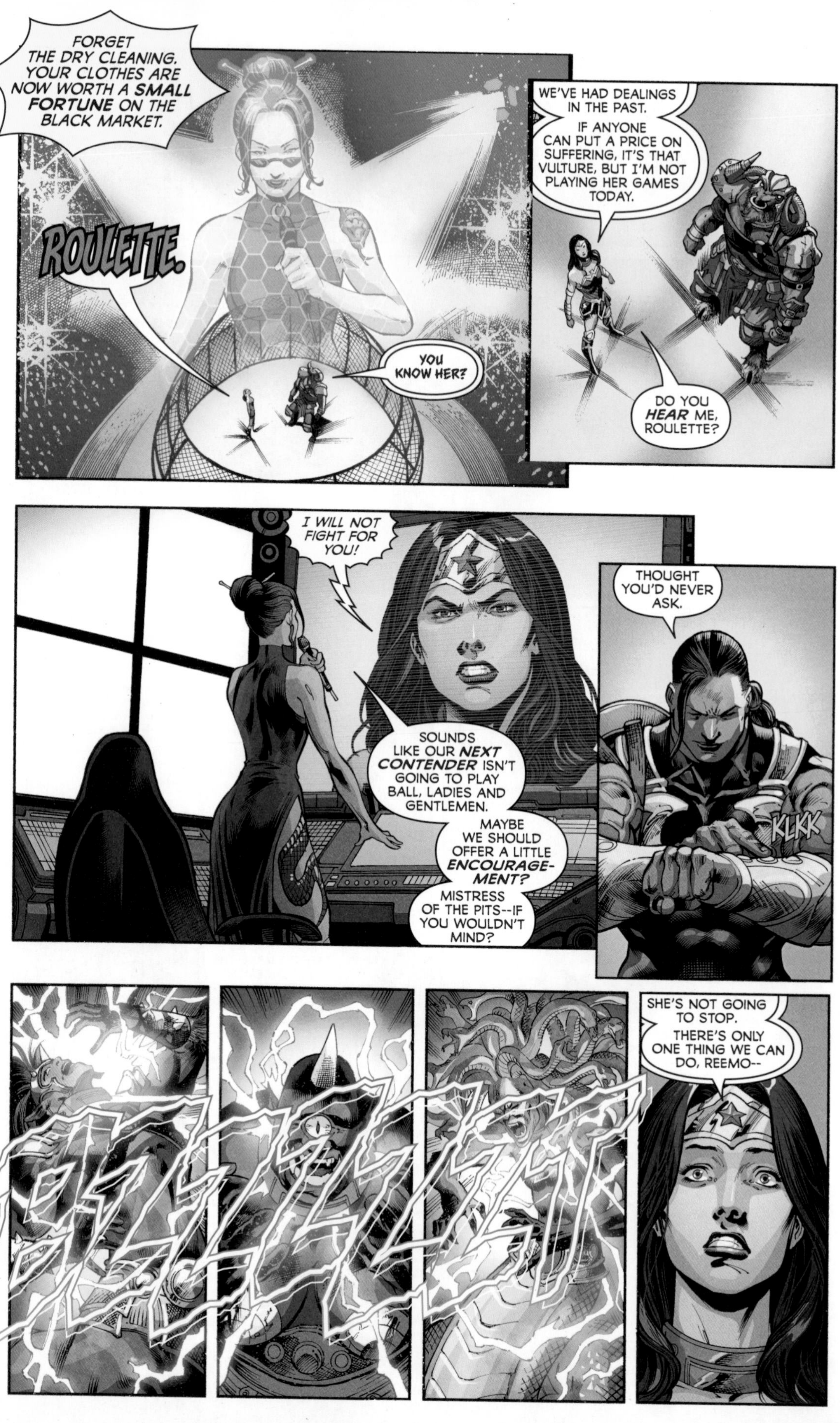
FORGET THE DRY CLEANING. YOUR CLOTHES ARE NOW WORTH A SMALL FORTUNE ON THE BLACK MARKET.
ROULETTE.
YOU KNOW HER?
WE'VE HAD DEALINGS IN THE PAST.
IF ANYONE CAN PUT A PRICE ON SUFFERING, IT'S THAT VULTURE, BUT I'M NOT PLAYING HER GAMES TODAY.
DO YOU HEAR ME, ROULETTE?
I WILL NOT FIGHT FOR YOU!
SOUNDS LIKE OUR NEXT CONTENDER ISN'T GOING TO PLAY BALL, LADIES AND GENTLEMEN.
MAYBE WE SHOULD OFFER A LITTLE ENCOURAGE-MENT?
MISTRESS OF THE PITS--IF YOU WOULDN'T MIND?
THOUGHT YOU'D NEVER ASK.
KLKK
SHE'S NOT GOING TO STOP.
THERE'S ONLY ONE THING WE CAN DO, REEMO--

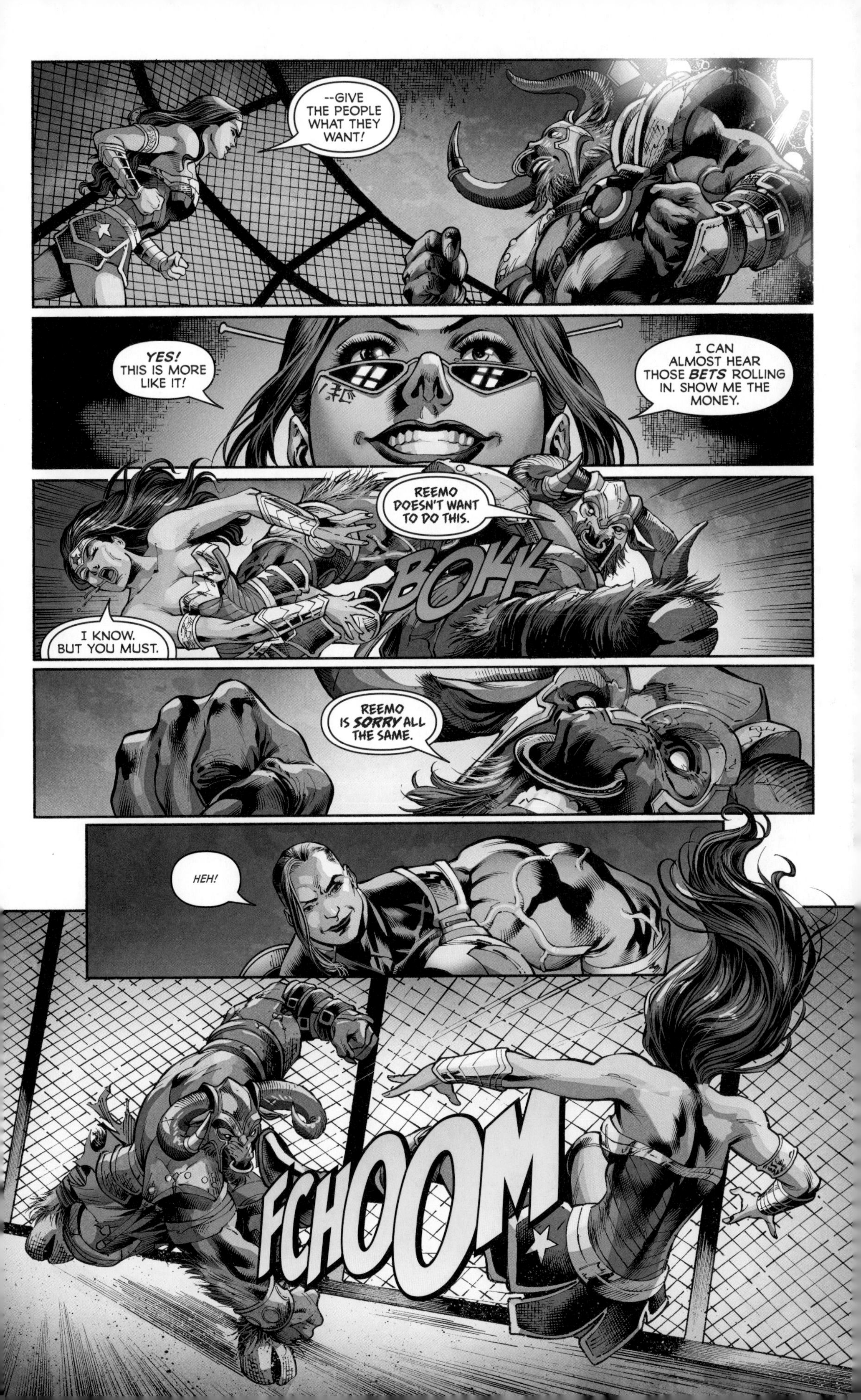
--GIVE THE PEOPLE WHAT THEY WANT!
YES! THIS IS MORE LIKE IT!
I CAN ALMOST HEAR THOSE BETS ROLLING IN. SHOW ME THE MONEY.
REEMO DOESN'T WANT TO DO THIS.
BOKK
I KNOW. BUT YOU MUST.
REEMO IS SORRY ALL THE SAME.
HEH!
FCHOOM

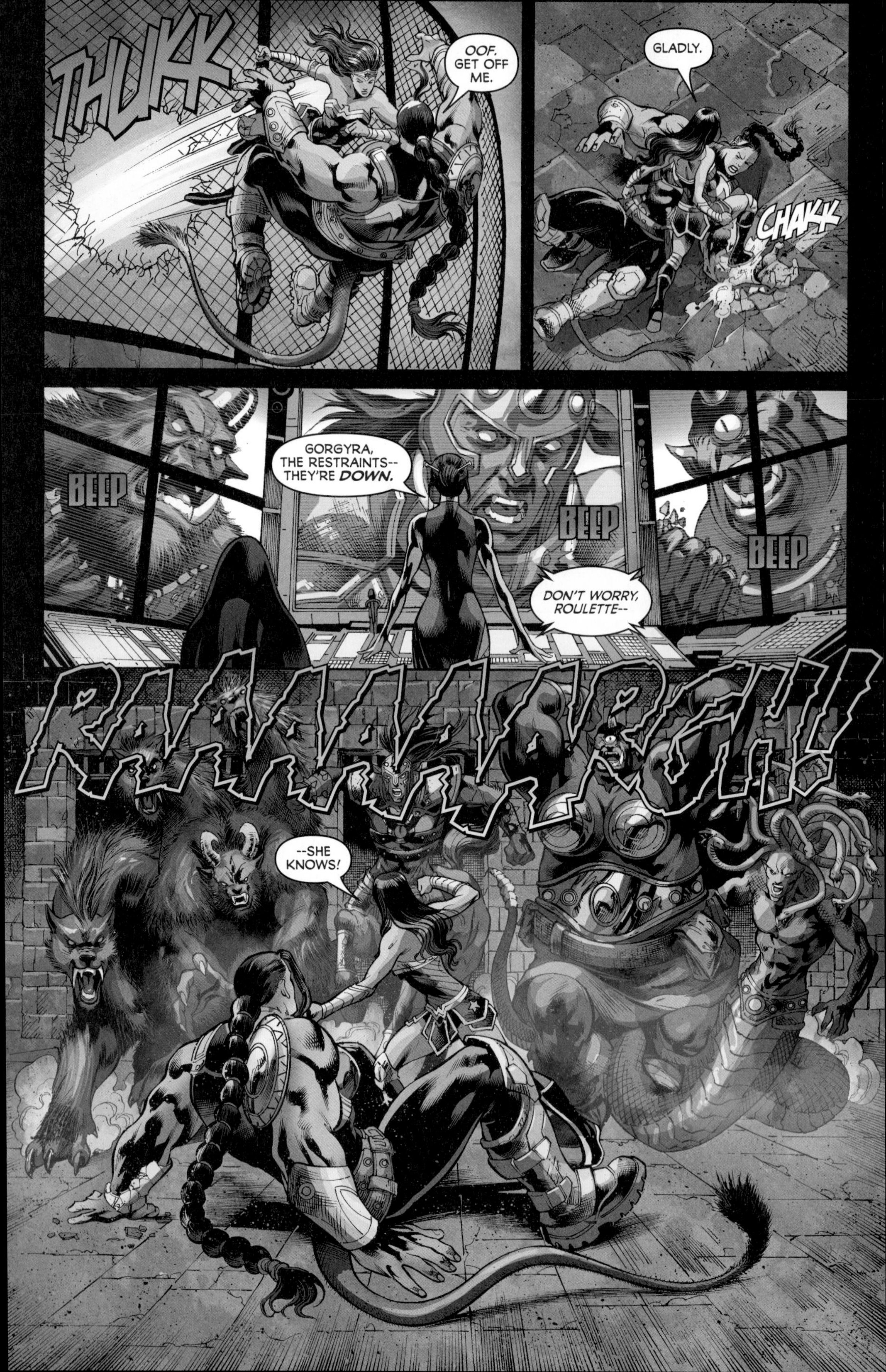
THUKK
OOF, GET OFF ME.
GLADLY.
CHAKK
GORGYRA, THE RESTRAINTS-- THEY'RE DOWN.
BEEP
BEEP
BEEP
DON'T WORRY, ROULETTE--
RAAAAARGH!
--SHE KNOWS!

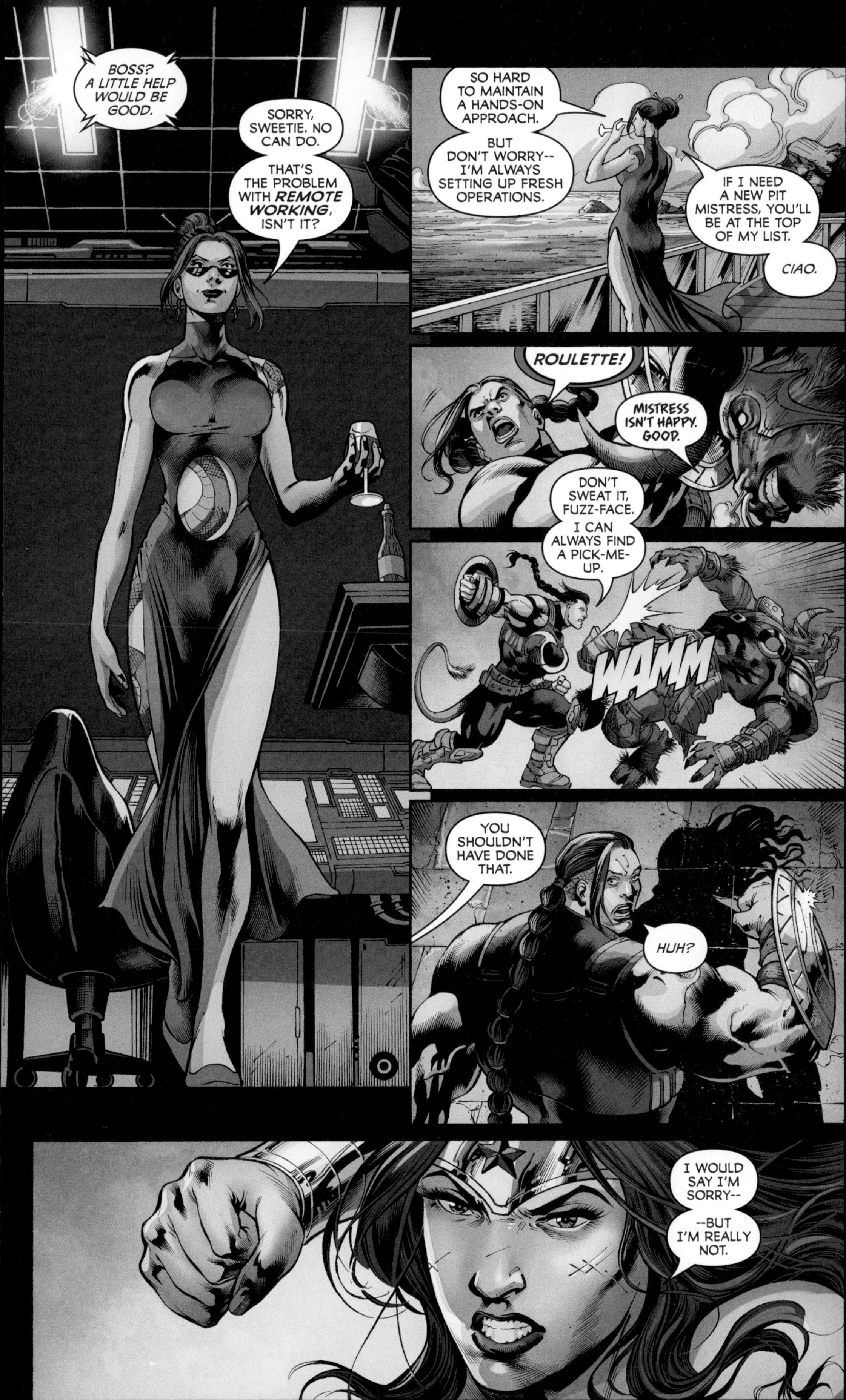
BOSS? A LITTLE HELP WOULD BE GOOD.
SORRY, SWEETIE. NO CAN DO.
THAT'S THE PROBLEM WITH ***REMOTE WORKING***, ISN'T IT?
SO HARD TO MAINTAIN A HANDS-ON APPROACH.
BUT DON'T WORRY-- I'M ALWAYS SETTING UP FRESH OPERATIONS.
IF I NEED A NEW PIT MISTRESS, YOU'LL BE AT THE TOP OF MY LIST.
CIAO.
ROULETTE!
MISTRESS ISN'T HAPPY. GOOD.
DON'T SWEAT IT, FUZZ-FACE. I CAN ALWAYS FIND A PICK-ME-UP.
WAMM
YOU SHOULDN'T HAVE DONE THAT.
HUH?
I WOULD SAY I'M SORRY--
--BUT I'M REALLY NOT.

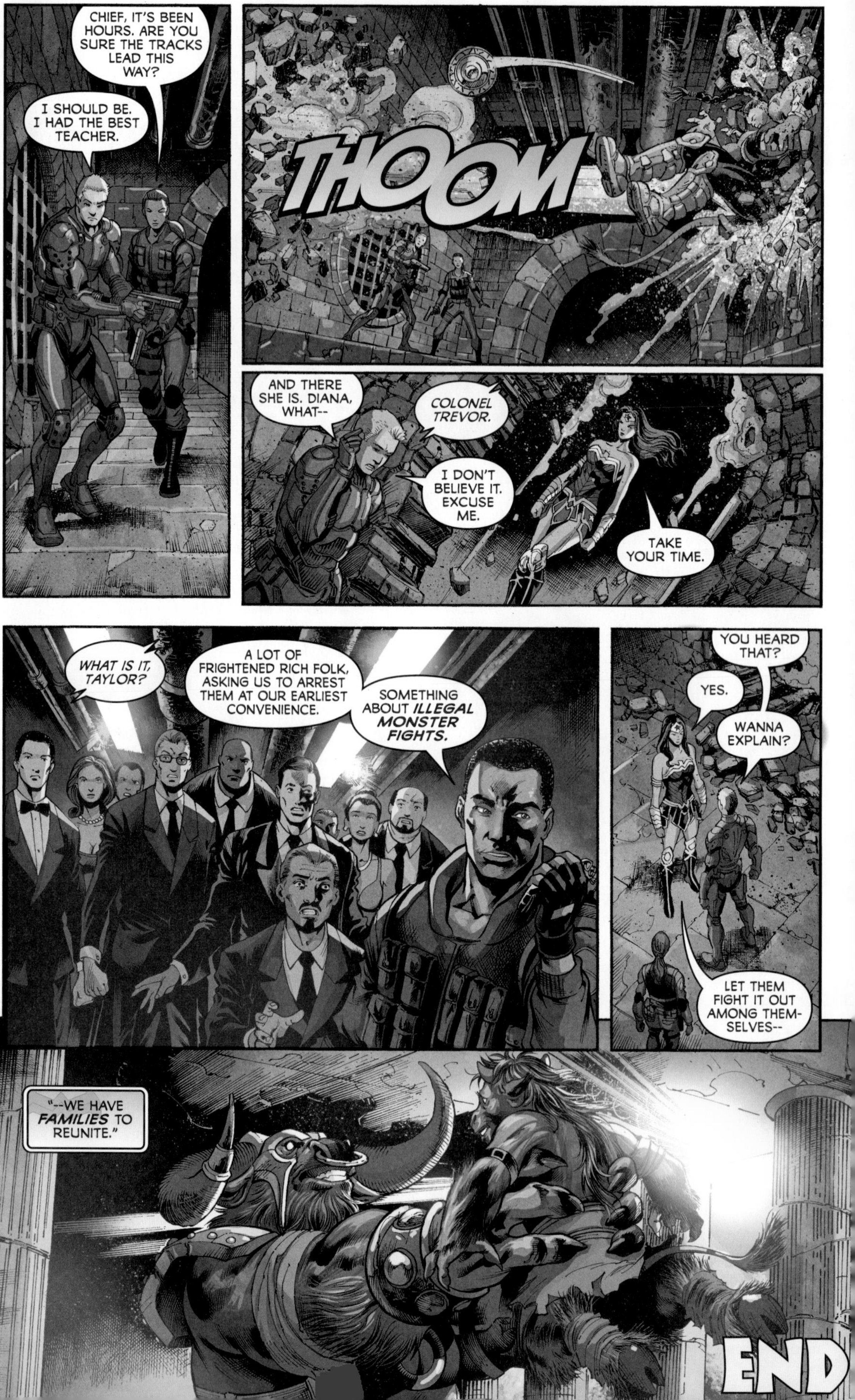
CHIEF, IT'S BEEN HOURS. ARE YOU SURE THE TRACKS LEAD THIS WAY?
I SHOULD BE. I HAD THE BEST TEACHER.
THOOM
AND THERE SHE IS. DIANA, WHAT--
COLONEL TREVOR.
I DON'T BELIEVE IT. EXCUSE ME.
TAKE YOUR TIME.
WHAT IS IT, TAYLOR?
A LOT OF FRIGHTENED RICH FOLK, ASKING US TO ARREST THEM AT OUR EARLIEST CONVENIENCE.
SOMETHING ABOUT *ILLEGAL MONSTER FIGHTS.*
YOU HEARD THAT?
YES.
WANNA EXPLAIN?
LET THEM FIGHT IT OUT AMONG THEM-SELVES--
"--WE HAVE *FAMILIES* TO REUNITE."
END

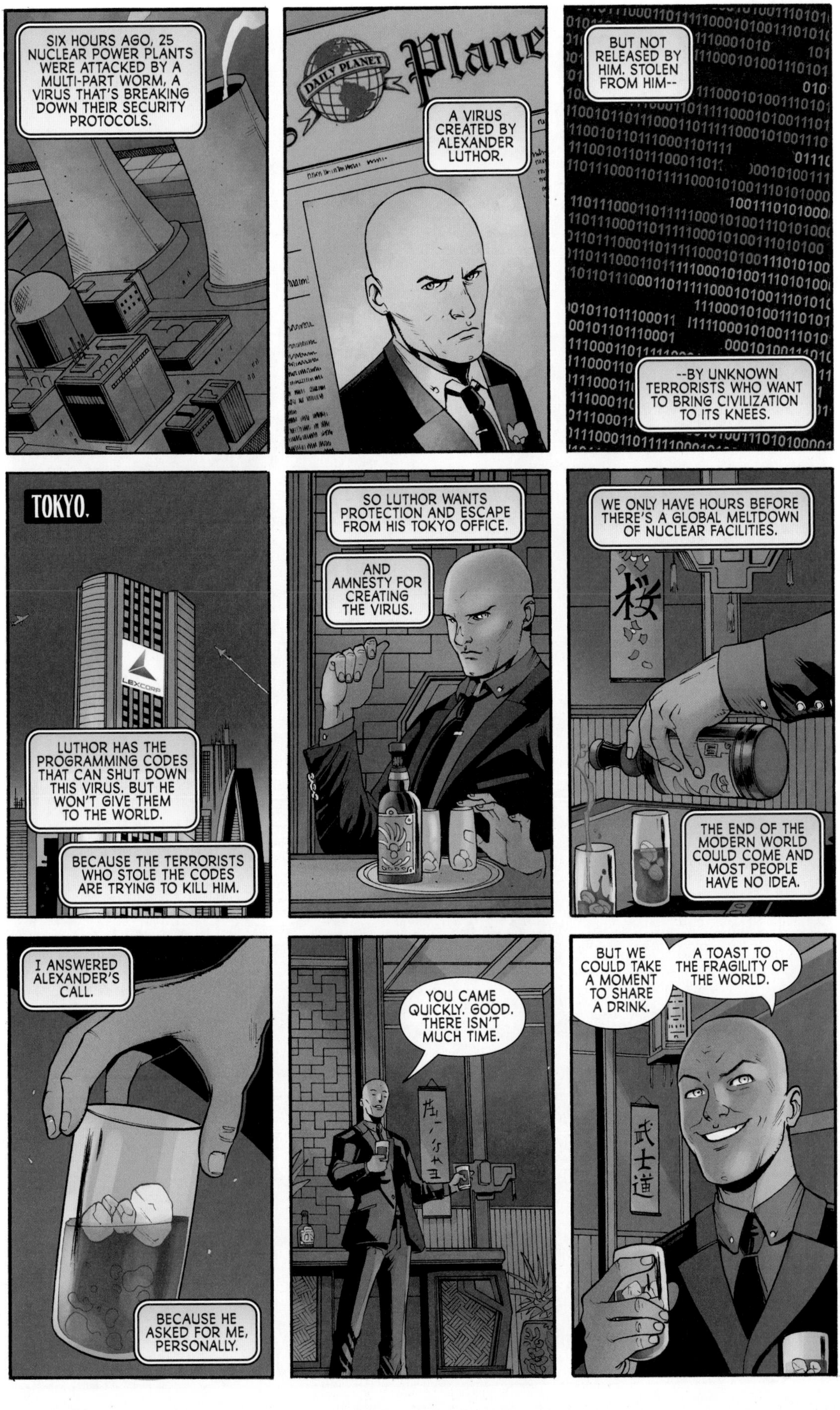
SIX HOURS AGO, 25 NUCLEAR POWER PLANTS WERE ATTACKED BY A MULTI-PART WORM, A VIRUS THAT'S BREAKING DOWN THEIR SECURITY PROTOCOLS.
DAILY PLANET
A VIRUS CREATED BY ALEXANDER LUTHOR.
BUT NOT RELEASED BY HIM. STOLEN FROM HIM--
--BY UNKNOWN TERRORISTS WHO WANT TO BRING CIVILIZATION TO ITS KNEES.
TOKYO.
LEXCORP
LUTHOR HAS THE PROGRAMMING CODES THAT CAN SHUT DOWN THIS VIRUS. BUT HE WON'T GIVE THEM TO THE WORLD.
BECAUSE THE TERRORISTS WHO STOLE THE CODES ARE TRYING TO KILL HIM.
SO LUTHOR WANTS PROTECTION AND ESCAPE FROM HIS TOKYO OFFICE.
AND AMNESTY FOR CREATING THE VIRUS.
WE ONLY HAVE HOURS BEFORE THERE'S A GLOBAL MELTDOWN OF NUCLEAR FACILITIES.
桜
THE END OF THE MODERN WORLD COULD COME AND MOST PEOPLE HAVE NO IDEA.
I ANSWERED ALEXANDER'S CALL.
BECAUSE HE ASKED FOR ME, PERSONALLY.
YOU CAME QUICKLY. GOOD. THERE ISN'T MUCH TIME.
BUT WE COULD TAKE A MOMENT TO SHARE A DRINK.
A TOAST TO THE FRAGILITY OF THE WORLD.
武士道

One Night in Tokyo

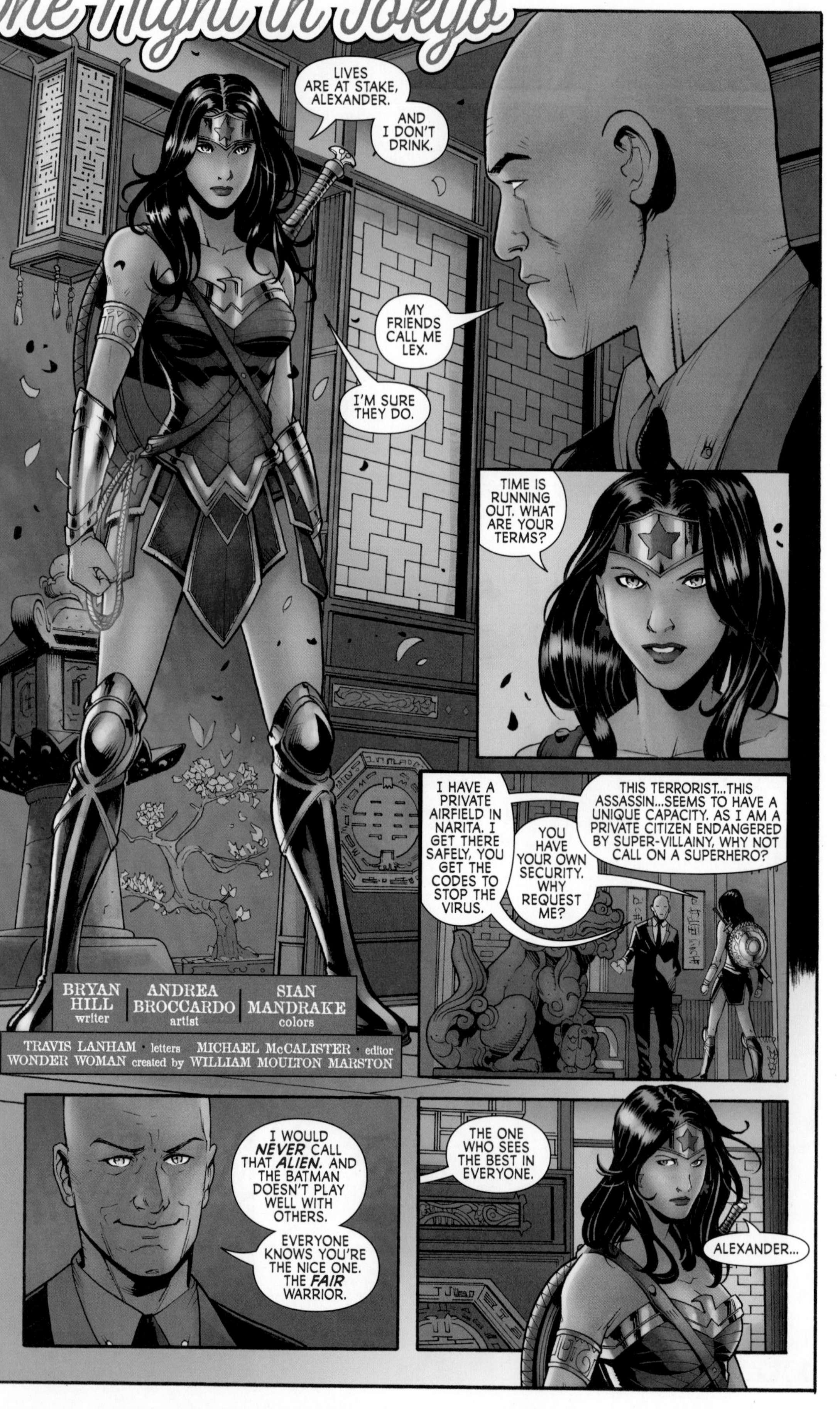
LIVES ARE AT STAKE, ALEXANDER.
AND I DON'T DRINK.
MY FRIENDS CALL ME LEX.
I'M SURE THEY DO.
BRYAN HILL writer | ANDREA BROCCARDO artist | SIAN MANDRAKE colors
TRAVIS LANHAM letters MICHAEL McCALISTER editor
WONDER WOMAN created by WILLIAM MOULTON MARSTON
TIME IS RUNNING OUT. WHAT ARE YOUR TERMS?
I HAVE A PRIVATE AIRFIELD IN NARITA. I GET THERE SAFELY, YOU GET THE CODES TO STOP THE VIRUS.
YOU HAVE YOUR OWN SECURITY. WHY REQUEST ME?
THIS TERRORIST...THIS ASSASSIN...SEEMS TO HAVE A UNIQUE CAPACITY. AS I AM A PRIVATE CITIZEN ENDANGERED BY SUPER-VILLAINY, WHY NOT CALL ON A SUPERHERO?
I WOULD NEVER CALL THAT ALIEN. AND THE BATMAN DOESN'T PLAY WELL WITH OTHERS.
EVERYONE KNOWS YOU'RE THE NICE ONE. THE FAIR WARRIOR.
THE ONE WHO SEES THE BEST IN EVERYONE.
ALEXANDER...

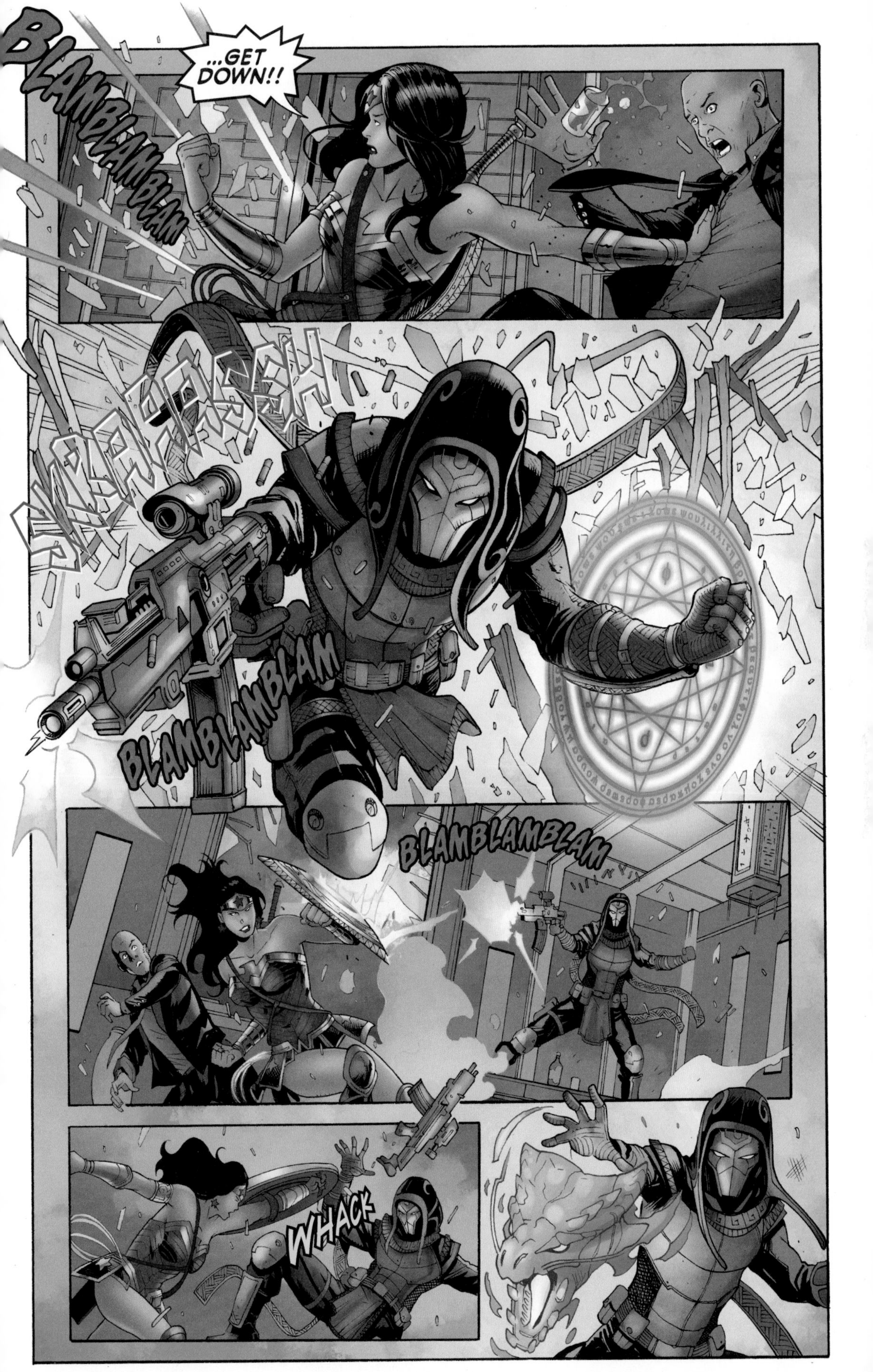

BLAMBLAMBLAMBLAM
...GET DOWN!!
SKRASSH
BLAMBLAMBLAM
BLAMBLAMBLAM
WHACK

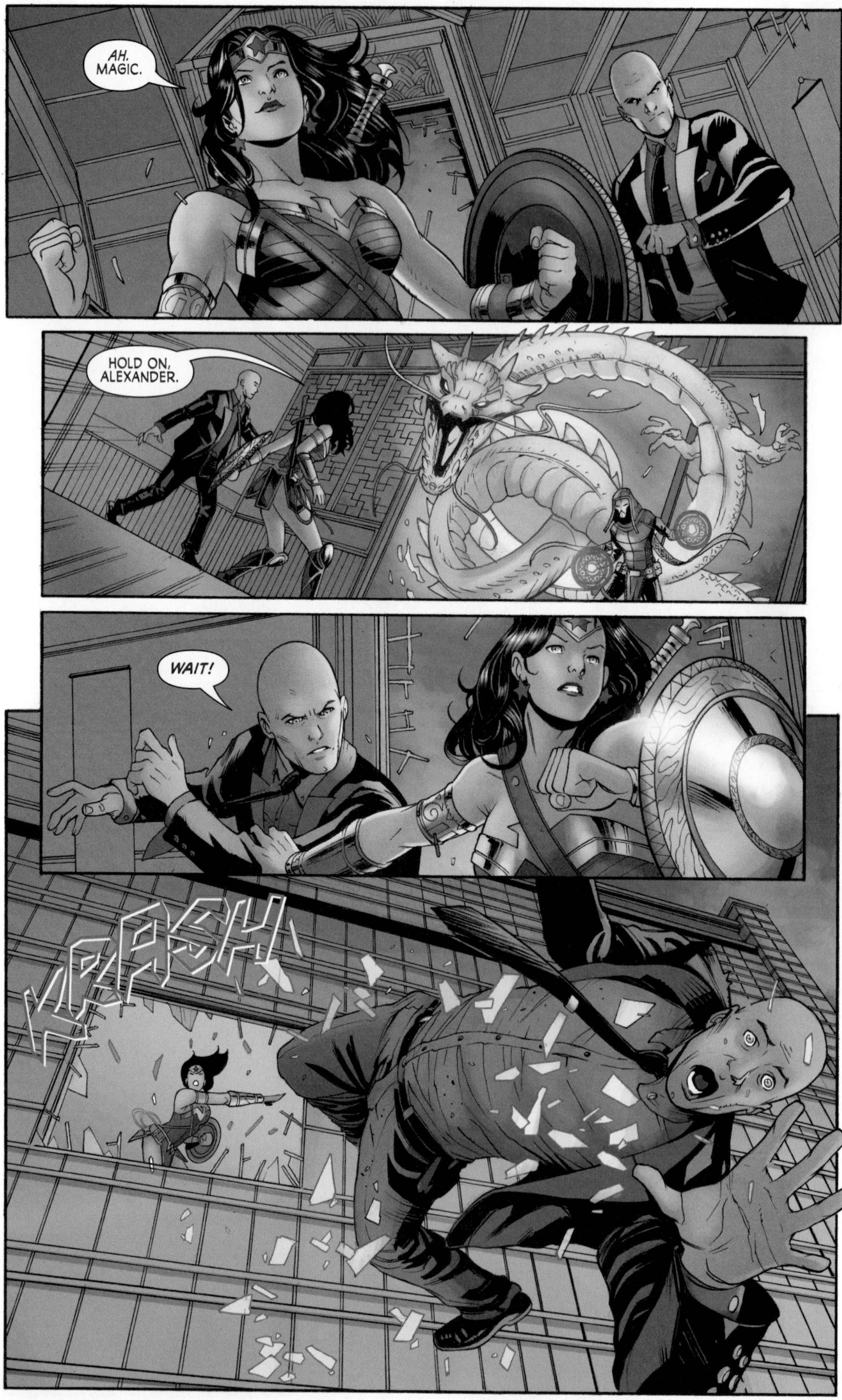

AH. MAGIC.
HOLD ON, ALEXANDER.
WAIT!
KRASH!

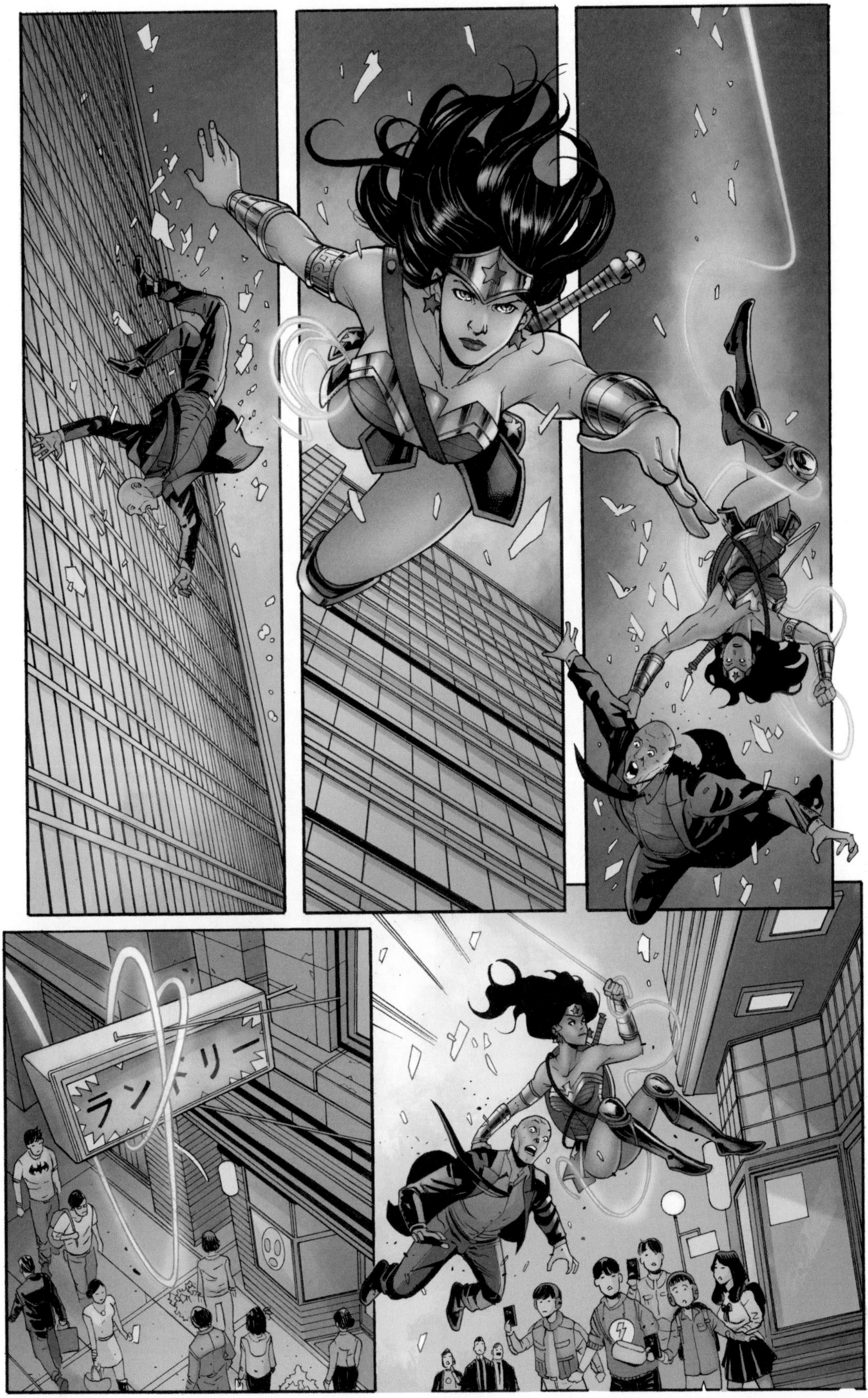
ランドリー

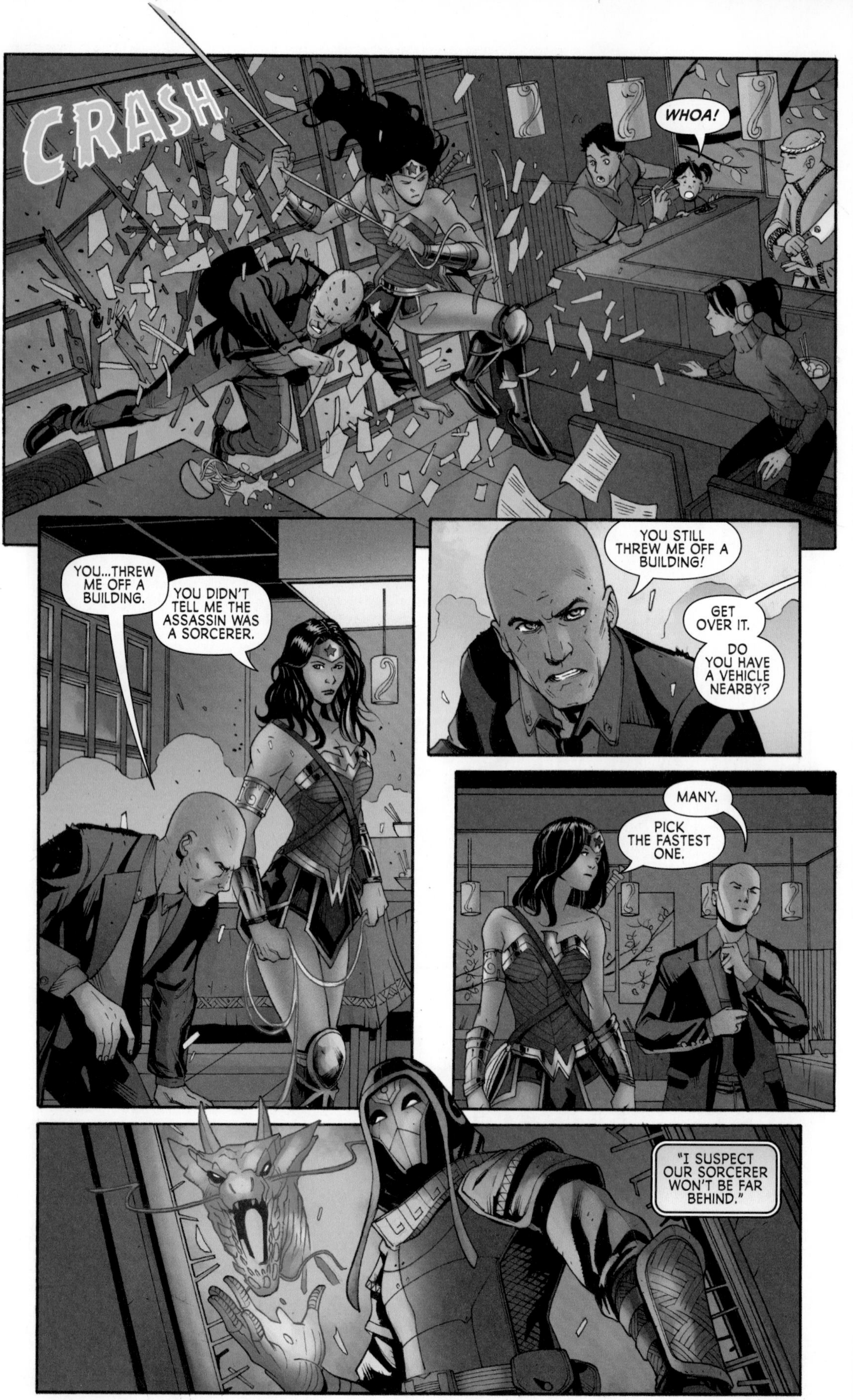
CRASH
WHOA!
YOU...THREW ME OFF A BUILDING.
YOU DIDN'T TELL ME THE ASSASSIN WAS A SORCERER.
YOU STILL THREW ME OFF A BUILDING!
GET OVER IT.
DO YOU HAVE A VEHICLE NEARBY?
MANY.
PICK THE FASTEST ONE.
"I SUSPECT OUR SORCERER WON'T BE FAR BEHIND."

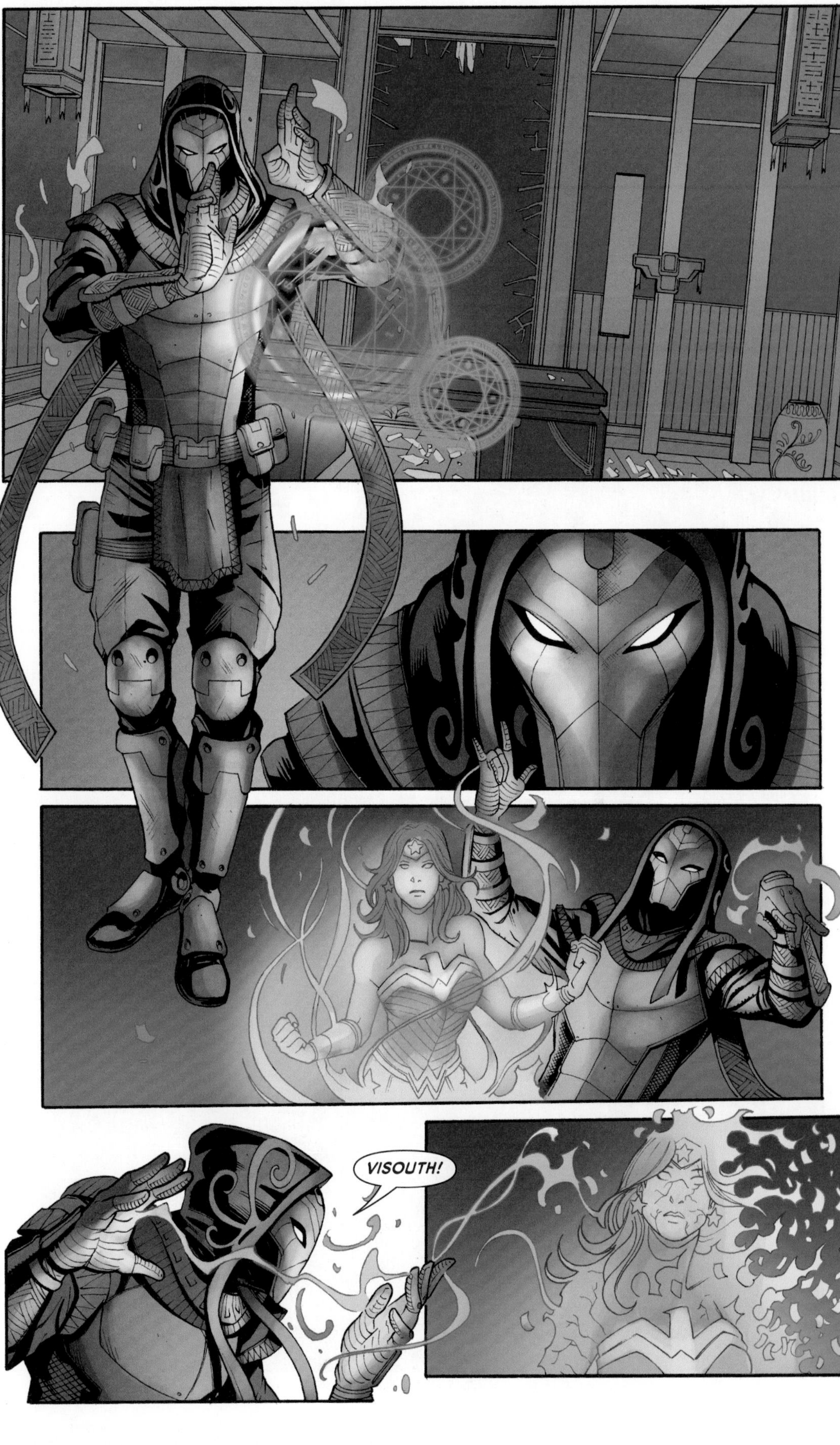
VISOUTH!

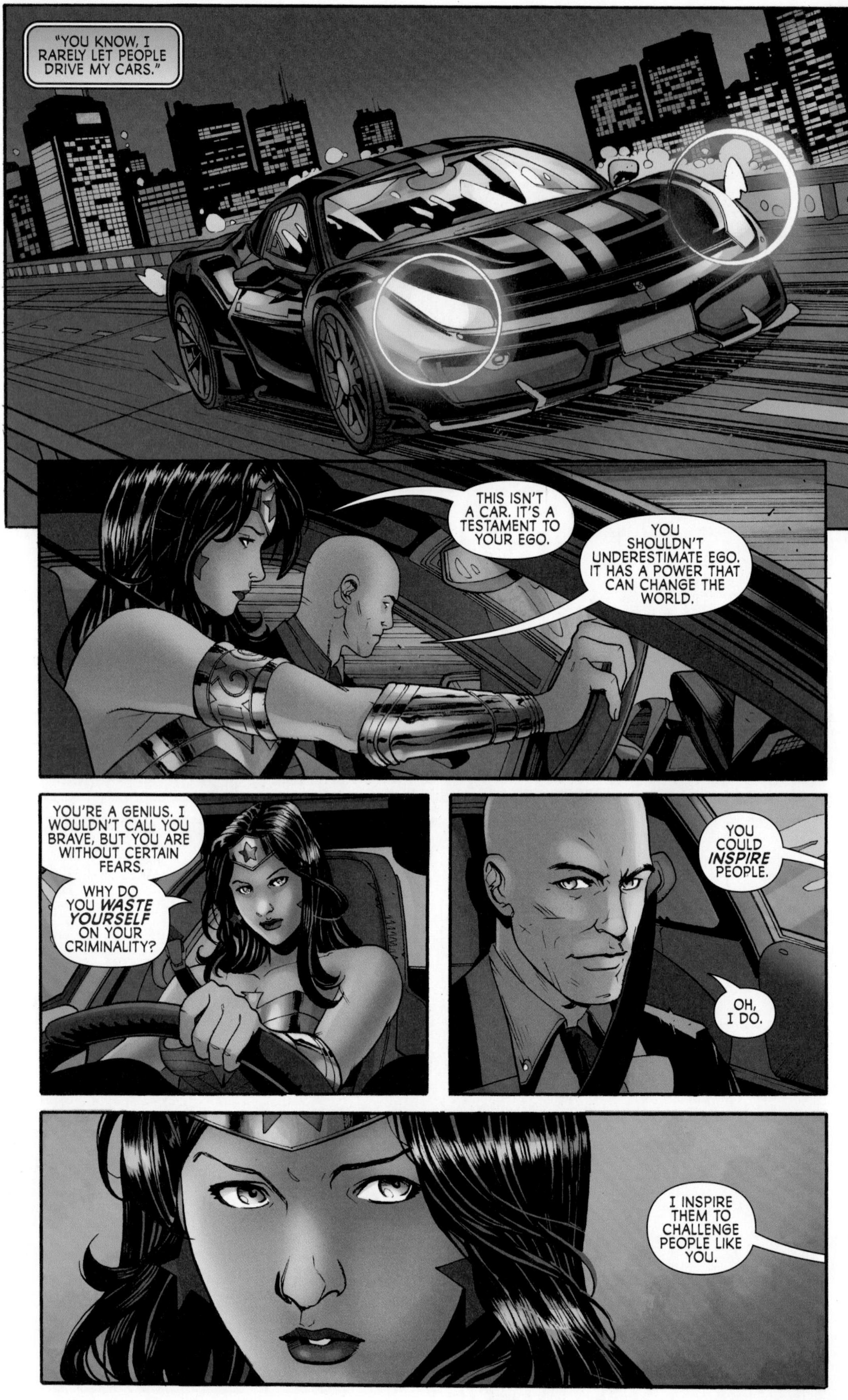
"YOU KNOW, I RARELY LET PEOPLE DRIVE MY CARS."
THIS ISN'T A CAR. IT'S A TESTAMENT TO YOUR EGO.
YOU SHOULDN'T UNDERESTIMATE EGO. IT HAS A POWER THAT CAN CHANGE THE WORLD.
YOU'RE A GENIUS. I WOULDN'T CALL YOU BRAVE, BUT YOU ARE WITHOUT CERTAIN FEARS.
WHY DO YOU *WASTE YOURSELF* ON YOUR CRIMINALITY?
YOU COULD *INSPIRE* PEOPLE.
OH, I DO.
I INSPIRE THEM TO CHALLENGE PEOPLE LIKE YOU.

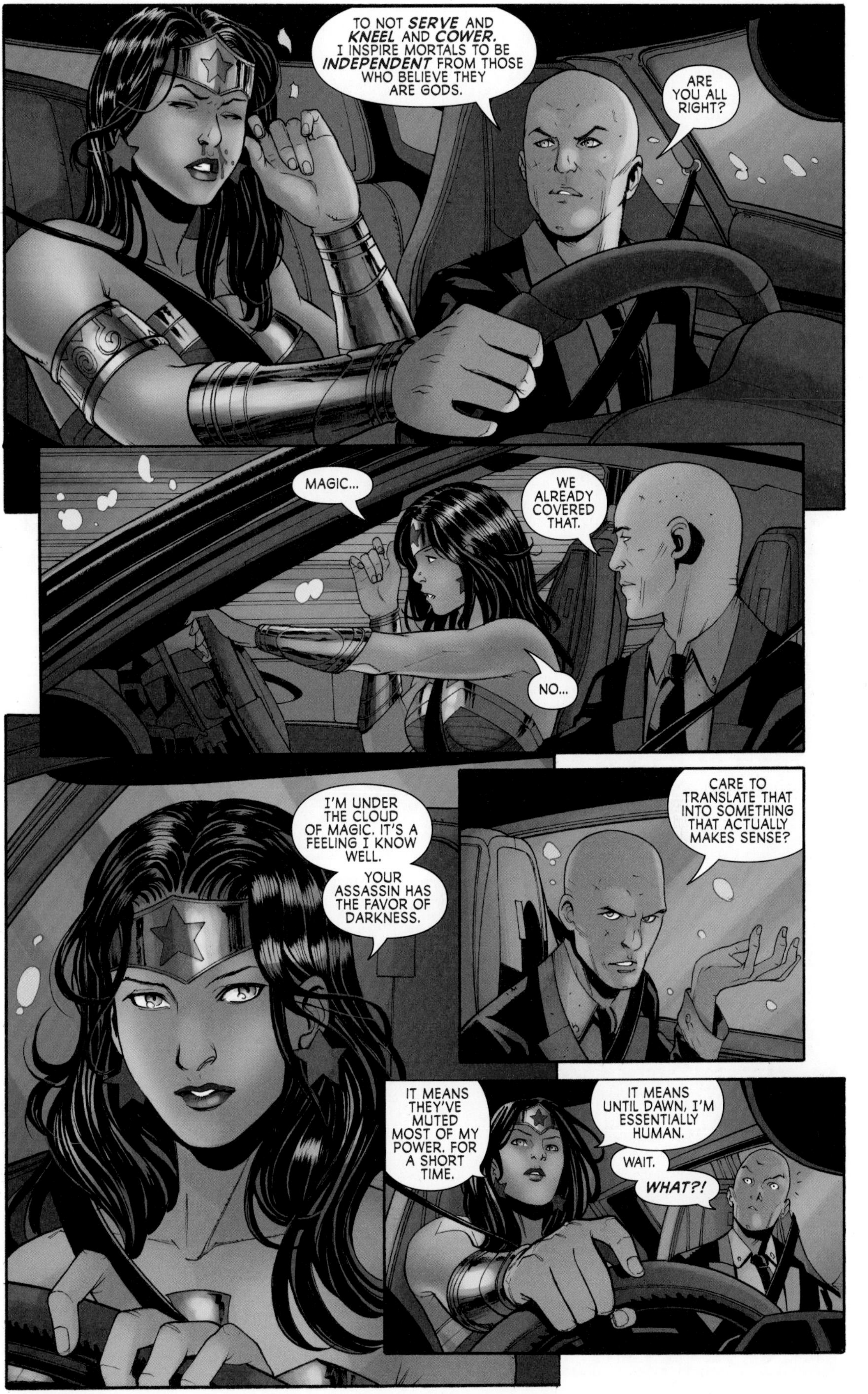
TO NOT **SERVE** AND **KNEEL** AND **COWER.** I INSPIRE MORTALS TO BE **INDEPENDENT** FROM THOSE WHO BELIEVE THEY ARE GODS.
ARE YOU ALL RIGHT?
MAGIC...
WE ALREADY COVERED THAT.
NO...
I'M UNDER THE CLOUD OF MAGIC. IT'S A FEELING I KNOW WELL.
YOUR ASSASSIN HAS THE FAVOR OF DARKNESS.
CARE TO TRANSLATE THAT INTO SOMETHING THAT ACTUALLY MAKES SENSE?
IT MEANS THEY'VE MUTED MOST OF MY POWER. FOR A SHORT TIME.
IT MEANS UNTIL DAWN, I'M ESSENTIALLY HUMAN.
WAIT.
WHAT?!

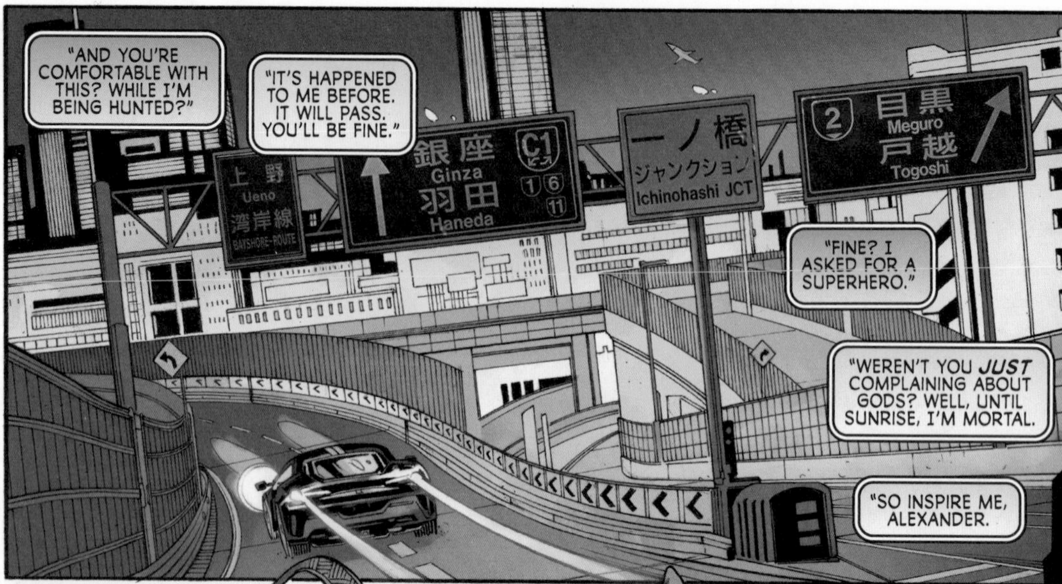
"AND YOU'RE COMFORTABLE WITH THIS? WHILE I'M BEING HUNTED?"
"IT'S HAPPENED TO ME BEFORE. IT WILL PASS. YOU'LL BE FINE."
上野 Ueno 湾岸線 BAYSHORE-ROUTE
銀座 Ginza 羽田 Haneda C1 1 6 11
一ノ橋 ジャンクション Ichinohashi JCT
2 目黒 Meguro 戸越 Togoshi
"FINE? I ASKED FOR A SUPERHERO."
"WEREN'T YOU *JUST* COMPLAINING ABOUT GODS? WELL, UNTIL SUNRISE, I'M MORTAL.
"SO INSPIRE ME, ALEXANDER.

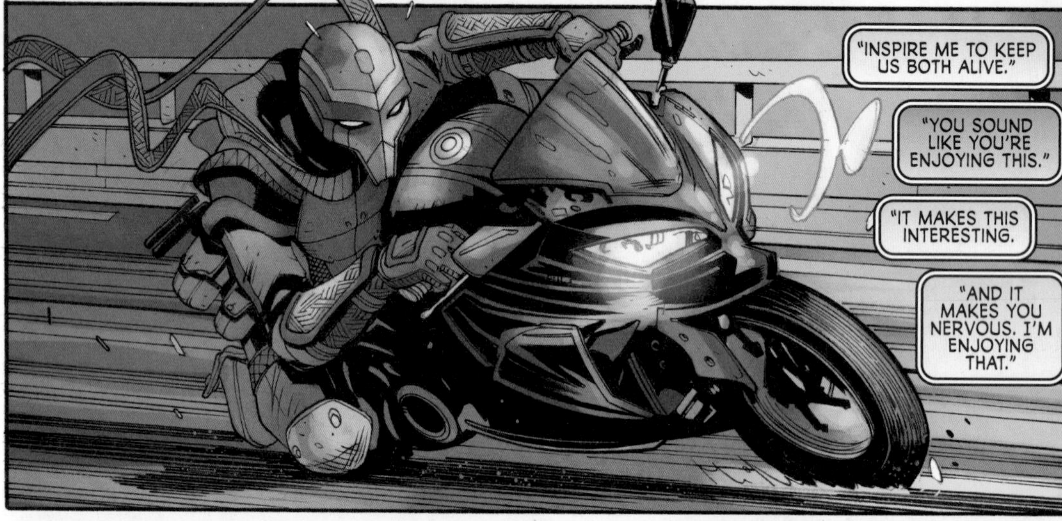
"INSPIRE ME TO KEEP US BOTH ALIVE."
"YOU SOUND LIKE YOU'RE ENJOYING THIS."
"IT MAKES THIS INTERESTING.
"AND IT MAKES YOU NERVOUS. I'M ENJOYING THAT."

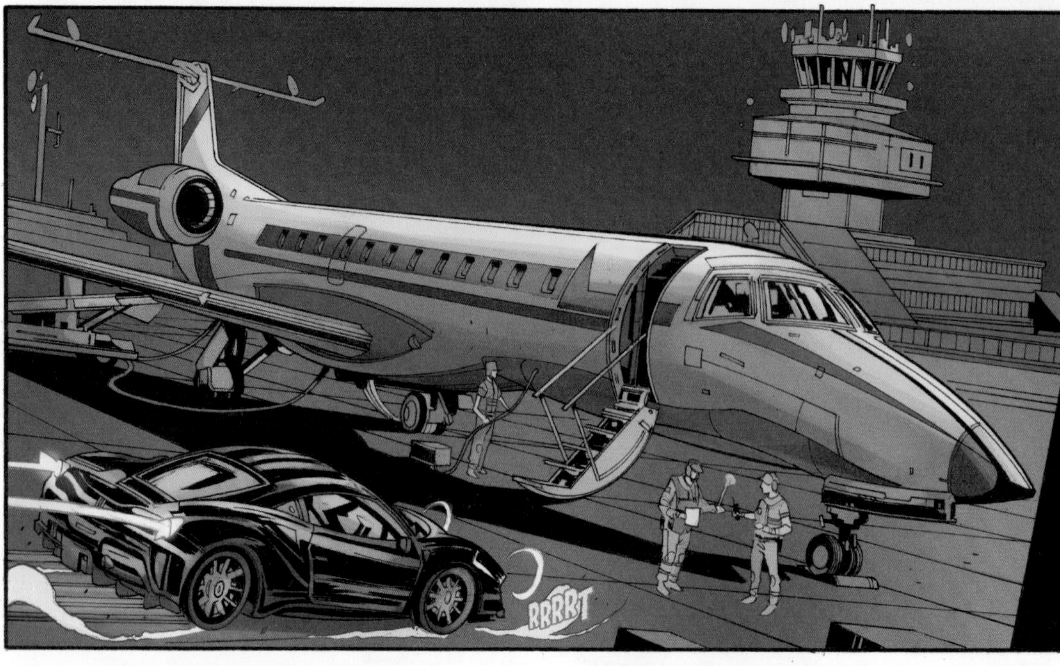
RRRRT

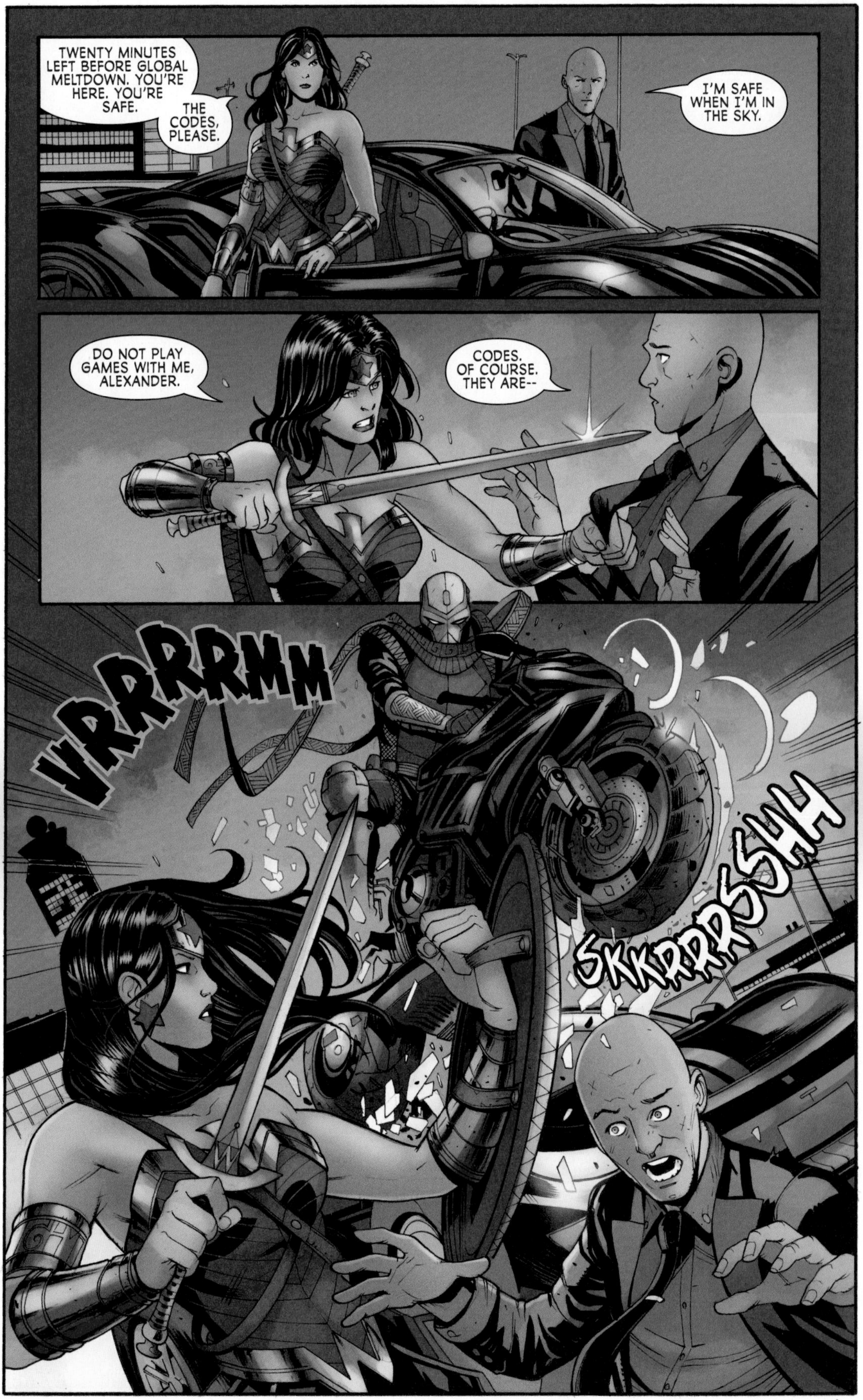
TWENTY MINUTES LEFT BEFORE GLOBAL MELTDOWN. YOU'RE HERE. YOU'RE SAFE.
THE CODES, PLEASE.
I'M SAFE WHEN I'M IN THE SKY.
DO NOT PLAY GAMES WITH ME, ALEXANDER.
CODES. OF COURSE. THEY ARE--
VRRRRMM
SKKRRRSSHH

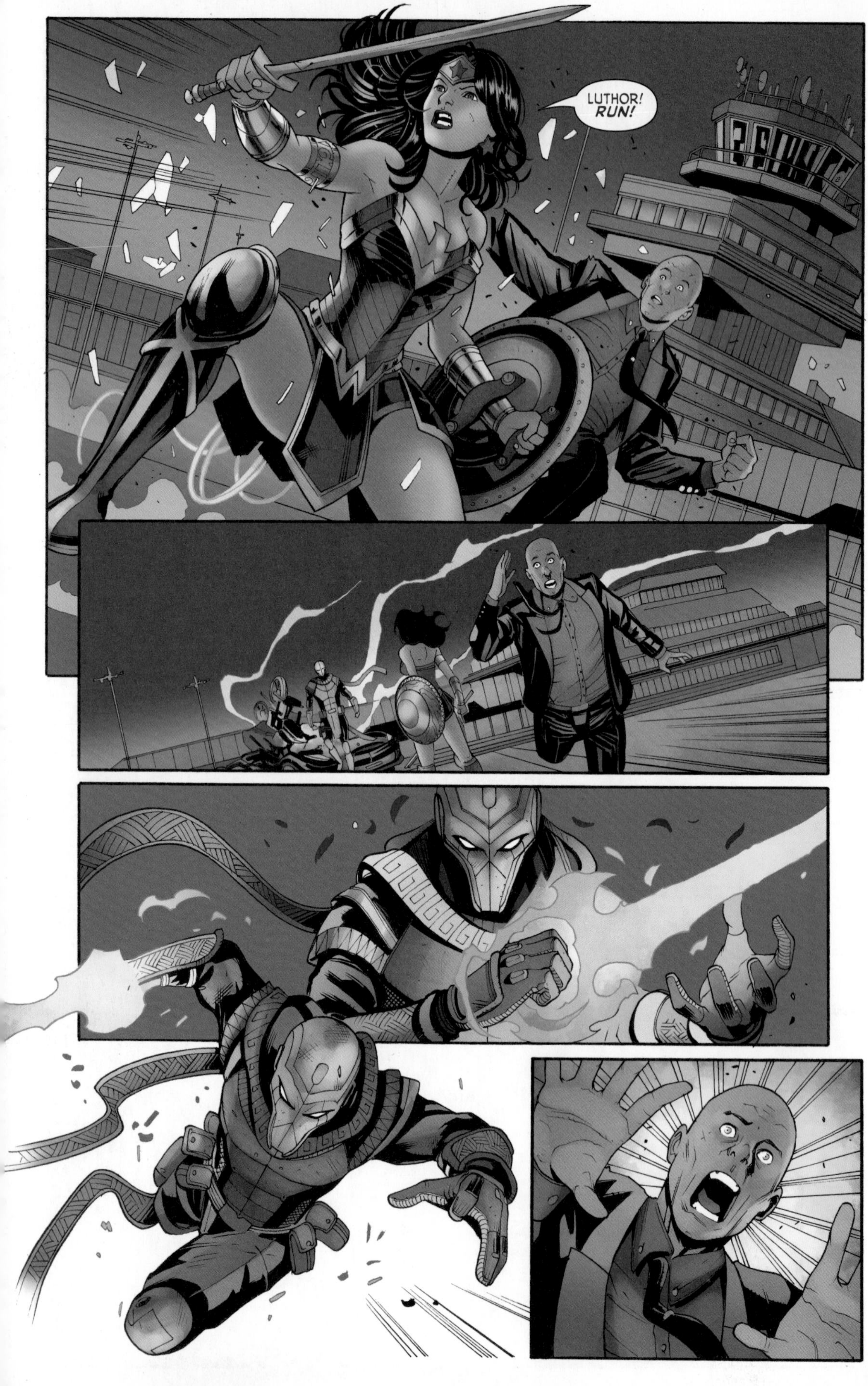
LUTHOR! RUN!

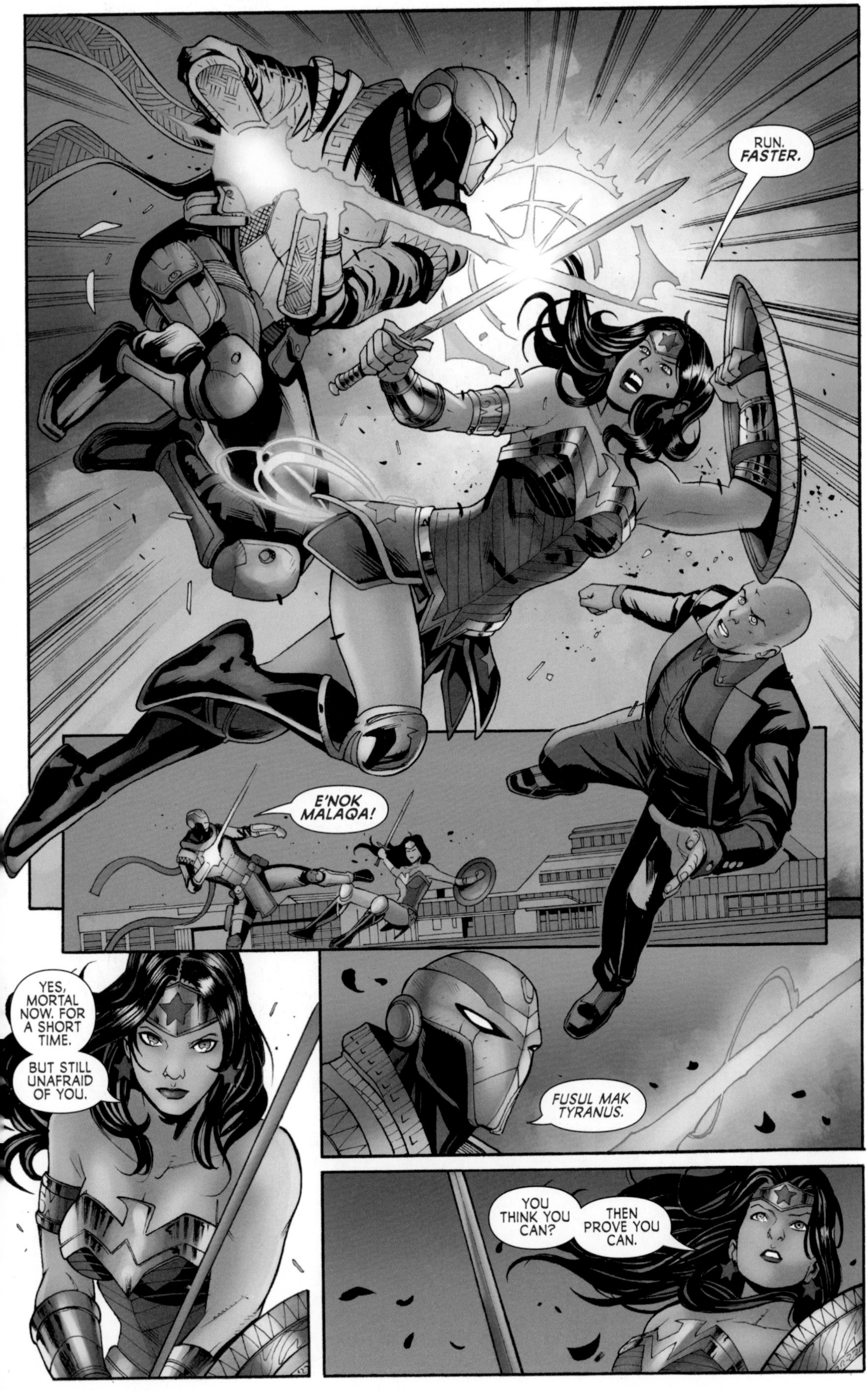
RUN. FASTER.
E'NOK MALAQA!
YES, MORTAL NOW. FOR A SHORT TIME.
BUT STILL UNAFRAID OF YOU.
FUSUL MAK TYRANUS.
YOU THINK YOU CAN?
THEN PROVE YOU CAN.

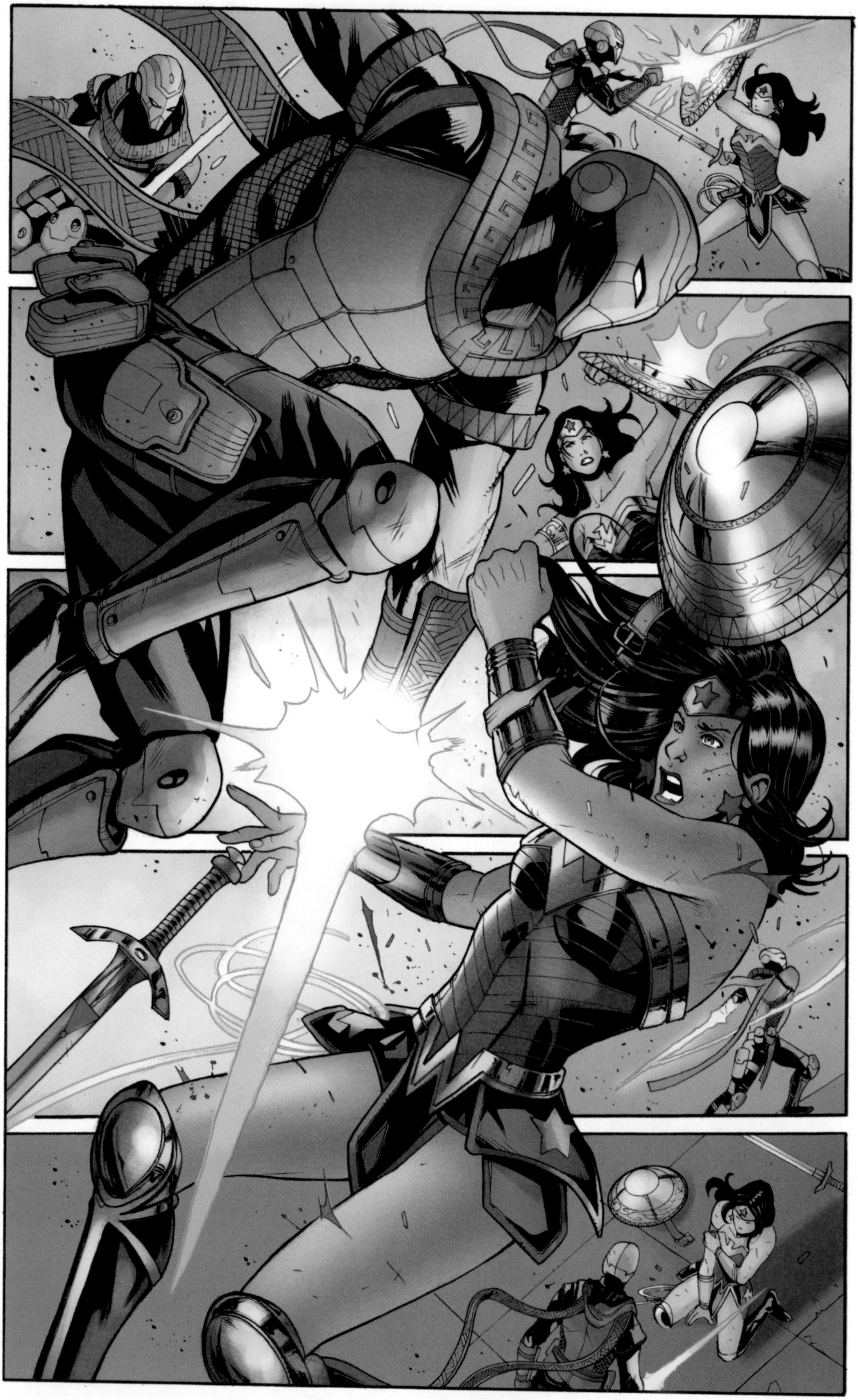

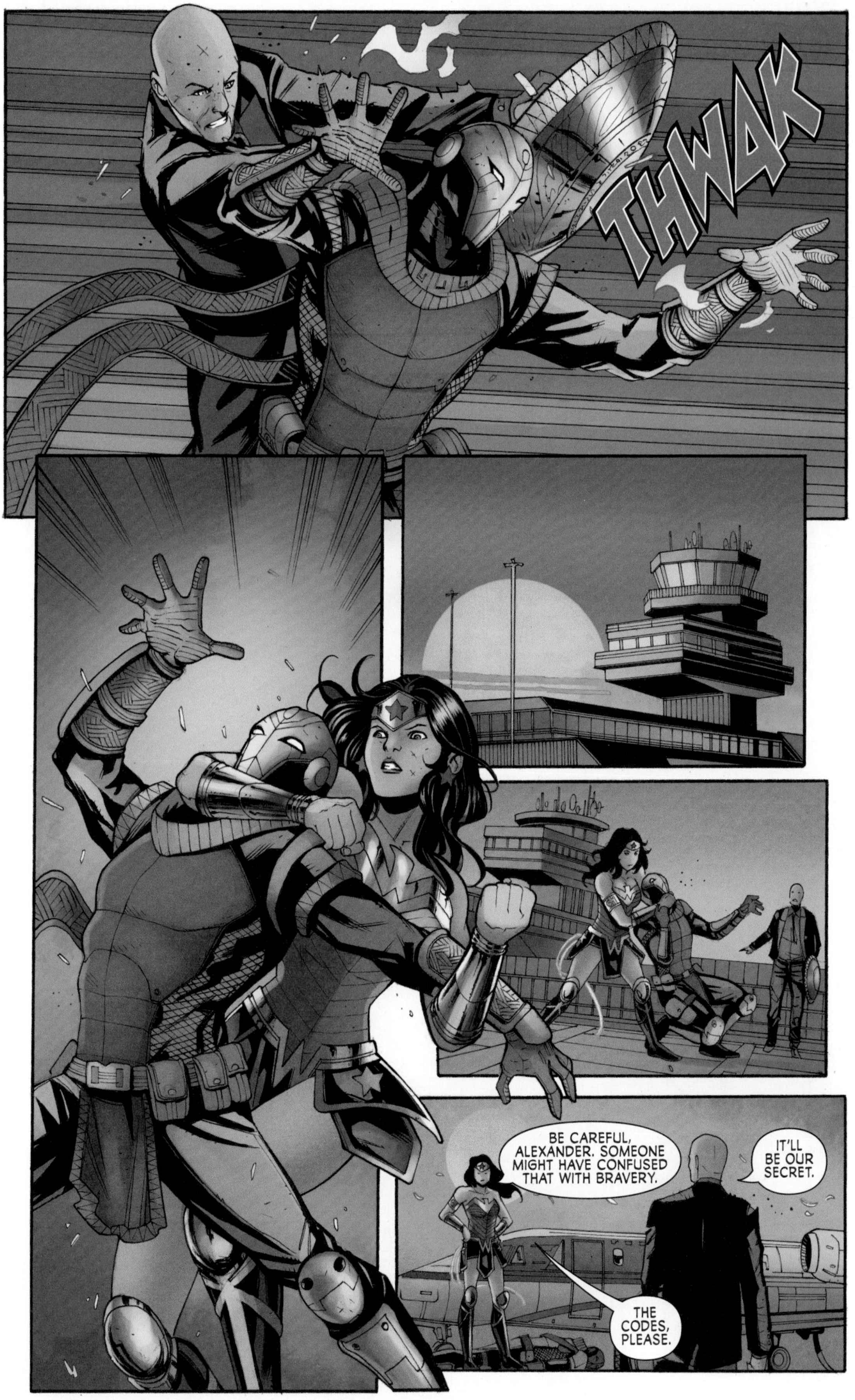
THWAK
BE CAREFUL, ALEXANDER. SOMEONE MIGHT HAVE CONFUSED THAT WITH BRAVERY.
IT'LL BE OUR SECRET.
THE CODES, PLEASE.

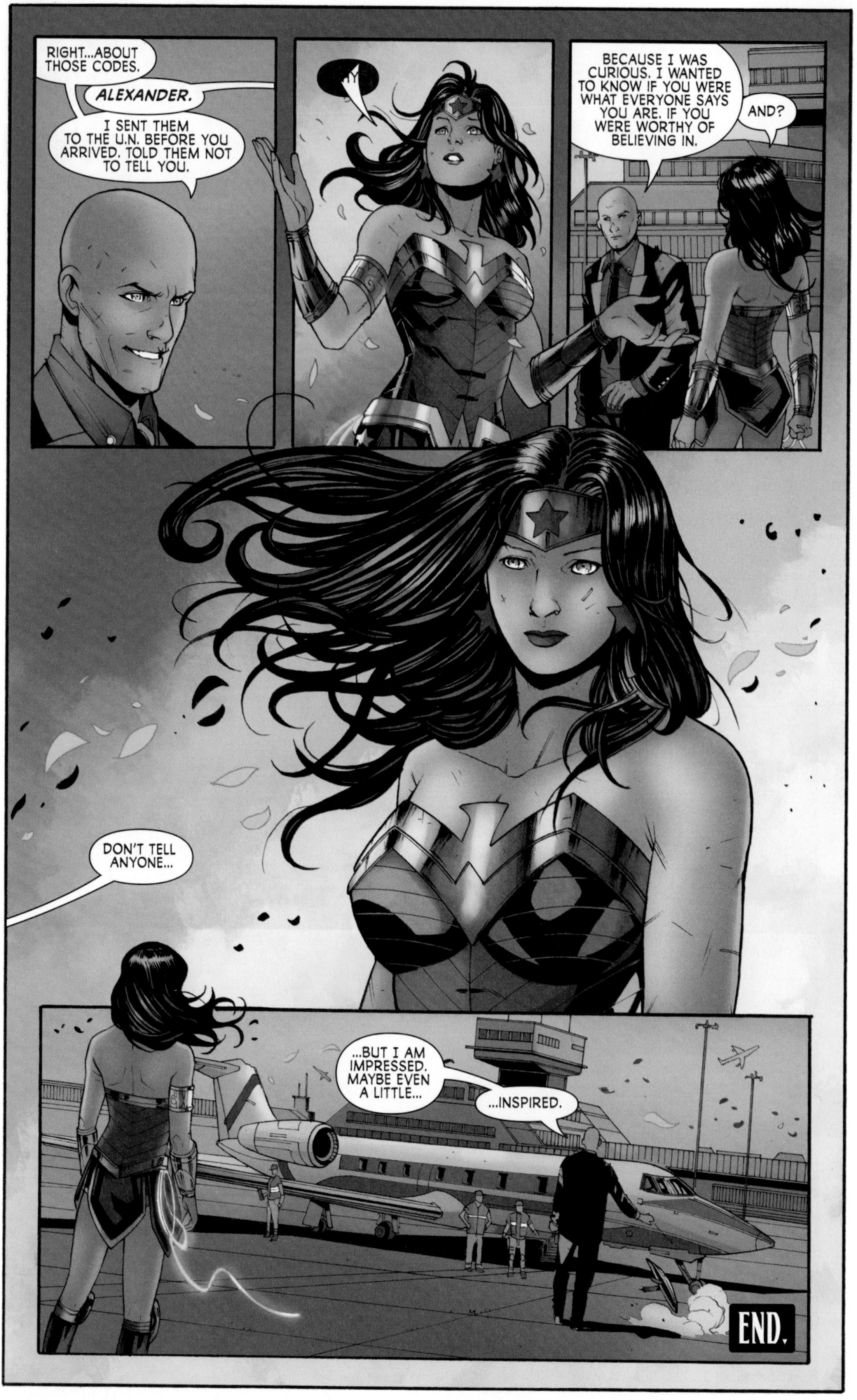
RIGHT...ABOUT THOSE CODES.
ALEXANDER.
I SENT THEM TO THE U.N. BEFORE YOU ARRIVED. TOLD THEM NOT TO TELL YOU.
BECAUSE I WAS CURIOUS. I WANTED TO KNOW IF YOU WERE WHAT EVERYONE SAYS YOU ARE. IF YOU WERE WORTHY OF BELIEVING IN.
AND?
DON'T TELL ANYONE...
...BUT I AM IMPRESSED. MAYBE EVEN A LITTLE...
...INSPIRED.
END.

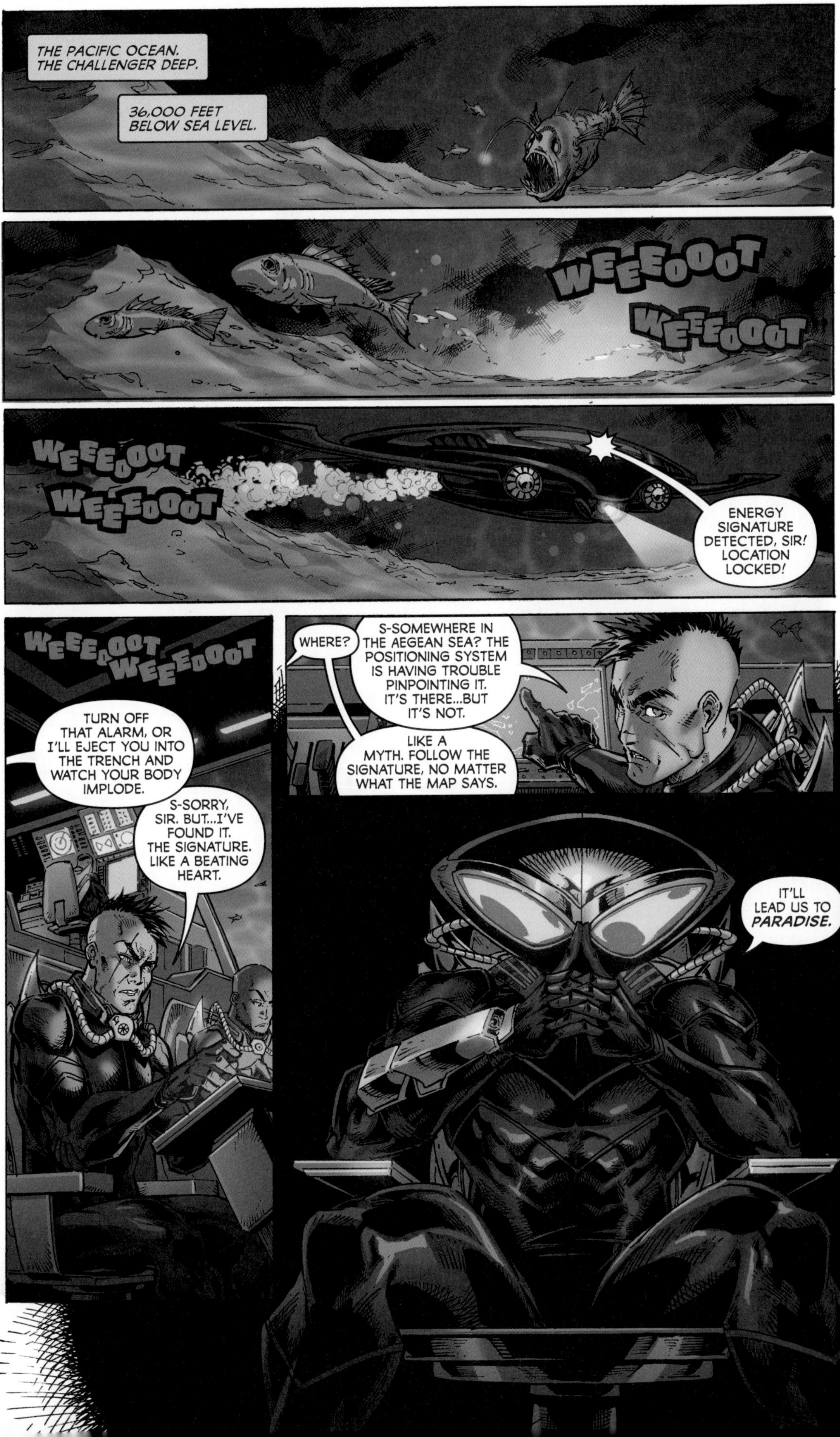
THE PACIFIC OCEAN. THE CHALLENGER DEEP.
36,000 FEET BELOW SEA LEVEL.
WEEEOOOT
WEEEOOOT
WEEEOOOT
WEEEOOOT
ENERGY SIGNATURE DETECTED, SIR! LOCATION LOCKED!
WEEEOOOT WEEEOOOT
WHERE?
S-SOMEWHERE IN THE AEGEAN SEA? THE POSITIONING SYSTEM IS HAVING TROUBLE PINPOINTING IT. IT'S THERE...BUT IT'S NOT.
LIKE A MYTH. FOLLOW THE SIGNATURE, NO MATTER WHAT THE MAP SAYS.
TURN OFF THAT ALARM, OR I'LL EJECT YOU INTO THE TRENCH AND WATCH YOUR BODY IMPLODE.
S-SORRY, SIR. BUT...I'VE FOUND IT. THE SIGNATURE. LIKE A BEATING HEART.
IT'LL LEAD US TO *PARADISE.*

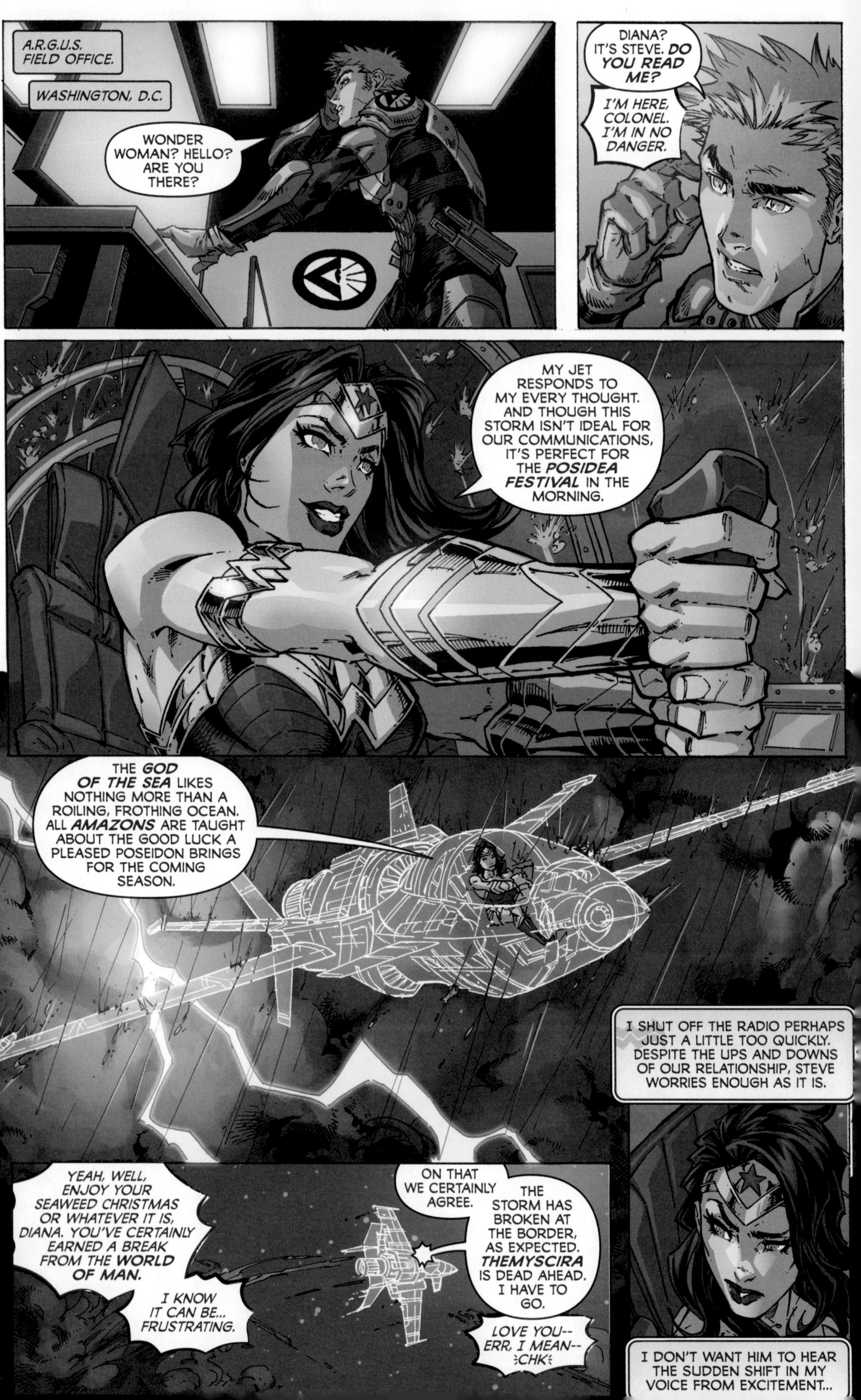
A.R.G.U.S. FIELD OFFICE.
WASHINGTON, D.C.
WONDER WOMAN? HELLO? ARE YOU THERE?
DIANA? IT'S STEVE. DO YOU READ ME?
I'M HERE, COLONEL. I'M IN NO DANGER.
MY JET RESPONDS TO MY EVERY THOUGHT. AND THOUGH THIS STORM ISN'T IDEAL FOR OUR COMMUNICATIONS, IT'S PERFECT FOR THE POSIDEA FESTIVAL IN THE MORNING.
THE GOD OF THE SEA LIKES NOTHING MORE THAN A ROILING, FROTHING OCEAN. ALL AMAZONS ARE TAUGHT ABOUT THE GOOD LUCK A PLEASED POSEIDON BRINGS FOR THE COMING SEASON.
I SHUT OFF THE RADIO PERHAPS JUST A LITTLE TOO QUICKLY. DESPITE THE UPS AND DOWNS OF OUR RELATIONSHIP, STEVE WORRIES ENOUGH AS IT IS.
YEAH, WELL, ENJOY YOUR SEAWEED CHRISTMAS OR WHATEVER IT IS, DIANA. YOU'VE CERTAINLY EARNED A BREAK FROM THE WORLD OF MAN.
I KNOW IT CAN BE... FRUSTRATING.
ON THAT WE CERTAINLY AGREE.
THE STORM HAS BROKEN AT THE BORDER, AS EXPECTED. THEMYSCIRA IS DEAD AHEAD. I HAVE TO GO.
LOVE YOU-- ERR, I MEAN-- CHK
I DON'T WANT HIM TO HEAR THE SUDDEN SHIFT IN MY VOICE FROM EXCITEMENT...

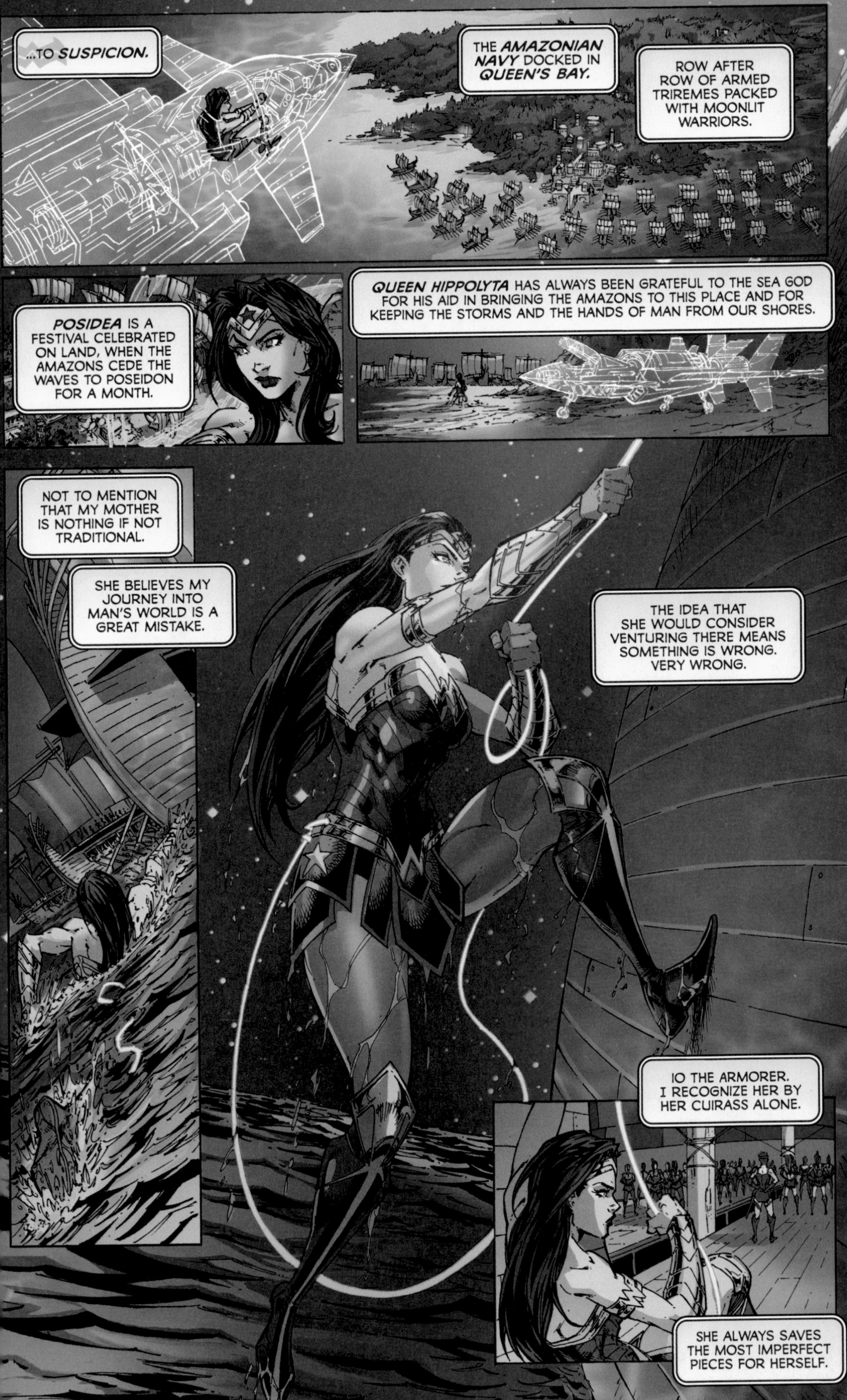
...TO SUSPICION.
THE AMAZONIAN NAVY DOCKED IN QUEEN'S BAY.
ROW AFTER ROW OF ARMED TRIREMES PACKED WITH MOONLIT WARRIORS.
POSIDEA IS A FESTIVAL CELEBRATED ON LAND, WHEN THE AMAZONS CEDE THE WAVES TO POSEIDON FOR A MONTH.
QUEEN HIPPOLYTA HAS ALWAYS BEEN GRATEFUL TO THE SEA GOD FOR HIS AID IN BRINGING THE AMAZONS TO THIS PLACE AND FOR KEEPING THE STORMS AND THE HANDS OF MAN FROM OUR SHORES.
NOT TO MENTION THAT MY MOTHER IS NOTHING IF NOT TRADITIONAL.
SHE BELIEVES MY JOURNEY INTO MAN'S WORLD IS A GREAT MISTAKE.
THE IDEA THAT SHE WOULD CONSIDER VENTURING THERE MEANS SOMETHING IS WRONG. VERY WRONG.
IO THE ARMORER. I RECOGNIZE HER BY HER CUIRASS ALONE.
SHE ALWAYS SAVES THE MOST IMPERFECT PIECES FOR HERSELF.

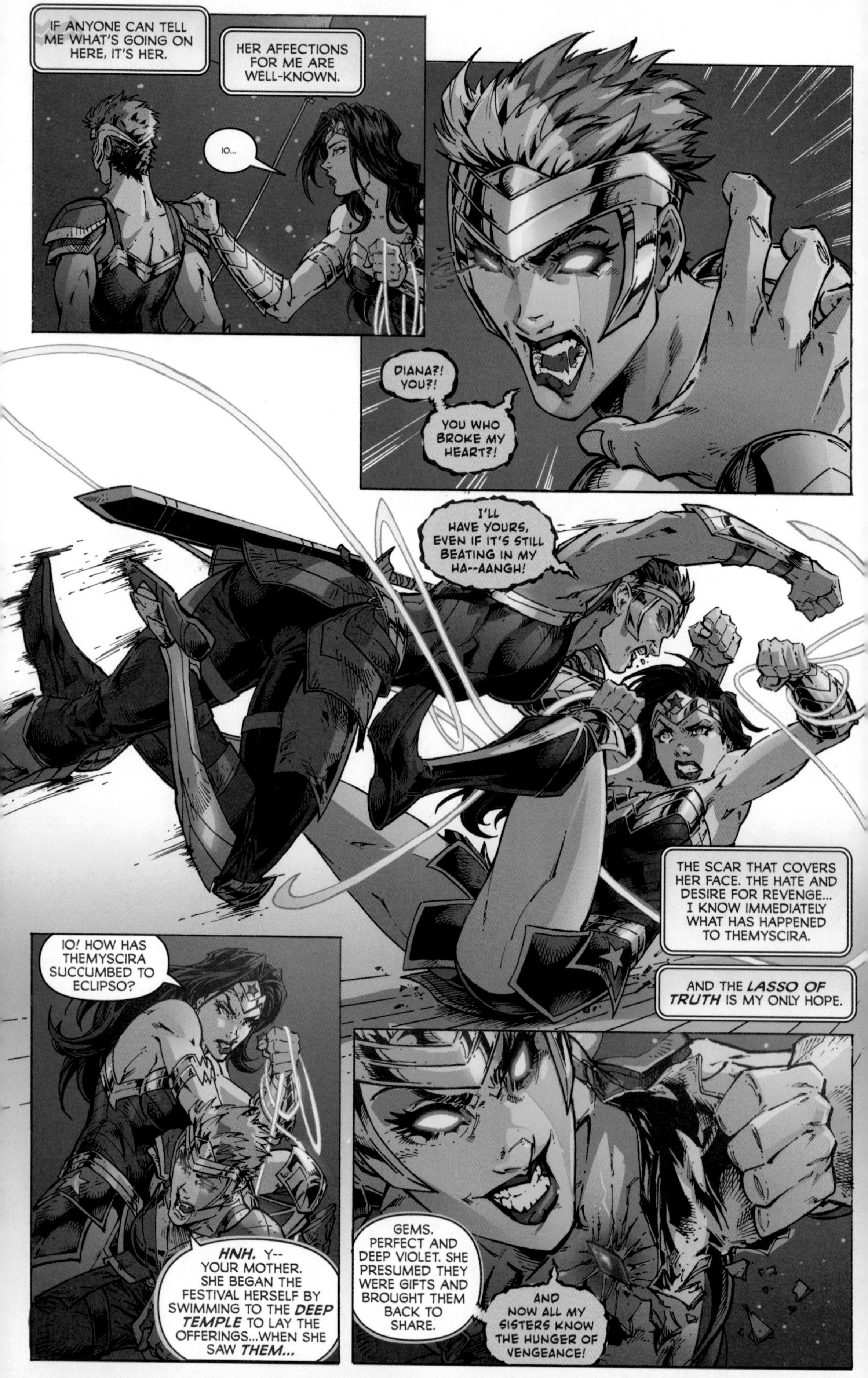
IF ANYONE CAN TELL ME WHAT'S GOING ON HERE, IT'S HER.
HER AFFECTIONS FOR ME ARE WELL-KNOWN.
IO...
DIANA?! YOU?!
YOU WHO BROKE MY HEART?!
I'LL HAVE YOURS, EVEN IF IT'S STILL BEATING IN MY HA--AANGH!
THE SCAR THAT COVERS HER FACE. THE HATE AND DESIRE FOR REVENGE... I KNOW IMMEDIATELY WHAT HAS HAPPENED TO THEMYSCIRA.
AND THE *LASSO OF TRUTH* IS MY ONLY HOPE.
IO! HOW HAS THEMYSCIRA SUCCUMBED TO ECLIPSO?
HNH. Y-- YOUR MOTHER. SHE BEGAN THE FESTIVAL HERSELF BY SWIMMING TO THE *DEEP TEMPLE* TO LAY THE OFFERINGS...WHEN SHE SAW *THEM...*
GEMS. PERFECT AND DEEP VIOLET. SHE PRESUMED THEY WERE GIFTS AND BROUGHT THEM BACK TO SHARE.
AND NOW ALL MY SISTERS KNOW THE HUNGER OF VENGEANCE!

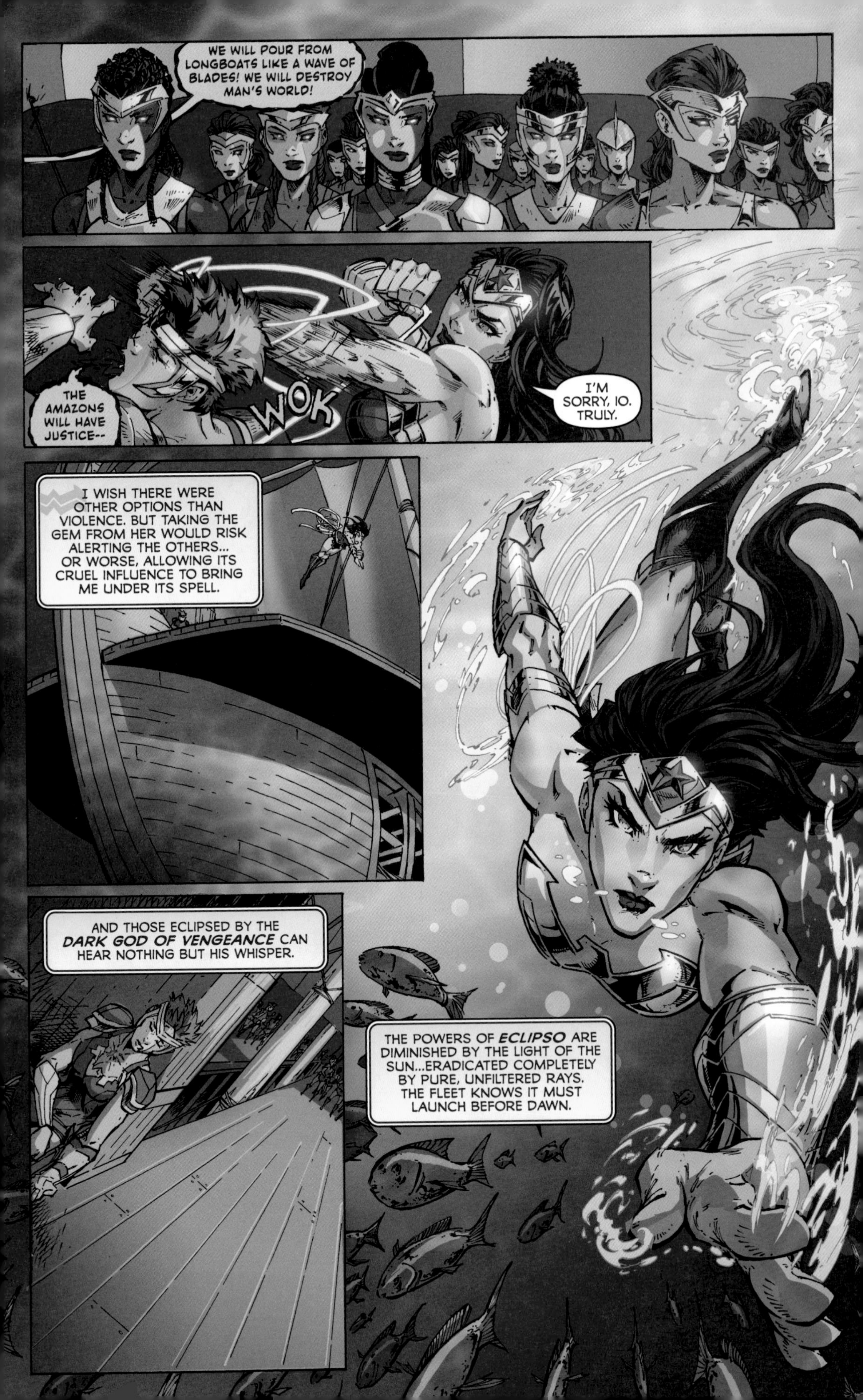

WE WILL POUR FROM LONGBOATS LIKE A WAVE OF BLADES! WE WILL DESTROY MAN'S WORLD!
THE AMAZONS WILL HAVE JUSTICE--
WOK
I'M SORRY, IO. TRULY.
I WISH THERE WERE OTHER OPTIONS THAN VIOLENCE. BUT TAKING THE GEM FROM HER WOULD RISK ALERTING THE OTHERS... OR WORSE, ALLOWING ITS CRUEL INFLUENCE TO BRING ME UNDER ITS SPELL.
AND THOSE ECLIPSED BY THE *DARK GOD OF VENGEANCE* CAN HEAR NOTHING BUT HIS WHISPER.
THE POWERS OF *ECLIPSO* ARE DIMINISHED BY THE LIGHT OF THE SUN...ERADICATED COMPLETELY BY PURE, UNFILTERED RAYS. THE FLEET KNOWS IT MUST LAUNCH BEFORE DAWN.

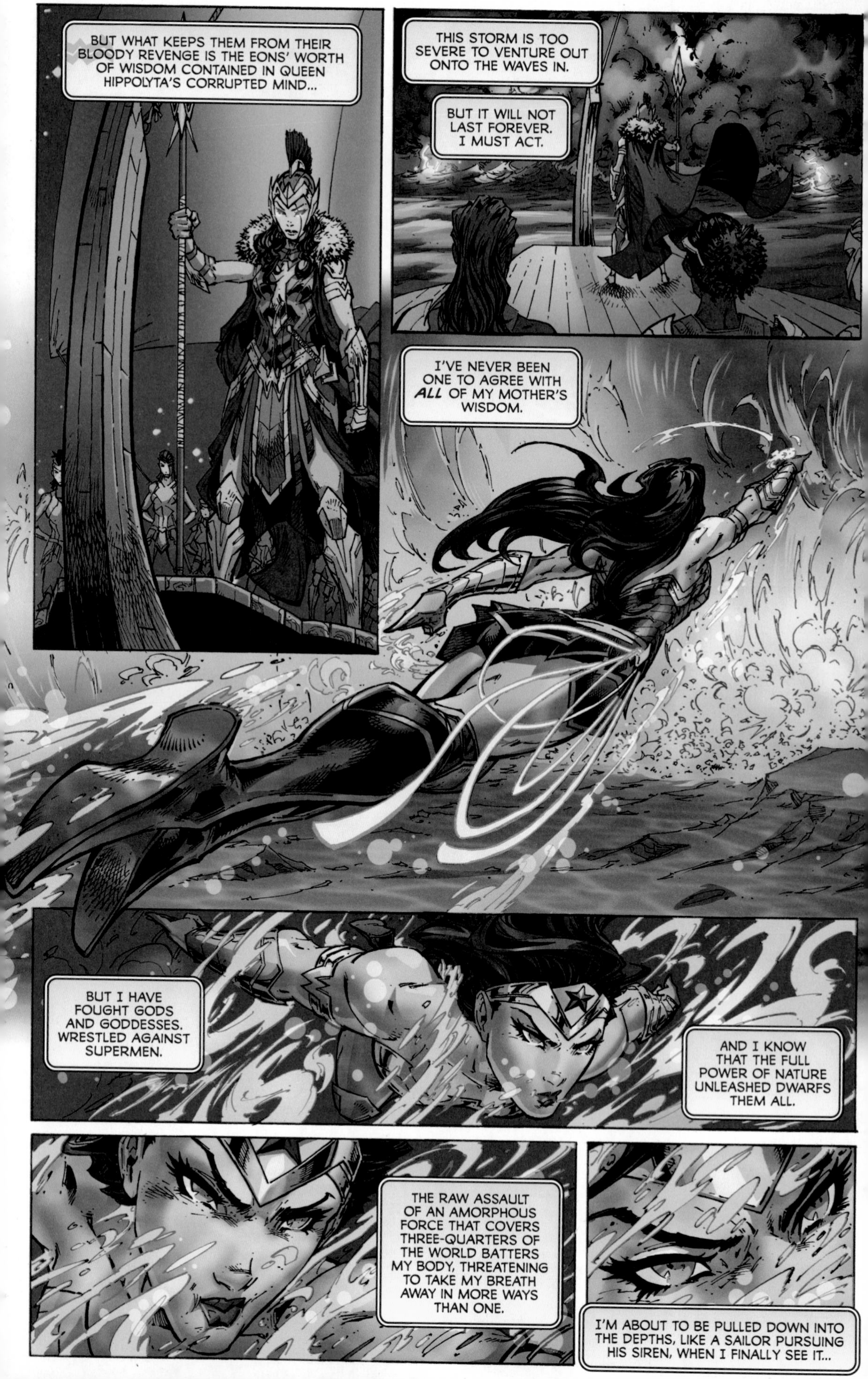
BUT WHAT KEEPS THEM FROM THEIR BLOODY REVENGE IS THE EONS' WORTH OF WISDOM CONTAINED IN QUEEN HIPPOLYTA'S CORRUPTED MIND...
THIS STORM IS TOO SEVERE TO VENTURE OUT ONTO THE WAVES IN.
BUT IT WILL NOT LAST FOREVER. I MUST ACT.
I'VE NEVER BEEN ONE TO AGREE WITH *ALL* OF MY MOTHER'S WISDOM.
BUT I HAVE FOUGHT GODS AND GODDESSES. WRESTLED AGAINST SUPERMEN.
AND I KNOW THAT THE FULL POWER OF NATURE UNLEASHED DWARFS THEM ALL.
THE RAW ASSAULT OF AN AMORPHOUS FORCE THAT COVERS THREE-QUARTERS OF THE WORLD BATTERS MY BODY, THREATENING TO TAKE MY BREATH AWAY IN MORE WAYS THAN ONE.
I'M ABOUT TO BE PULLED DOWN INTO THE DEPTHS, LIKE A SAILOR PURSUING HIS SIREN, WHEN I FINALLY SEE IT...

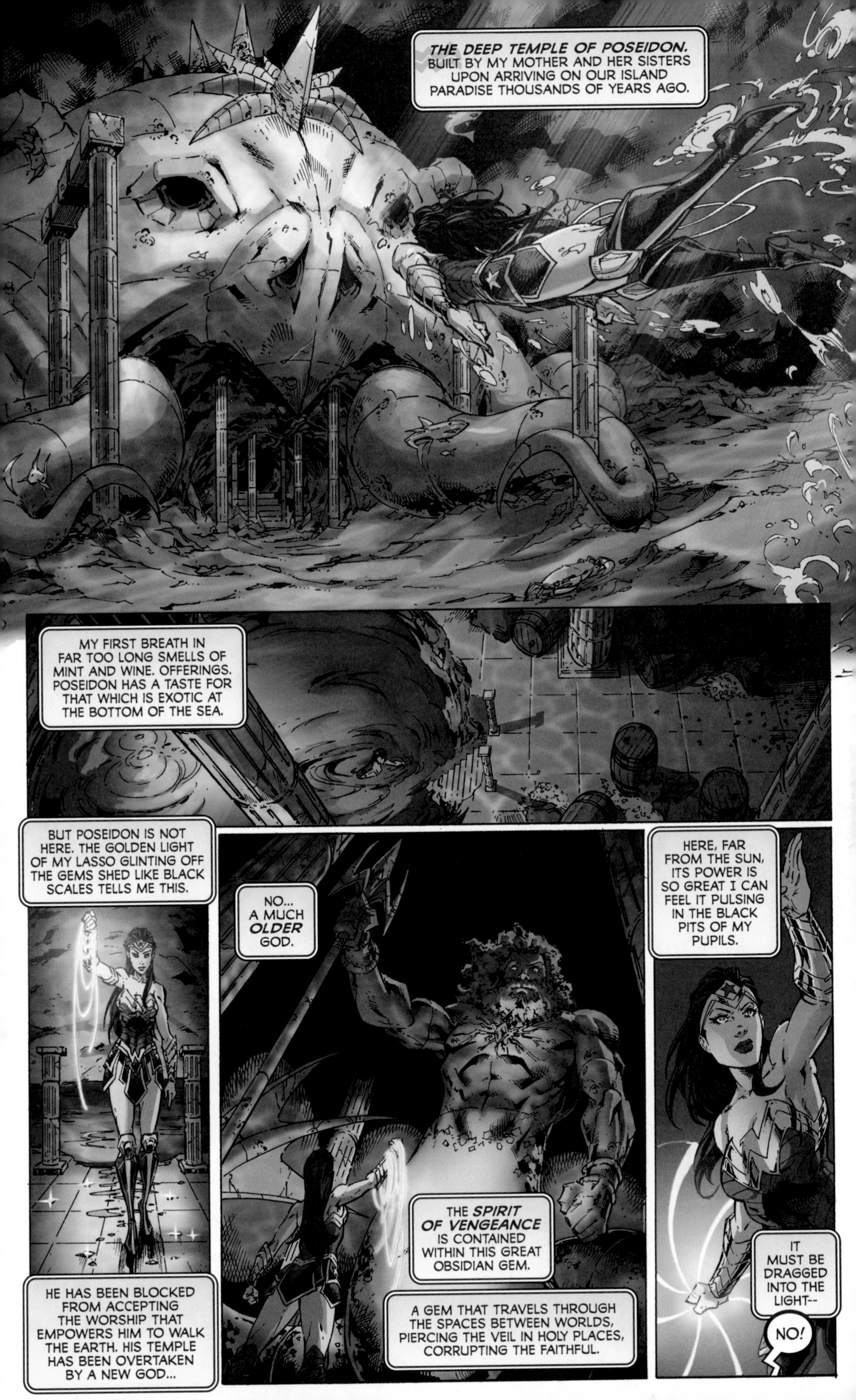

THE DEEP TEMPLE OF POSEIDON. BUILT BY MY MOTHER AND HER SISTERS UPON ARRIVING ON OUR ISLAND PARADISE THOUSANDS OF YEARS AGO.
MY FIRST BREATH IN FAR TOO LONG SMELLS OF MINT AND WINE. OFFERINGS. POSEIDON HAS A TASTE FOR THAT WHICH IS EXOTIC AT THE BOTTOM OF THE SEA.
BUT POSEIDON IS NOT HERE. THE GOLDEN LIGHT OF MY LASSO GLINTING OFF THE GEMS SHED LIKE BLACK SCALES TELLS ME THIS.
HE HAS BEEN BLOCKED FROM ACCEPTING THE WORSHIP THAT EMPOWERS HIM TO WALK THE EARTH. HIS TEMPLE HAS BEEN OVERTAKEN BY A NEW GOD...
NO... A MUCH OLDER GOD.
THE SPIRIT OF VENGEANCE IS CONTAINED WITHIN THIS GREAT OBSIDIAN GEM.
A GEM THAT TRAVELS THROUGH THE SPACES BETWEEN WORLDS, PIERCING THE VEIL IN HOLY PLACES, CORRUPTING THE FAITHFUL.
HERE, FAR FROM THE SUN, ITS POWER IS SO GREAT I CAN FEEL IT PULSING IN THE BLACK PITS OF MY PUPILS.
IT MUST BE DRAGGED INTO THE LIGHT--
NO!

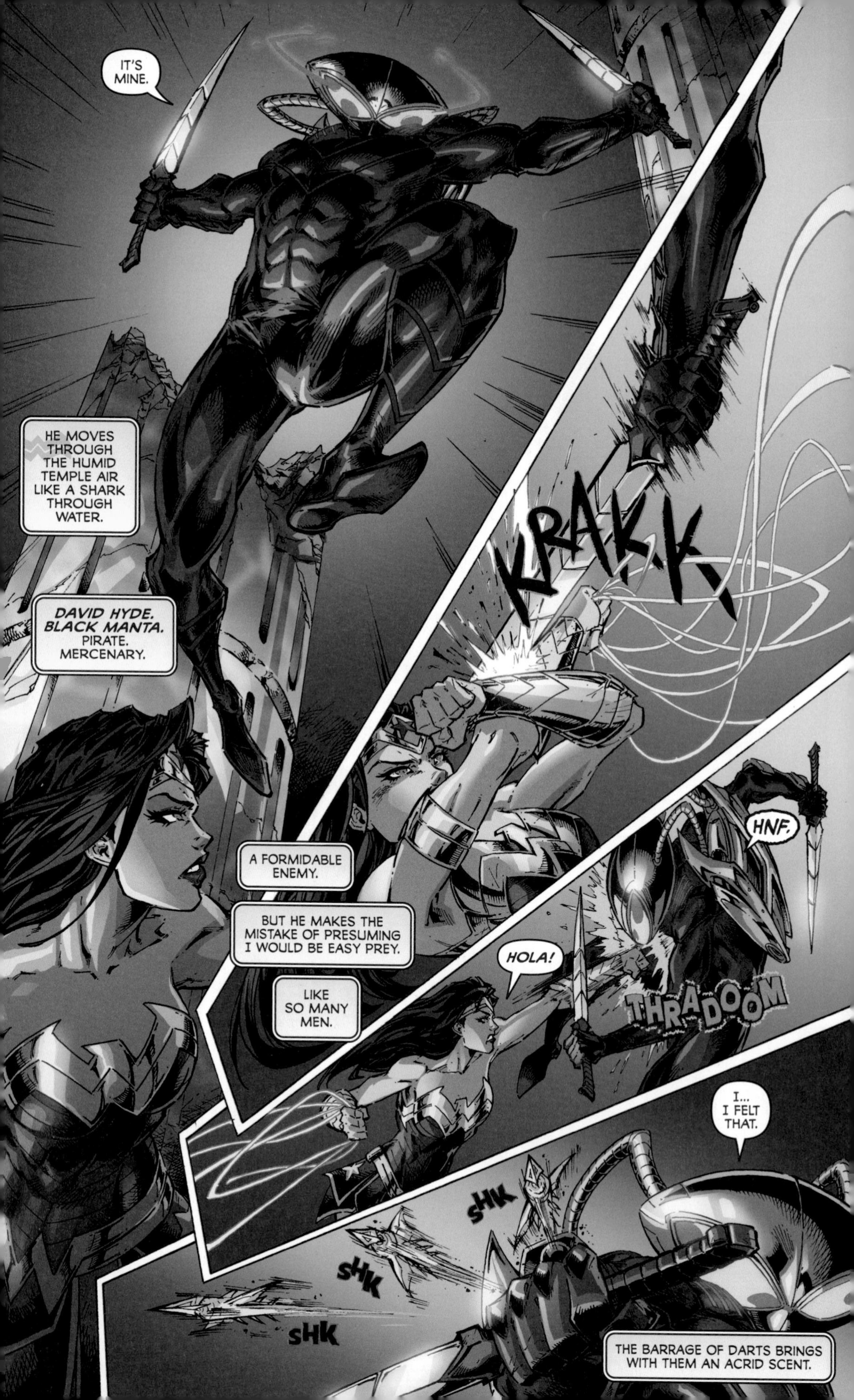
IT'S MINE.
HE MOVES THROUGH THE HUMID TEMPLE AIR LIKE A SHARK THROUGH WATER.
DAVID HYDE. BLACK MANTA. PIRATE. MERCENARY.
KRAKK
A FORMIDABLE ENEMY.
BUT HE MAKES THE MISTAKE OF PRESUMING I WOULD BE EASY PREY.
LIKE SO MANY MEN.
HNF.
HOLA!
THRADOOM
I... I FELT THAT.
SHK
SHK
SHK
THE BARRAGE OF DARTS BRINGS WITH THEM AN ACRID SCENT.

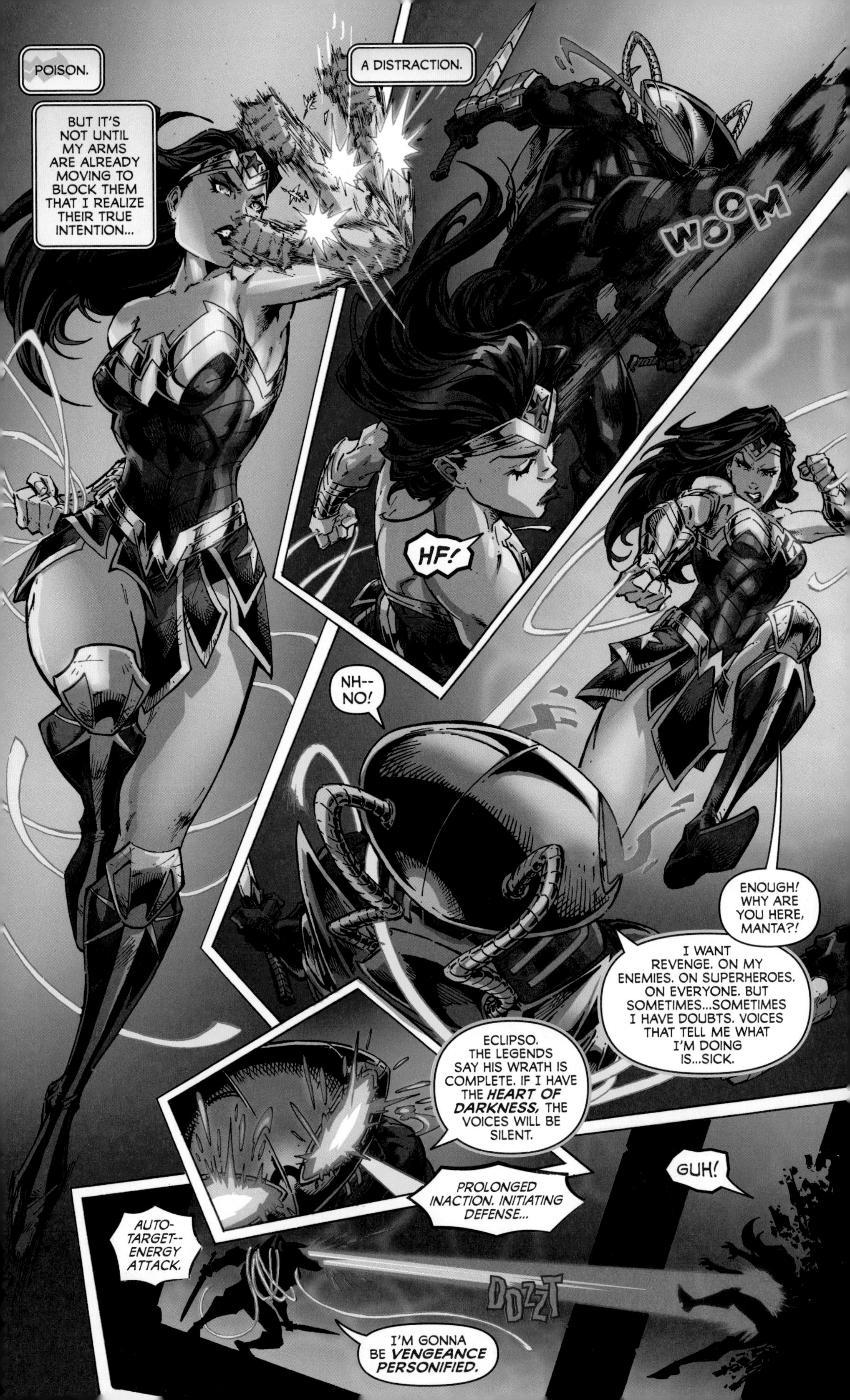
POISON.
BUT IT'S NOT UNTIL MY ARMS ARE ALREADY MOVING TO BLOCK THEM THAT I REALIZE THEIR TRUE INTENTION...
A DISTRACTION.
WOOOM
HF!
NH-- NO!
ENOUGH! WHY ARE YOU HERE, MANTA?!
I WANT REVENGE. ON MY ENEMIES. ON SUPERHEROES. ON EVERYONE. BUT SOMETIMES...SOMETIMES I HAVE DOUBTS. VOICES THAT TELL ME WHAT I'M DOING IS...SICK.
ECLIPSO. THE LEGENDS SAY HIS WRATH IS COMPLETE. IF I HAVE THE HEART OF DARKNESS, THE VOICES WILL BE SILENT.
PROLONGED INACTION. INITIATING DEFENSE...
GUH!
AUTO-TARGET-- ENERGY ATTACK.
DOZZT
I'M GONNA BE VENGEANCE PERSONIFIED.

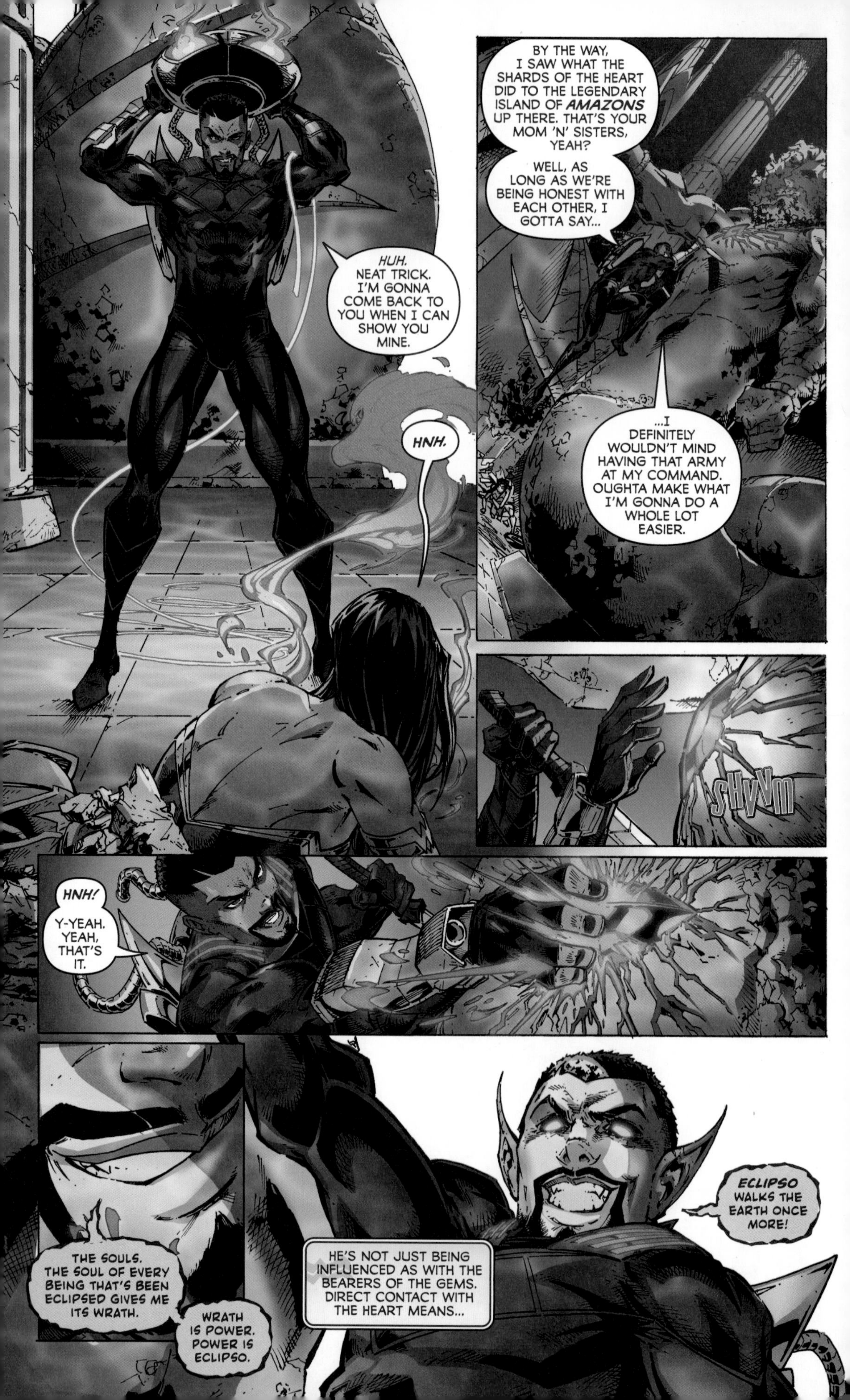
HUH. NEAT TRICK. I'M GONNA COME BACK TO YOU WHEN I CAN SHOW YOU MINE.
HNH.
BY THE WAY, I SAW WHAT THE SHARDS OF THE HEART DID TO THE LEGENDARY ISLAND OF AMAZONS UP THERE. THAT'S YOUR MOM 'N' SISTERS, YEAH?
WELL, AS LONG AS WE'RE BEING HONEST WITH EACH OTHER, I GOTTA SAY...
...I DEFINITELY WOULDN'T MIND HAVING THAT ARMY AT MY COMMAND. OUGHTA MAKE WHAT I'M GONNA DO A WHOLE LOT EASIER.
SHVVM
HNH!
Y-YEAH. YEAH, THAT'S IT.
THE SOULS. THE SOUL OF EVERY BEING THAT'S BEEN ECLIPSED GIVES ME ITS WRATH.
WRATH IS POWER. POWER IS ECLIPSO.
HE'S NOT JUST BEING INFLUENCED AS WITH THE BEARERS OF THE GEMS. DIRECT CONTACT WITH THE HEART MEANS...
ECLIPSO WALKS THE EARTH ONCE MORE!

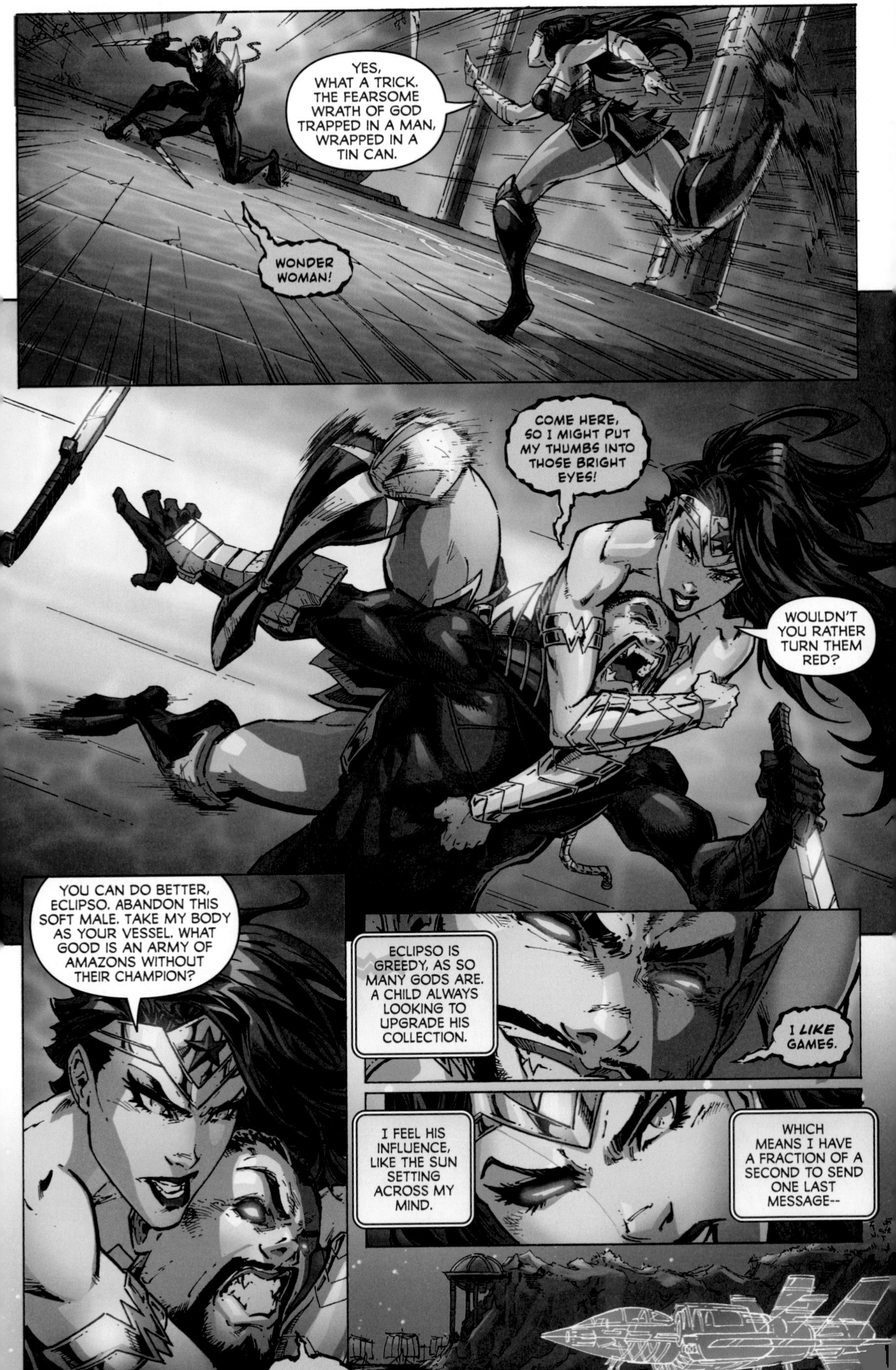
YES, WHAT A TRICK. THE FEARSOME WRATH OF GOD TRAPPED IN A MAN, WRAPPED IN A TIN CAN.
WONDER WOMAN!
COME HERE, SO I MIGHT PUT MY THUMBS INTO THOSE BRIGHT EYES!
WOULDN'T YOU RATHER TURN THEM RED?
YOU CAN DO BETTER, ECLIPSO. ABANDON THIS SOFT MALE. TAKE MY BODY AS YOUR VESSEL. WHAT GOOD IS AN ARMY OF AMAZONS WITHOUT THEIR CHAMPION?
YOU PLAY GAMES.
ECLIPSO IS GREEDY, AS SO MANY GODS ARE. A CHILD ALWAYS LOOKING TO UPGRADE HIS COLLECTION.
I LIKE GAMES.
I FEEL HIS INFLUENCE, LIKE THE SUN SETTING ACROSS MY MIND.
WHICH MEANS I HAVE A FRACTION OF A SECOND TO SEND ONE LAST MESSAGE--
THRRRMMMM

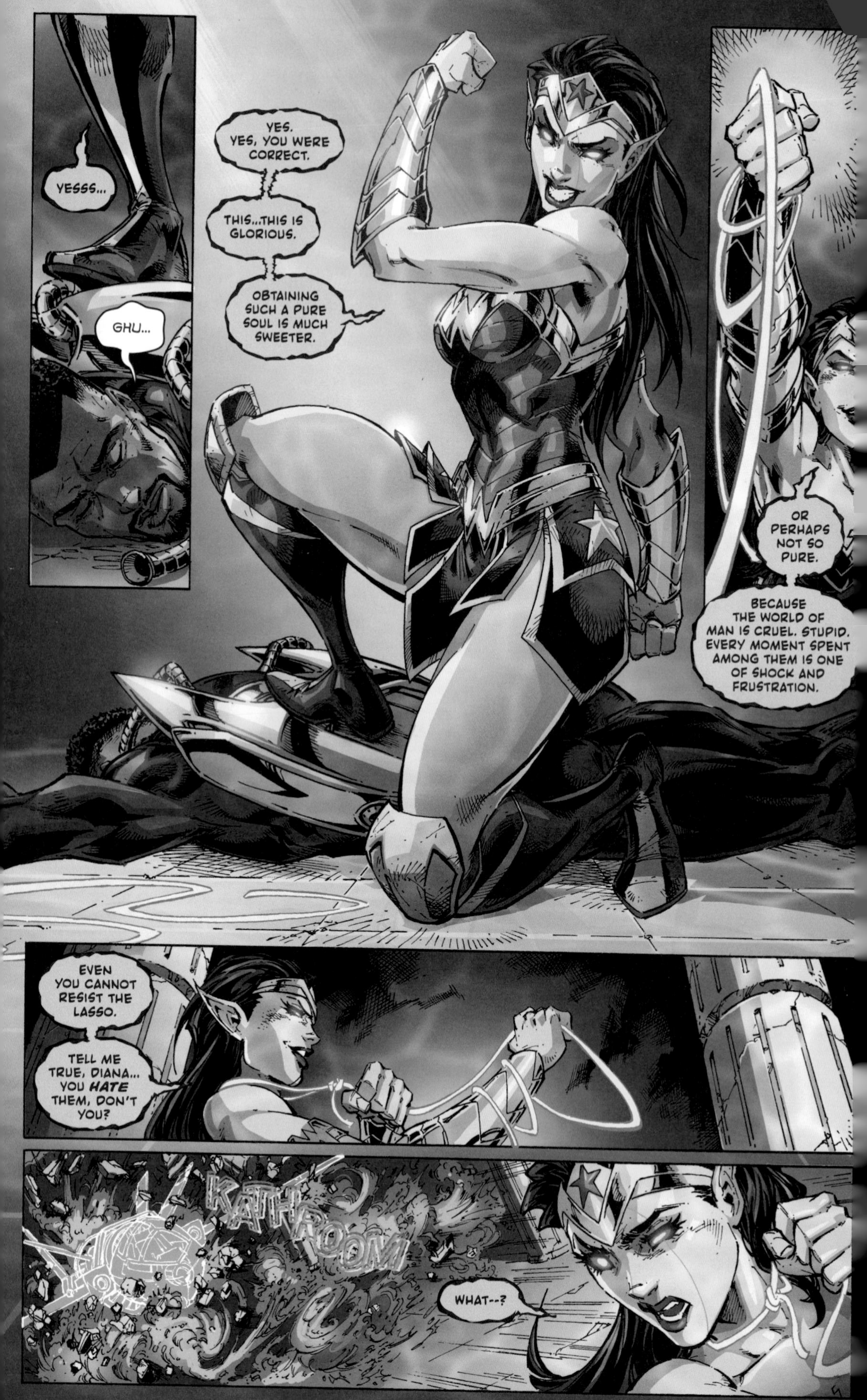
YESSS...
GHU...
YES. YES, YOU WERE CORRECT.
THIS...THIS IS GLORIOUS.
OBTAINING SUCH A PURE SOUL IS MUCH SWEETER.
OR PERHAPS NOT SO PURE.
BECAUSE THE WORLD OF MAN IS CRUEL. STUPID. EVERY MOMENT SPENT AMONG THEM IS ONE OF SHOCK AND FRUSTRATION.
EVEN YOU CANNOT RESIST THE LASSO.
TELL ME TRUE, DIANA... YOU *HATE* THEM, DON'T YOU?
KATHROOM
WHAT--?

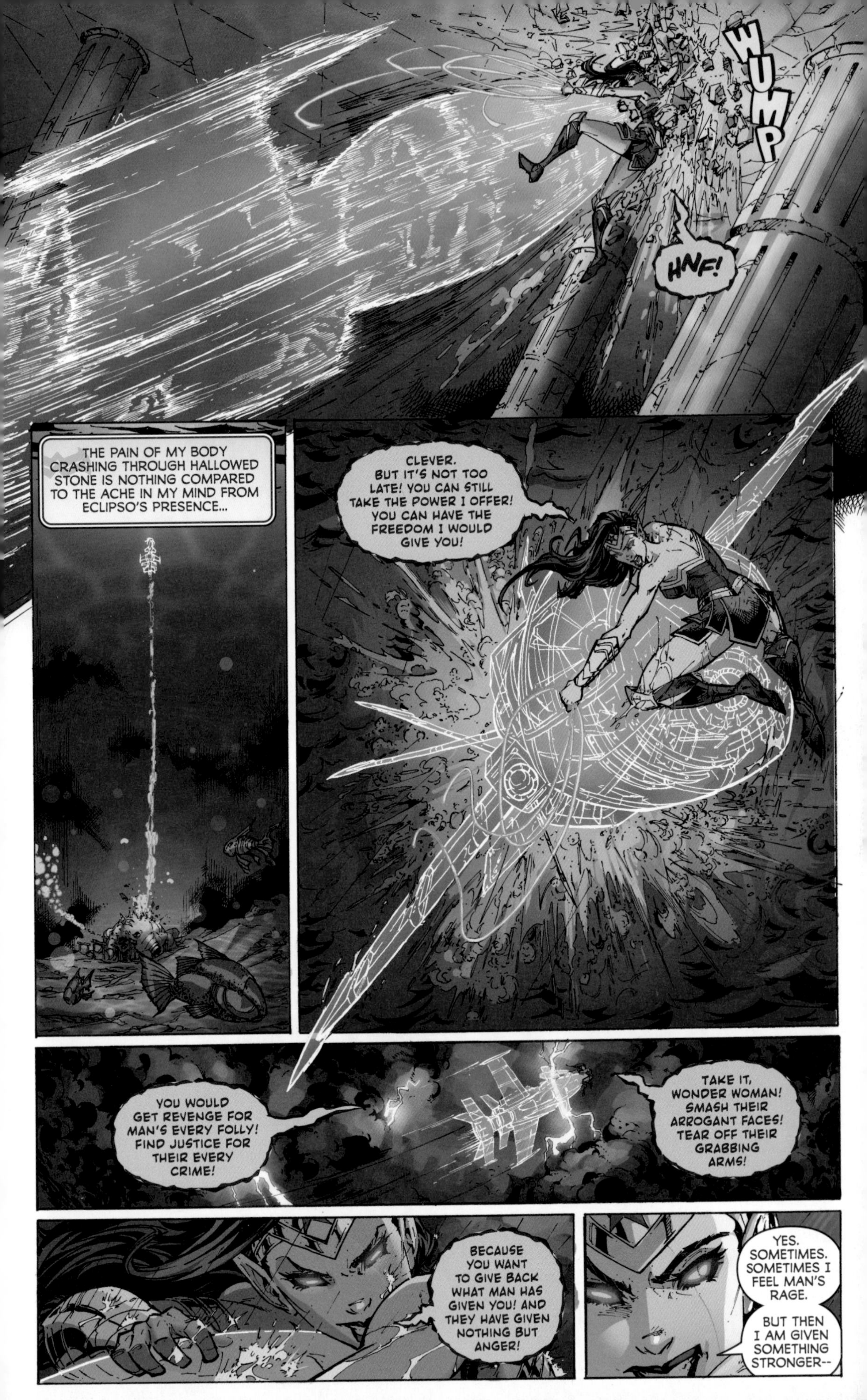
WUMP
HNF!
THE PAIN OF MY BODY CRASHING THROUGH HALLOWED STONE IS NOTHING COMPARED TO THE ACHE IN MY MIND FROM ECLIPSO'S PRESENCE...
CLEVER. BUT IT'S NOT TOO LATE! YOU CAN STILL TAKE THE POWER I OFFER! YOU CAN HAVE THE FREEDOM I WOULD GIVE YOU!
YOU WOULD GET REVENGE FOR MAN'S EVERY FOLLY! FIND JUSTICE FOR THEIR EVERY CRIME!
TAKE IT, WONDER WOMAN! SMASH THEIR ARROGANT FACES! TEAR OFF THEIR GRABBING ARMS!
BECAUSE YOU WANT TO GIVE BACK WHAT MAN HAS GIVEN YOU! AND THEY HAVE GIVEN NOTHING BUT ANGER!
YES. SOMETIMES. SOMETIMES I FEEL MAN'S RAGE.
BUT THEN I AM GIVEN SOMETHING STRONGER--

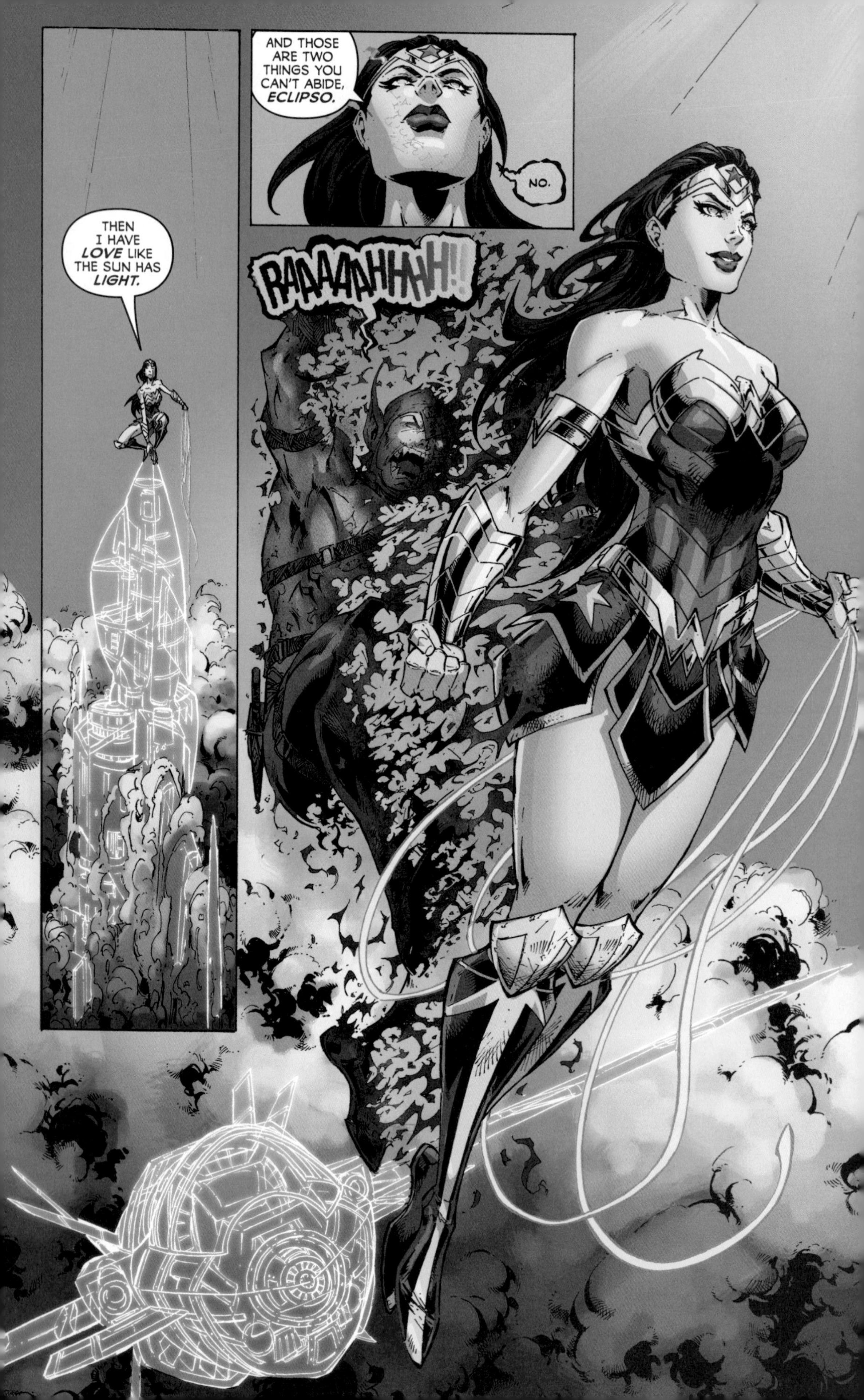
AND THOSE ARE TWO THINGS YOU CAN'T ABIDE, ECLIPSO.
NO.
THEN I HAVE LOVE LIKE THE SUN HAS LIGHT.
RAAAAAHHHH!!

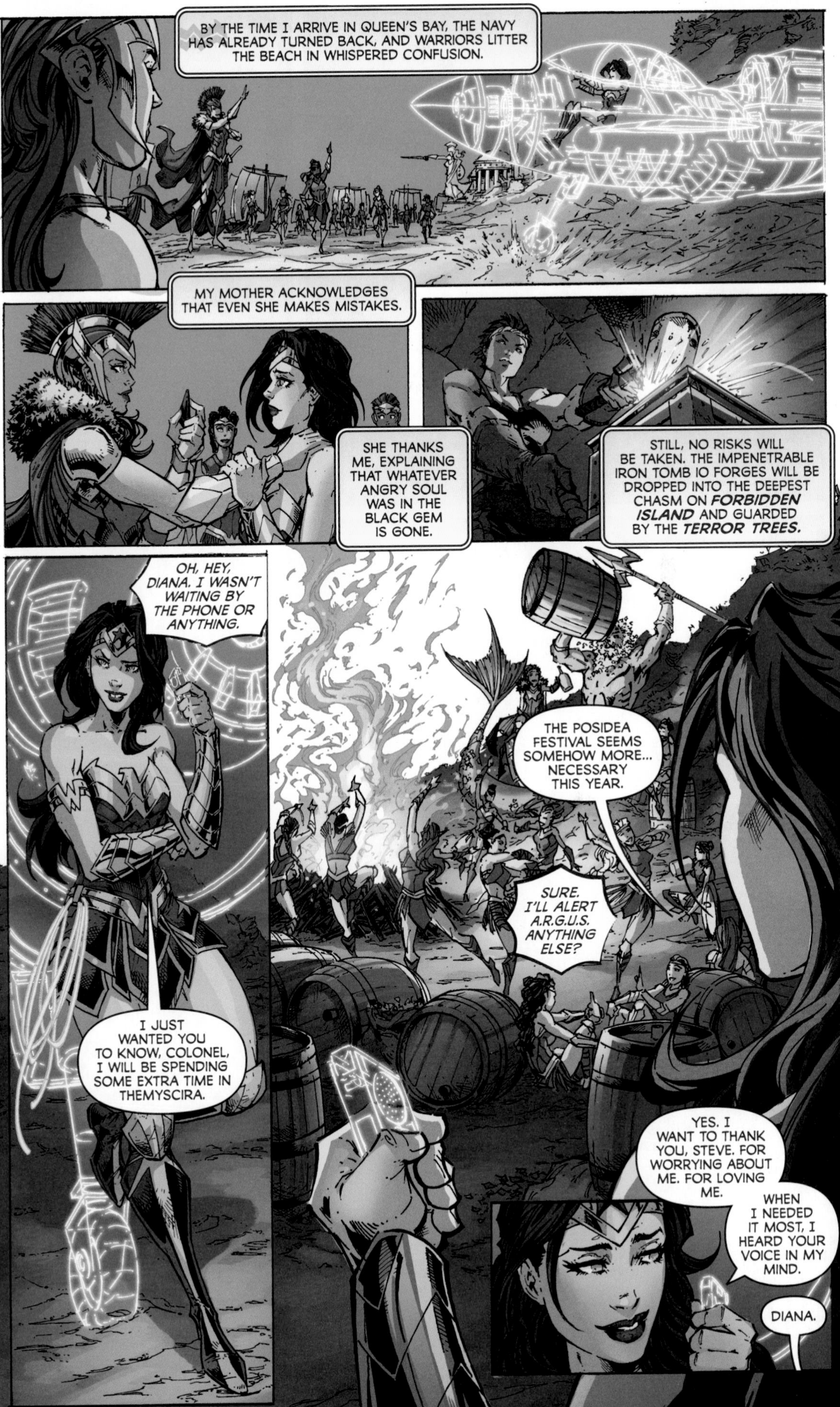

BY THE TIME I ARRIVE IN QUEEN'S BAY, THE NAVY HAS ALREADY TURNED BACK, AND WARRIORS LITTER THE BEACH IN WHISPERED CONFUSION.
MY MOTHER ACKNOWLEDGES THAT EVEN SHE MAKES MISTAKES.
SHE THANKS ME, EXPLAINING THAT WHATEVER ANGRY SOUL WAS IN THE BLACK GEM IS GONE.
STILL, NO RISKS WILL BE TAKEN. THE IMPENETRABLE IRON TOMB IO FORGES WILL BE DROPPED INTO THE DEEPEST CHASM ON *FORBIDDEN ISLAND* AND GUARDED BY THE *TERROR TREES.*
OH, HEY, DIANA. I WASN'T WAITING BY THE PHONE OR ANYTHING.
THE POSIDEA FESTIVAL SEEMS SOMEHOW MORE... NECESSARY THIS YEAR.
SURE. I'LL ALERT A.R.G.U.S. ANYTHING ELSE?
I JUST WANTED YOU TO KNOW, COLONEL, I WILL BE SPENDING SOME EXTRA TIME IN THEMYSCIRA.
YES. I WANT TO THANK YOU, STEVE. FOR WORRYING ABOUT ME. FOR LOVING ME.
WHEN I NEEDED IT MOST, I HEARD YOUR VOICE IN MY MIND.
DIANA.

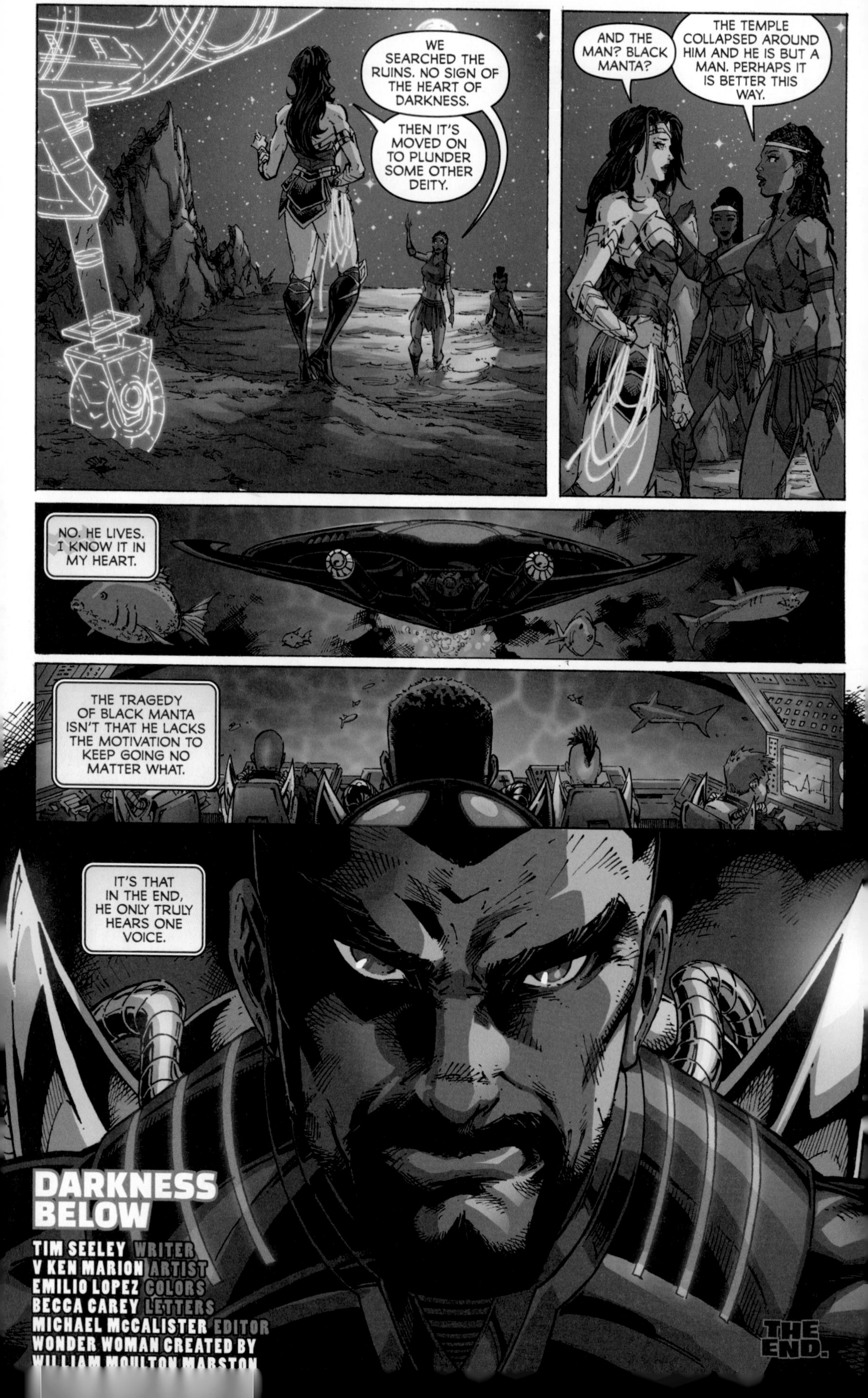

WE SEARCHED THE RUINS. NO SIGN OF THE HEART OF DARKNESS.
THEN IT'S MOVED ON TO PLUNDER SOME OTHER DEITY.
AND THE MAN? BLACK MANTA?
THE TEMPLE COLLAPSED AROUND HIM AND HE IS BUT A MAN. PERHAPS IT IS BETTER THIS WAY.
NO. HE LIVES. I KNOW IT IN MY HEART.
THE TRAGEDY OF BLACK MANTA ISN'T THAT HE LACKS THE MOTIVATION TO KEEP GOING NO MATTER WHAT.
IT'S THAT IN THE END, HE ONLY TRULY HEARS ONE VOICE.
DARKNESS BELOW
TIM SEELEY WRITER
V KEN MARION ARTIST
EMILIO LOPEZ COLORS
BECCA CAREY LETTERS
MICHAEL McCALISTER EDITOR
WONDER WOMAN CREATED BY
WILLIAM MOULTON MARSTON
THE END.

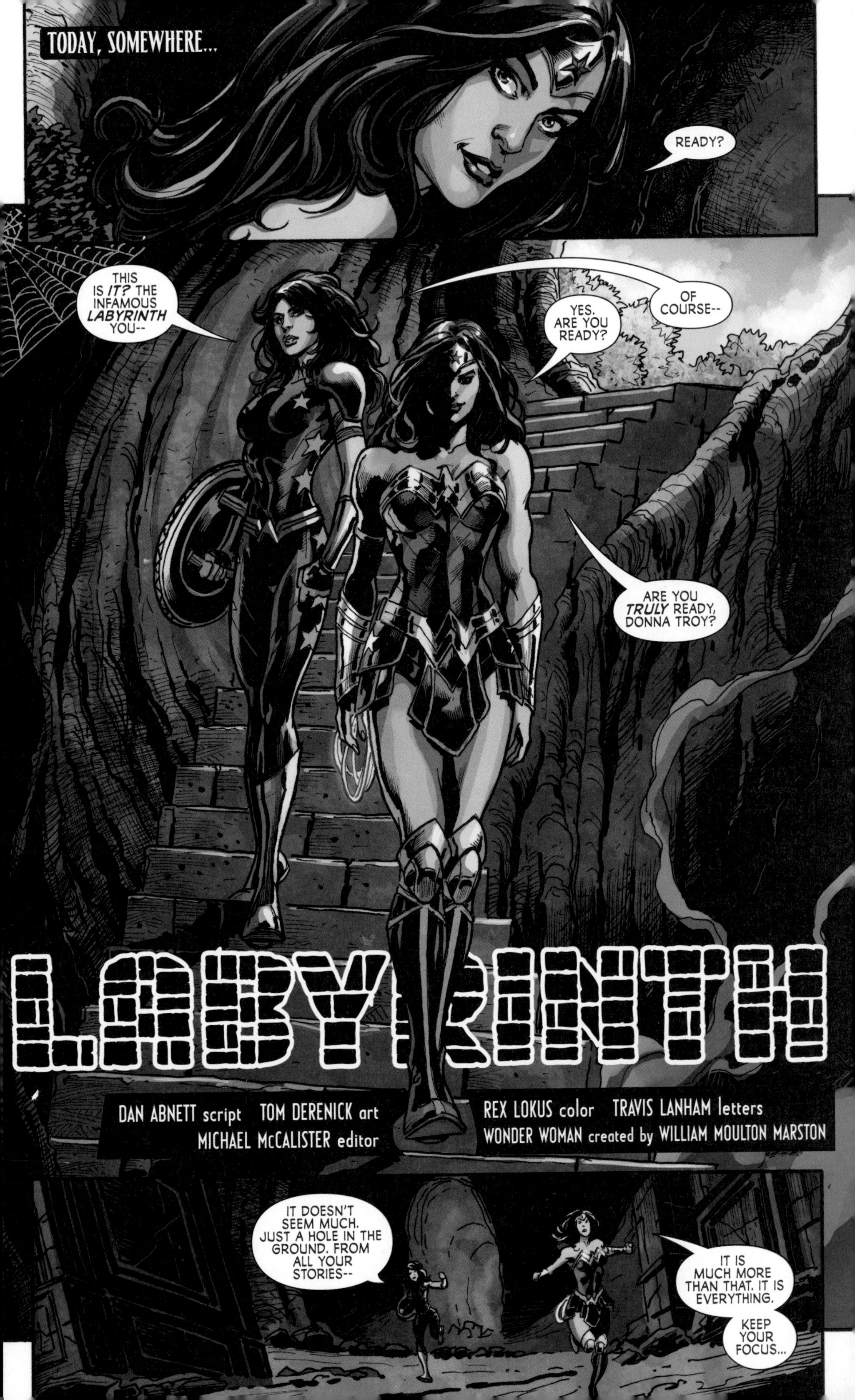
TODAY, SOMEWHERE...
READY?
THIS IS IT? THE INFAMOUS LABYRINTH YOU--
OF COURSE--
YES. ARE YOU READY?
ARE YOU TRULY READY, DONNA TROY?
LABYRINTH
DAN ABNETT script TOM DERENICK art
MICHAEL McCALISTER editor
REX LOKUS color TRAVIS LANHAM letters
WONDER WOMAN created by WILLIAM MOULTON MARSTON
IT DOESN'T SEEM MUCH. JUST A HOLE IN THE GROUND. FROM ALL YOUR STORIES--
IT IS MUCH MORE THAN THAT. IT IS EVERYTHING.
KEEP YOUR FOCUS...

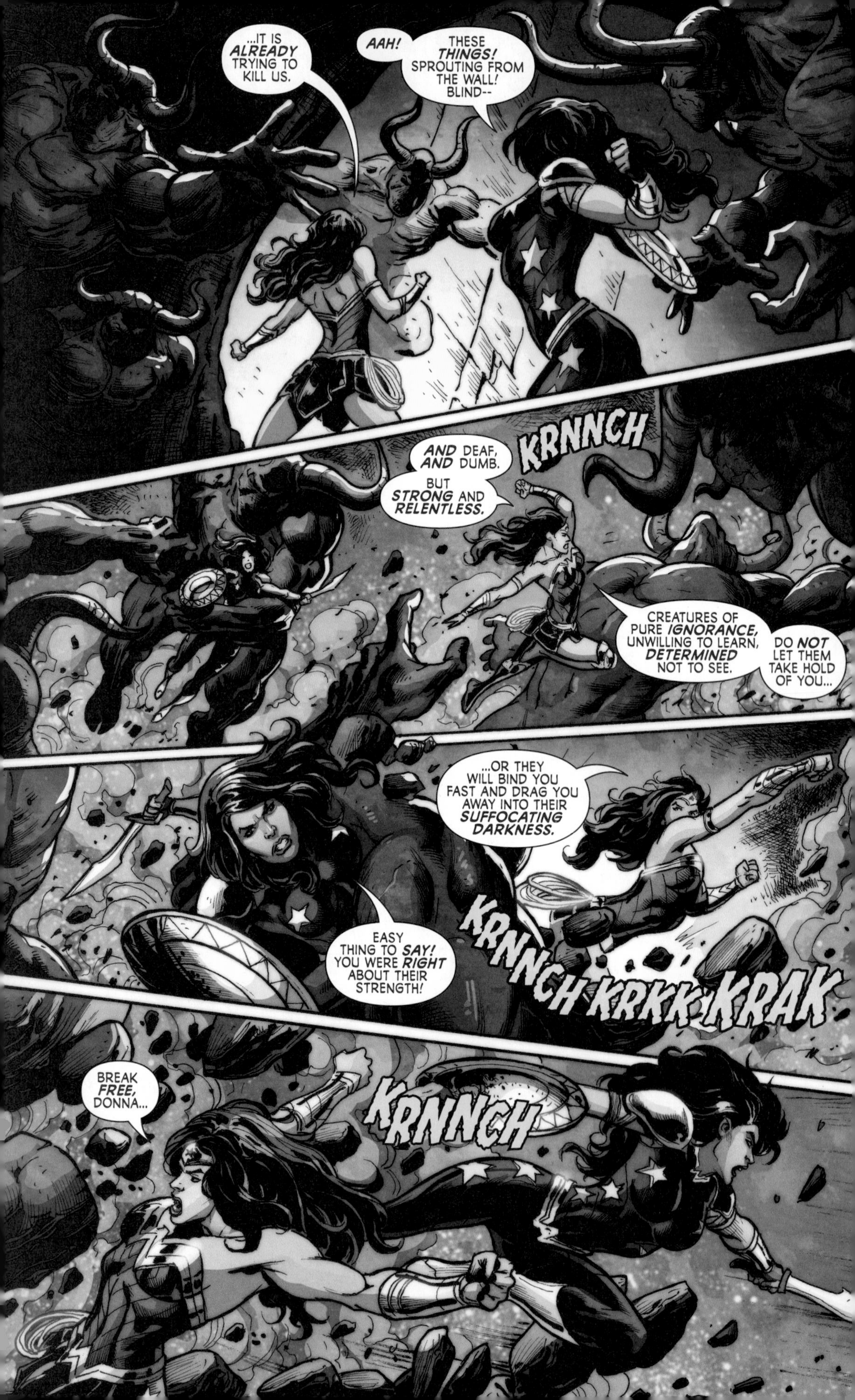
...IT IS *ALREADY* TRYING TO KILL US.
AAH!
THESE *THINGS!* SPROUTING FROM THE WALL! BLIND--
KRNNCH
AND DEAF, *AND* DUMB. BUT *STRONG* AND *RELENTLESS.*
CREATURES OF PURE *IGNORANCE,* UNWILLING TO LEARN, *DETERMINED* NOT TO SEE.
DO *NOT* LET THEM TAKE HOLD OF YOU...
...OR THEY WILL BIND YOU FAST AND DRAG YOU AWAY INTO THEIR *SUFFOCATING DARKNESS.*
EASY THING TO *SAY!* YOU WERE *RIGHT* ABOUT THEIR STRENGTH!
KRNNCH KRKK KRAK
BREAK *FREE,* DONNA...
KRNNCH

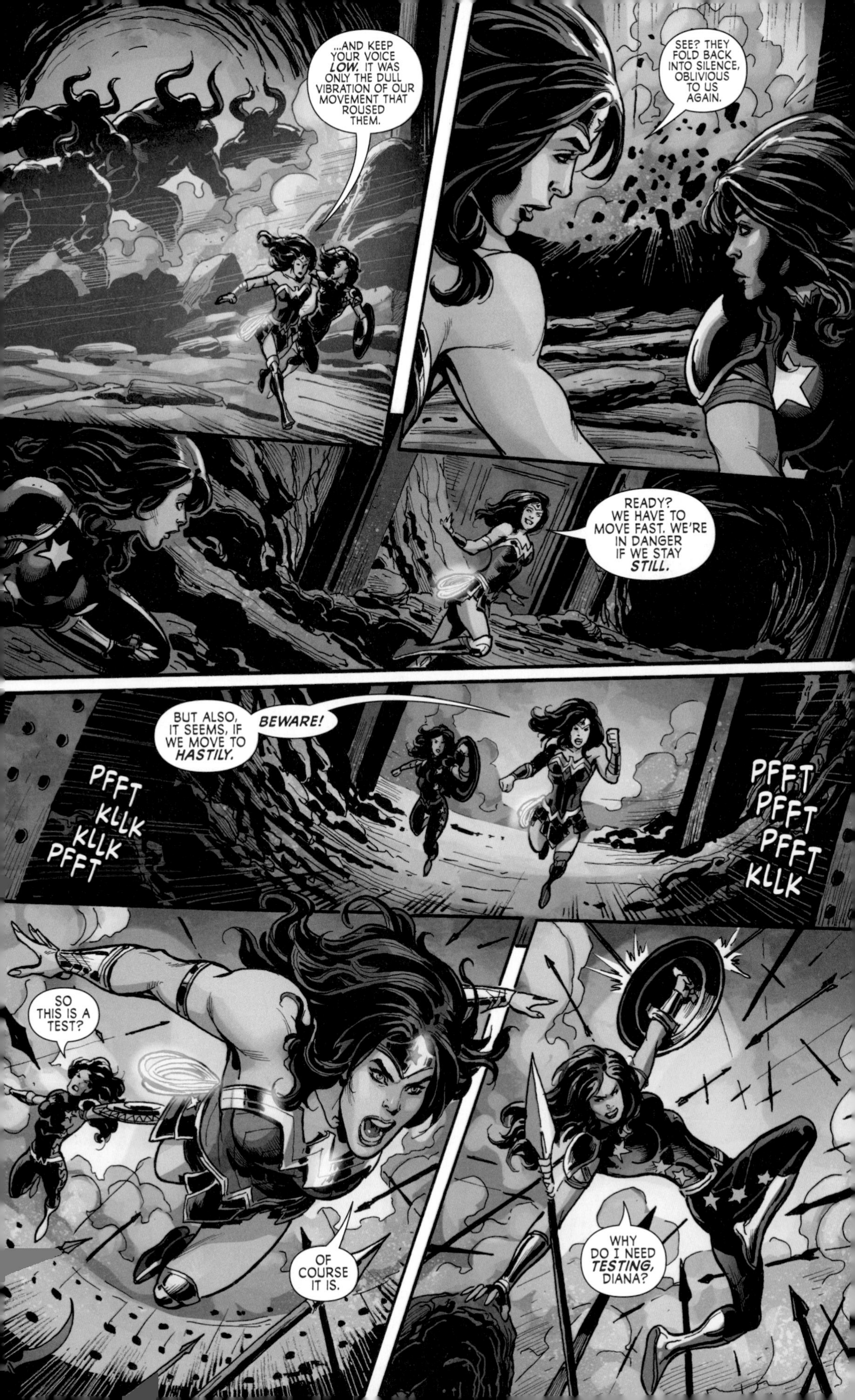
...AND KEEP YOUR VOICE LOW. IT WAS ONLY THE DULL VIBRATION OF OUR MOVEMENT THAT ROUSED THEM.
SEE? THEY FOLD BACK INTO SILENCE, OBLIVIOUS TO US AGAIN.
READY? WE HAVE TO MOVE FAST. WE'RE IN DANGER IF WE STAY STILL.
BUT ALSO, IT SEEMS, IF WE MOVE TO HASTILY.
BEWARE!
PFFT KLLK KLLK PFFT
PFFT PFFT PFFT KLLK
SO THIS IS A TEST?
OF COURSE IT IS.
WHY DO I NEED TESTING, DIANA?

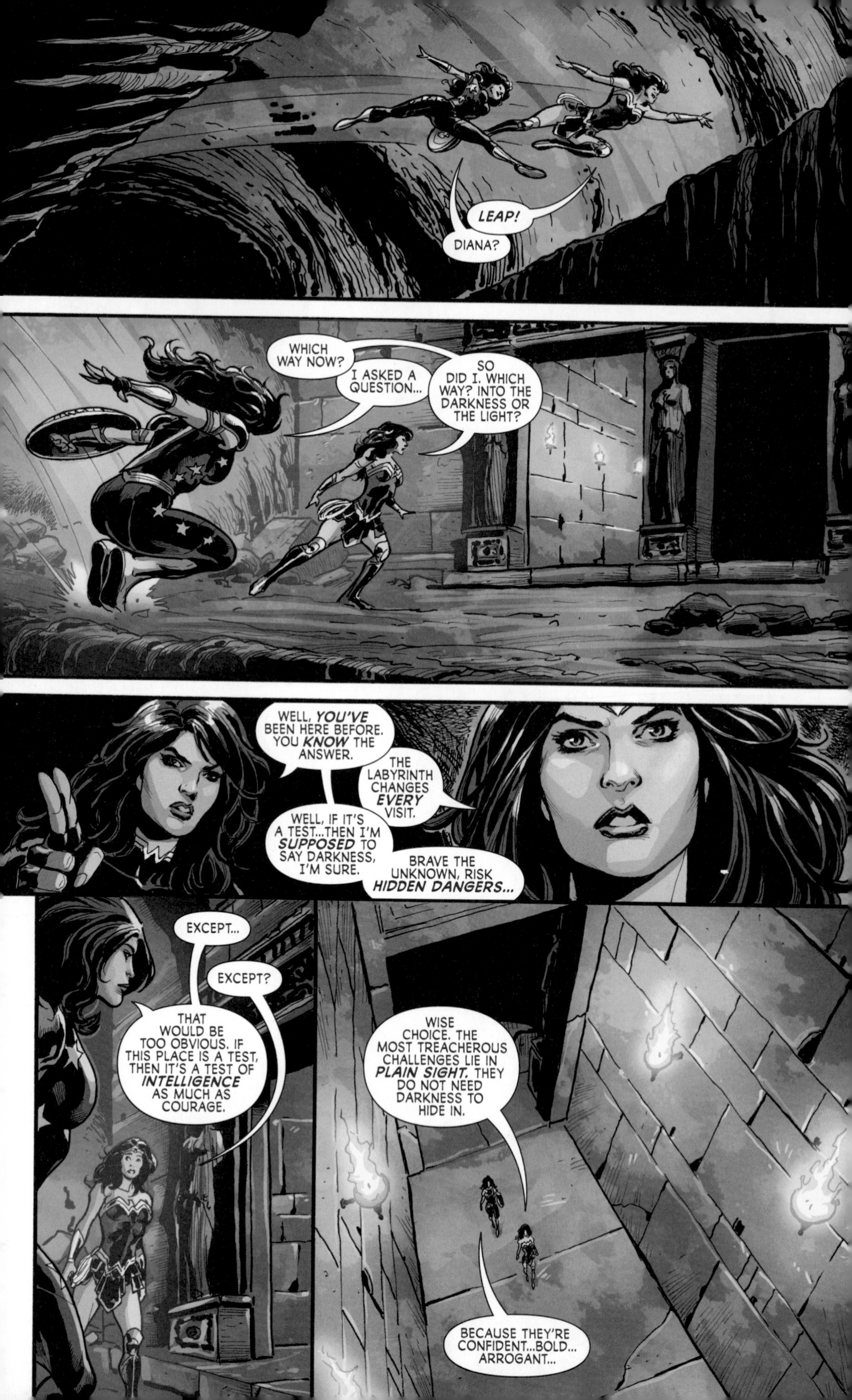
LEAP!
DIANA?
WHICH WAY NOW?
I ASKED A QUESTION...
SO DID I. WHICH WAY? INTO THE DARKNESS OR THE LIGHT?
WELL, YOU'VE BEEN HERE BEFORE. YOU KNOW THE ANSWER.
THE LABYRINTH CHANGES EVERY VISIT.
WELL, IF IT'S A TEST...THEN I'M SUPPOSED TO SAY DARKNESS, I'M SURE.
BRAVE THE UNKNOWN, RISK HIDDEN DANGERS...
EXCEPT...
EXCEPT?
THAT WOULD BE TOO OBVIOUS. IF THIS PLACE IS A TEST, THEN IT'S A TEST OF INTELLIGENCE AS MUCH AS COURAGE.
WISE CHOICE. THE MOST TREACHEROUS CHALLENGES LIE IN PLAIN SIGHT. THEY DO NOT NEED DARKNESS TO HIDE IN.
BECAUSE THEY'RE CONFIDENT...BOLD... ARROGANT...

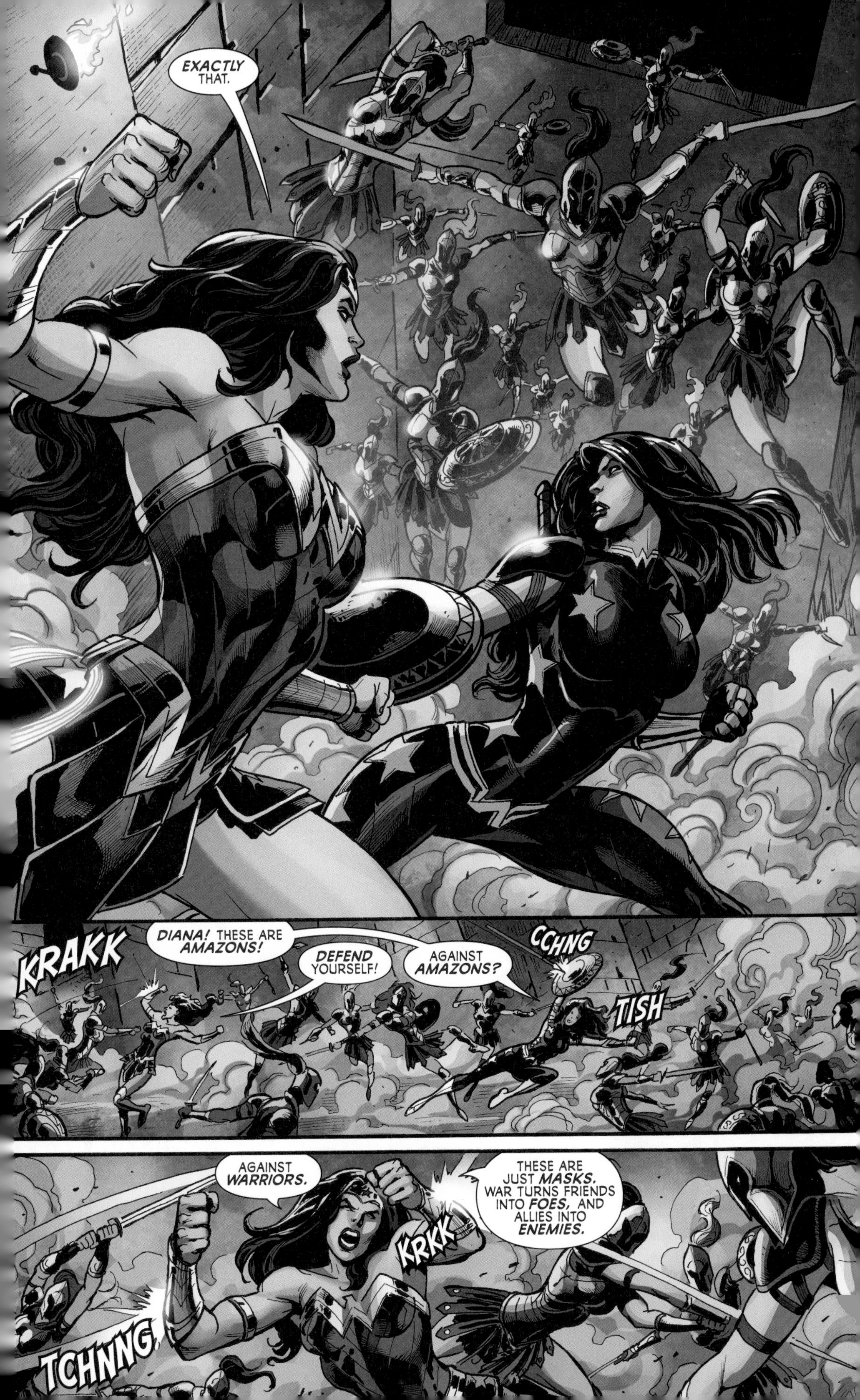
EXACTLY THAT.
KRAKK
DIANA! THESE ARE AMAZONS!
DEFEND YOURSELF!
AGAINST AMAZONS?
CCHNG
TISH
AGAINST WARRIORS.
THESE ARE JUST MASKS. WAR TURNS FRIENDS INTO FOES, AND ALLIES INTO ENEMIES.
KRKK
TCHNNG

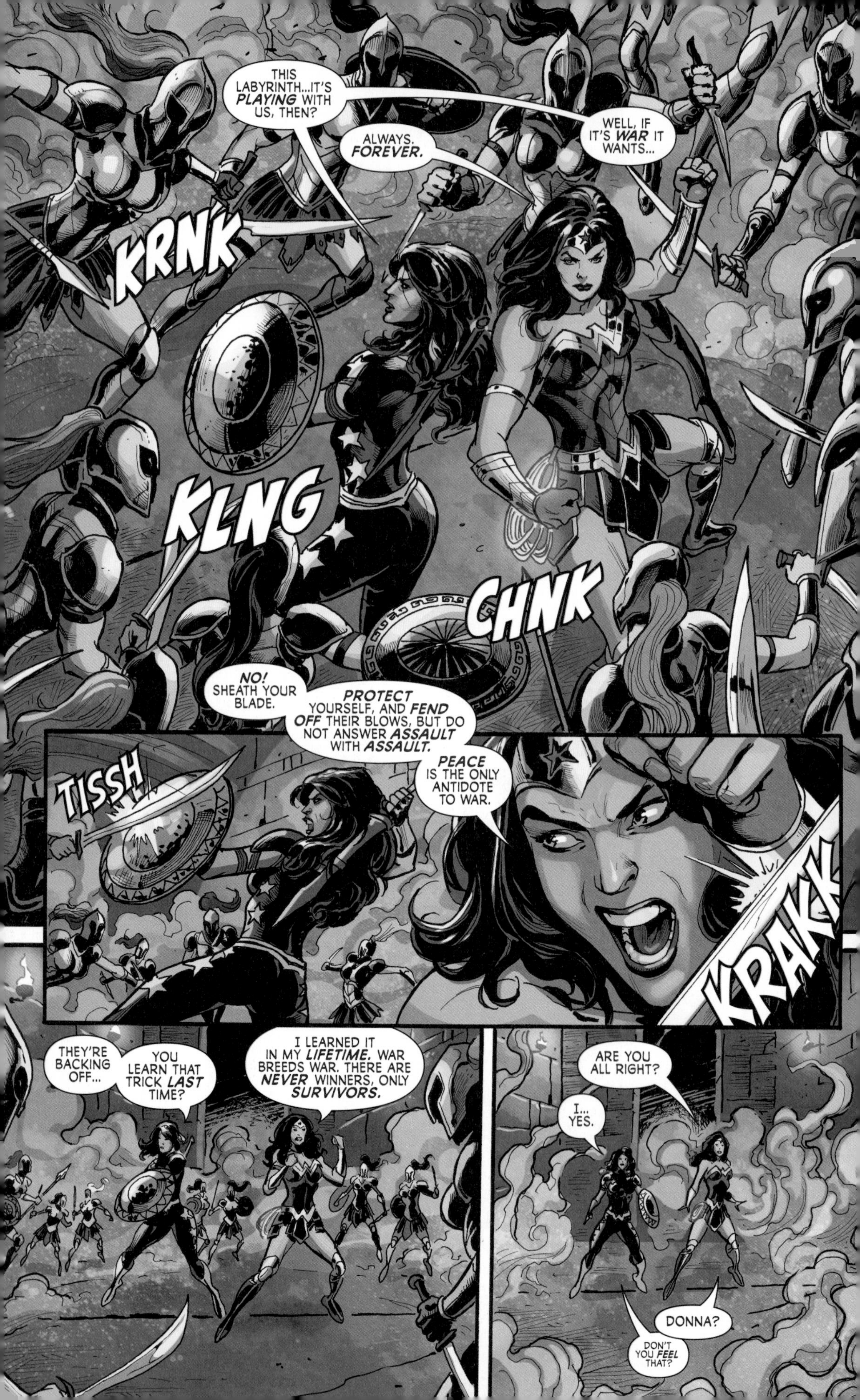

THIS LABYRINTH...IT'S *PLAYING* WITH US, THEN?
ALWAYS. *FOREVER.*
WELL, IF IT'S *WAR* IT WANTS...
KRNK
KLNG
CHNK
NO! SHEATH YOUR BLADE.
PROTECT YOURSELF, AND *FEND OFF* THEIR BLOWS, BUT DO NOT ANSWER *ASSAULT* WITH *ASSAULT.*
PEACE IS THE ONLY ANTIDOTE TO WAR.
TISSH
KRAKK
THEY'RE BACKING OFF...
YOU LEARN THAT TRICK *LAST* TIME?
I LEARNED IT IN MY *LIFETIME.* WAR BREEDS WAR. THERE ARE *NEVER* WINNERS, ONLY *SURVIVORS.*
ARE YOU ALL RIGHT?
I... YES.
DONNA?
DON'T YOU *FEEL* THAT?

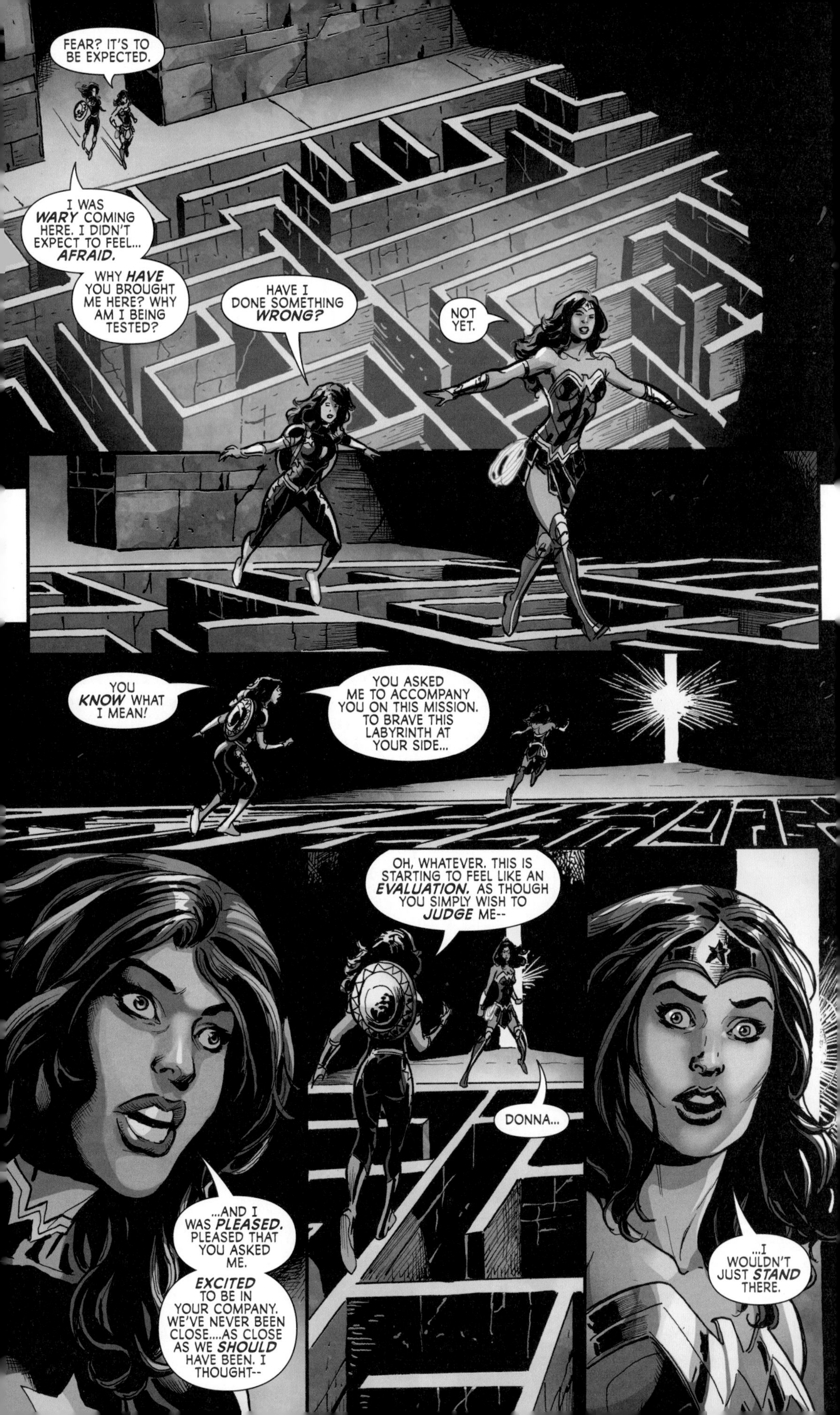
FEAR? IT'S TO BE EXPECTED.
I WAS WARY COMING HERE. I DIDN'T EXPECT TO FEEL... AFRAID.
WHY HAVE YOU BROUGHT ME HERE? WHY AM I BEING TESTED?
HAVE I DONE SOMETHING WRONG?
NOT YET.
YOU KNOW WHAT I MEAN!
YOU ASKED ME TO ACCOMPANY YOU ON THIS MISSION. TO BRAVE THIS LABYRINTH AT YOUR SIDE...
...AND I WAS PLEASED. PLEASED THAT YOU ASKED ME.
EXCITED TO BE IN YOUR COMPANY. WE'VE NEVER BEEN CLOSE....AS CLOSE AS WE SHOULD HAVE BEEN. I THOUGHT--
OH, WHATEVER. THIS IS STARTING TO FEEL LIKE AN EVALUATION. AS THOUGH YOU SIMPLY WISH TO JUDGE ME--
DONNA...
...I WOULDN'T JUST STAND THERE.

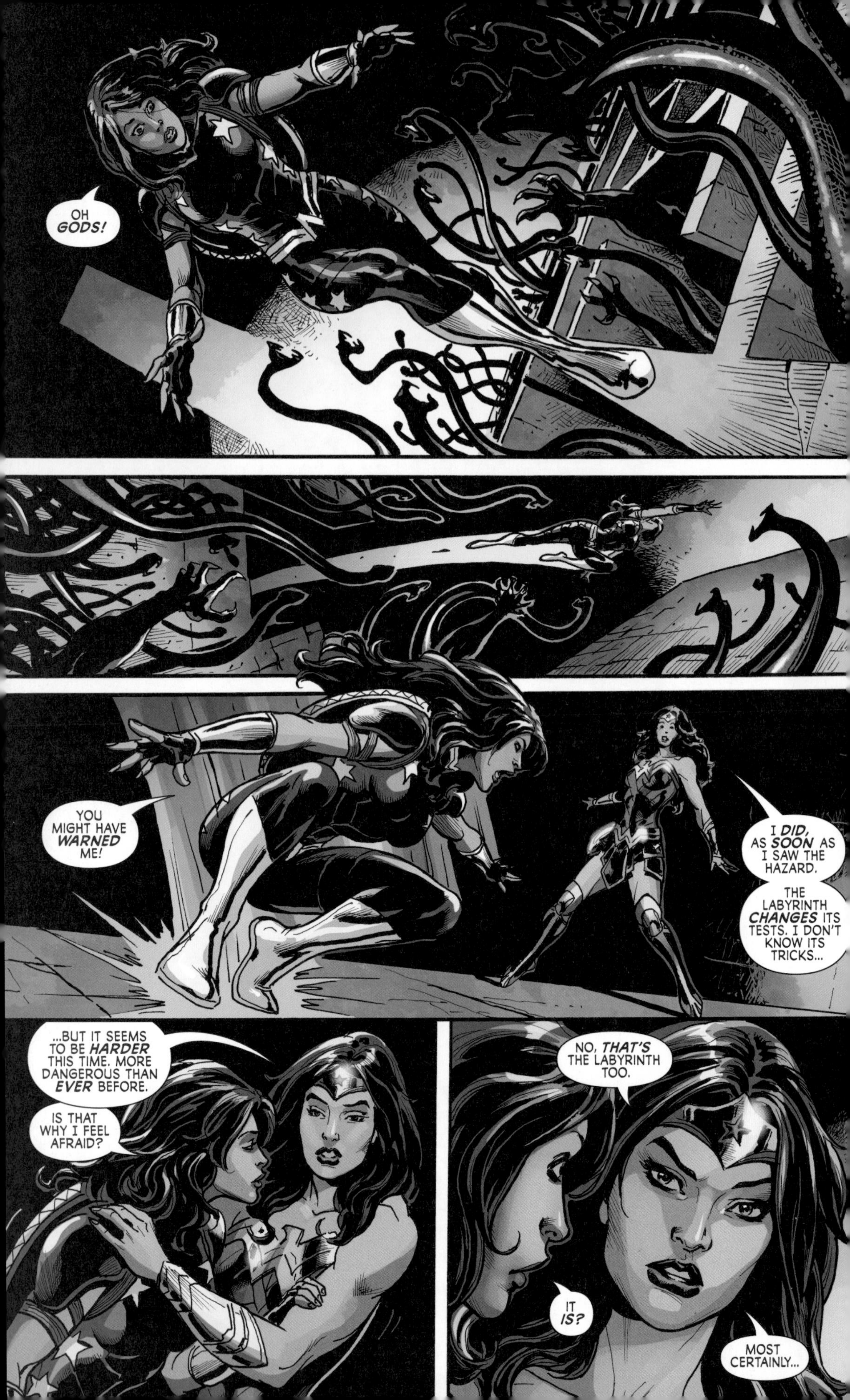
OH GODS!
YOU MIGHT HAVE WARNED ME!
I DID, AS SOON AS I SAW THE HAZARD.
THE LABYRINTH CHANGES ITS TESTS. I DON'T KNOW ITS TRICKS...
...BUT IT SEEMS TO BE HARDER THIS TIME. MORE DANGEROUS THAN EVER BEFORE.
IS THAT WHY I FEEL AFRAID?
NO, THAT'S THE LABYRINTH TOO.
IT IS?
MOST CERTAINLY...

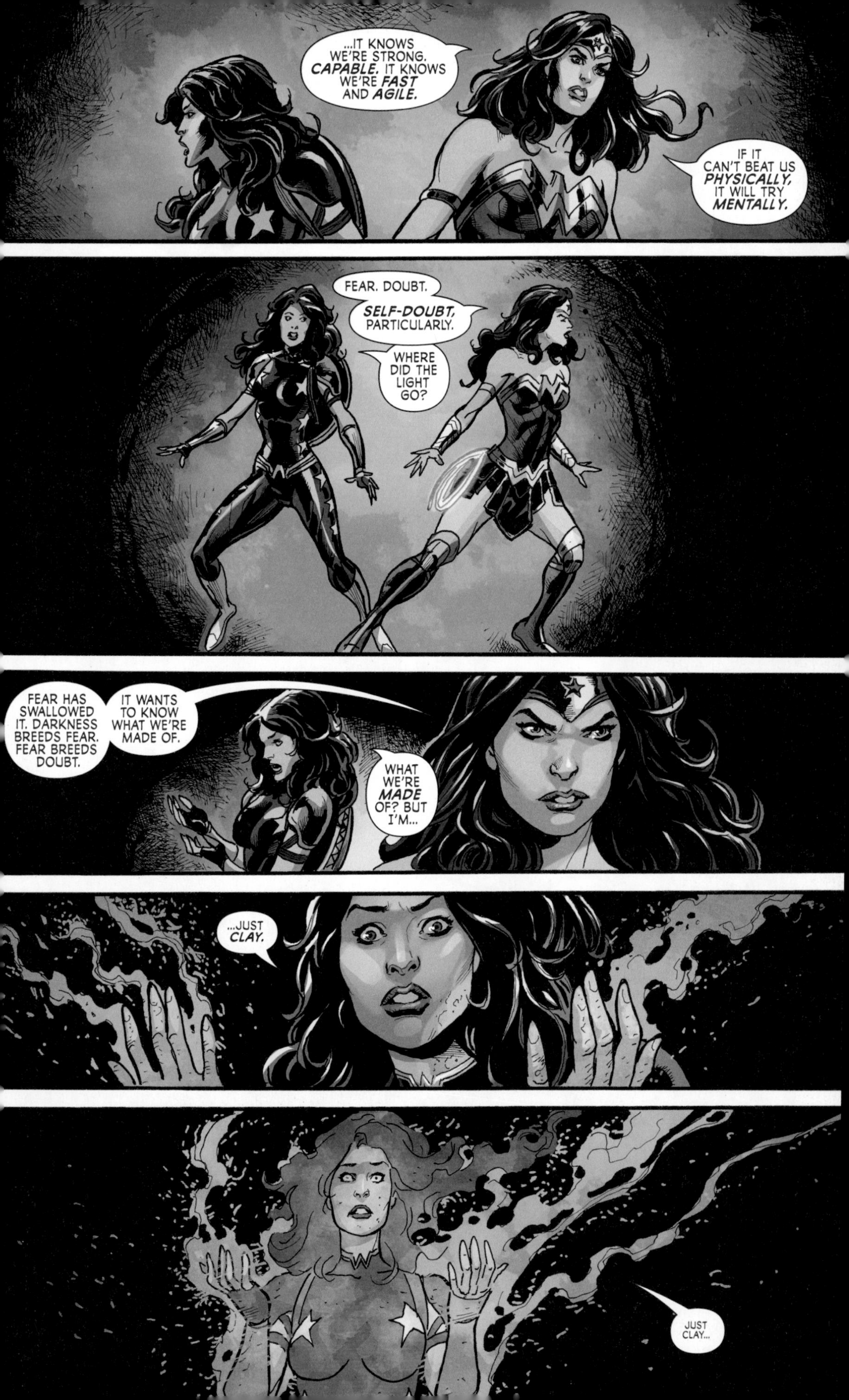
...IT KNOWS WE'RE STRONG. CAPABLE. IT KNOWS WE'RE FAST AND AGILE.
IF IT CAN'T BEAT US PHYSICALLY, IT WILL TRY MENTALLY.
FEAR. DOUBT.
SELF-DOUBT, PARTICULARLY.
WHERE DID THE LIGHT GO?
FEAR HAS SWALLOWED IT. DARKNESS BREEDS FEAR. FEAR BREEDS DOUBT.
IT WANTS TO KNOW WHAT WE'RE MADE OF.
WHAT WE'RE MADE OF? BUT I'M...
...JUST CLAY.
JUST CLAY...

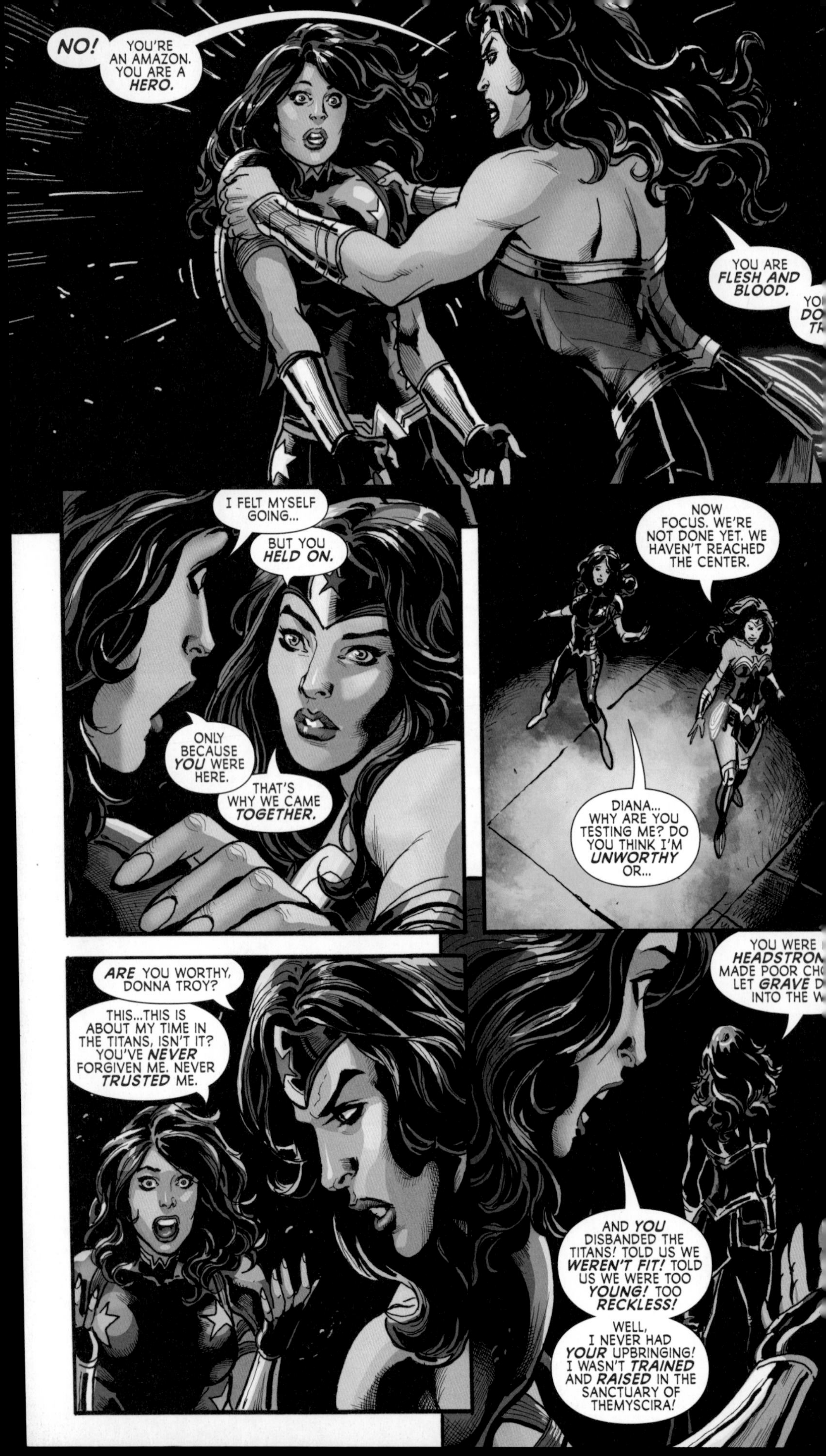
NO!
YOU'RE AN AMAZON. YOU ARE A HERO.
YOU ARE FLESH AND BLOOD.
I FELT MYSELF GOING...
BUT YOU HELD ON.
ONLY BECAUSE YOU WERE HERE.
THAT'S WHY WE CAME TOGETHER.
NOW FOCUS. WE'RE NOT DONE YET. WE HAVEN'T REACHED THE CENTER.
DIANA... WHY ARE YOU TESTING ME? DO YOU THINK I'M UNWORTHY OR...
ARE YOU WORTHY, DONNA TROY?
THIS...THIS IS ABOUT MY TIME IN THE TITANS, ISN'T IT? YOU'VE NEVER FORGIVEN ME. NEVER TRUSTED ME.
YOU WERE
AND YOU DISBANDED THE TITANS! TOLD US WE WEREN'T FIT! TOLD US WE WERE TOO YOUNG! TOO RECKLESS!
WELL, I NEVER HAD YOUR UPBRINGING! I WASN'T TRAINED AND RAISED IN THE SANCTUARY OF THEMYSCIRA!

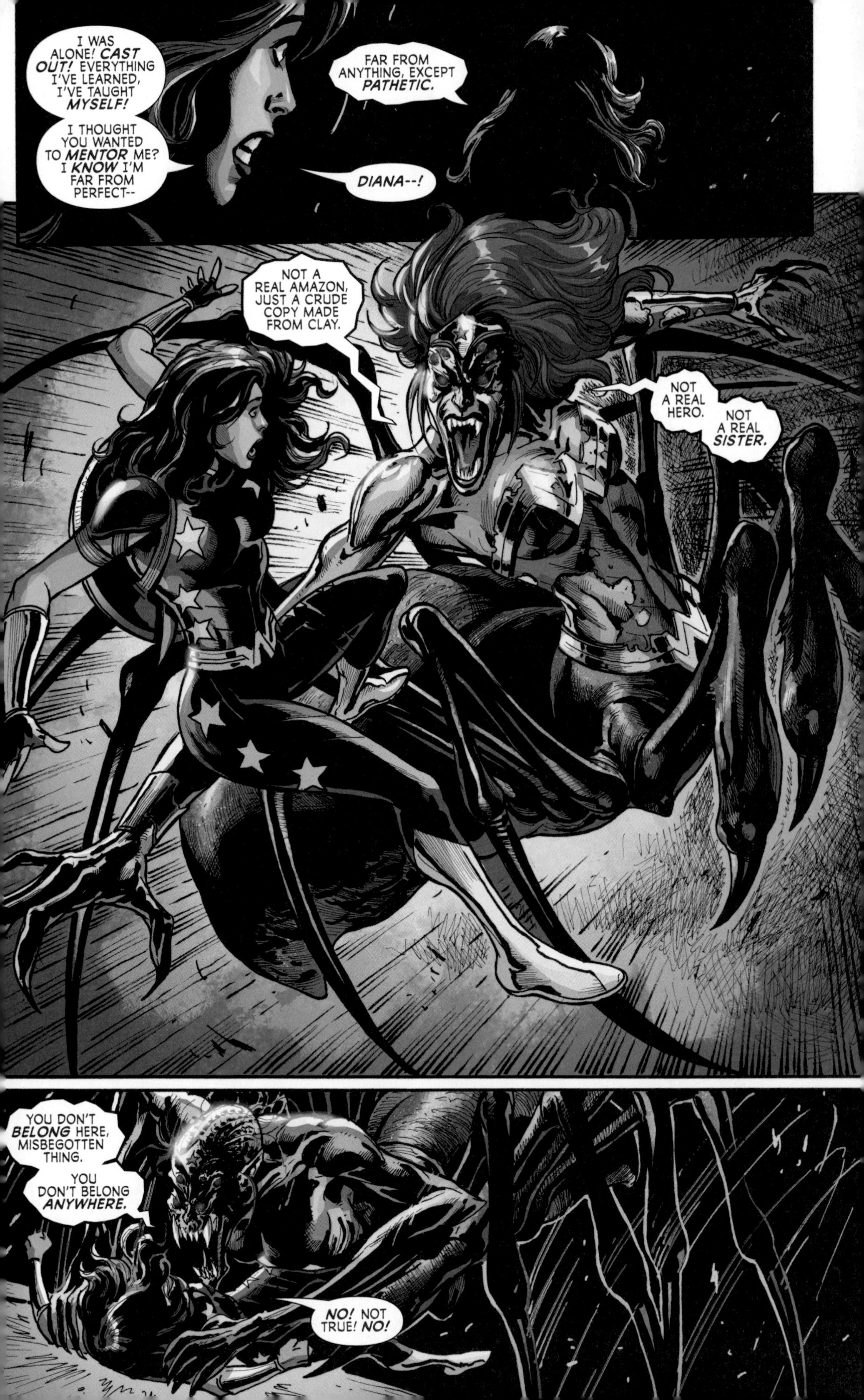
I WAS ALONE! CAST OUT! EVERYTHING I'VE LEARNED, I'VE TAUGHT MYSELF!
I THOUGHT YOU WANTED TO MENTOR ME? I KNOW I'M FAR FROM PERFECT--
FAR FROM ANYTHING, EXCEPT PATHETIC.
DIANA--!
NOT A REAL AMAZON, JUST A CRUDE COPY MADE FROM CLAY.
NOT A REAL HERO.
NOT A REAL SISTER.
YOU DON'T BELONG HERE, MISBEGOTTEN THING.
YOU DON'T BELONG ANYWHERE.
NO! NOT TRUE! NO!

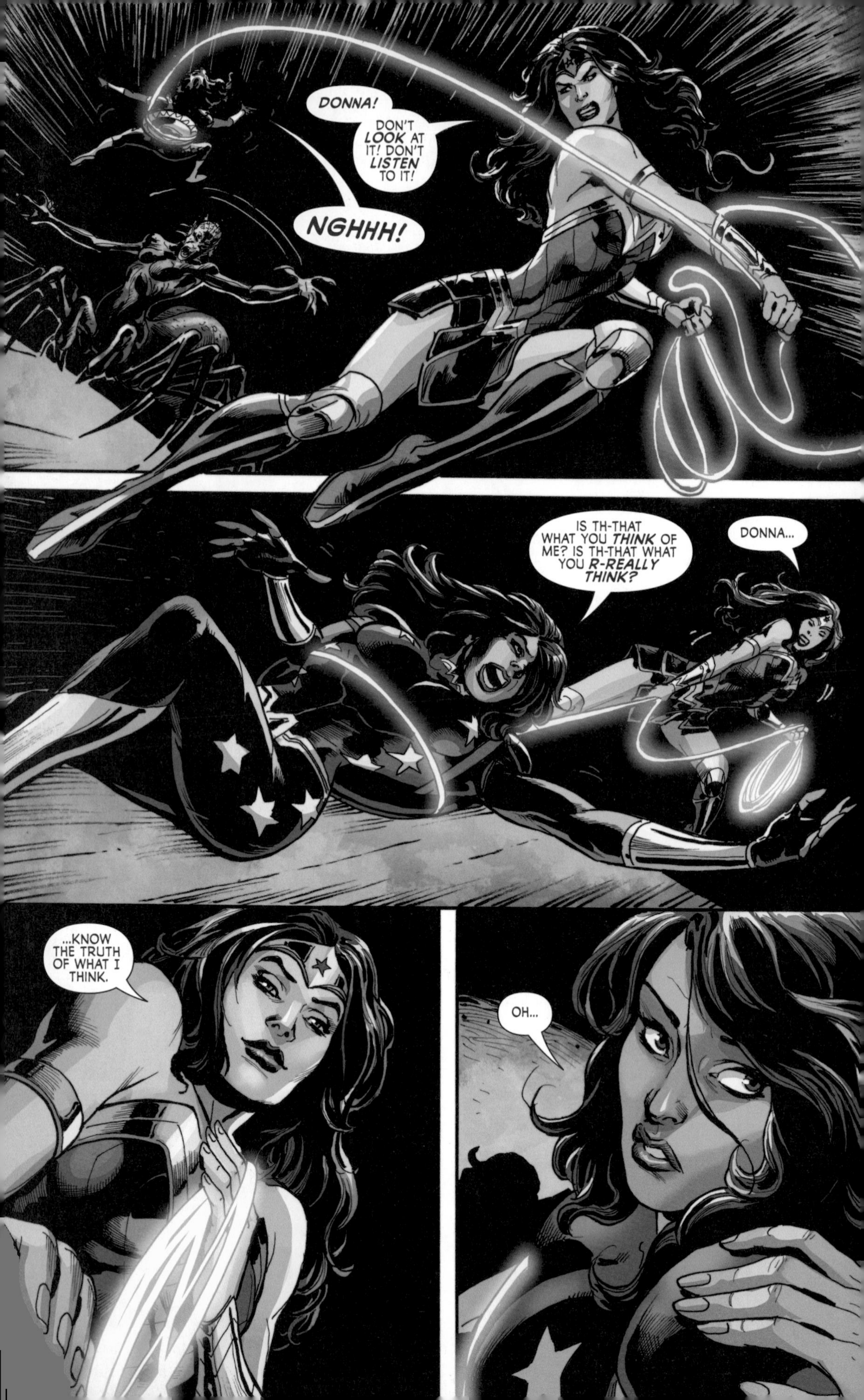
DONNA!
DON'T LOOK AT IT! DON'T LISTEN TO IT!
NGHHH!
IS TH-THAT WHAT YOU THINK OF ME? IS TH-THAT WHAT YOU R-REALLY THINK?
DONNA...
...KNOW THE TRUTH OF WHAT I THINK.
OH...

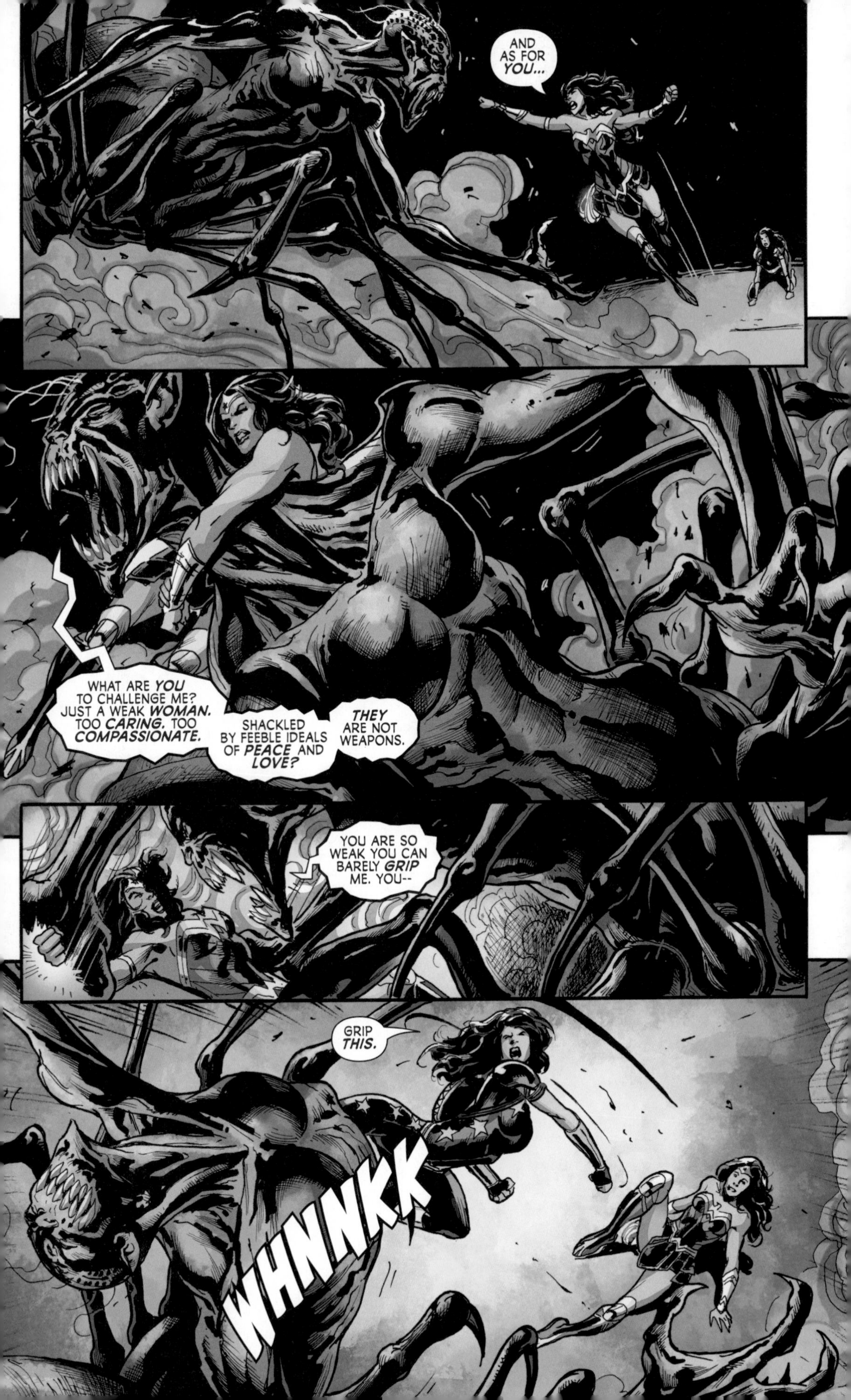
AND AS FOR YOU...
WHAT ARE YOU TO CHALLENGE ME? JUST A WEAK WOMAN. TOO CARING. TOO COMPASSIONATE.
SHACKLED BY FEEBLE IDEALS OF PEACE AND LOVE?
THEY ARE NOT WEAPONS.
YOU ARE SO WEAK YOU CAN BARELY GRIP ME. YOU--
GRIP THIS.
WHNNKK

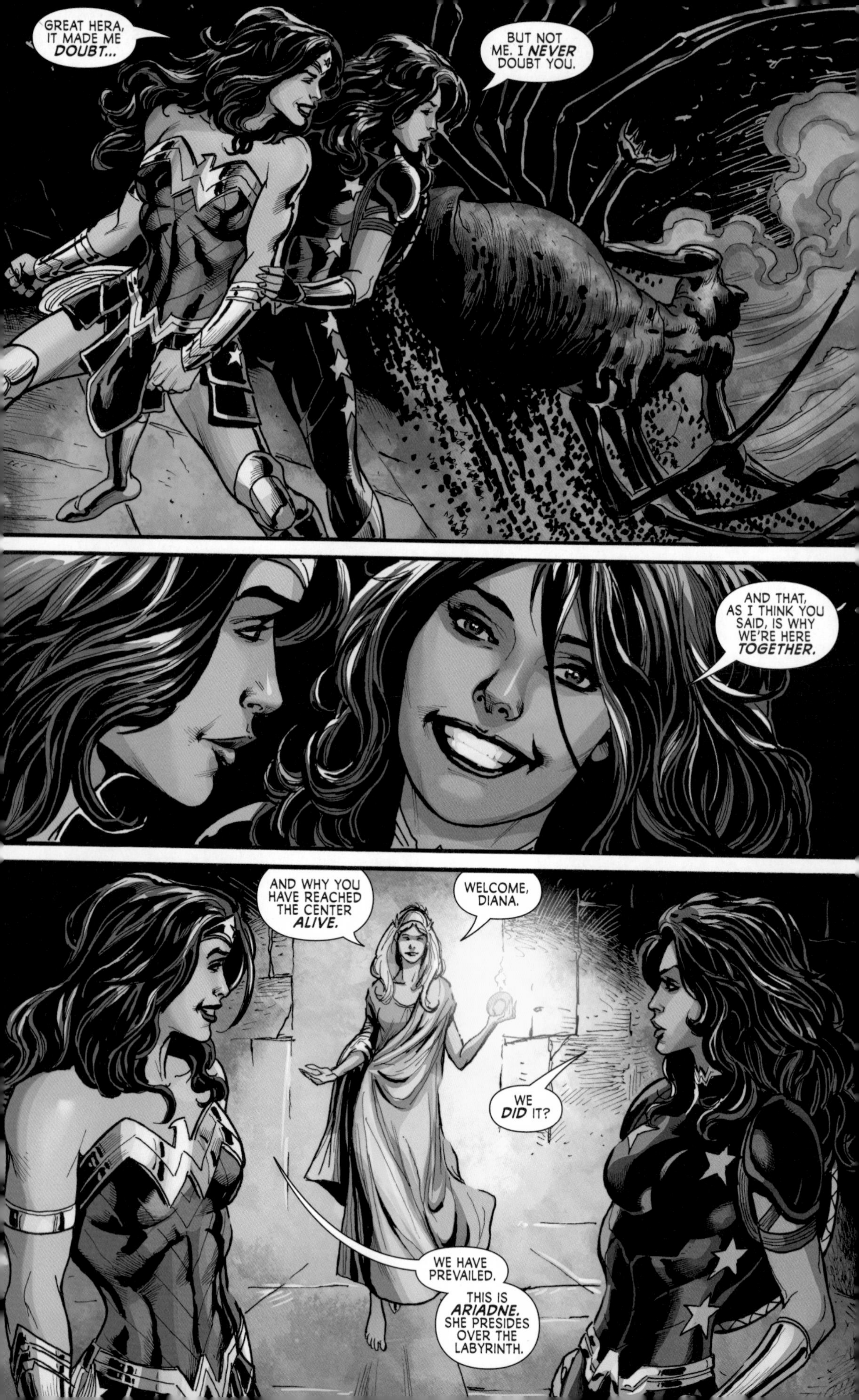
GREAT HERA, IT MADE ME DOUBT...
BUT NOT ME. I NEVER DOUBT YOU.
AND THAT, AS I THINK YOU SAID, IS WHY WE'RE HERE TOGETHER.
AND WHY YOU HAVE REACHED THE CENTER ALIVE.
WELCOME, DIANA.
WE DID IT?
WE HAVE PREVAILED.
THIS IS ARIADNE. SHE PRESIDES OVER THE LABYRINTH.

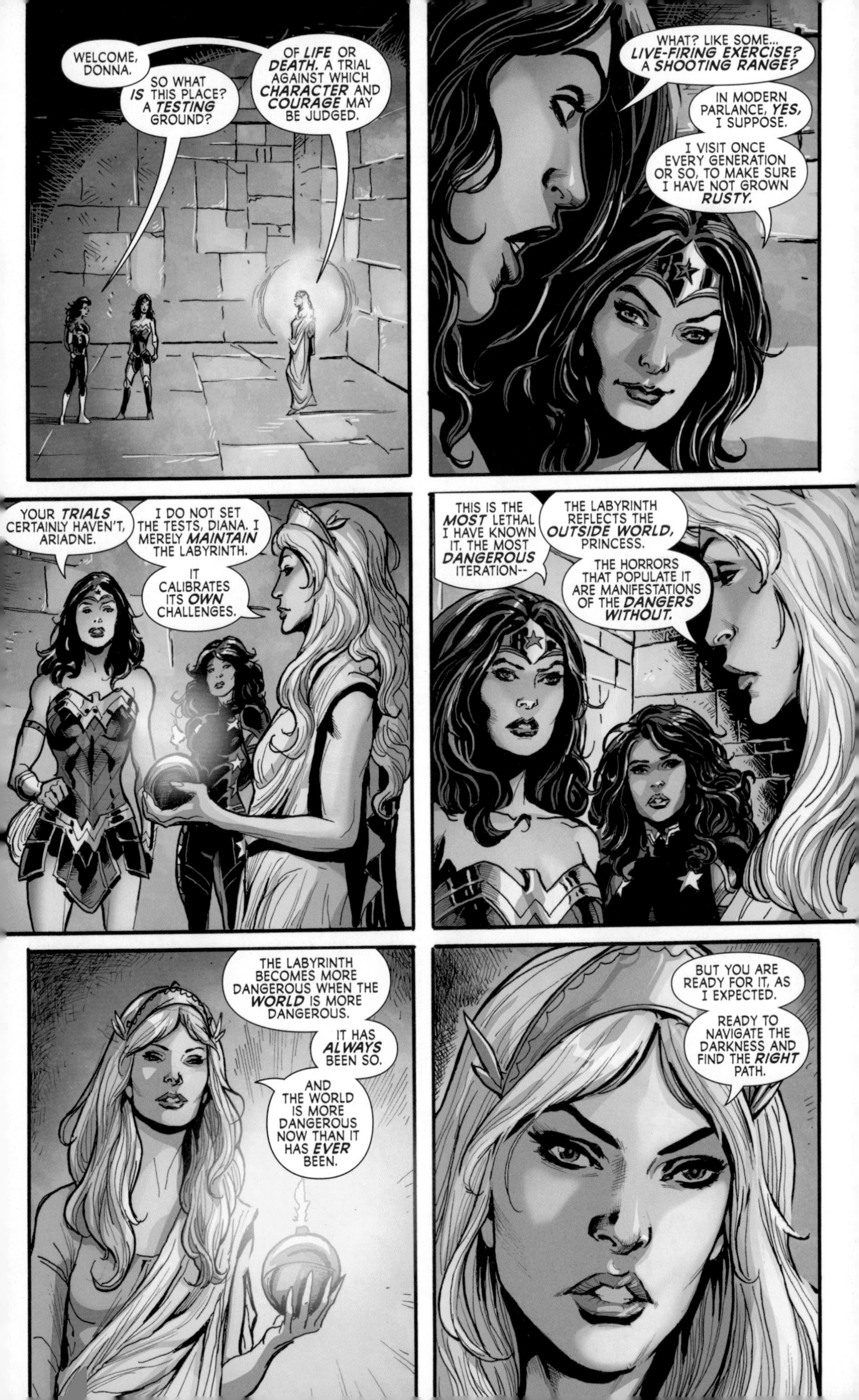

WELCOME, DONNA.
SO WHAT IS THIS PLACE? A TESTING GROUND?
OF LIFE OR DEATH. A TRIAL AGAINST WHICH CHARACTER AND COURAGE MAY BE JUDGED.
WHAT? LIKE SOME... LIVE-FIRING EXERCISE? A SHOOTING RANGE?
IN MODERN PARLANCE, YES, I SUPPOSE.
I VISIT ONCE EVERY GENERATION OR SO, TO MAKE SURE I HAVE NOT GROWN RUSTY.
YOUR TRIALS CERTAINLY HAVEN'T, ARIADNE.
I DO NOT SET THE TESTS, DIANA. I MERELY MAINTAIN THE LABYRINTH.
IT CALIBRATES ITS OWN CHALLENGES.
THIS IS THE MOST LETHAL I HAVE KNOWN IT. THE MOST DANGEROUS ITERATION--
THE LABYRINTH REFLECTS THE OUTSIDE WORLD, PRINCESS.
THE HORRORS THAT POPULATE IT ARE MANIFESTATIONS OF THE DANGERS WITHOUT.
THE LABYRINTH BECOMES MORE DANGEROUS WHEN THE WORLD IS MORE DANGEROUS.
IT HAS ALWAYS BEEN SO.
AND THE WORLD IS MORE DANGEROUS NOW THAN IT HAS EVER BEEN.
BUT YOU ARE READY FOR IT, AS I EXPECTED.
READY TO NAVIGATE THE DARKNESS AND FIND THE RIGHT PATH.

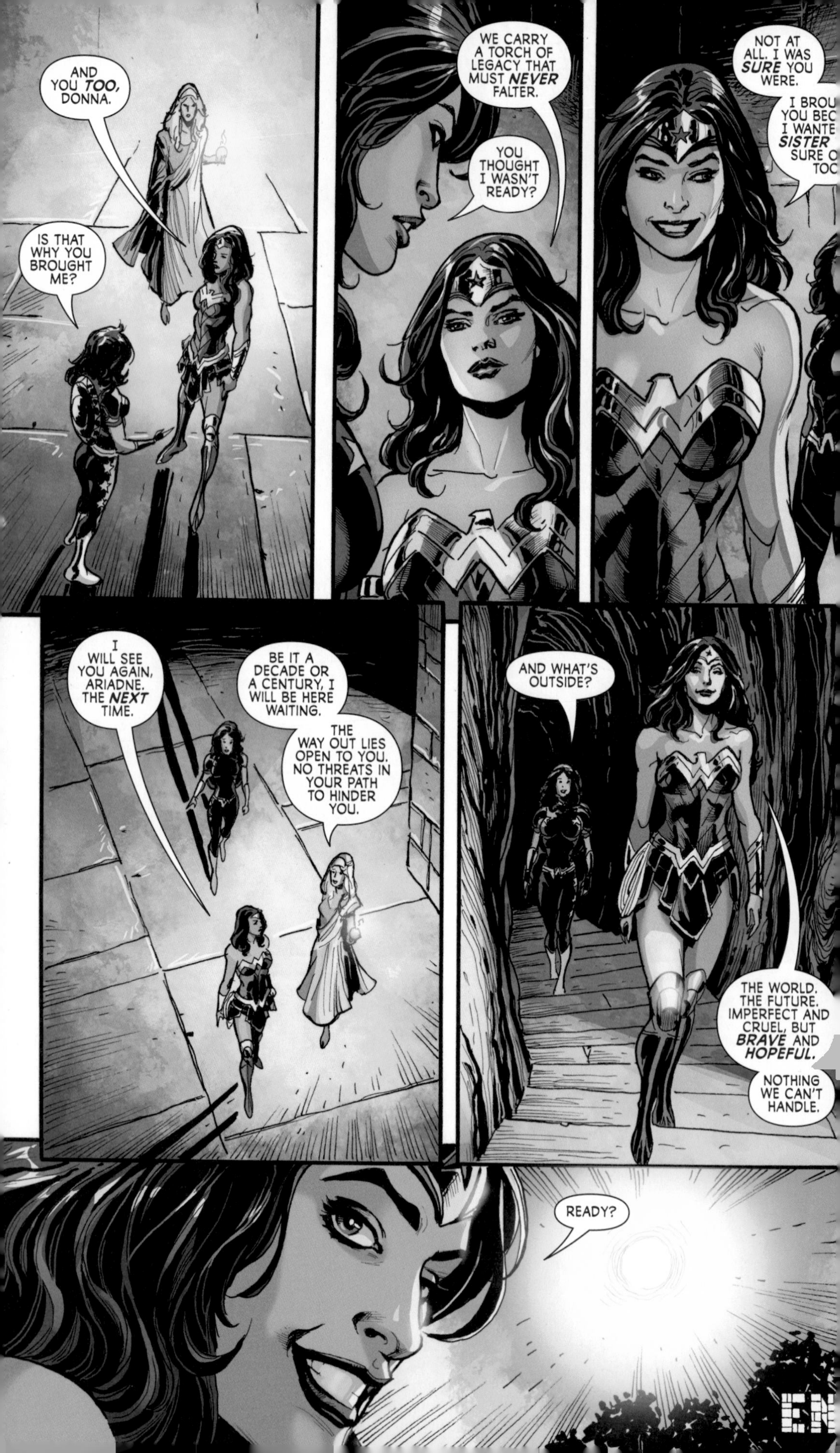
AND YOU *TOO,* DONNA.
IS THAT WHY YOU BROUGHT ME?
WE CARRY A TORCH OF LEGACY THAT MUST *NEVER* FALTER.
YOU THOUGHT I WASN'T READY?
NOT AT ALL. I WAS *SURE* YOU WERE.
I WILL SEE YOU AGAIN, ARIADNE. THE *NEXT* TIME.
BE IT A DECADE OR A CENTURY, I WILL BE HERE WAITING.
THE WAY OUT LIES OPEN TO YOU. NO THREATS IN YOUR PATH TO HINDER YOU.
AND WHAT'S OUTSIDE?
THE WORLD. THE FUTURE. IMPERFECT AND CRUEL, BUT *BRAVE* AND *HOPEFUL.*
NOTHING WE CAN'T HANDLE.
READY?

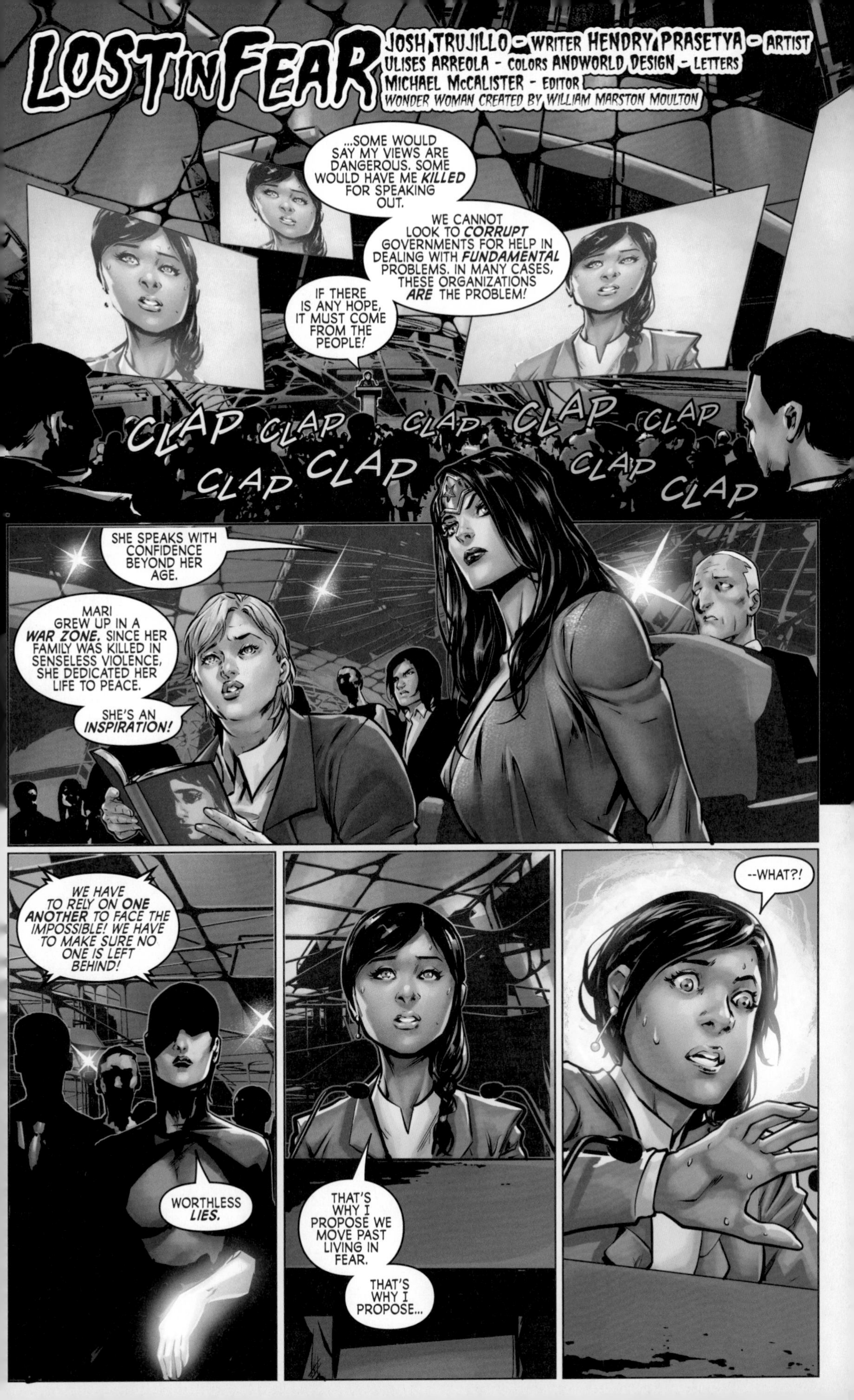
LOST IN FEAR
JOSH TRUJILLO - WRITER HENDRY PRASETYA - ARTIST
ULISES ARREOLA - COLORS ANDWORLD DESIGN - LETTERS
MICHAEL McCALISTER - EDITOR
WONDER WOMAN CREATED BY WILLIAM MARSTON MOULTON
...SOME WOULD SAY MY VIEWS ARE DANGEROUS. SOME WOULD HAVE ME KILLED FOR SPEAKING OUT.
WE CANNOT LOOK TO CORRUPT GOVERNMENTS FOR HELP IN DEALING WITH FUNDAMENTAL PROBLEMS. IN MANY CASES, THESE ORGANIZATIONS ARE THE PROBLEM!
IF THERE IS ANY HOPE, IT MUST COME FROM THE PEOPLE!
CLAP CLAP CLAP CLAP CLAP CLAP CLAP CLAP CLAP
SHE SPEAKS WITH CONFIDENCE BEYOND HER AGE.
MARI GREW UP IN A WAR ZONE. SINCE HER FAMILY WAS KILLED IN SENSELESS VIOLENCE, SHE DEDICATED HER LIFE TO PEACE.
SHE'S AN INSPIRATION!
WE HAVE TO RELY ON ONE ANOTHER TO FACE THE IMPOSSIBLE! WE HAVE TO MAKE SURE NO ONE IS LEFT BEHIND!
WORTHLESS LIES.
THAT'S WHY I PROPOSE WE MOVE PAST LIVING IN FEAR.
THAT'S WHY I PROPOSE...
--WHAT?!

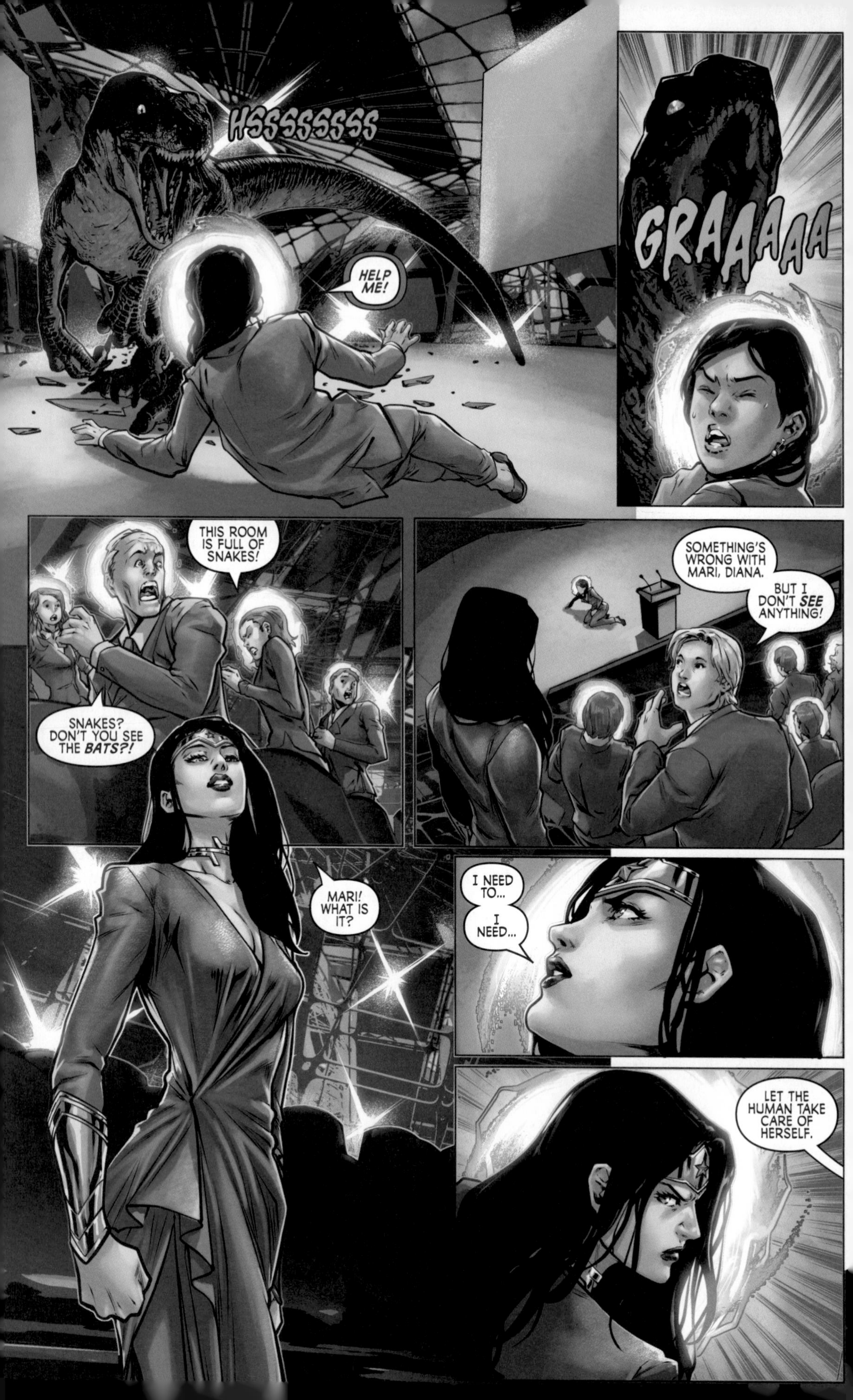
HSSSSSSSS
HELP ME!
GRAAAAA
THIS ROOM IS FULL OF SNAKES!
SNAKES? DON'T YOU SEE THE *BATS?!*
SOMETHING'S WRONG WITH MARI, DIANA.
BUT I DON'T *SEE* ANYTHING!
MARI! WHAT IS IT?
I NEED TO...
I NEED...
LET THE HUMAN TAKE CARE OF HERSELF.

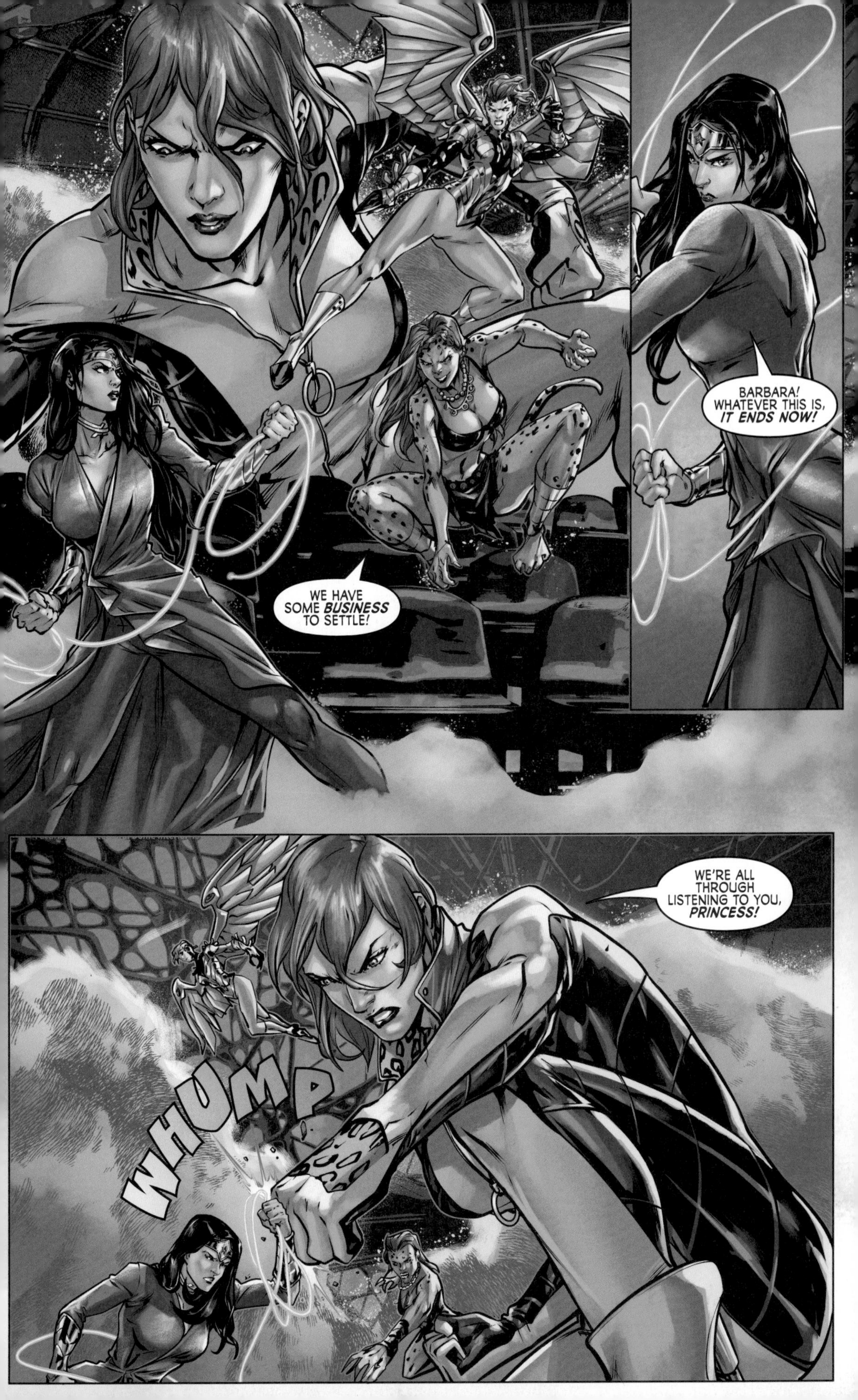
BARBARA! WHATEVER THIS IS, IT ENDS NOW!
WE HAVE SOME BUSINESS TO SETTLE!
WE'RE ALL THROUGH LISTENING TO YOU, PRINCESS!
WHUMP

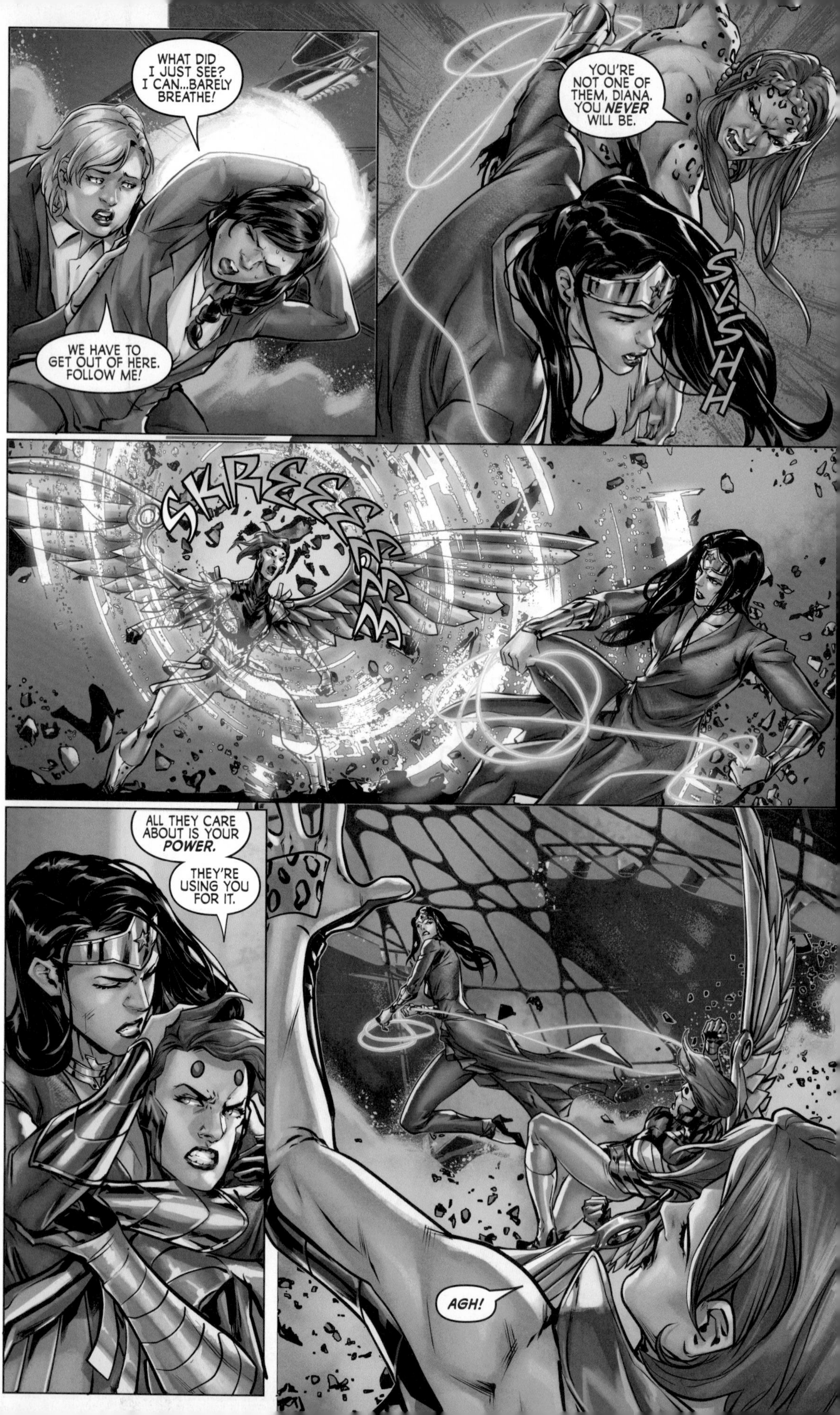
WHAT DID I JUST SEE? I CAN...BARELY BREATHE!
WE HAVE TO GET OUT OF HERE. FOLLOW ME!
YOU'RE NOT ONE OF THEM, DIANA. YOU *NEVER* WILL BE.
SVSHH
SKREEEEEEM
ALL THEY CARE ABOUT IS YOUR ***POWER.***
THEY'RE USING YOU FOR IT.
AGH!

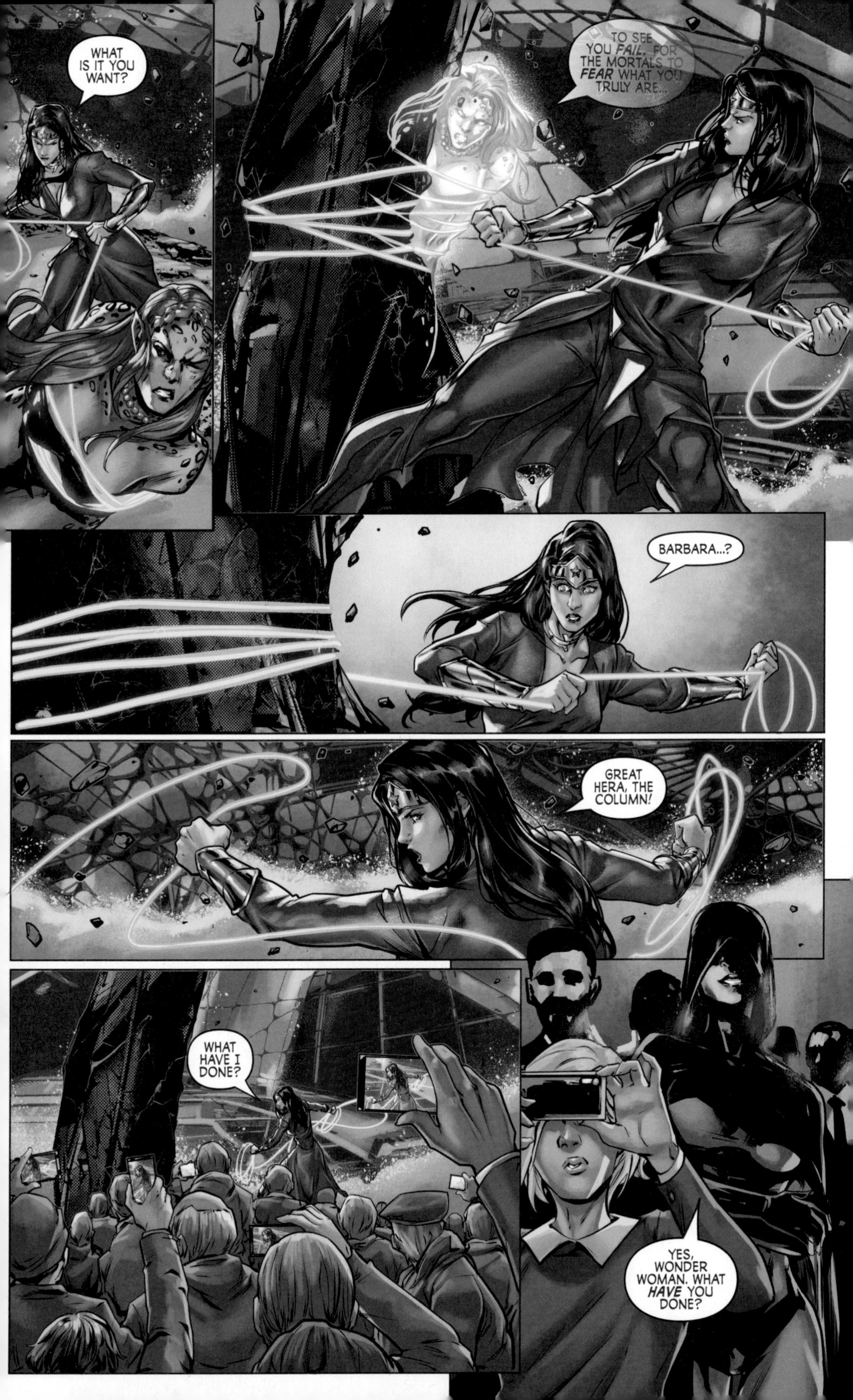
WHAT IS IT YOU WANT?
TO SEE YOU FAIL, FOR THE MORTALS TO FEAR WHAT YOU TRULY ARE...
BARBARA...?
GREAT HERA, THE COLUMN!
WHAT HAVE I DONE?
YES, WONDER WOMAN. WHAT HAVE YOU DONE?

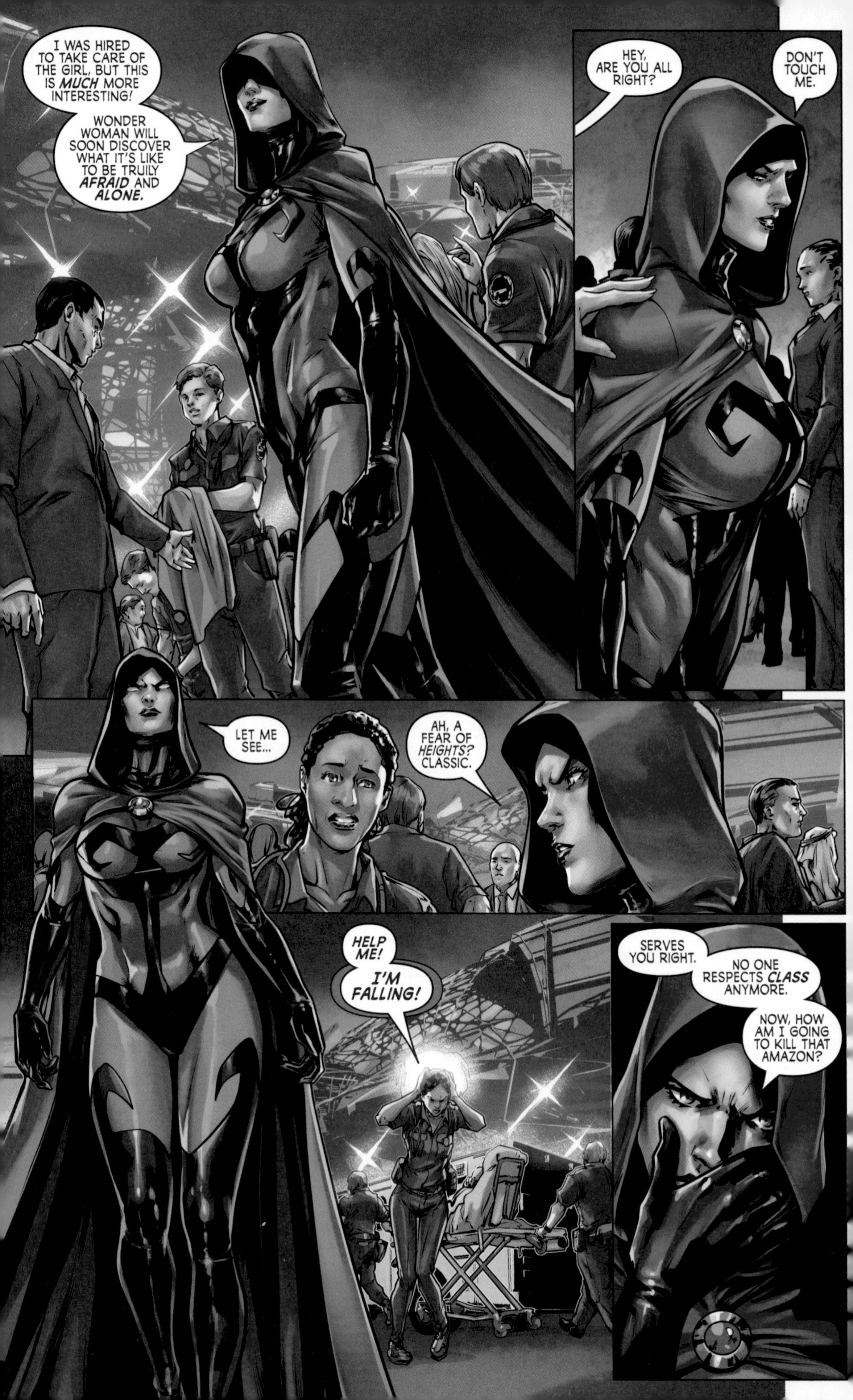
I WAS HIRED TO TAKE CARE OF THE GIRL, BUT THIS IS *MUCH* MORE INTERESTING!
WONDER WOMAN WILL SOON DISCOVER WHAT IT'S LIKE TO BE TRUILY ***AFRAID*** AND ***ALONE.***
HEY, ARE YOU ALL RIGHT?
DON'T TOUCH ME.
LET ME SEE...
AH, A FEAR OF *HEIGHTS?* CLASSIC.
HELP ME!
I'M FALLING!
SERVES YOU RIGHT.
NO ONE RESPECTS ***CLASS*** ANYMORE.
NOW, HOW AM I GOING TO KILL THAT AMAZON?

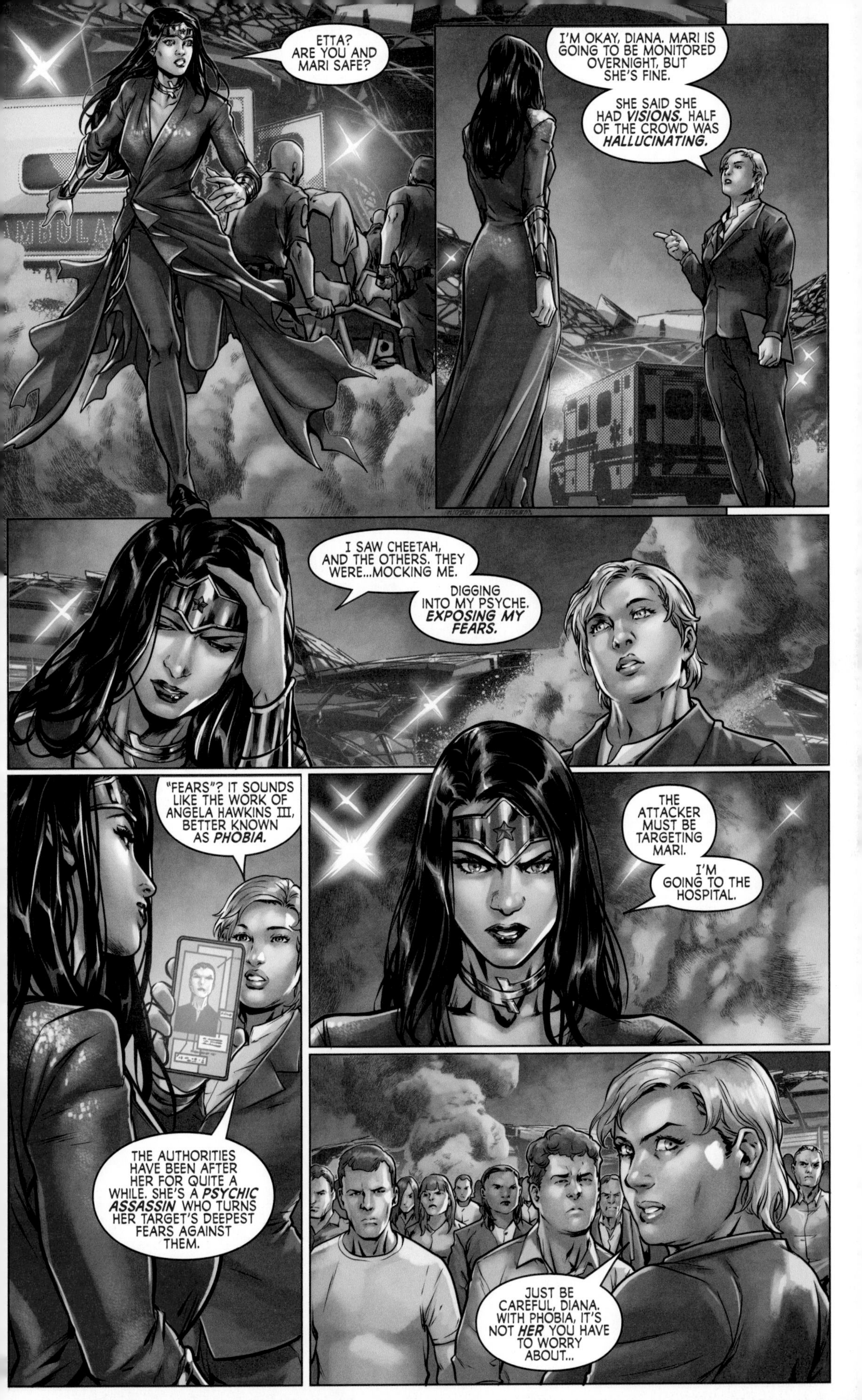
ETTA? ARE YOU AND MARI SAFE?
I'M OKAY, DIANA. MARI IS GOING TO BE MONITORED OVERNIGHT, BUT SHE'S FINE.
SHE SAID SHE HAD VISIONS. HALF OF THE CROWD WAS HALLUCINATING.
AMBULA
I SAW CHEETAH, AND THE OTHERS. THEY WERE...MOCKING ME.
DIGGING INTO MY PSYCHE. EXPOSING MY FEARS.
"FEARS"? IT SOUNDS LIKE THE WORK OF ANGELA HAWKINS III, BETTER KNOWN AS PHOBIA.
THE AUTHORITIES HAVE BEEN AFTER HER FOR QUITE A WHILE. SHE'S A PSYCHIC ASSASSIN WHO TURNS HER TARGET'S DEEPEST FEARS AGAINST THEM.
THE ATTACKER MUST BE TARGETING MARI.
I'M GOING TO THE HOSPITAL.
JUST BE CAREFUL, DIANA. WITH PHOBIA, IT'S NOT HER YOU HAVE TO WORRY ABOUT...

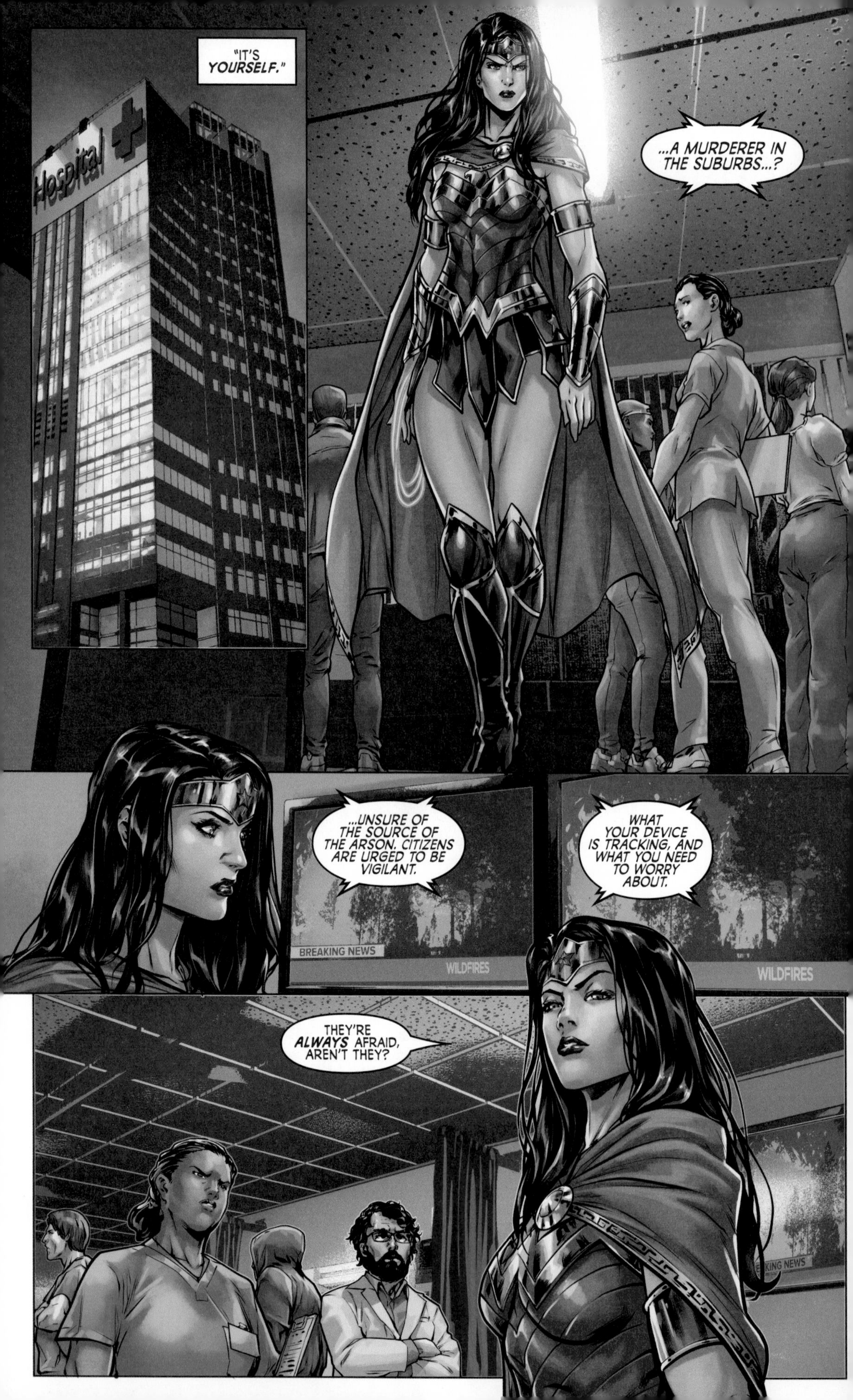
"IT'S
YOURSELF."
Hospital
...A MURDERER IN
THE SUBURBS...?
...UNSURE OF
THE SOURCE OF
THE ARSON. CITIZENS
ARE URGED TO BE
VIGILANT.
BREAKING NEWS
WILDFIRES
WHAT
YOUR DEVICE
IS TRACKING, AND
WHAT YOU NEED
TO WORRY
ABOUT.
WILDFIRES
THEY'RE
ALWAYS AFRAID,
AREN'T THEY?

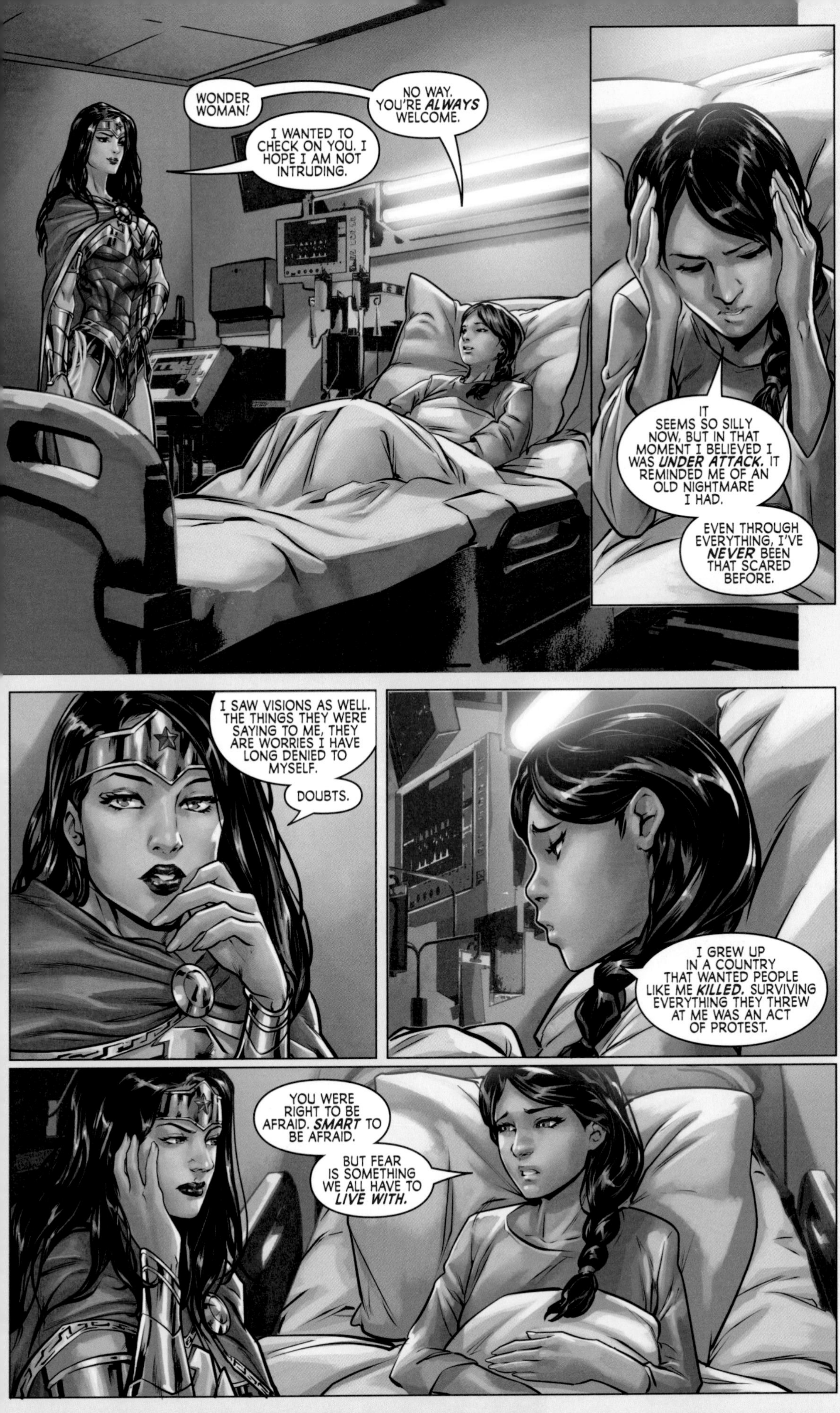

WONDER WOMAN!
I WANTED TO CHECK ON YOU. I HOPE I AM NOT INTRUDING.
NO WAY. YOU'RE ALWAYS WELCOME.
IT SEEMS SO SILLY NOW, BUT IN THAT MOMENT I BELIEVED I WAS UNDER ATTACK. IT REMINDED ME OF AN OLD NIGHTMARE I HAD.
EVEN THROUGH EVERYTHING, I'VE NEVER BEEN THAT SCARED BEFORE.
I SAW VISIONS AS WELL. THE THINGS THEY WERE SAYING TO ME, THEY ARE WORRIES I HAVE LONG DENIED TO MYSELF.
DOUBTS.
I GREW UP IN A COUNTRY THAT WANTED PEOPLE LIKE ME KILLED. SURVIVING EVERYTHING THEY THREW AT ME WAS AN ACT OF PROTEST.
YOU WERE RIGHT TO BE AFRAID. SMART TO BE AFRAID.
BUT FEAR IS SOMETHING WE ALL HAVE TO LIVE WITH.

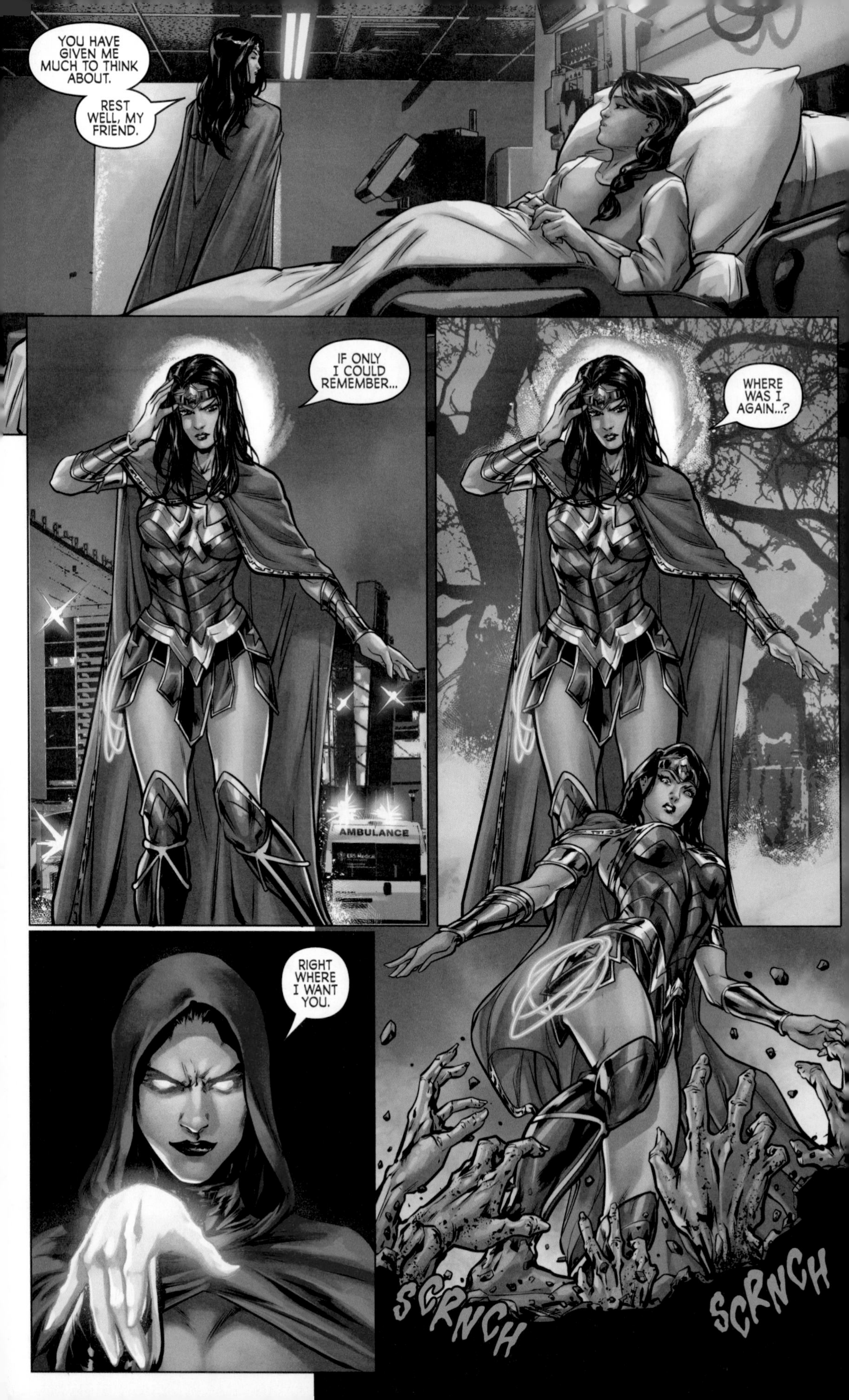
YOU HAVE GIVEN ME MUCH TO THINK ABOUT.
REST WELL, MY FRIEND.
IF ONLY I COULD REMEMBER...
WHERE WAS I AGAIN...?
AMBULANCE
RIGHT WHERE I WANT YOU.
SCRNCH
SCRNCH

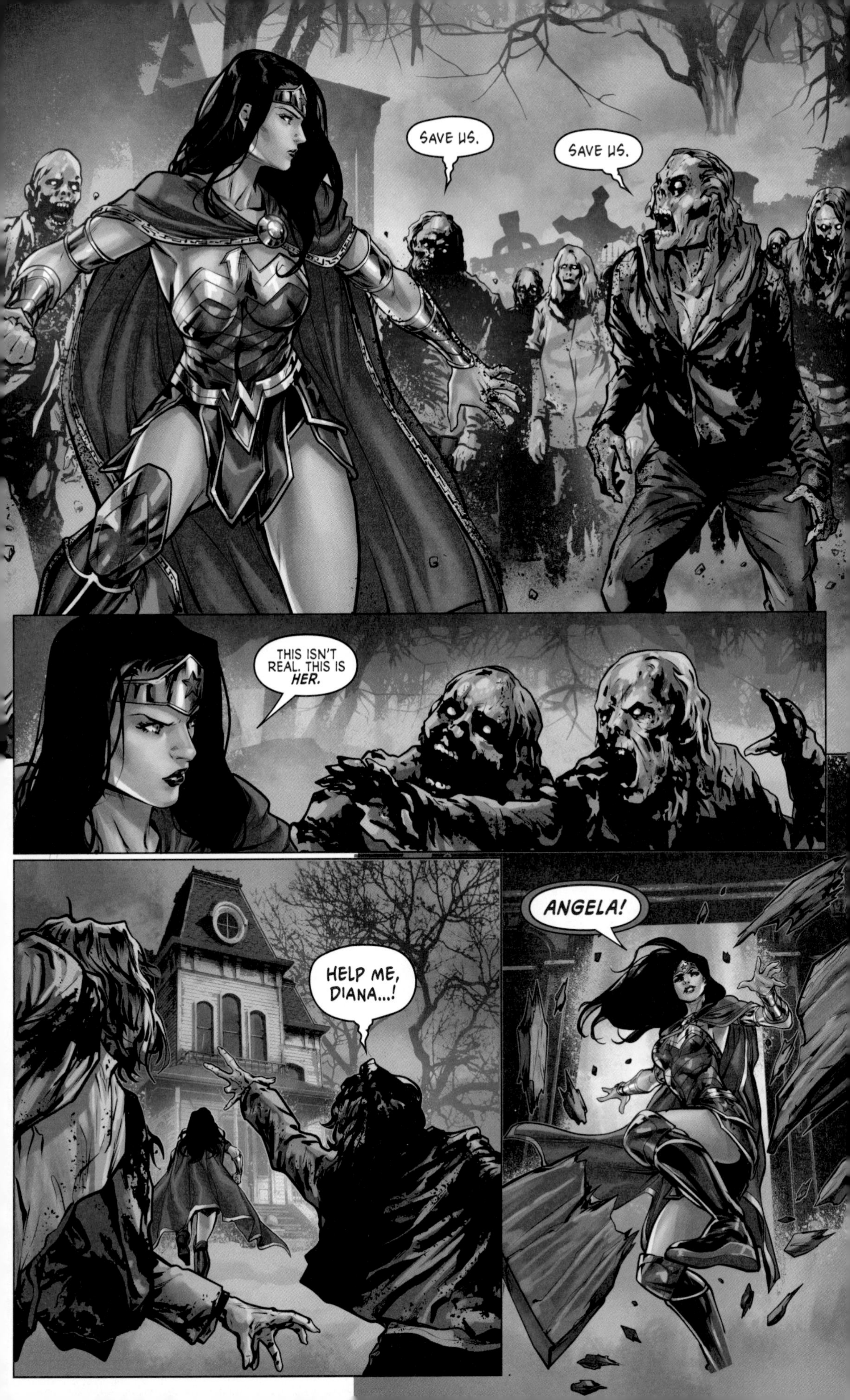
SAVE US.
SAVE US.
THIS ISN'T REAL. THIS IS HER.
HELP ME, DIANA...!
ANGELA!

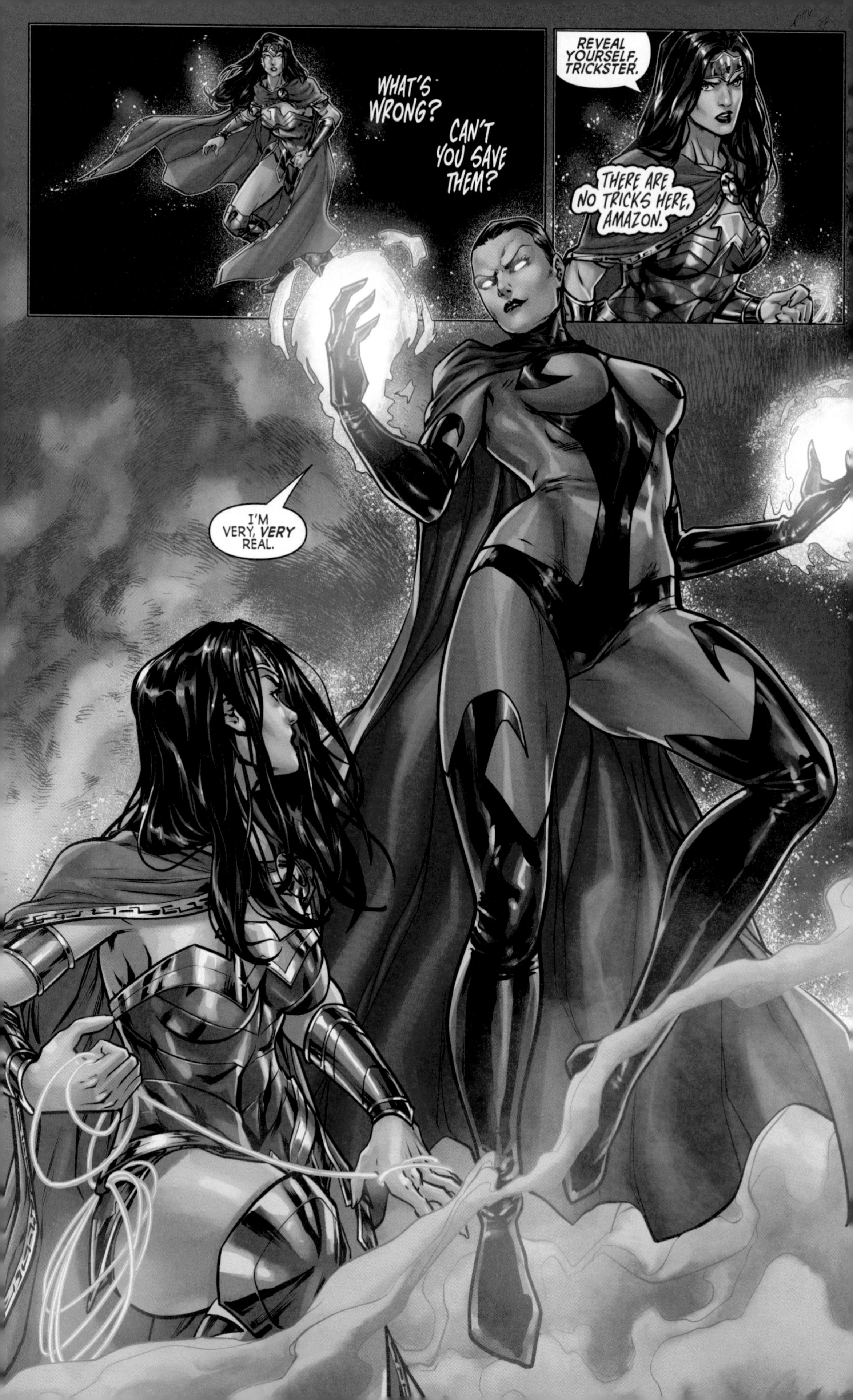
WHAT'S WRONG?
CAN'T YOU SAVE THEM?
REVEAL YOURSELF, TRICKSTER.
THERE ARE NO TRICKS HERE, AMAZON.
I'M VERY, VERY REAL.

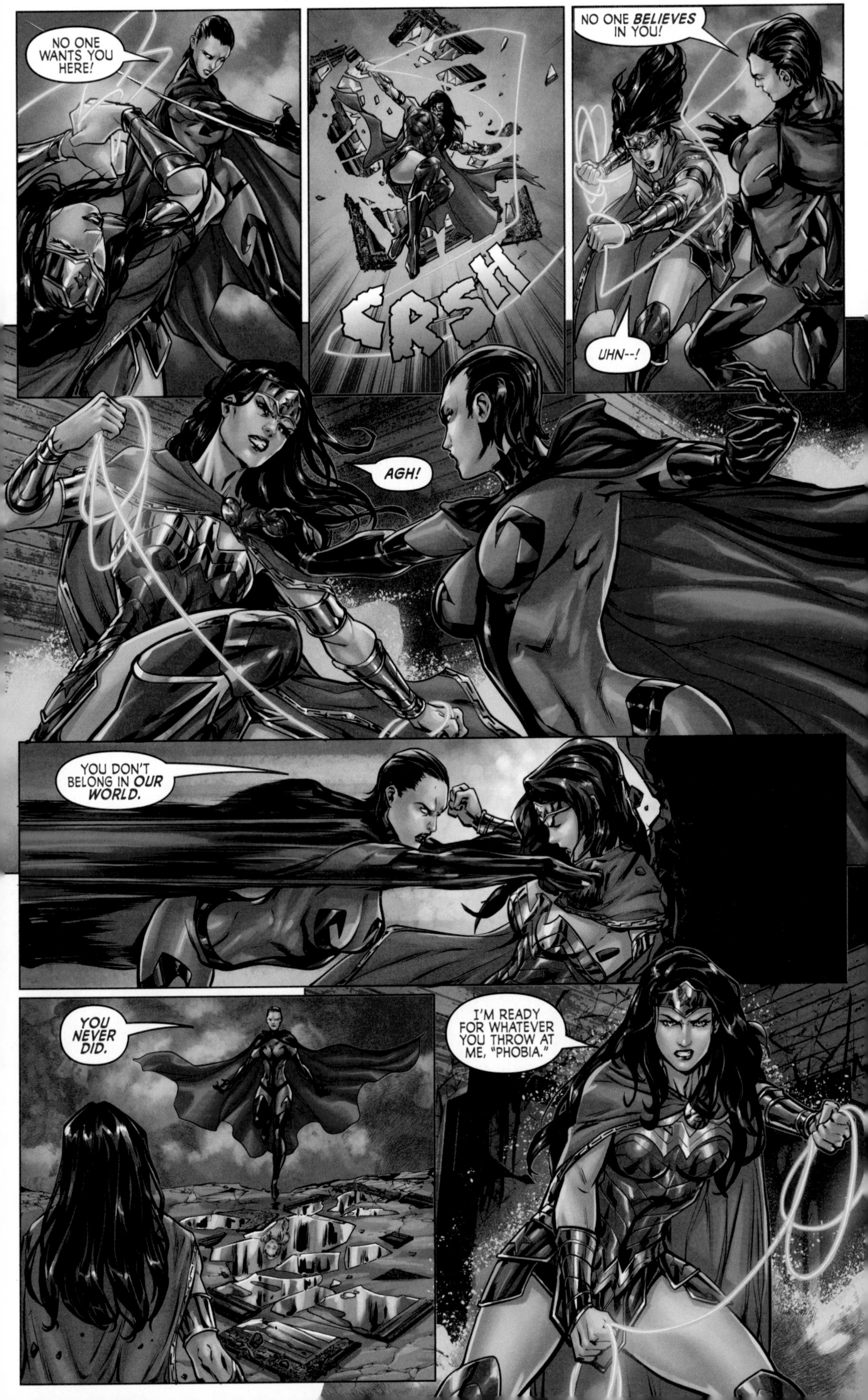
NO ONE WANTS YOU HERE!
CRSH
NO ONE *BELIEVES* IN YOU!
UHN--!
AGH!
YOU DON'T BELONG IN *OUR WORLD.*
YOU NEVER DID.
I'M READY FOR WHATEVER YOU THROW AT ME, "PHOBIA."

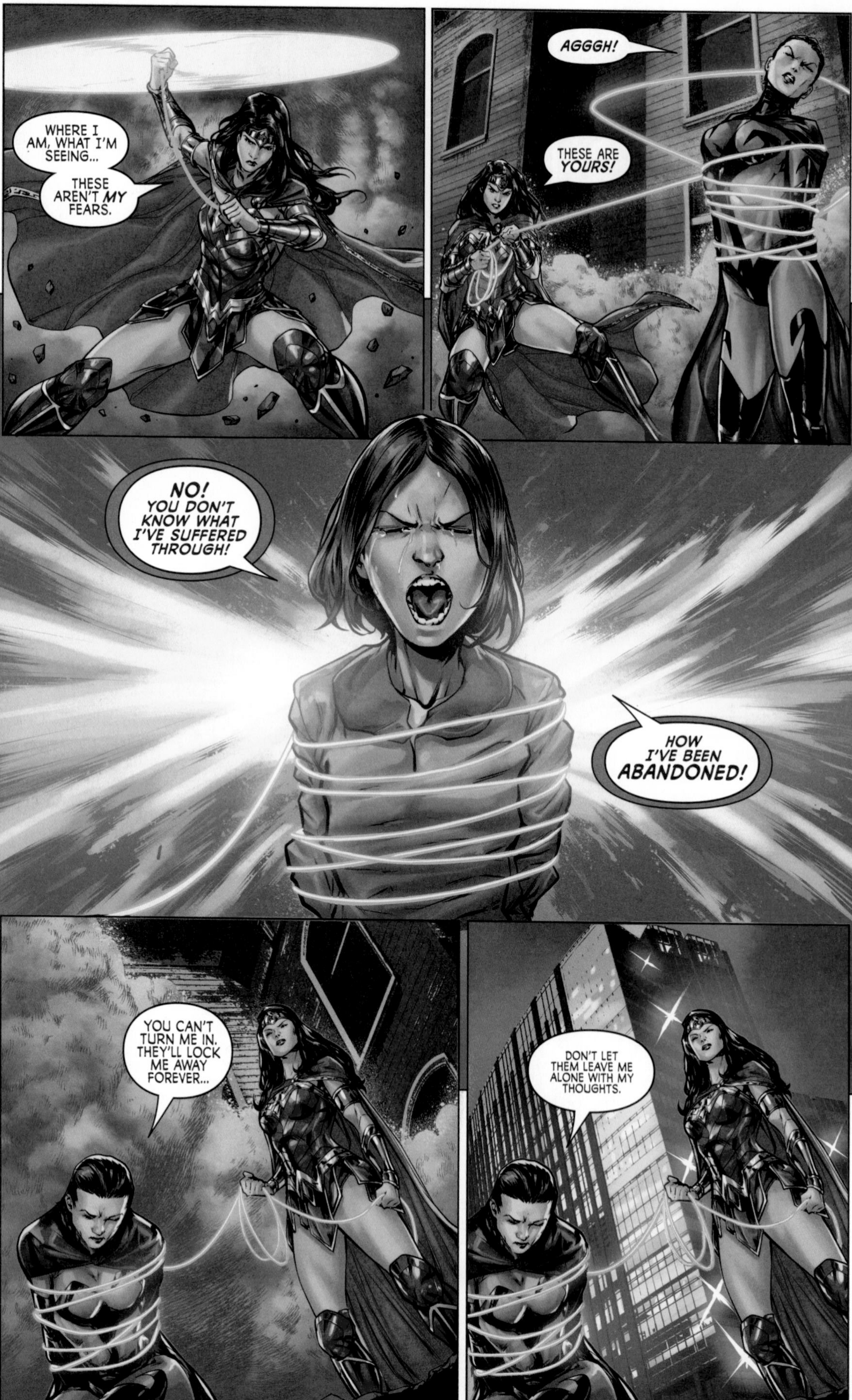
WHERE I AM, WHAT I'M SEEING...
THESE AREN'T MY FEARS.
AGGGH!
THESE ARE YOURS!
NO! YOU DON'T KNOW WHAT I'VE SUFFERED THROUGH!
HOW I'VE BEEN ABANDONED!
YOU CAN'T TURN ME IN. THEY'LL LOCK ME AWAY FOREVER...
DON'T LET THEM LEAVE ME ALONE WITH MY THOUGHTS.

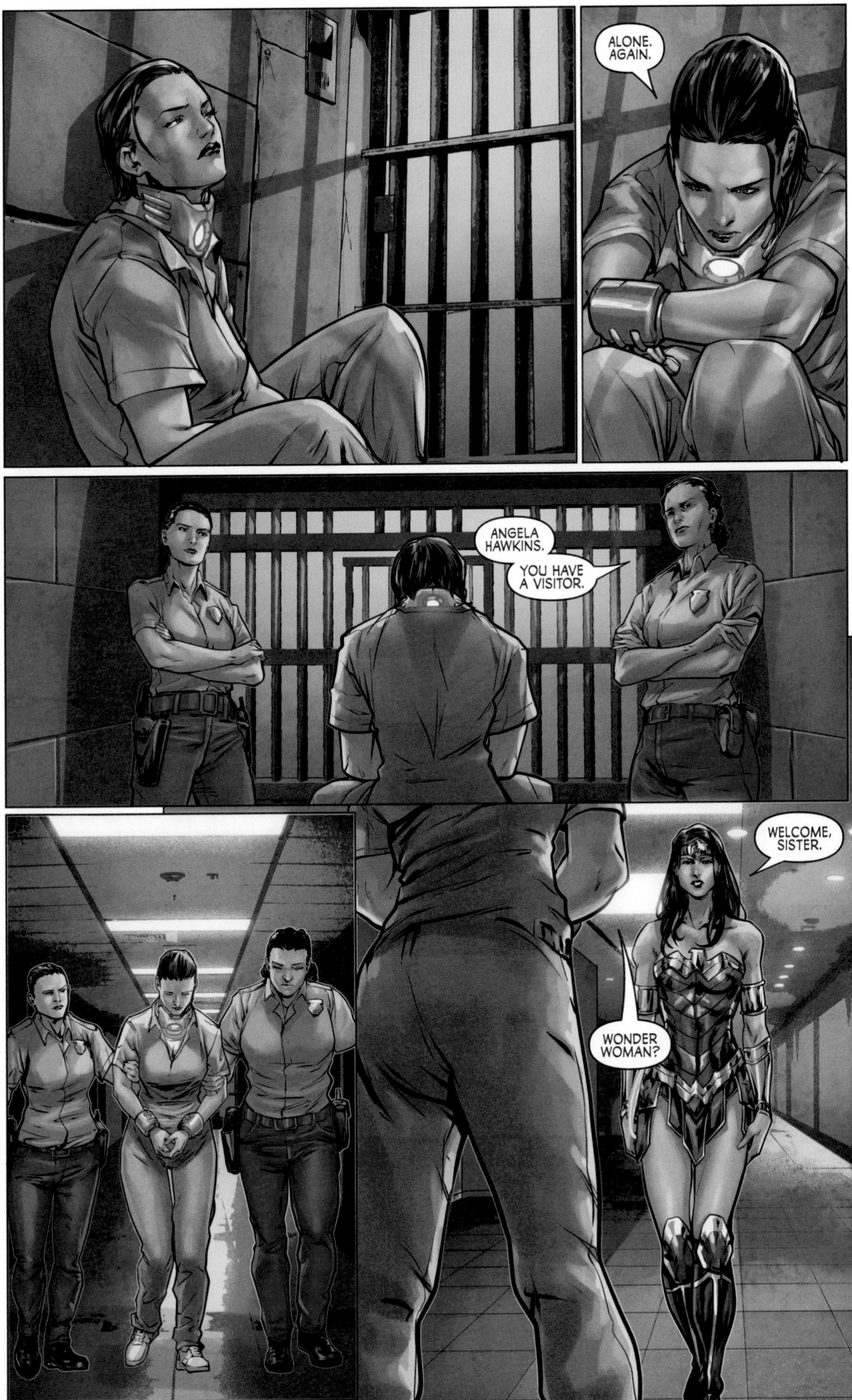
ALONE. AGAIN.
ANGELA HAWKINS.
YOU HAVE A VISITOR.
WELCOME, SISTER.
WONDER WOMAN?

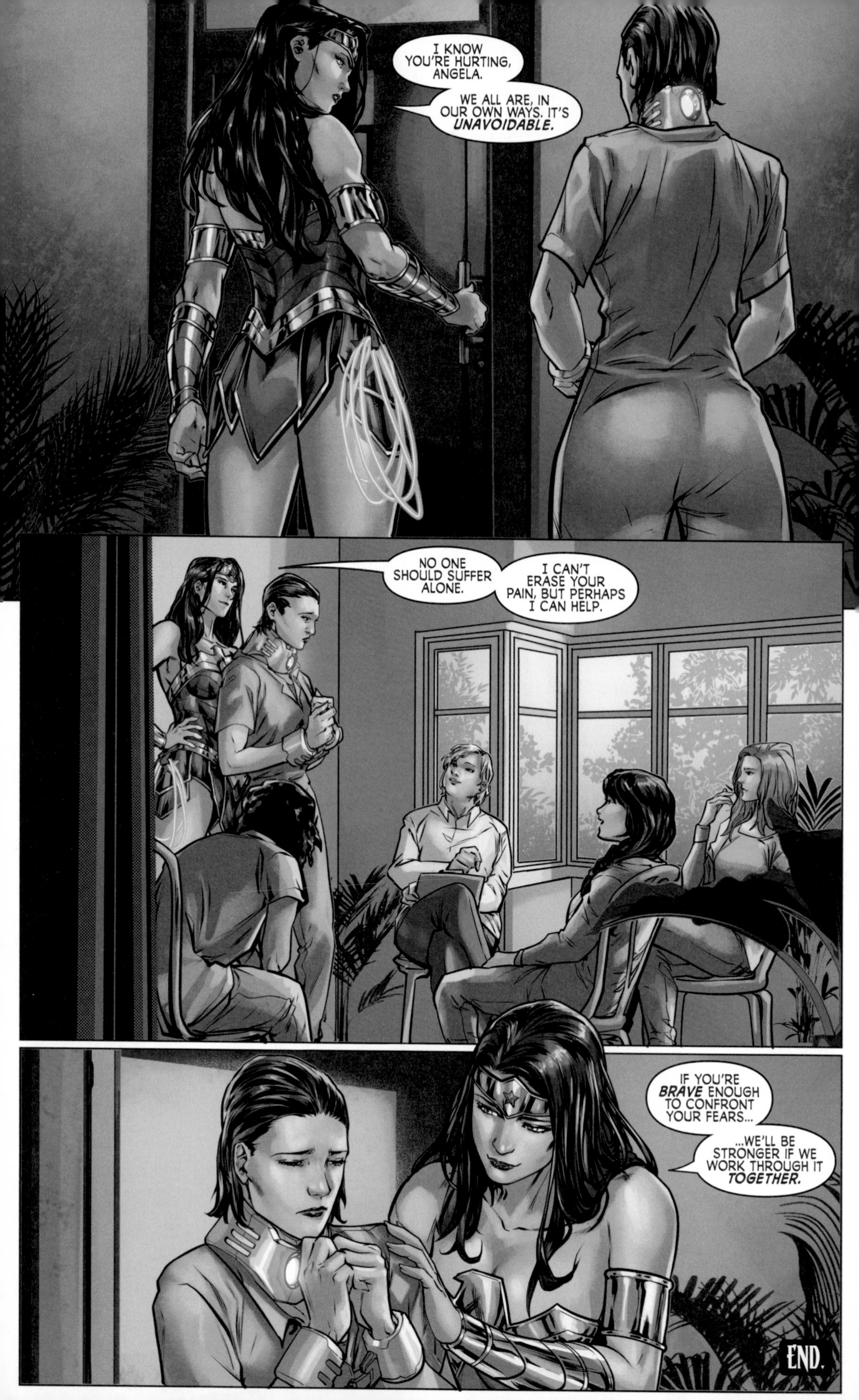
I KNOW YOU'RE HURTING, ANGELA.
WE ALL ARE, IN OUR OWN WAYS. IT'S *UNAVOIDABLE.*
NO ONE SHOULD SUFFER ALONE.
I CAN'T ERASE YOUR PAIN, BUT PERHAPS I CAN HELP.
IF YOU'RE *BRAVE* ENOUGH TO CONFRONT YOUR FEARS...
...WE'LL BE STRONGER IF WE WORK THROUGH IT *TOGETHER.*
END.

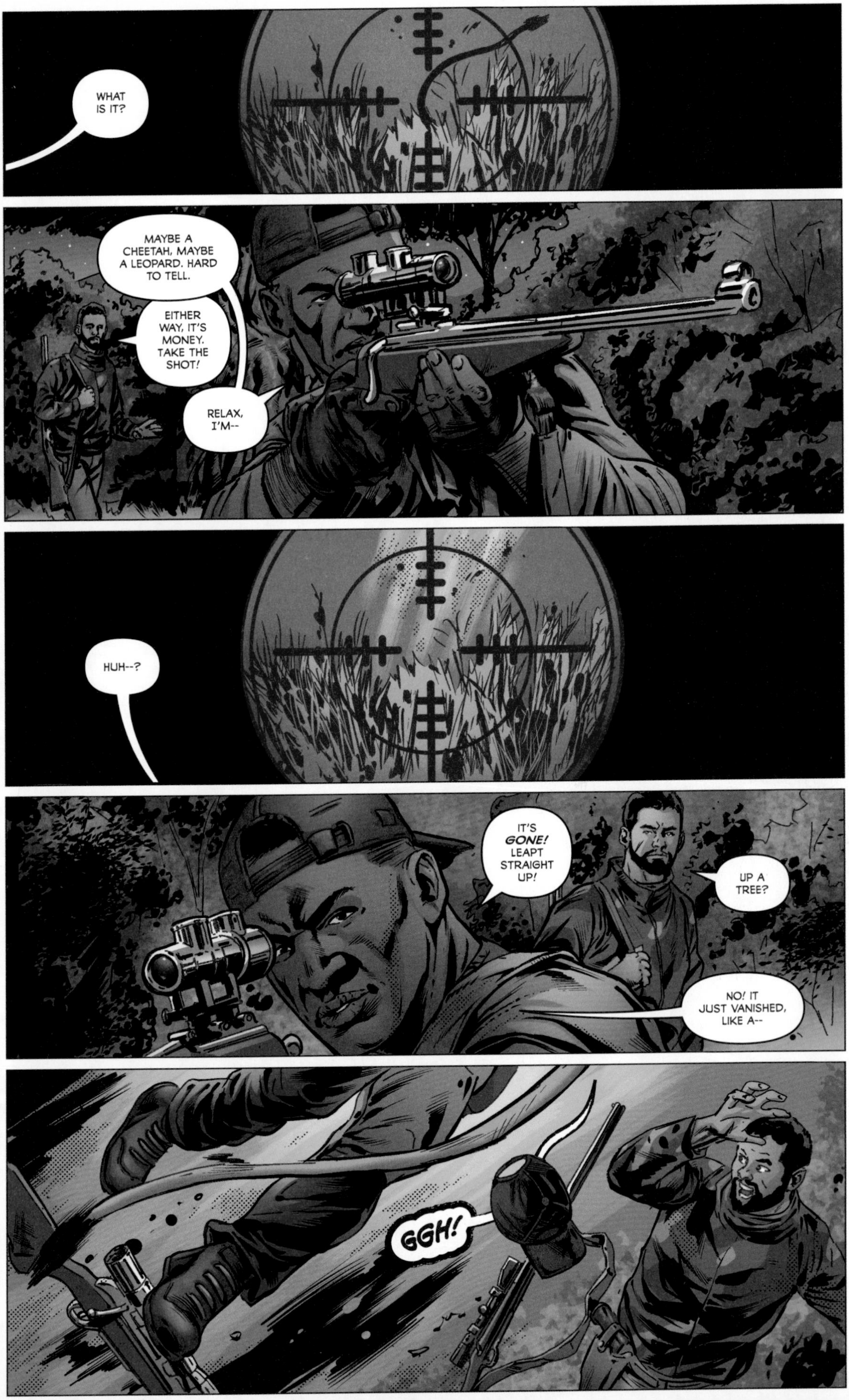
WHAT IS IT?
MAYBE A CHEETAH, MAYBE A LEOPARD. HARD TO TELL.
EITHER WAY, IT'S MONEY. TAKE THE SHOT!
RELAX, I'M--
HUH--?
IT'S *GONE!* LEAPT STRAIGHT UP!
UP A TREE?
NO! IT JUST VANISHED, LIKE A--
GGH!

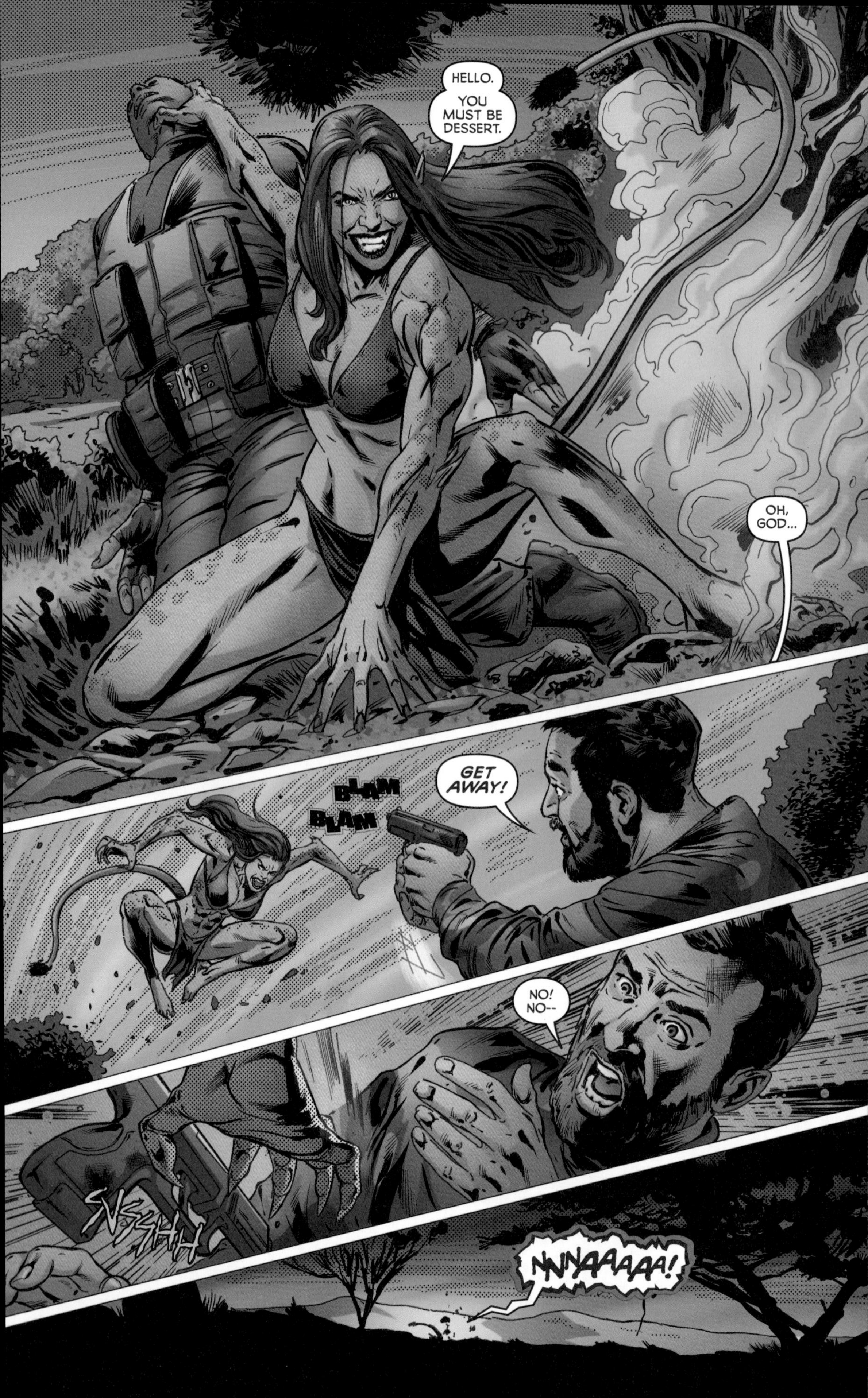
HELLO.
YOU MUST BE DESSERT.
OH, GOD...
GET AWAY!
BLAM
BLAM
NO! NO--
HISSSH
NNYAAAAA!

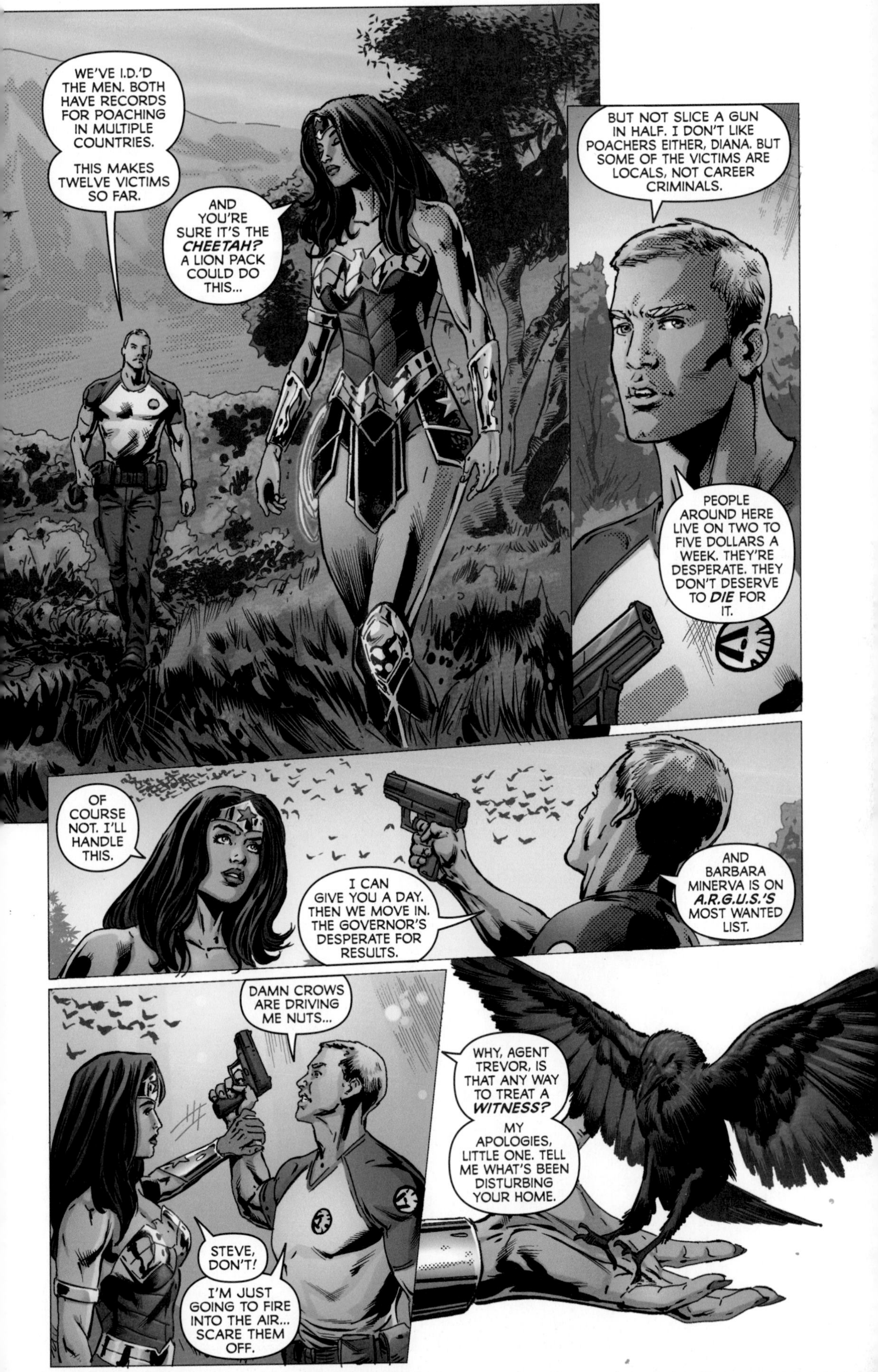

WE'VE I.D.'D THE MEN. BOTH HAVE RECORDS FOR POACHING IN MULTIPLE COUNTRIES.
THIS MAKES TWELVE VICTIMS SO FAR.
AND YOU'RE SURE IT'S THE CHEETAH? A LION PACK COULD DO THIS...
BUT NOT SLICE A GUN IN HALF. I DON'T LIKE POACHERS EITHER, DIANA. BUT SOME OF THE VICTIMS ARE LOCALS, NOT CAREER CRIMINALS.
PEOPLE AROUND HERE LIVE ON TWO TO FIVE DOLLARS A WEEK. THEY'RE DESPERATE. THEY DON'T DESERVE TO DIE FOR IT.
AND BARBARA MINERVA IS ON A.R.G.U.S.'S MOST WANTED LIST.
OF COURSE NOT. I'LL HANDLE THIS.
I CAN GIVE YOU A DAY. THEN WE MOVE IN. THE GOVERNOR'S DESPERATE FOR RESULTS.
DAMN CROWS ARE DRIVING ME NUTS...
STEVE, DON'T!
I'M JUST GOING TO FIRE INTO THE AIR... SCARE THEM OFF.
WHY, AGENT TREVOR, IS THAT ANY WAY TO TREAT A WITNESS?
MY APOLOGIES, LITTLE ONE. TELL ME WHAT'S BEEN DISTURBING YOUR HOME.

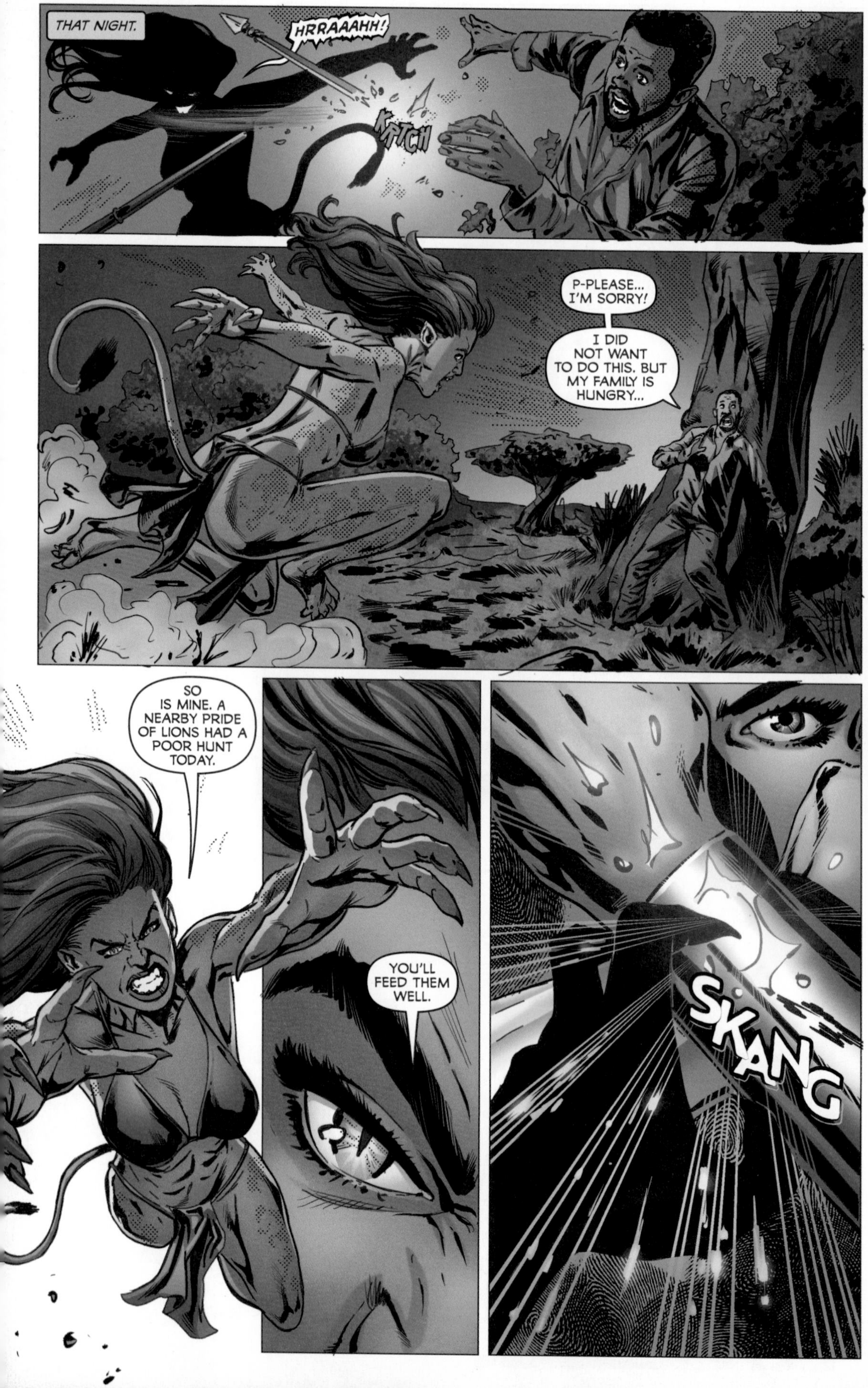
THAT NIGHT.
HRRAAAHH!
KRTCH
P-PLEASE... I'M SORRY!
I DID NOT WANT TO DO THIS. BUT MY FAMILY IS HUNGRY...
SO IS MINE. A NEARBY PRIDE OF LIONS HAD A POOR HUNT TODAY.
YOU'LL FEED THEM WELL.
SKANG

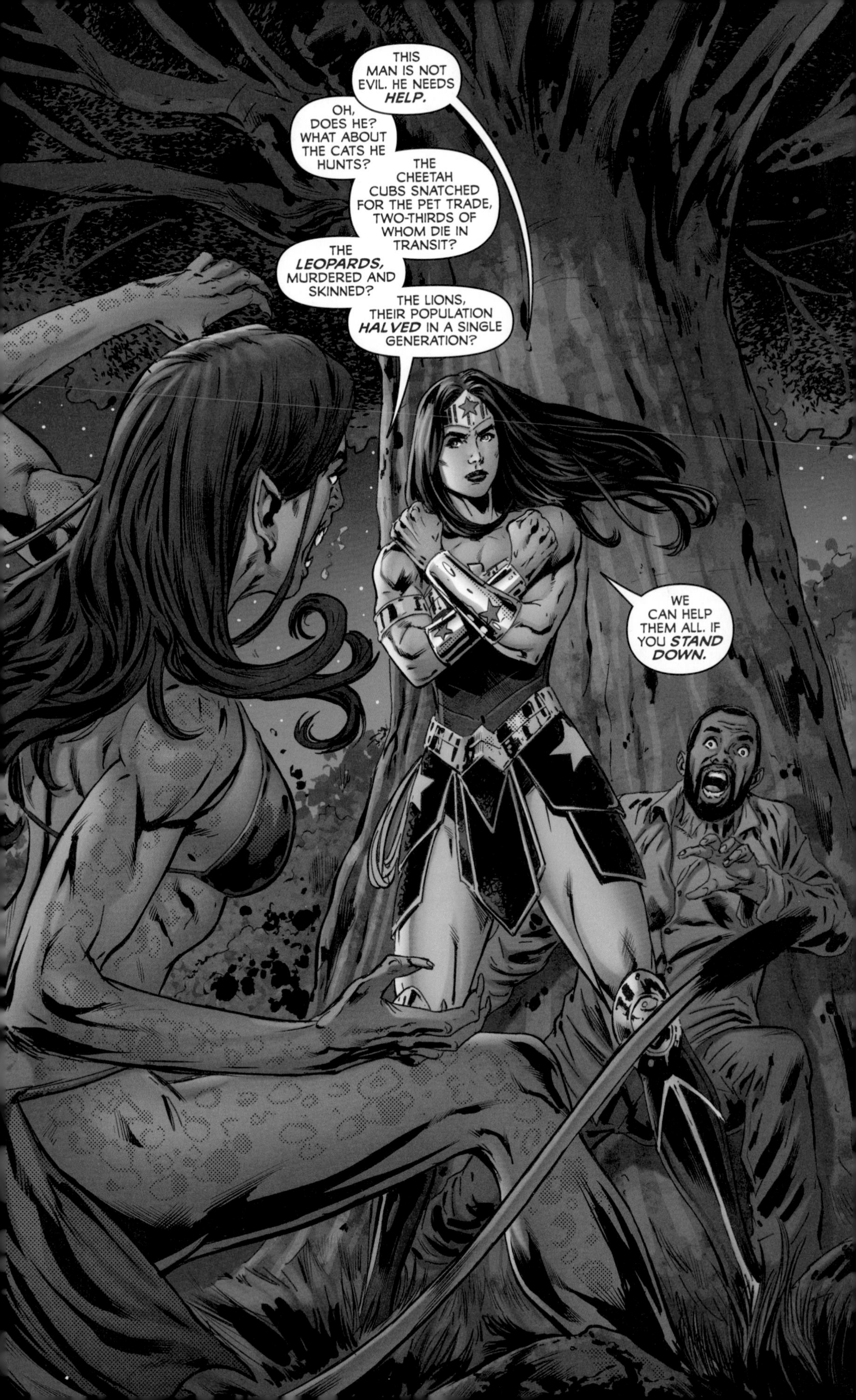
THIS MAN IS NOT EVIL. HE NEEDS ***HELP.***
OH, DOES HE? WHAT ABOUT THE CATS HE HUNTS?
THE CHEETAH CUBS SNATCHED FOR THE PET TRADE, TWO-THIRDS OF WHOM DIE IN TRANSIT?
THE ***LEOPARDS,*** MURDERED AND SKINNED?
THE LIONS, THEIR POPULATION ***HALVED*** IN A SINGLE GENERATION?
WE CAN HELP THEM ALL. IF YOU ***STAND DOWN.***

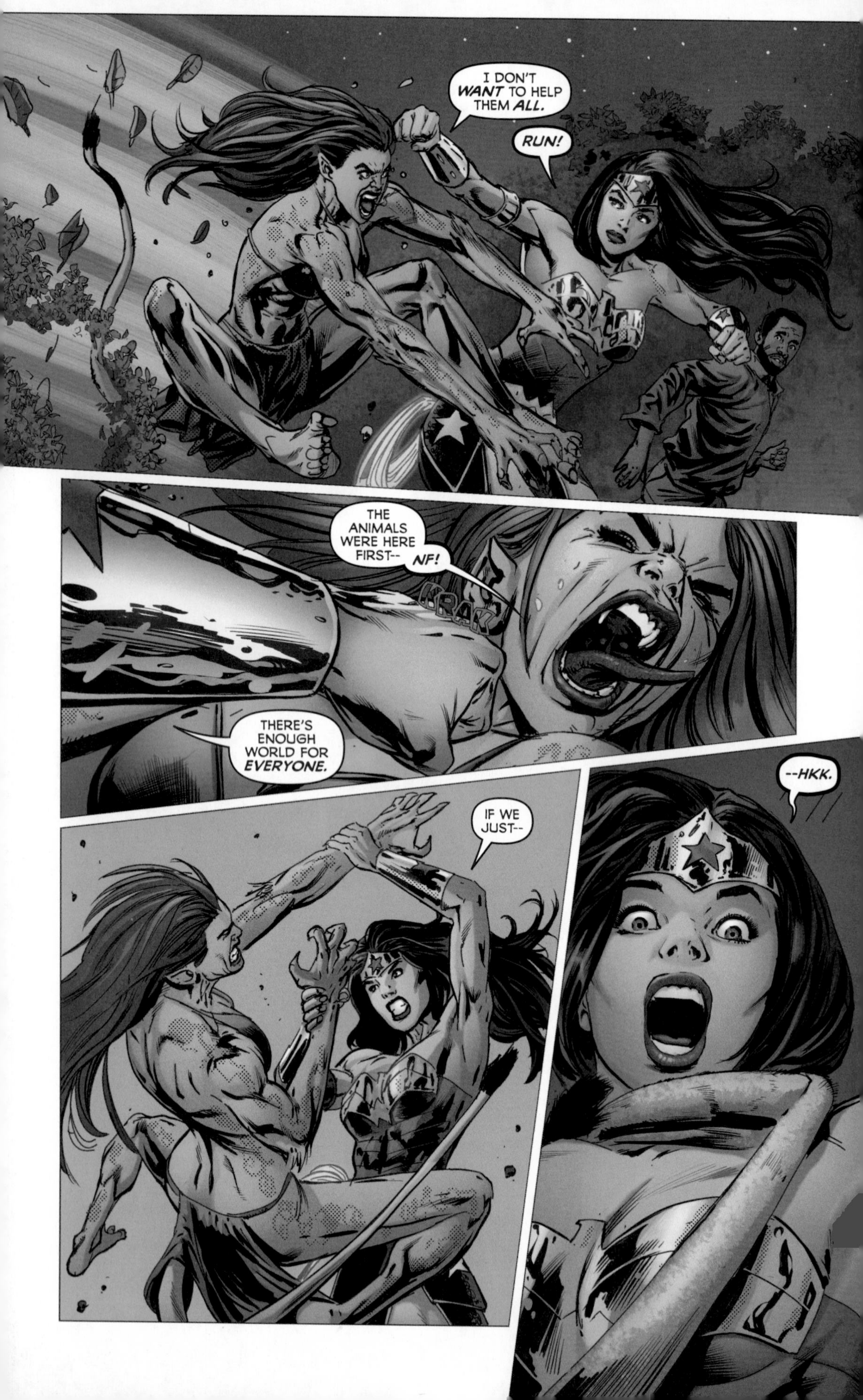
I DON'T *WANT* TO HELP THEM *ALL.*
RUN!
THE ANIMALS WERE HERE FIRST--
NF!
KRAK
THERE'S ENOUGH WORLD FOR *EVERYONE.*
IF WE JUST--
--HKK.

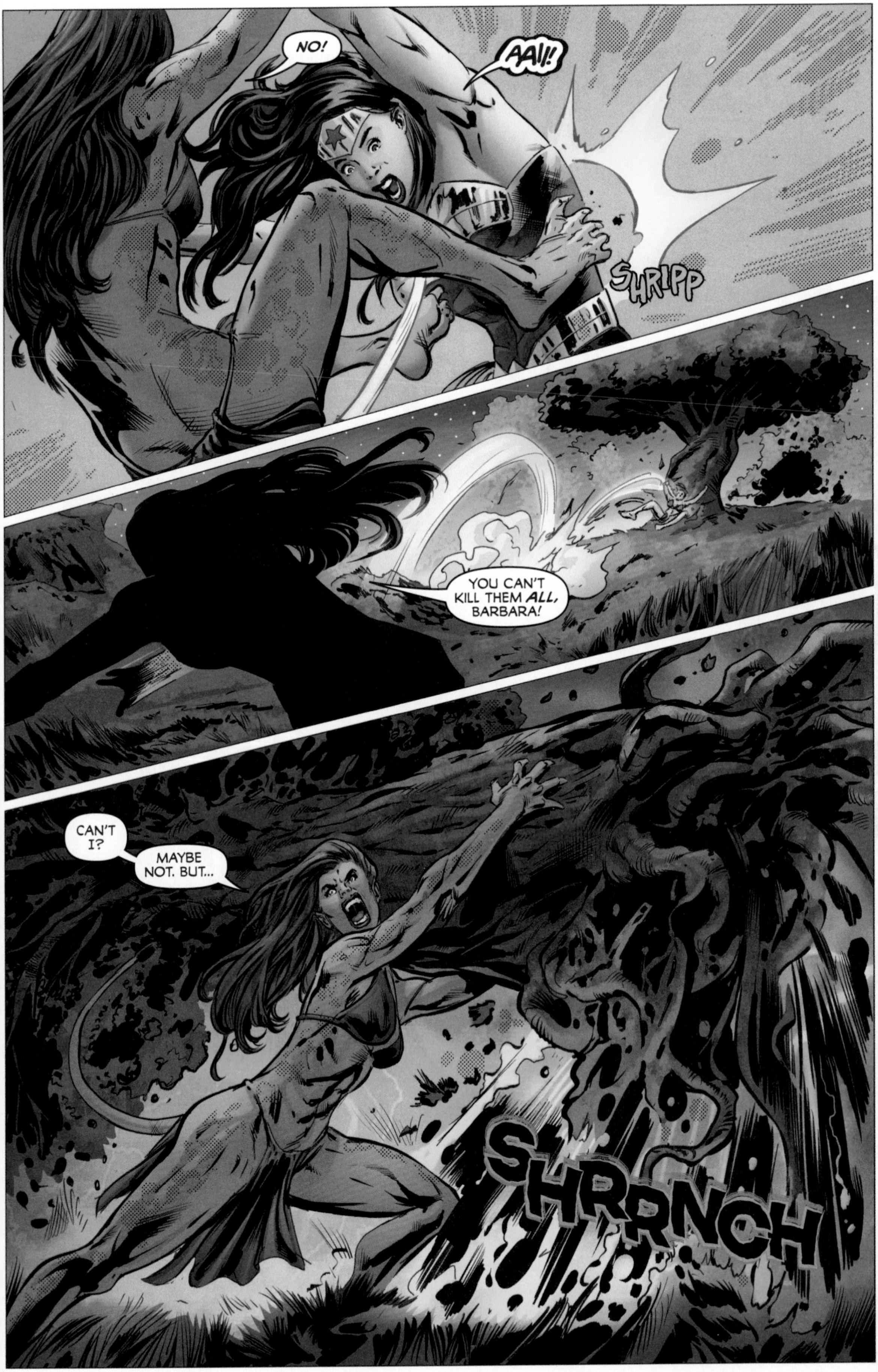
NO!
AAII!
SHRIPP
YOU CAN'T KILL THEM ALL, BARBARA!
CAN'T I?
MAYBE NOT. BUT...
SHRRNCH

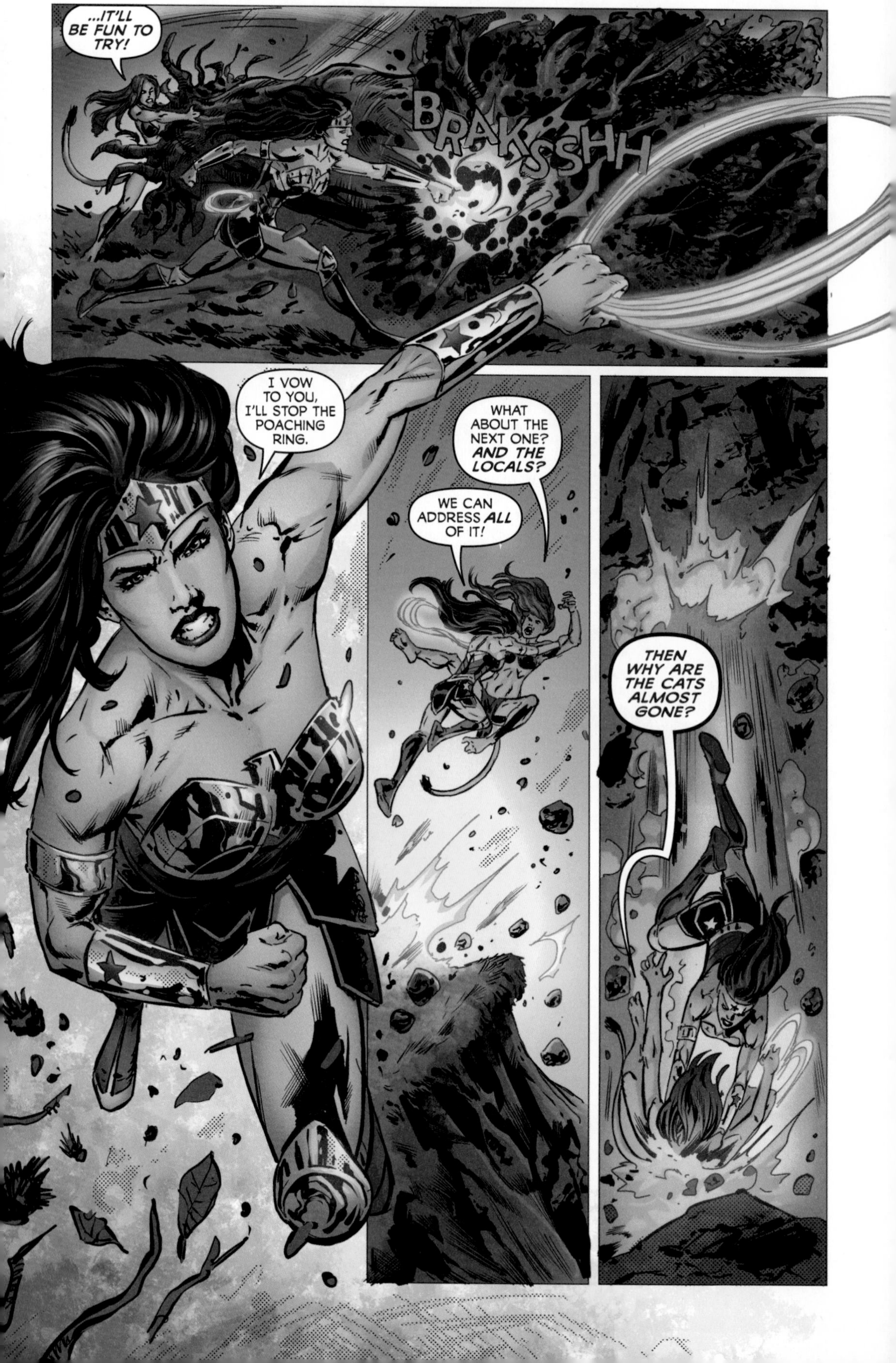
...IT'LL BE FUN TO TRY!
BRAKSSHH
I VOW TO YOU, I'LL STOP THE POACHING RING.
WHAT ABOUT THE NEXT ONE? AND THE LOCALS?
WE CAN ADDRESS ALL OF IT!
THEN WHY ARE THE CATS ALMOST GONE?

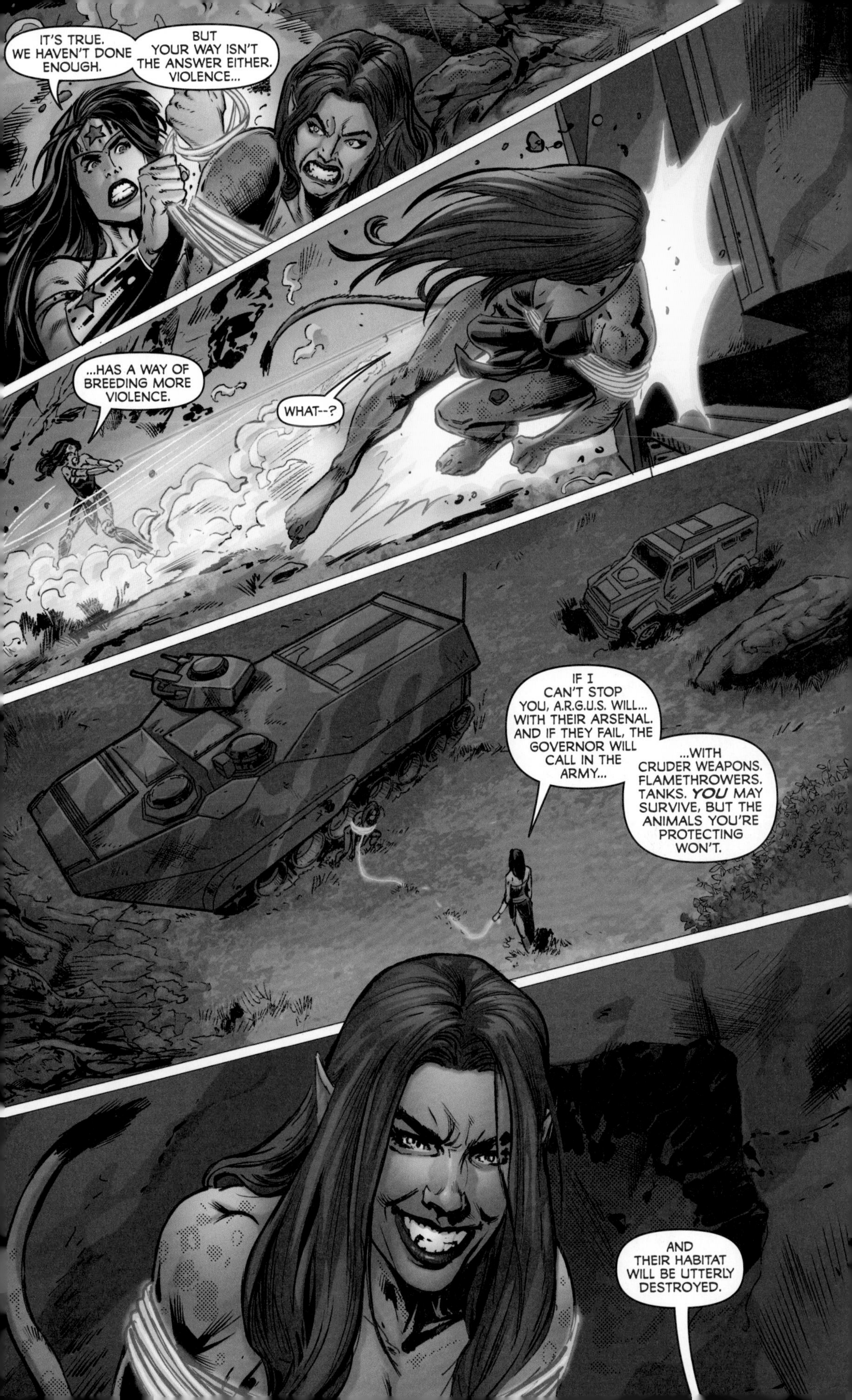
IT'S TRUE. WE HAVEN'T DONE ENOUGH.
BUT YOUR WAY ISN'T THE ANSWER EITHER. VIOLENCE...
...HAS A WAY OF BREEDING MORE VIOLENCE.
WHAT--?
IF I CAN'T STOP YOU, A.R.G.U.S. WILL... WITH THEIR ARSENAL. AND IF THEY FAIL, THE GOVERNOR WILL CALL IN THE ARMY...
...WITH CRUDER WEAPONS. FLAMETHROWERS. TANKS. YOU MAY SURVIVE, BUT THE ANIMALS YOU'RE PROTECTING WON'T.
AND THEIR HABITAT WILL BE UTTERLY DESTROYED.

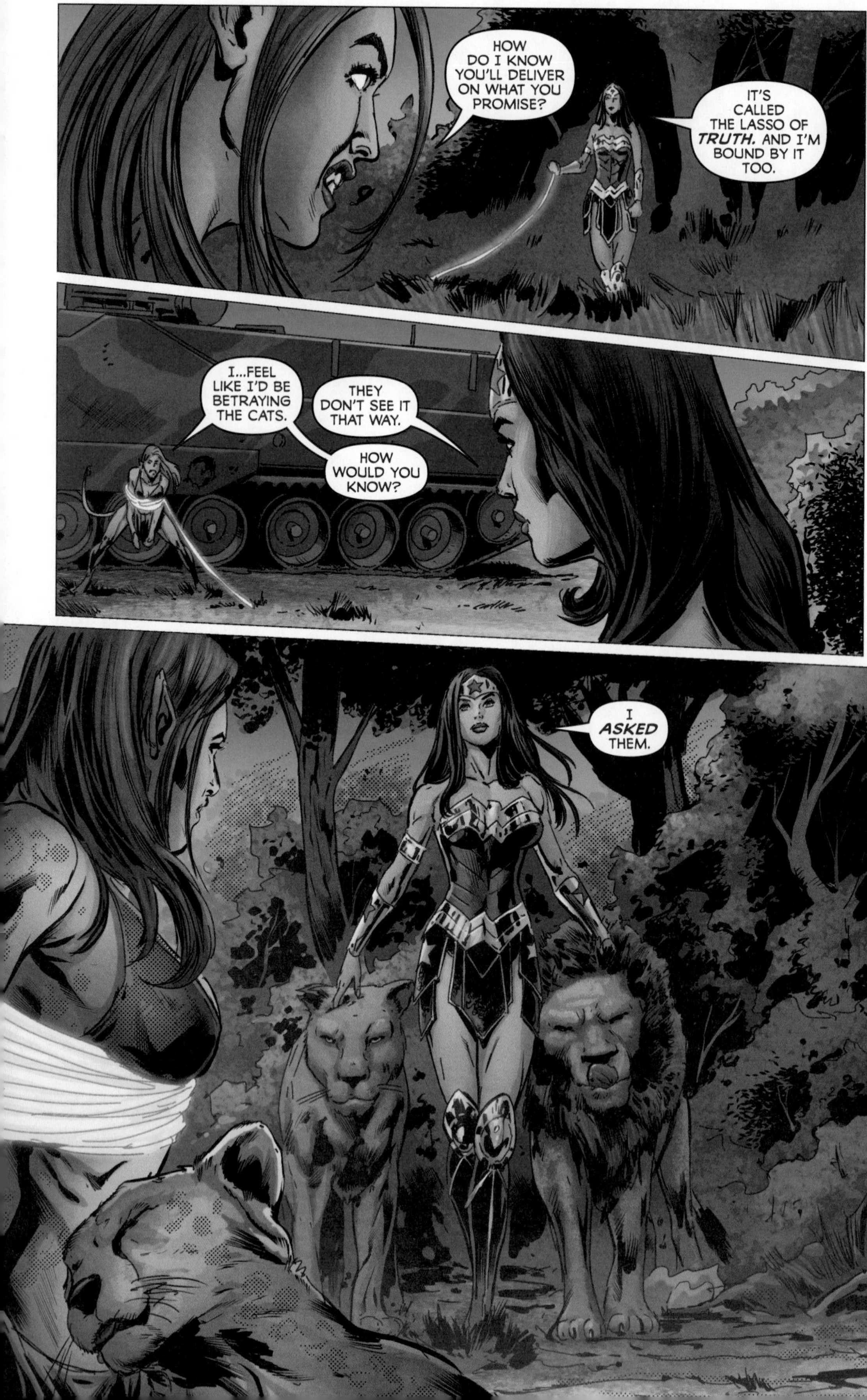
HOW DO I KNOW YOU'LL DELIVER ON WHAT YOU PROMISE?
IT'S CALLED THE LASSO OF *TRUTH.* AND I'M BOUND BY IT TOO.
I...FEEL LIKE I'D BE BETRAYING THE CATS.
THEY DON'T SEE IT THAT WAY.
HOW WOULD YOU KNOW?
I *ASKED* THEM.

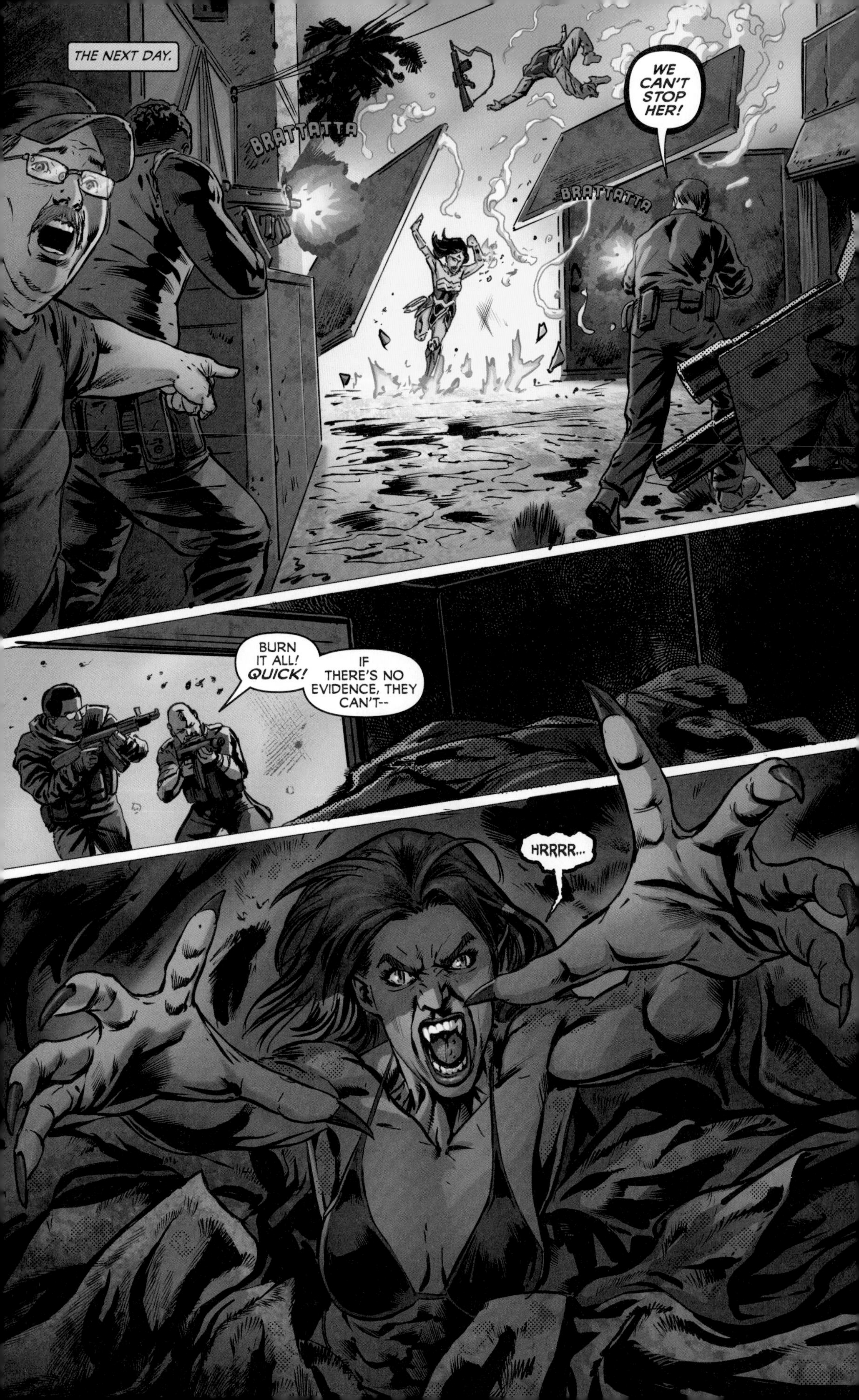
THE NEXT DAY.
BRATTATTA
WE CAN'T STOP HER!
BRATTATTA
BURN IT ALL! QUICK!
IF THERE'S NO EVIDENCE, THEY CAN'T--
HRRRR...

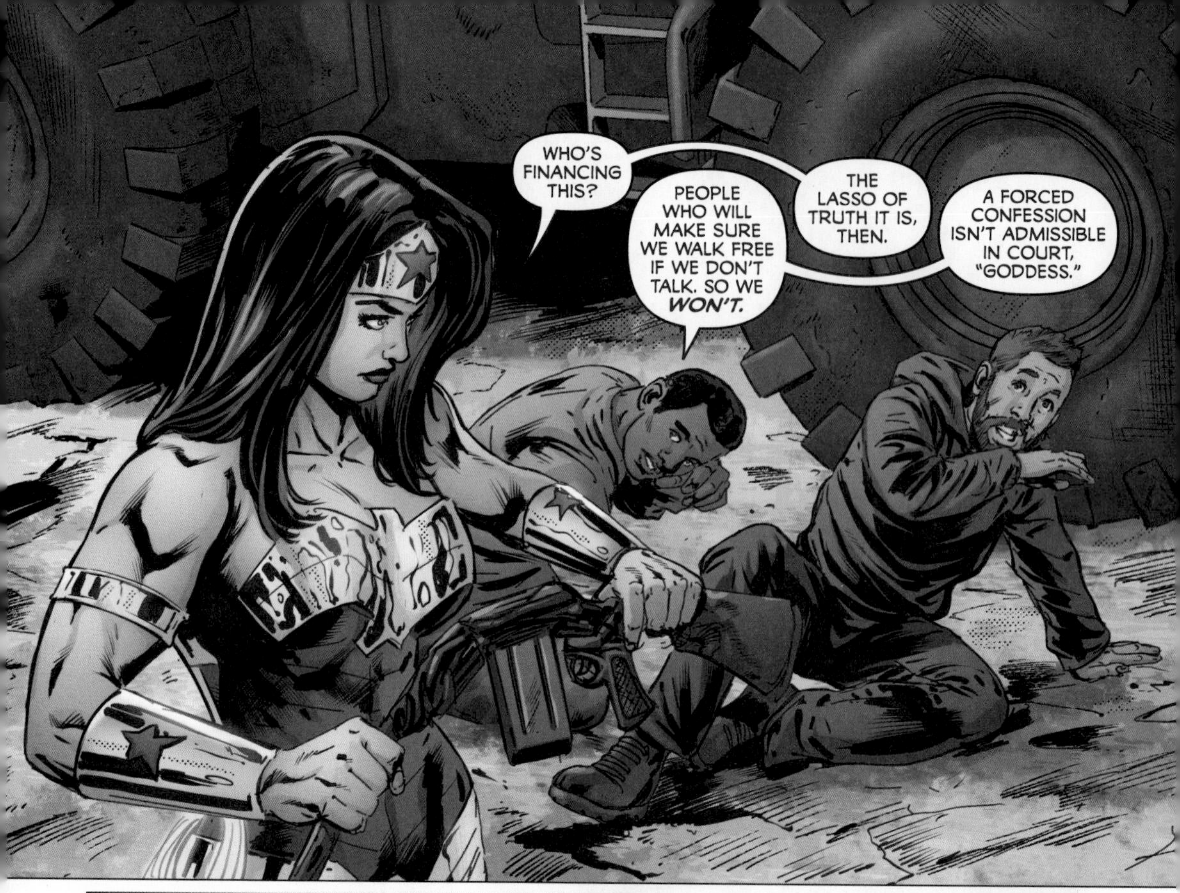
WHO'S FINANCING THIS?
PEOPLE WHO WILL MAKE SURE WE WALK FREE IF WE DON'T TALK. SO WE WON'T.
THE LASSO OF TRUTH IT IS, THEN.
A FORCED CONFESSION ISN'T ADMISSIBLE IN COURT, "GODDESS."
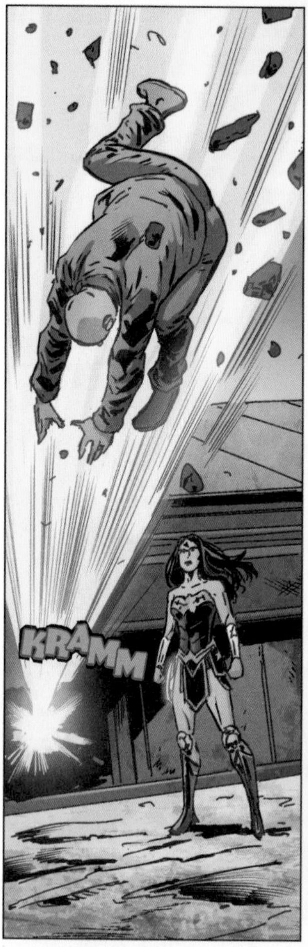
KRAMM
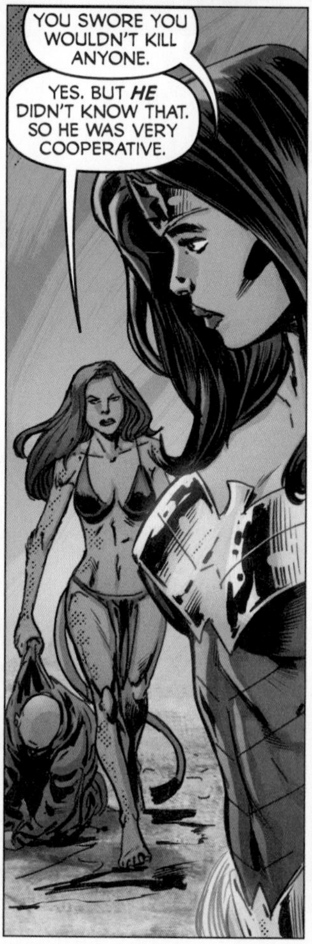
YOU SWORE YOU WOULDN'T KILL ANYONE.
YES. BUT HE DIDN'T KNOW THAT. SO HE WAS VERY COOPERATIVE.
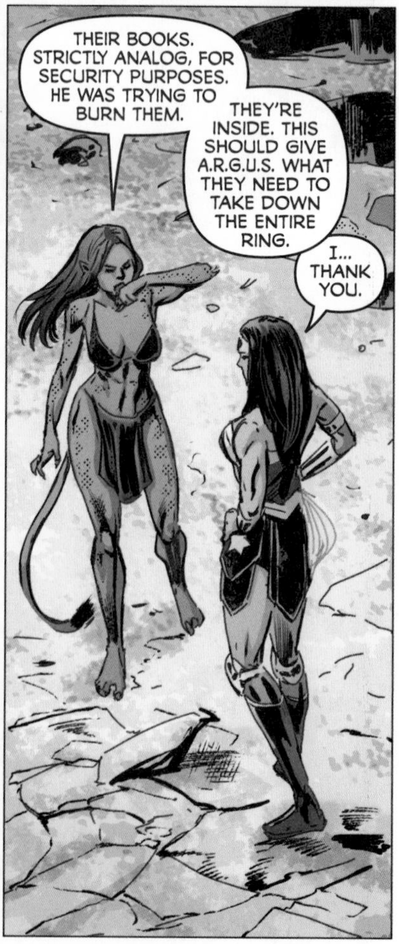
THEIR BOOKS. STRICTLY ANALOG, FOR SECURITY PURPOSES. HE WAS TRYING TO BURN THEM.
THEY'RE INSIDE. THIS SHOULD GIVE A.R.G.U.S. WHAT THEY NEED TO TAKE DOWN THE ENTIRE RING.
I... THANK YOU.

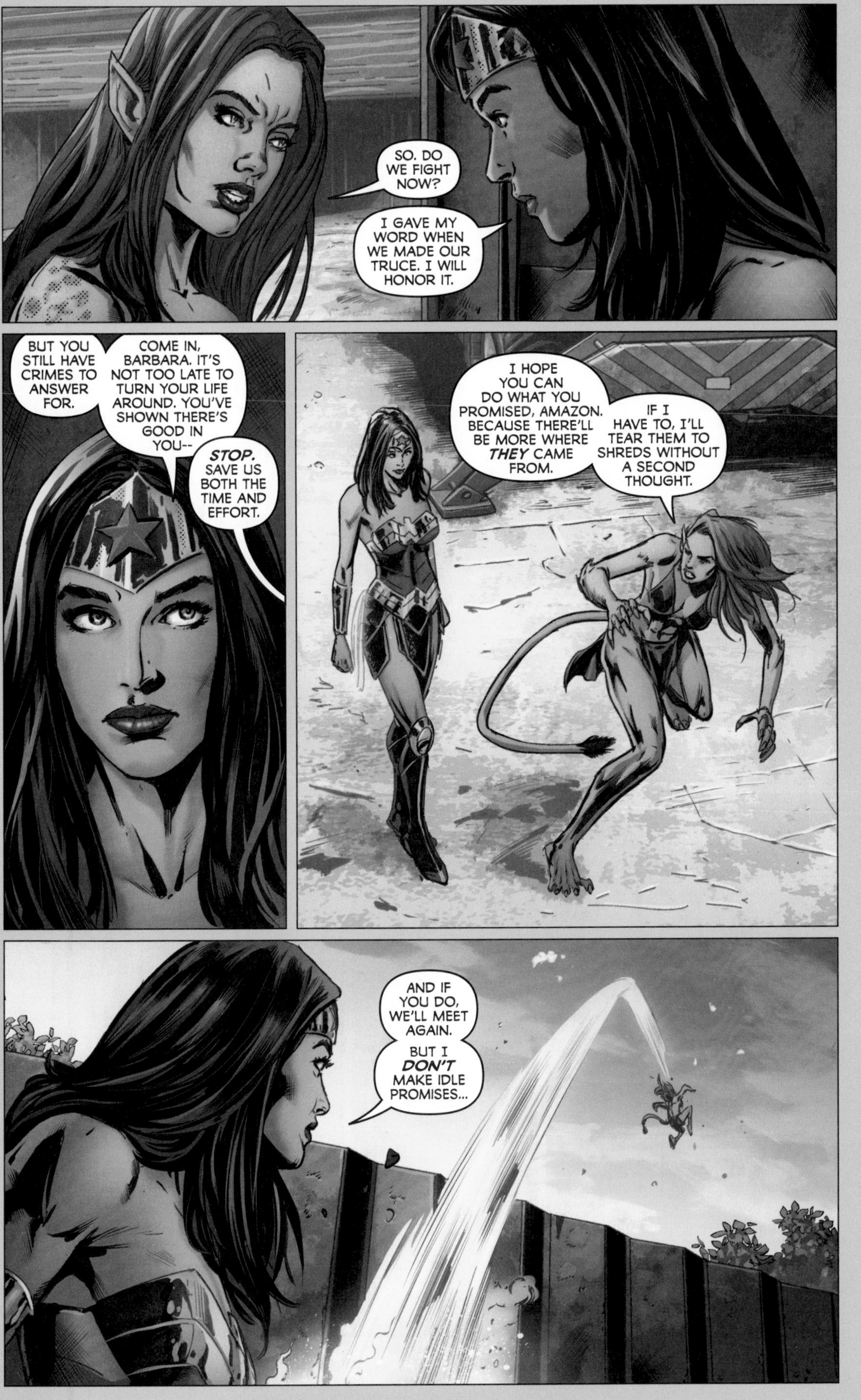
SO. DO WE FIGHT NOW?
I GAVE MY WORD WHEN WE MADE OUR TRUCE. I WILL HONOR IT.
BUT YOU STILL HAVE CRIMES TO ANSWER FOR.
COME IN, BARBARA. IT'S NOT TOO LATE TO TURN YOUR LIFE AROUND. YOU'VE SHOWN THERE'S GOOD IN YOU--
STOP. SAVE US BOTH THE TIME AND EFFORT.
I HOPE YOU CAN DO WHAT YOU PROMISED, AMAZON. BECAUSE THERE'LL BE MORE WHERE THEY CAME FROM.
IF I HAVE TO, I'LL TEAR THEM TO SHREDS WITHOUT A SECOND THOUGHT.
AND IF YOU DO, WE'LL MEET AGAIN.
BUT I DON'T MAKE IDLE PROMISES...

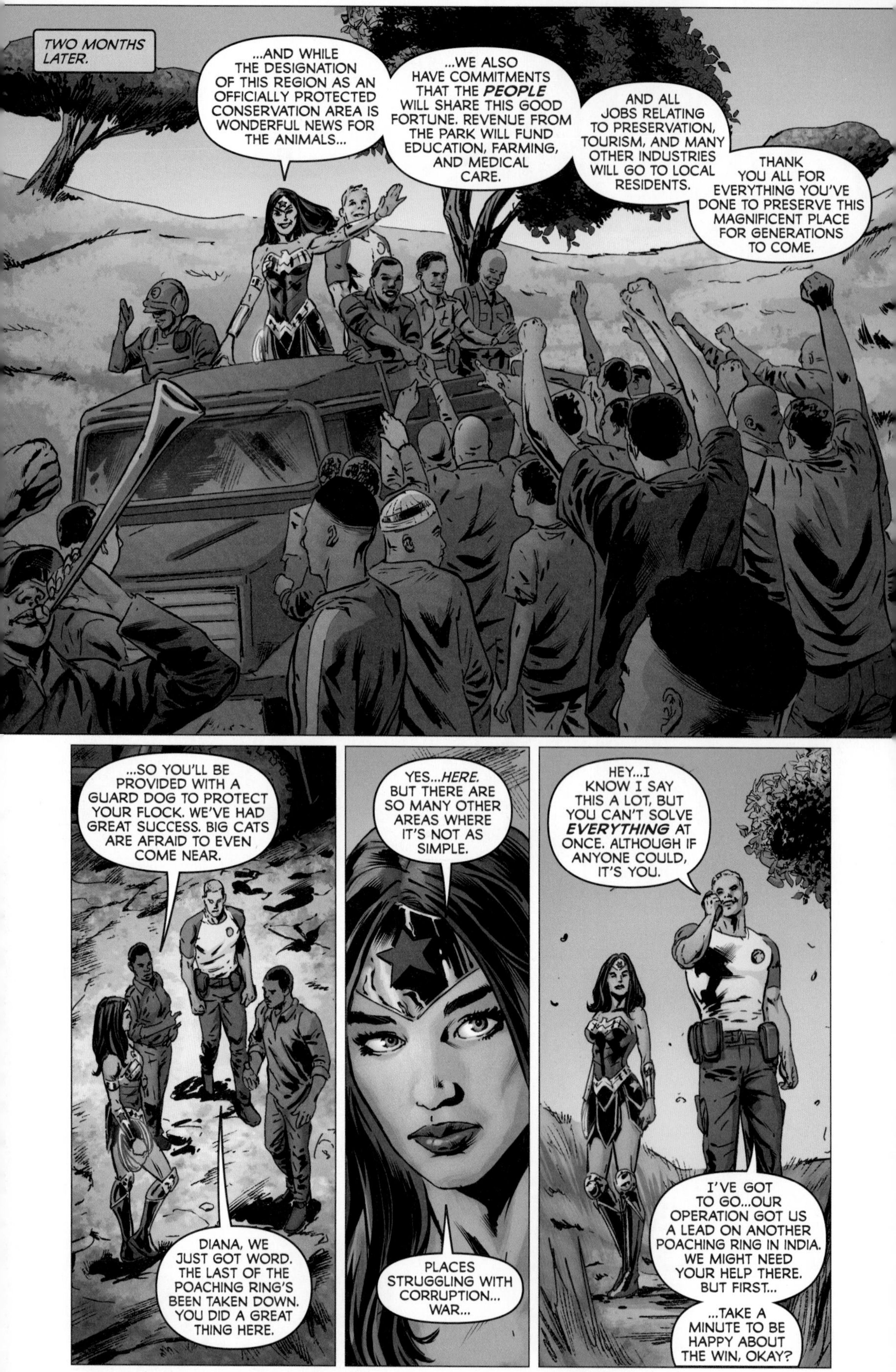
TWO MONTHS LATER.
...AND WHILE THE DESIGNATION OF THIS REGION AS AN OFFICIALLY PROTECTED CONSERVATION AREA IS WONDERFUL NEWS FOR THE ANIMALS...
...WE ALSO HAVE COMMITMENTS THAT THE PEOPLE WILL SHARE THIS GOOD FORTUNE. REVENUE FROM THE PARK WILL FUND EDUCATION, FARMING, AND MEDICAL CARE.
AND ALL JOBS RELATING TO PRESERVATION, TOURISM, AND MANY OTHER INDUSTRIES WILL GO TO LOCAL RESIDENTS.
THANK YOU ALL FOR EVERYTHING YOU'VE DONE TO PRESERVE THIS MAGNIFICENT PLACE FOR GENERATIONS TO COME.
...SO YOU'LL BE PROVIDED WITH A GUARD DOG TO PROTECT YOUR FLOCK. WE'VE HAD GREAT SUCCESS. BIG CATS ARE AFRAID TO EVEN COME NEAR.
DIANA, WE JUST GOT WORD. THE LAST OF THE POACHING RING'S BEEN TAKEN DOWN. YOU DID A GREAT THING HERE.
YES...HERE. BUT THERE ARE SO MANY OTHER AREAS WHERE IT'S NOT AS SIMPLE.
PLACES STRUGGLING WITH CORRUPTION... WAR...
HEY...I KNOW I SAY THIS A LOT, BUT YOU CAN'T SOLVE EVERYTHING AT ONCE. ALTHOUGH IF ANYONE COULD, IT'S YOU.
I'VE GOT TO GO...OUR OPERATION GOT US A LEAD ON ANOTHER POACHING RING IN INDIA. WE MIGHT NEED YOUR HELP THERE. BUT FIRST...
...TAKE A MINUTE TO BE HAPPY ABOUT THE WIN, OKAY?

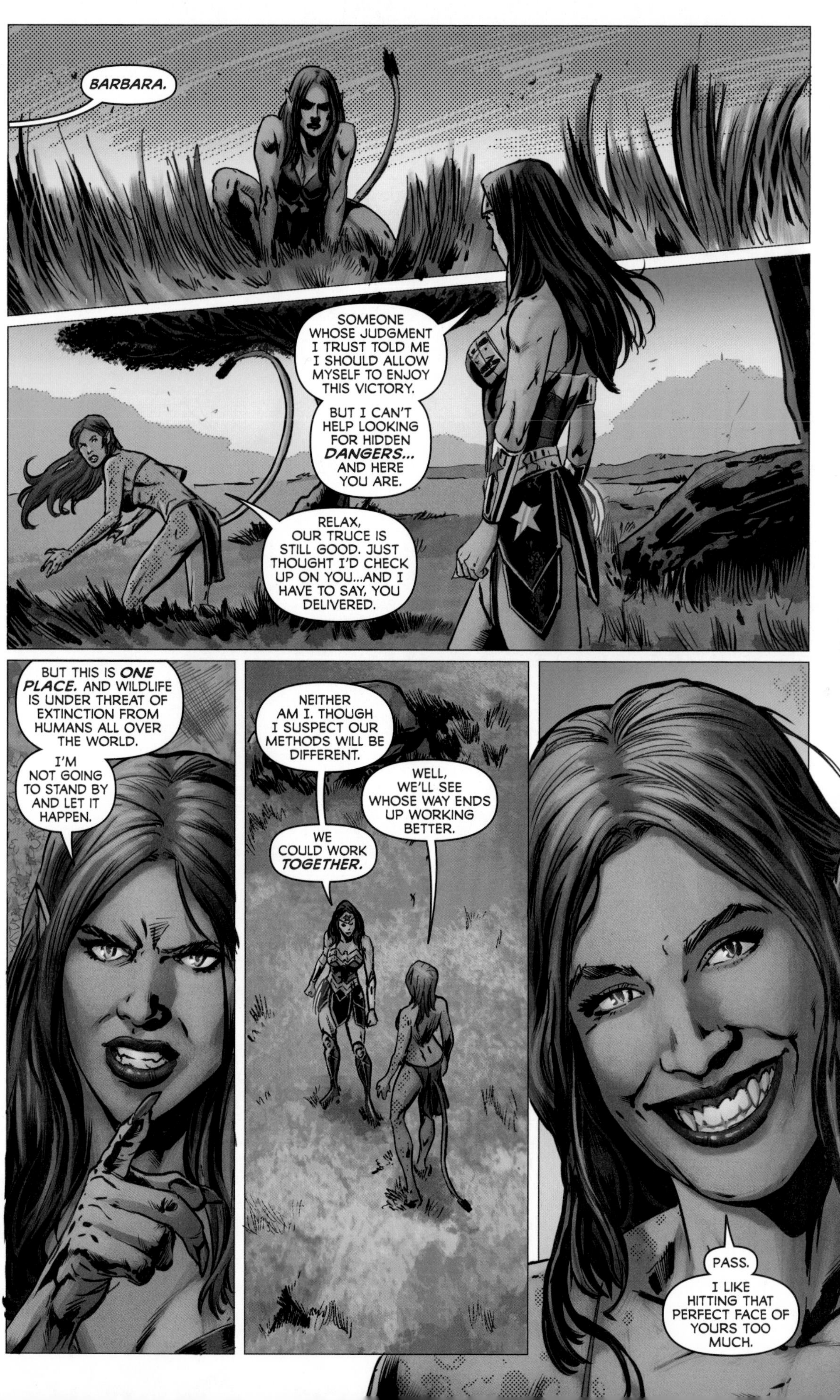
BARBARA.
SOMEONE WHOSE JUDGMENT I TRUST TOLD ME I SHOULD ALLOW MYSELF TO ENJOY THIS VICTORY.
BUT I CAN'T HELP LOOKING FOR HIDDEN *DANGERS...* AND HERE YOU ARE.
RELAX, OUR TRUCE IS STILL GOOD. JUST THOUGHT I'D CHECK UP ON YOU...AND I HAVE TO SAY, YOU DELIVERED.
BUT THIS IS *ONE PLACE.* AND WILDLIFE IS UNDER THREAT OF EXTINCTION FROM HUMANS ALL OVER THE WORLD.
I'M NOT GOING TO STAND BY AND LET IT HAPPEN.
NEITHER AM I. THOUGH I SUSPECT OUR METHODS WILL BE DIFFERENT.
WELL, WE'LL SEE WHOSE WAY ENDS UP WORKING BETTER.
WE COULD WORK *TOGETHER.*
PASS.
I LIKE HITTING THAT PERFECT FACE OF YOURS TOO MUCH.

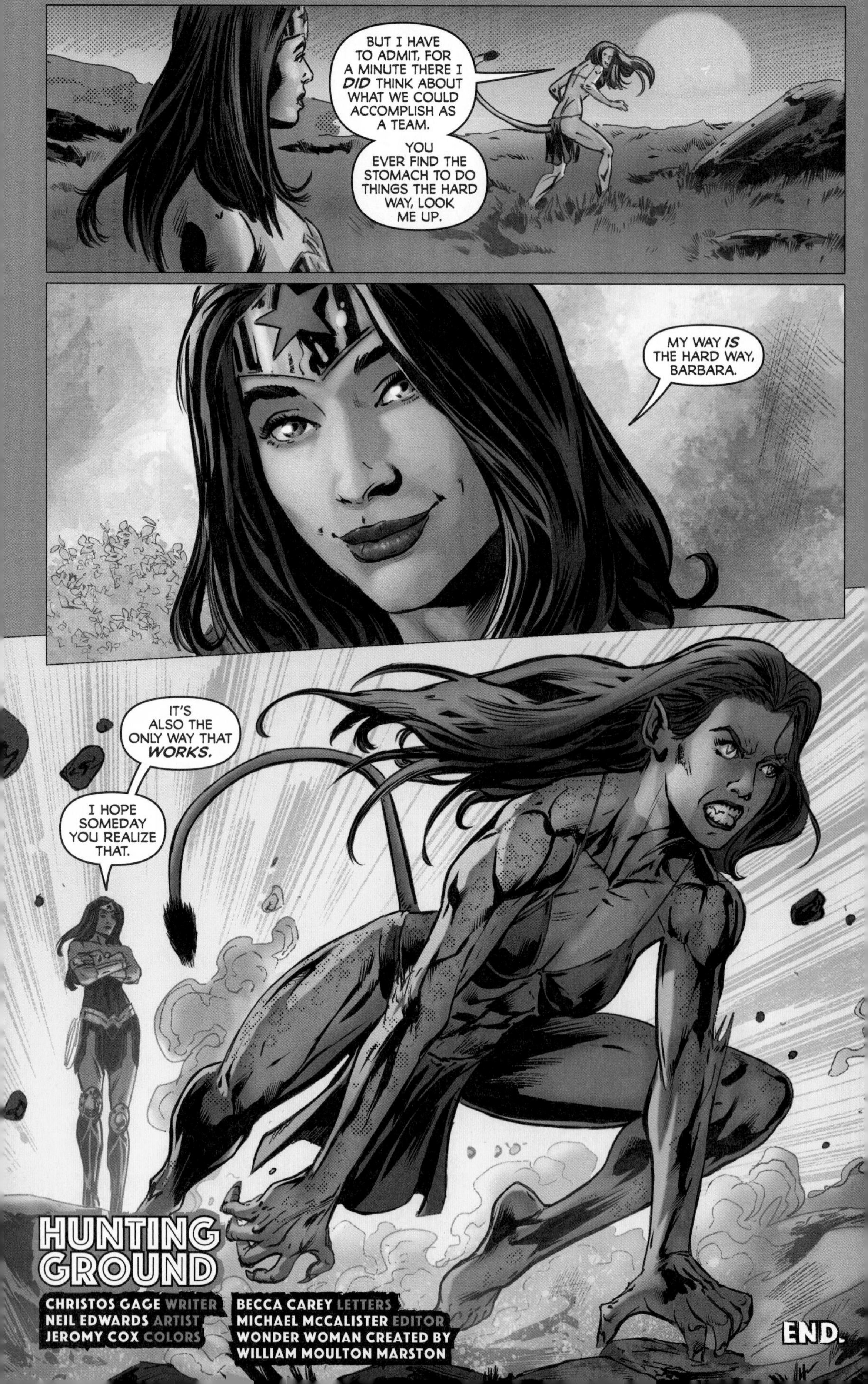
BUT I HAVE TO ADMIT, FOR A MINUTE THERE I *DID* THINK ABOUT WHAT WE COULD ACCOMPLISH AS A TEAM.
YOU EVER FIND THE STOMACH TO DO THINGS THE HARD WAY, LOOK ME UP.
MY WAY *IS* THE HARD WAY, BARBARA.
IT'S ALSO THE ONLY WAY THAT *WORKS.*
I HOPE SOMEDAY YOU REALIZE THAT.
HUNTING GROUND
CHRISTOS GAGE WRITER
NEIL EDWARDS ARTIST
JEROMY COX COLORS
BECCA CAREY LETTERS
MICHAEL MCCALISTER EDITOR
WONDER WOMAN CREATED BY WILLIAM MOULTON MARSTON
END.

"Clear storytelling at its best. It's an intriguing concept and easy to grasp."
– THE NEW YORK TIMES

"Azzarello is rebuilding the mythology of Wonder Woman."
– CRAVE ONLINE

WONDER WOMAN
VOL. 1: BLOOD
BRIAN AZZARELLO
with CLIFF CHIANG

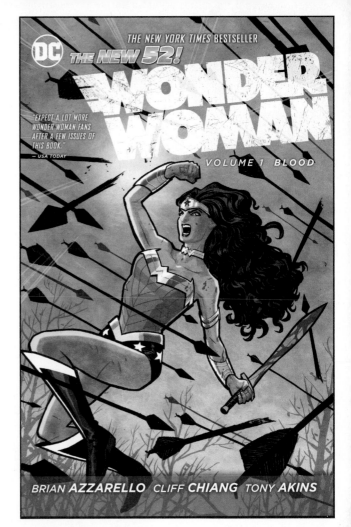

**WONDER WOMAN
VOL. 2: GUTS**

**WONDER WOMAN
VOL. 3: IRON**

READ THE ENTIRE EPIC!

WONDER WOMAN VOL. 4:
WAR

WONDER WOMAN VOL. 5:
FLESH

WONDER WOMAN VOL. 6:
BONES

WONDER WOMAN VOL. 7:
WAR-TORN

WONDER WOMAN VOL. 8:
A TWIST OF FATE

WONDER WOMAN VOL. 9:
RESURRECTION

"Greg Rucka and company have created a compelling narrative for fans of the Amazing Amazon." **– NERDIST**

"(A) heartfelt and genuine take on Diana's origin." **– NEWSARAMA**

DC UNIVERSE REBIRTH

WONDER WOMAN

VOL. 1: THE LIES
GREG RUCKA
with LIAM SHARP

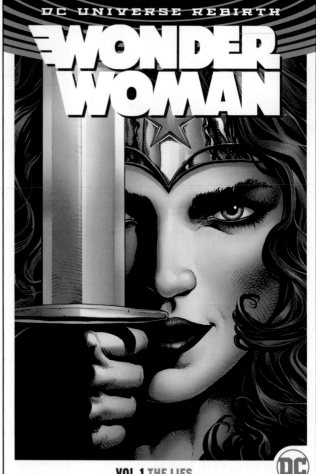

VOL.1 THE LIES
GREG RUCKA • LIAM SHARP • LAURA MARTIN

JUSTICE LEAGUE VOL. 1:
THE EXTINCTION MACHINES

SUPERGIRL VOL. 1:
REIGN OF THE SUPERMEN

BATGIRL VOL. 1:
BEYOND BURNSIDE

Get more DC graphic novels wherever comics and books are sold!